D0794500

STEEL CANVAS
The Art of American Arms

STEEL CANVAS

★ *The Art of American Arms* ★

R.L.WILSON

FOREWORD BY WILLIAM R. CHANEY
Chairman, TIFFANY & Co.

Photography by Peter Beard,
G. Allan Brown, Douglas Sandberg, and Jonathan Shorey

CHARTWELL
BOOKS, INC.

Other books by R. L. Wilson

The Peacemakers: Arms and Adventure in the American West*
Winchester: An American Legend*
Colt: An American Legend*
Winchester Engraving
Colt Engraving
Winchester: The Golden Age of American Gunmaking and the
   Winchester 1 of 1000
Samuel Colt Presents
The Arms Collection of Colonel Colt
L. D. Nimschke, Firearms Engraver
The Rampant Colt
Colt Commemorative Firearms (two editions)
Theodore Roosevelt, Outdoorsman (two editions)
Antique Arms Annual (editor)
The Book of Colt Firearms
The Book of Colt Engraving
The Book of Winchester Engraving
Colt Pistols (with R. E. Hable)
Colt Handguns (Japanese)
Paterson Colt Pistol Variations (with P. R. Phillips)
The Colt Heritage
The Deringer in America (with L. D. Eberhart, two volumes)
Colt's Dates of Manufacture
*Also in French, German, and Italian editions.

This edition published in 2004 by CHARTWELL BOOKS
A division of BOOK SALES, INC.
114 Northfield Avenue, Edison, New Jersey 08837

Published by arrangement with R. L. Wilson
Book and cover design: Martin Moskof
Design assistant: George Brady

Library of Congress Cataloging-in-Publication Data
Wilson, R. L. (Robert Lawrence)
   Steel canvas: the art of American arms / R. L. Wilson:
   photography by Peter Beard . . . [et al.]
      p.   cm.
   Includes bibliographical references and inced.
   ISBN: 0-7858-1891-X
   1. Firearms—United States—Decoration.   2. Engraving
(Metalwork)—United States—Themes, motives.   3. Chasing
(Metalwork)—United States—Themes, motives.   I. Title.
NK6520.W55 1995   739.7′42′0973—dc20   94-19344

Printed in China

Front endpaper: From top left, cased Remington New Model Army, no. 29, factory engraved and with etched cylinder and loading lever and ivory grips; gold-inlaid and engraved Colt Model 1851 Navy, no. 23498, a tribute (c. 1992) to the artistry of Gustave Young, by modern master Paul Lantuch; pair of S&W No. 2 Army revolvers with etched decoration attributed to Tiffany & Co. or contemporary New York–based artisan, nos. 26510 and 29950; S&W New Model No. 3, no. 27916, factory engraved c. 1892; exhibition embellished and cased Colt Single Action Army, no. 50932, engraved by Gustave Young and positioned on lid of its rare leather-on-wood, velvet-lined case; cut-for-shoulder-stock Colt Model 1860 Army, no. 183226, with leaf-style scrollwork; *from center left,* rare example of a gun engraver's pattern book, by G. Ernst (Zella, Germany), c. 1840; left-handed Sharps Model 1853 Sporting Rifle engraved by Gustave Young for factory exhibition use; cartridges and screwdrivers from Cased Winchester Model 1876 rifle presented to Colonel Gzowski, no. 53072, of .50-95 Express caliber, an extraordinary gift to Queen Victoria's A.D.C. for Canada, 1884 (note bird's-eye maple case and selected pages from a rare copy of Winchester's Highly Finished Arms catalogue of 1897); Gustave Young–engraved Colt Third Model Dragoon revolvers *at right,* from rare rosewood cased set, nos. 16474 and 16476—author discovered documentation for these revolvers in factory ledgers, indicating shipment April 30, 1884; they were factory showguns for many years. (Private collection).

Frontispiece: Masterpieces of arms: relief-sculpted and engraved Winchester Model 1866 rifle, no. 109651, by J. Ulrich, *above* title page from Winchester's Highly Finished Arms catalogue of 1897; Colt Single Action Army *at center,* no. 40958SA, from a pair by Frank E. Hendricks; standing *at left* is the finest pre–World War II Colt Single Action Army no. 50932, nickel plated and blued with checkered ivory grips; S&W *at top left* New Model No. 3, no. 27916, in .44 caliber; Tiffany & Co. silver-mounted Art Nouveau Winchester Model 1886 *at bottom* Paris Exposition 1900 showgun, no. 120528; *above* the Winchester a deluxe Colt Model 1851 Navy, no. 23498, done in Gustave Young style by Paul Lantuch; pair of rhinoceros sidelocks from .577 Holland & Holland double-barrel rifle, no. 35577, with engraving and sculpted steel by K. C. Hunt; steel eagle patchbox engraved by Gustave Young on the unique left-handed Sharps Paris Exposition Model 1853 sporting rifle, with etched cylinder from Remington New Model Army no. 29 to *left* of buttplate; *top* pistol a tribute to late-seventeenth-century flintlock Parisian gunmaking by modern master

Monte Mandarino, from a work in progress; folding knives *at left center* by H. Frank and a Victorinox Swiss Army by Andrew Bourbon; *at bottom,* the American Eagle by Tiffany & Co., commissioned, in a series limited to ten Colt Model 1860 Army revolvers, by the U.S. Historical Society, Richmond, Virginia, 1992. Blue leather casing made by Arno Werner for pair of Colt Single Action Army revolvers gold-inlaid, engraved, and ivory-gripped by John E. Warren. (Private collection).

Back endpaper: Six contemporary masterpieces of flintlock arms by Monte Mandarino, tributes to European and American gunmakers from the seventeenth and eighteenth centuries. *At top,* curly maple–stocked German long rifle, c. 1720, the relief-carved stock inlaid with silver wire representing the influence of the French baroque style of twenty-five years earlier; flush gold inlaid and engraved barrel and chiseled and engraved steel mounts; engraving by Daniel Goodwin; 38-inch, .58-caliber barrel. *Second down,* a maple-stocked and relief-carved American longrifle, representing the "transitional" style from the heavier, shorter Germanic Jaeger rifle to the longer and more slender Pennsylvania or Kentucky rifle; the stepped wrist and heavier butt of the Jaeger rifle are combined with the lighter, longer barrel of the evolving longrifle; the flintlock pistol one of a pair of Louis XIV Parisian holster pistols of the 1690 period; pistol with its mate and the gold-mounted fowling piece *below* comprise a set, or "garniture," and are gold-inlaid and chiseled "en suite"; pistol decorated with scenes depicting war and confrontation, while its mate is decorated with scenes of peace and victory; 14-inch smoothbore barrels of 20-bore; *third long gun down,* a Georgian rifle of the 1740 period, with pattern-welded barrel by Judson Brennan and the Getz brothers; English walnut stock profusely inlaid with sheet silver and silver wire, with mounts of chiseled steel done in the English rococo manner; .58 caliber, with 28-inch barrel; *fourth long gun down,* a Louis XIV Parisian fowling piece of the 1690 period, the English walnut stock heavily inlaid with 22-karat sheet gold and gold wire; the mounts heavily chiseled steel rendered in the French baroque manner, as is the barrel; foresight a 22-karat gold carp swimming toward the muzzle, its dorsal fin serving as the sight blade; 48-inch barrel of 20-bore; American or Kentucky longrifle reflecting general style and architecture of the Lancaster County (Pennsylvania) school of gunmaking, c. the Revolutionary War; .50-caliber Douglas swamped barrel of 42 inches; relief-carved maple stock with designs showing strong influence of rococo style; steel mounts, engraved by Daniel Goodwin, former Colt factory engraver. Pattern book and loose page *at left center* by G. Ernst, Zella, c. 1840; page *at right center* from Winchester's Highly Finished Arms catalogue of 1897. Colt Model 1860 Army revolver, *top right,* the American Eagle by Tiffany & Co., commissioned by the U.S. Historical Society and engraved and gold-mounted by Andrew Bourbon. Pair of Colt Single Action Army revolvers by John E. Warren, gold-inlaid, engraved, with carved ivory grips and finished in gray case hardening and bluing, c. 1970. (Private collection).

Contents

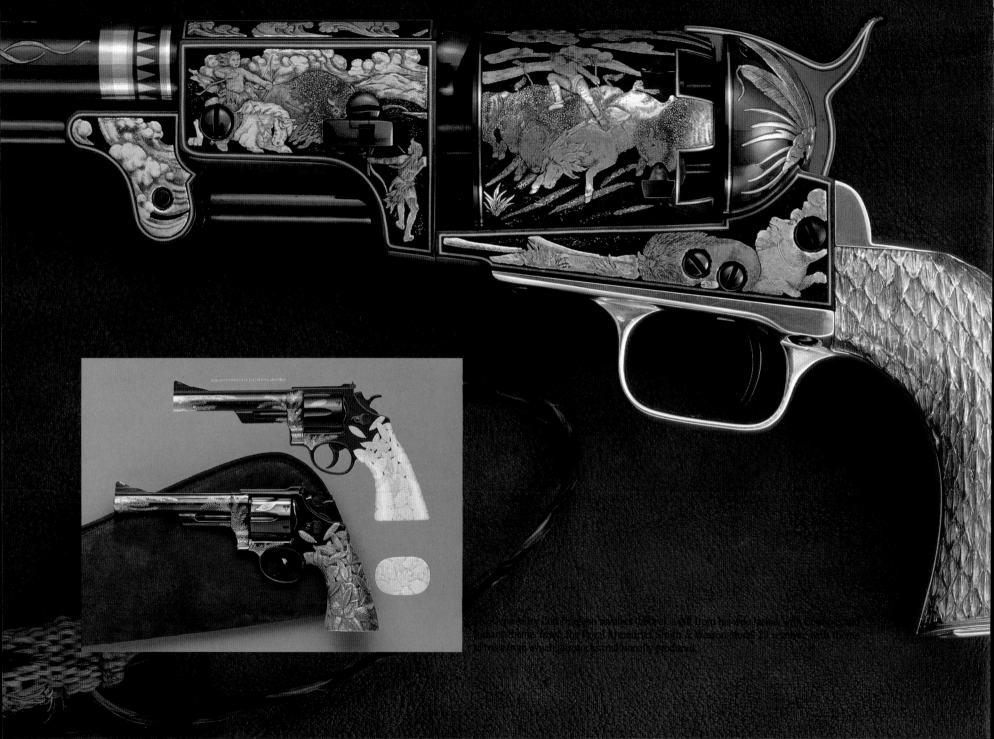

Foreword

Since 1837, Tiffany & Co. has been recognized around the world as a premier source of fine jewelry and silver creations. However, the range of the company's design expertise also extends to the realm of decorative arms. As chairman of Tiffany & Co. and a great admirer of decorative arms, I am extremely pleased that R. L. Wilson has chosen to highlight our achievements in this handsome and fascinating volume.

During the Civil War, many savvy retailers such as Charles Lewis Tiffany began supplying military equipage to the Union Army. Although the company had established itself as a premier source for household silver by this time, the war had adversely affected the sales of such items. Making the best of the situation, Tiffany began applying its silversmithing techniques to presentation swords and firearms.

The elaborate designs and variety of techniques used in Tiffany swords made the firm America's preeminent swordmaker. Over the next fifty years, Tiffany's decorative firearms would achieve the same artistic status as its swords.

Tiffany & Co. revived the art in the early 1980's because of such very special commissions in collaboration with R. L. Wilson as a Colt revolver for Gene Autry's eighty-first birthday and a Smith & Wesson revolver for the Royal Armouries–H. M. Tower of London. Wilson's enthusiasm for decorative arms is inspiring and contagious. His lavish chronicle of the medium, *Steel Canvas,* is the definitive history of decorative arms.

Through this volume, R. L. Wilson documents and celebrates the unique art of decorative arms. *Steel Canvas* is as much a treasure as any of the firearms found within its pages. It is gratifying to know that Tiffany's contributions to the art will endure through the publication of this engaging book.

William R. Chaney
Chairman, TIFFANY & CO.

Introduction

In their foreword to Christie's 1985 auction catalogue benefitting the Arms and Armor Department of New York's Metropolitan Museum of Art, Philippe de Montebello (director), and A. O. Sulzberger (chairman of the museum's board of trustees, and also chairman of the board of *The New York Times*), summed up succinctly and eloquently the universal appeal of arms and armor:

> Collecting arms and armor has been the pastime for noblemen and kings for centuries. There is an obvious romance and mystique about armor and early firearms. At the height of their skill, armorers chiseled steel to make it look like the fashionable clothing of the day, with pleats, sashes, and stitchery all finely engraved and embossed into the metal. Since the introduction of black powder, armorers, jewelers, wood sculptors, and engravers have continually competed to create ever more beautiful masterpieces, each new invention surpassing the others in beauty and technology. One of the earliest drawings of a wheel-lock mechanism can be found in Leonardo da Vinci's *Codex Atlanticus*, for even this great inventor was fascinated with the skill and ingenuity to be found in the diverse firing systems of the sixteenth century. From mid-sixteenth-century matchlocks covered with intricate ivory inlay, flintlock pistols from Napoleon's gunmaker with minute golden stars set directly in the blued steel, the elegant and precise shotguns of Holland & Holland from London to the precision engineering of the modern-day Colt are just a few examples of the evolution of this fascinating art of the engraver and gunmaker. . . .

Those who appreciate beauty in its myriad forms can admire the artistry in fine arms—one need not be a target shooter, hunter, or collector. Engraving and related embellishments are traditional areas in arms and form a common bond, from the earliest weapons to the most modern sporting rifles, with other fields of decorative arts—particularly in metal, wood, and ivory. It is possible to sense a certain communication with the original owner of an engraved arm simply by studying its decorative details. Yet despite the broad interest in the subject, relatively little has been published on the history of arms engraving. A great deal, on the other hand, has been published on the unique, pioneering role of firearms in the evolution of technology, machine tools, mass production, and parts interchangeability—a history that long predates Henry Ford and the automobile.

Considering all the trades that together make a fine gun or edged weapon, only filing, polishing, and engraving employ the same basic tools that have been in use for some five centuries. An engraver from centuries past would feel very much at home if he stepped up to a modern workbench to cut a Colt Peacemaker revolver. His only real concern would be the increased hardness of the metal. Prior to the mid-twentieth century, having to fight tough steels was virtually unheard of. Today many steels (including stainless) are so hard that even in their so-called soft state they are extremely difficult to engrave.

Arms engraving has been a field bound by tradition. To trace the story from the beginning in Colonial times is to see the development of an American style of decoration based largely on European roots. These generic styles were never abandoned, and many have been retained virtually unaltered. Many pieces embellished today

Encircling freshly engraved Ruger Red Label over-and-under shotgun receiver, forend iron, top lever, and triggerguard are engravers' samples, plastic castings of contemporary firearms engravings, and steel dies and hubs (by Alvin A. White). The Winchester Model 1873 receiver, with voluptuous reclining nude, by Marty Rabeno, as is the floorplate with the elephant and scroll motif. Floorplates with grand slam of bighorn sheep, and with small game motifs and mountain lion, by Sam Welch. Floorplate bear motif at *upper left* by Ralph Bone, as is the Celtic decor on the Walther PPK slide. Floorplate at *upper right* by Arnold Griebel. Left and right sides of .22 autoloading rifle frame by Robert Swartley. Cigarette lighter and blued-steel sample plate on wood base by Carlton Ennis. Dentists' technique of casting in white plastic has proven ideal for documenting engravings.

employ the same scroll designs popular with craftsmen and clients of the nineteenth century. There has been relatively little "modern art" in modern arms engraving. Animals, human figures, and other motifs are generally expected to be realistic, not abstract. Scrollwork, though usually an abstraction itself, is traditionally of vine styles, leaf and floral designs, arabesques, banknote scrolls, and so forth. Gauguin, Picasso, and Pollack have had limited effect on the decoration of arms. Tiffany & Co., however, since the mid-nineteenth century, has been at the forefront of the exquisite and the original in American arms, whenever the firm was actively involved.

But, in general terms, the prevailing style in American arms engraving has been Germanic scrollwork. Some German-born engravers are active today on American arms, and most American-born engravers use a scroll with Germanic roots as their most popular style.

Since World War II there has been a veritable explosion of interest in all fields of fine and decorative arts. Quality arms skyrocketed in price and in popularity. In the mid-1970s they joined fine furniture, silver, and rare coins as among the most highly valued objects in collecting. Spurred on by inflation (and then by the lack of it), the uncertainty of many traditional investments, and by periodic low interest levels on savings, the buying of collectibles continues to set new price and volume records with great rapidity.

Arms and armor subjects are a key element in this phenomenon. Arms collectors have known all along what others are only now discovering: that firearms and edged weapons (each and every one a unique object) represent a fascinating field that combines the various appeals of art, craftsmanship, history, mechanics, and romance.

Consider further that approximately 20 million hunting licenses are sold in America annually (hunting is a $40 billion annual domestic business), that millions throughout the world are familiar with arms because of sporting interest and mili-tary service, that a number of museums in the United States and Europe recognize fine arms as their main drawing card, that TV and movies often show arms in roman-tic and adventurous settings, that the Wild West (where a gun was a portable body-guard) is the single most attractive historical element in America's past, and that arms collecting offers sweet escape from the ever-increasing lunacy of modern life.

The most active and enthusiastic connoisseurs of American arms engraving and its history are collectors of antique arms and our present-day crop of engravers and their patrons: tens of thousands of enthusiastic sportsmen and collectors. And every day brings new devotees to the art of the arms engraver and embellisher.

Considering all the fields of metalwork craftsmanship and manufacturing in modern times, there is at least one flourishing example that maintains, at its upper levels, the highest standards, and deserves recognition and preservation as an Amer-ican decorative art form with distinctive traditions and achievements in product and style. That field is fine guns and knives.

After nearly a lifetime of research, study, and collecting of arms, I am just as enthusiastic about, and devoted to, the field as I was as a little boy with a paper route, enduring the extremely severe Minnesota weather to earn a few dollars to spend on my budding collection and library. My sincere interests are by no means limited to arms, but this is the field that I continue to find the most challenging, fascinating, and appealing of any within the vast umbrella of subjects in the realm of antiques and the decorative arts.

R. L. Wilson
Castle View
Hadlyme, Connecticut

Education is the key to understanding firearms, their value and significance—historic, artistic, and technical. All my adult life I have enjoyed firearms: researching and writing about them, placing them in museums and collections, and (not least) using them. Yet I have always realized that people can misuse them, thus making firearms controversial to some. Collectors, curators, historians, antiquarians, sport-, target-, and silhouette-handgun shooters, local club marksmen through Olympic-level international competitors, gunsmiths, engravers, trap-, skeet-, and sporting clay–shotgun shooters, historical reenactors, muzzle loading devotees, air-gun and pellet shooters, handloaders and cartridge enthusiasts, and decent, law-abiding citizens who are gun owners—all face this dilemma.

There is a nonprofit foundation that is single-mindedly dedicated to education on firearms safety. More than that, this group supports an educational understanding of the appreciation of firearms—something close to my heart (as can be seen from this book). So I am dedicating this work to that organization, for its promotion of correct values in the magical world of firearms:
To the NRA Foundation,
a nonprofit institution dedicated to
education in firearms safety,
an understanding of the appreciation of firearms,
and their responsible ownership and use.

And to
Robert M. Lee,
conservationist, sportsman, adventurer, explorer, author,
entrepreneur, and collector nonpareil;
founder and president of
Hunting World, Incorporated;
and creator of the Hunting World Collection
of fine luggage and leather products, extraordinary Swiss watches,
sporting clothing, and outdoor sporting accessories;
whose expertise and connoisseurship on,
and dedication to,
fine, rare, and beautiful arms,
and whose enthusiastic support of the author
have been vital in the creation of this book.

STEEL CANVAS
The Art of American Arms

SIMONIN FECIT

LE LANGVEDOC A PARIS

2

Chapter 1
Five Centuries of Deluxe Arms

From the time weapons advanced beyond mere bludgeoning implements picked up from nature, they have been imbued with almost mystical qualities, revered far more than their utilitarian functions would indicate. The cruciform sword of the medieval northern European was a symbol of holy purpose; the Gothic armor of the fourteenth and fifteenth centuries reflected all the sweeping grace of the great cathedrals of the same period, the elegance of line actually enhancing its ability to deflect weapon blows.

Perhaps the first embellishment of arms began with etched inscriptions on sword blades. Incantations on blades made the wielder mighty in battle, and later, when makers began signing their blades, the names of the most successful were often counterfeited by less able makers. The celebrated Andrea Ferara, who may or may not have been an actual bladesmith, inspired such awe

Page 6 from the engraving pattern book (1684) of Claude Simonin. The volume was composed of designs that could be adapted to deluxe flintlock firearms, thus allowing engravers the advantage of sources to copy, rather than having to create the embellishments themselves. The serpentine shape at top was for the upper part of a buttplate.

that the name on a blade was akin to a good luck charm. E. Andrew Mowbray, in his notes to Lord Archibald Campbell's *Scottish Swords from the Battlefield at Culloden,* states:

> The roots for this tradition are really very simple. The proper tempering of a blade was dependent upon intently watching its changing color while under heat, then suddenly quenching in any one of several secret and usually appalling liquids or semiliquids. The observance of this phenomenon of changing blade color during tempering could best be effected after dark. Therefore much of the smith's work was nocturnal. The flickering lights, the moving shadows, and the rhythmic din of a forge in action convinced the man in the street that the swordsmith had some sort of pact with the forces of darkness. The Solingen guild made capital of this and a common belief arose that the carrying of a Solingen blade with its "running wolf" guild mark made a man bulletproof. Getting shot was only evidence of having a spurious blade.

Armor styles reflected the changing civil fashions, and armorers were called upon to represent not only the line and pleating of fabric in the steel of breastplates, backplates, pauldrons, and the other elements of a plate "har-

ness," but also the enrichment of brocade and lace. In the late fifteenth and early sixteenth centuries, the use of etching to render designs on the steel surface became popular (the metal was too hard to engrave in the manner that gold, silver, and brass were being decorated at the time). After coating the whole surface with an acid-resistant substance, designs were delicately scratched through. The plate was then dipped in acid, which bit deep into the metal where it was exposed. Finally, the acid was removed and the etched area highlighted with a pigment or with gold.

Later in the sixteenth century, every inch of surface was covered with foliate designs, vividly realistic depictions of battles, panoplies of weapons, coats of arms, and Christian symbolism. Armor, which was losing its importance in battle, had become exclusively an *objet d'art,* worn for parade and festival.

Early Firearms

As firearms developed over this same period, they were also given the artist's attentions. Early matchlocks, being primarily military arms, are only rarely found with decorations applied. But the longarms and pistols that

Etched and gilded, these swords represent the most exquisite of fifteenth-century metalwork on arms and armor. Made for the governor of Milan, c. 1495. From the Kunsthistorisches Museum, Vienna.

Adam and Eve on Tyrolian powder flask of carved ivory, with Welsperg coat of arms. Relief carving accentuated by background colored brown; the mounts gilded; c. 1550. From the Victoria and Albert Museum, London.

Etched and gilded for the Holy Roman Emperor Rudolph II, armor from the workshop of Anton Peffenhauser, Augsburg, 1571; one of many historic armors and arms at the Kunsthistorisches Museum.

used the later wheel-lock ignition system, a forerunner of the familiar flintlock, were another matter altogether. Complex products of precision engineering, these guns were often given lavish treatment: the wooden stocks inlaid with marquetry, stag horn, and mother-of-pearl; the barrels, locks, and other metal furniture etched or engraved and damascened or gilded in gold and silver.

This tradition of engraving the finest of firearms for the most prestigious of patrons has continued to our own age. The Italian firm of Beretta, still in the hands of the founding family, has made and embellished arms from the Renaissance to the present; the famous English firm of J. Purdey & Sons, creator of coveted shotguns, dates from 1814; and America's own Remington Arms Company began in 1816, though the somewhat later Colt firm (founded 1836) was far more prolific in the creation of embellished guns.

It is a matter of historical irony that the arms industry, which pioneered the Industrial Revolution, still relies on a high degree of handwork for its best-quality products. Most of the custom makers depend on hand fitting and finishing, making each gun produced unique. Only one contemporary firm, the relatively young (founded in 1968) Ivo Fabbri of Brescia, Italy, among the finest of today's gunmakers, has been able to apply mechanical wizardry and computers to produce arms of uniformly superb quality with a minimum of handwork.

But at the point the engraver takes over, the process becomes exclusively a hand operation. And while an

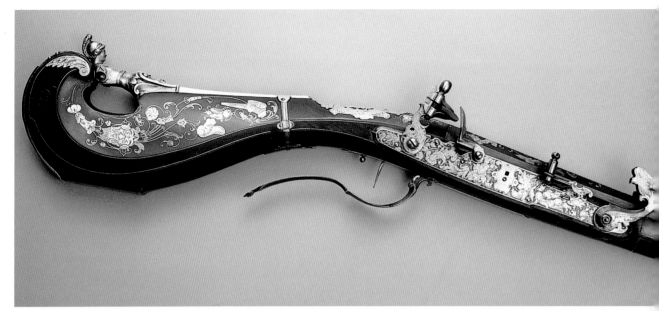

From the Cabinet of Arms of King Louis XIII. By F. DuClos, dated 1636. Early flintlock with matchlock, using superposed load system. Stock decorated with silver inlays; gilded bronze Atlanta rested under the shooter's chin.

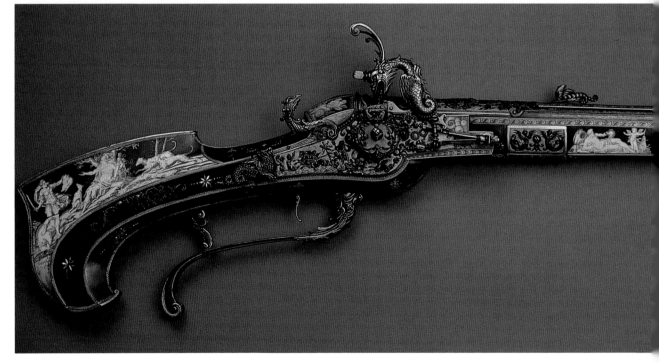

The rich tradition of embellishment established by the European gunmakers is represented here by a chiseled, gilded, engraved, and exquisitely stocked wheel-lock and matchlock gun, c. 1600; the metal decoration is by the German artisan Emanuel Sadeler, the stockwork by Adam Vischer, both of Munich. The action (or lock) makers emerged from guilds of locksmiths, the embellishers in metalwork from armorers' guilds and related groups of metal decorators; stockmakers came largely from furniture specialists.

indifferent gun, no matter how beautifully embellished, is still indifferent, a fine one is more greatly sought after and valued if the applied art is of an equal quality.

Pattern Books, Wheel-locks, and Flintlocks

For centuries, engraving was carried out largely from patterns, which were often recorded in the form of books. The earliest were for use on the products of the goldsmith—cups, bowls, and the like—and the designs had to be adapted in the gunsmith's shop to fit the distinctive contours of a gunlock. As demand grew for engraved arms, however, engravers began to issue patterns specifically for gun use. Among the earliest are a series of wheel-lock engravings in the French style from the late sixteenth century, attributed to a follower of the Parisian engraver Androuet Ducerceau. The French, particularly the Parisian school, were the most important and influential of gun engravers at this time. In 1685, when the Edict of Nantes—which had granted freedom of worship to Huguenots—was revoked, French Huguenot gunsmiths migrated to other European capitals, carrying their skills with them. In their new locations they tended to adopt and refine the local styles rather than maintain their own.

The invention of the wheel-lock (c. 1517) is generally attributed to southern Germany, and the cities of Nuremberg, Augsburg, Munich, and Dresden (along with neighboring countries, such as the Netherlands and Denmark) dominated most of the sixteenth-century production. The greatest collection of these early wheel-locks is that gathered by the Holy Roman Emperor

Encouraged by the Imperial Court, Russian gunmaking (at Tula) developed a high level of workmanship under French influence. Flintlock sporting gun from an elaborate garniture of arms made for the Empress Elizabeth, in the French style, at Tula, c. 1752. Chiseled and gilded mounts, with the stock silver-inlaid.

Sculpted steel became a distinctive characteristic of Italian gunmakers, from the late sixteenth century into the eighteenth. The Brescians were the masters of this technique and style. This pair of flintlocks signed AQUA FRESCA A BARGI—1681.

6

Double cased pairs of flintlock pistols by Nicholas Noël Boutet, gunmaker to Napoleon. Boutet was known for the wide range of luxurious appointments, including cast and chased mounts of gold, silver, and steel, gold- and silver-inlaid or masterfully carved stocks, and engraved, chiseled and/or inlaid locks and barrels. Boutet described himself as an artist; his workshops were at Versailles.

Presentation set of flintlock pistols, from the state of Connecticut to Commodore Thomas McDonough. By Simeon North, Middle-town, Connecticut, c. 1818. One of two such pairs; the state's commission stipulated that all work would be done within the state, thus showcasing native craftsmanship. Mounts of gold and of gilded silver. The sets proved to be the finest American flintlock pistols made. A national treasure, they are displayed at the National Museum of American History, Smithsonian Institution.

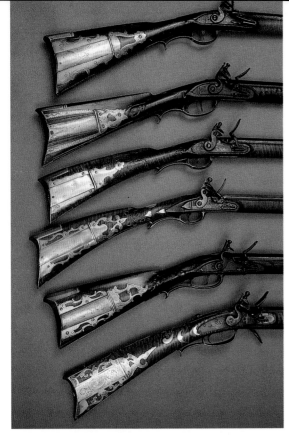

The American longrifle (or Kentucky rifle) of various schools and periods: late eighteenth and early nineteenth centuries. These arms represent America's first notable contribution to the history of embellished firearms. The craftsmen were largely Germanic. In style and execution the work ranged from somewhat primitive to quite sophisticated and refined, reflecting a range from folk artist to the highest caliber of master gunmaker.

Cased shotgun of Napoleon III; ebonized case finish with engraved flush brass-inlaid lid and sides. Crown above N engraved on stock escutcheon at top of wrist and on case lid escutcheon. Sculpted silver and silver gilt; stock of select walnut. Locks with sculpted steel, and gold inlay and damascene. Note game motifs; Napoleon, a nephew of Napoleon Bonaparte, was a keen hunter and sportsman. Silver buttplate with touchmark on toe. The exquisite case, gold-embossed inside lid: FIRMIN GAYMU / 20, PAS-SAGE DE L'OPERA / PARIS. Gold relief markings on barrel rib. Smoothbore 30-inch damascus barrels; bottoms marked EUGENE BERNARD (right barrel) and CANONNIER A PARIS (left barrel), with gold cartouche stamp inlaid to rear of each marking. Engraved bright steel bullet mold and patch cutter. A silk cloth was fitted to cover case interior (not shown).

9

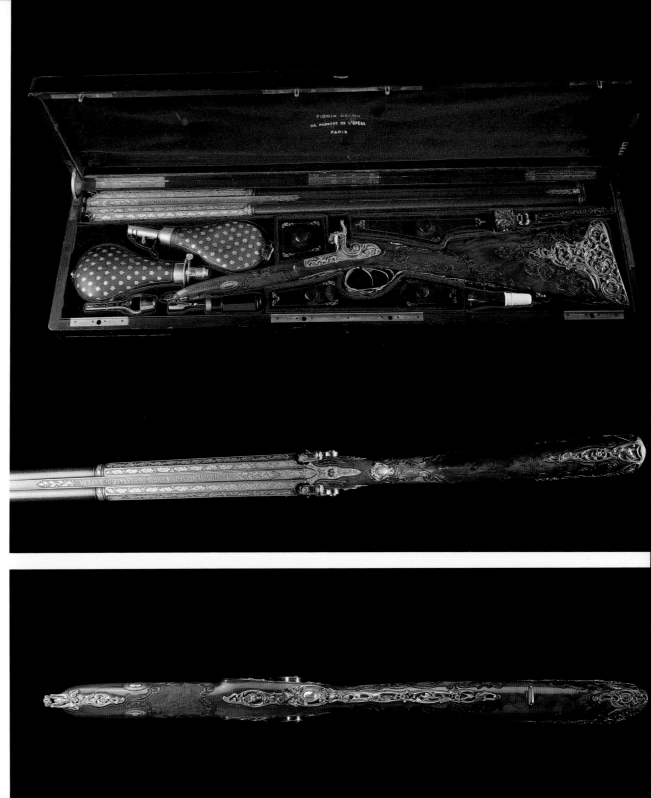

Examples of a particular style of mid-nineteenth-century embellishment, pistols (and even longarms) like this ebony-stocked pair by A. Gauvain (Paris) were heavily influenced by the Gothic revival in European art. The style was popular on deluxe guns of French, Belgian, German, and Austrian production, of the mid- to late nineteenth century. Note the *horror vacui,* the maker's need to decorate and cover every bit of surface. The grapes symbolized the celebration to follow a shooting contest. Vestiges of this garish style, particularly in game scenes and scrolls, continue in popularity to this day with the German and Austrian engravers and stockmakers.

Three deluxe Colt revolvers, engraved and inlaid by German-born and -trained Gustave Young, for presentation by Colonel Colt to Czar Nicholas I, 1853–54. These arms were used by Colt as display pieces, then taken to Russia and presented to the czar in a personal audience. The set constitutes the ultimate in the decoration of the Colt revolver in the nineteenth century; these were the most elaborate of American arms made up to that time. Young's execution, nevertheless, appears restrained when compared to contemporary European decoration. The Puritan ethic, which inhibited expression, had already taken hold with immigrant Young.

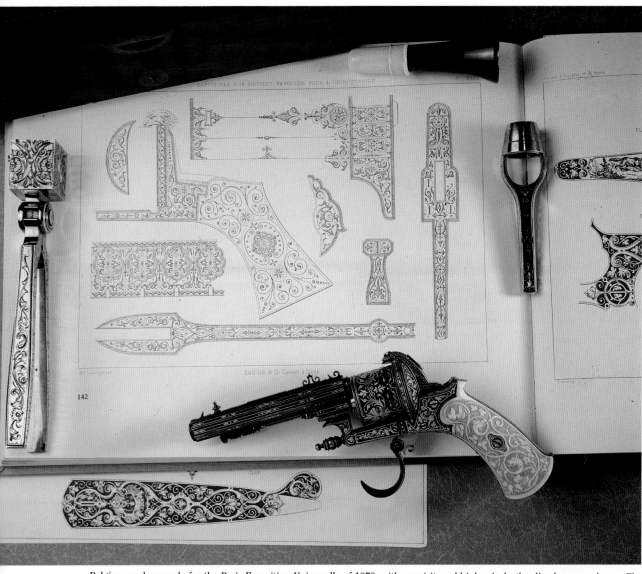

Charles V, which now resides in the Real Armeria, in Madrid.

Late in the century, France also began to make wheel-locks, but with a distinctive style characterized by a smaller lockplate, as well as with mechanical differences. Italy's wheel-lock production, begun about the same time, essentially adopted the German style.

France took preeminence from Germany in the art of gunmaking in the seventeenth century and is credited with the development of the flintlock ignition system. French firearms combine a beauty and delicacy of form with a high degree of technical achievement. The ascendency of France in this arena was not a little encouraged by King Louis XIII. At the age of ten, Louis already owned seven guns. Three years later, his collection totaled fifty, and he was adding to it regularly. A true arms enthusiast, he spent a great deal of time taking down and cleaning his own guns, and his *cabinet d'armes,* which eventually numbered several hundred firearms, remained intact until the French Revolution. Louis XIV ordered an inventory of it in 1673. The inventory numbers were stamped in the stocks, so that today many pieces can be traced to Louis's collection, although exactly what happened to the rest is unknown, owing to the confusion of the times. If Louis XIV was the Sun King, then Louis XIII was the Gun King.

While Italian makers did not develop a distinctive school of gunmaking, the area around Brescia in the north produced a style of embellishment, featuring pierced and chiseled renderings of birds, animals, human figures, and monsters, all surrounded by baroque foliate scrollwork, which earned them renown in the seventeenth century. Nor were the southern Italians idle. J. F. Hayward, in *European Firearms,* the guide to the arms collection at London's Victoria and Albert Museum, wrote:

In Southern Italy a type of chiselled ornament was adopted, by comparison with which even the florid Brescian style seems restrained. The lock was chiselled with grotesque masks carved in very high relief, and with figure sculpture executed in the round. This style

Belgian revolver made for the Paris Exposition Universelle of 1878, with exquisite gold inlay, in leather-lined rosewood case. The Charles Claesen pattern book, c. 1856, is reproduced from *Master French Gunsmiths Designs,* by Stephen V. Grancsay, late curator, Department of Arms and Armor, The Metropolitan Museum of Art, and a distinguished scholar of embellished arms. Gold inlaid on top of barrel: MATHES FRERES. Flush gold inlaid on bottom of trigger: EXPOSITION / UNIVERSELLE / PARIS [gold dot] 1878. Six-shot .36-caliber pinfire, with 4-inch faceted barrel. Decorated with piercing and relief and flush gold inlaying; blued and polished steel; carved ivory grips. Accessories from Napoleon III cased shotgun. Gustave Young probably resorted to the Claesen pattern book for his more demanding commissions.

Unique Winchester Model 1866 rifle, with frame, forend cap, and buttplate of solid silver; engraved by L. D. Nimschke and signed by the German-born and -trained craftsman seven times. Nimschke's extraordinary work scrapbook documented much of his output, including this *solid silver* rifle, made for a presentation by the president of Peru to the president of Bolivia. One of two pages from Nimschke's scrapbook reveals prints pulled to document this formidable commission. Note borders differing from the standard in decorative arts of the day; the scrollwork is a variation of Renaissance style, made popular with the publication in 1856 of Owen Jones's *The Grammar of Ornament.*

The influence of German and Austrian engraving is evident on this Smith & Wesson revolver decorated by R. J. Kornbrath, c. 1935. Born in Ferlach, Austria, Kornbrath worked in Hartford, Connecticut, in the years 1910–37.

Gold-embellished Purdey shotgun, from a matched and cased pair, completed c. 1981. The engraver, K. C. Hunt, a freelance in London, has done more firearms for royalty, world leaders, and other distinguished clientele than any other craftsman alive today. Sample plate cast in silver from gold-inlaid steel original, made by Hunt c. 1968 on commission from author.

of ornament has been associated with Naples, mainly because somewhat similar designs are found on the cup hilts of rapiers signed by Neapolitan masters.

It was also during the seventeenth century that elaborately inlaid stocks began to lose favor. Instead, greater care was placed in the selection of fine woods, especially walnuts, whose natural beauty complemented the sculptured and engraved steel mountings. The engraver was becoming paramount in the embellishing of arms.

Engraving Tools and Techniques

The methods of engraving, and the tools used, have remained virtually unchanged to the present. Slender chisels in various shapes, called scribers, are used in one hand and tapped with the small jeweler's hammer in the other, to form the basic design and shading. The graver, a shortened scriber with a bulbous wooden handle, is used by one hand alone to produce fine detail. Vises hold the piece being worked, magnifying glasses permit the artist to see the minute detail, and draftsman's dividers complete the equipment. The rest depends on the artistry of the craftsman.

A common practice after completing engraving on a particular element of a gun's furniture was to pull a proof on paper directly from the engraved surface. Known today as "gunmakers' pulls," these were kept in the artist's shop, possibly to prevent, but sometimes surely to permit, duplication in the future. Today they provide a record of many designs executed on pieces that have been lost and occasionally serve to identify the engraver of an unattributed piece that has survived.

The finest of embellished arms in Colonial America were imported from Europe. By the eighteenth century, even in Europe, the extravagant encrustations of bone, ivory, pearl, silver, and gold, the profuse relief chiseling, engraving, and etching on barrels, were waning. Again from Hayward, this time his book *The Art of the Gunmaker*: "The attitude of both gunmaker and his customer changed during the last decades of the 18th century. Whereas previously a fine gun had to be richly

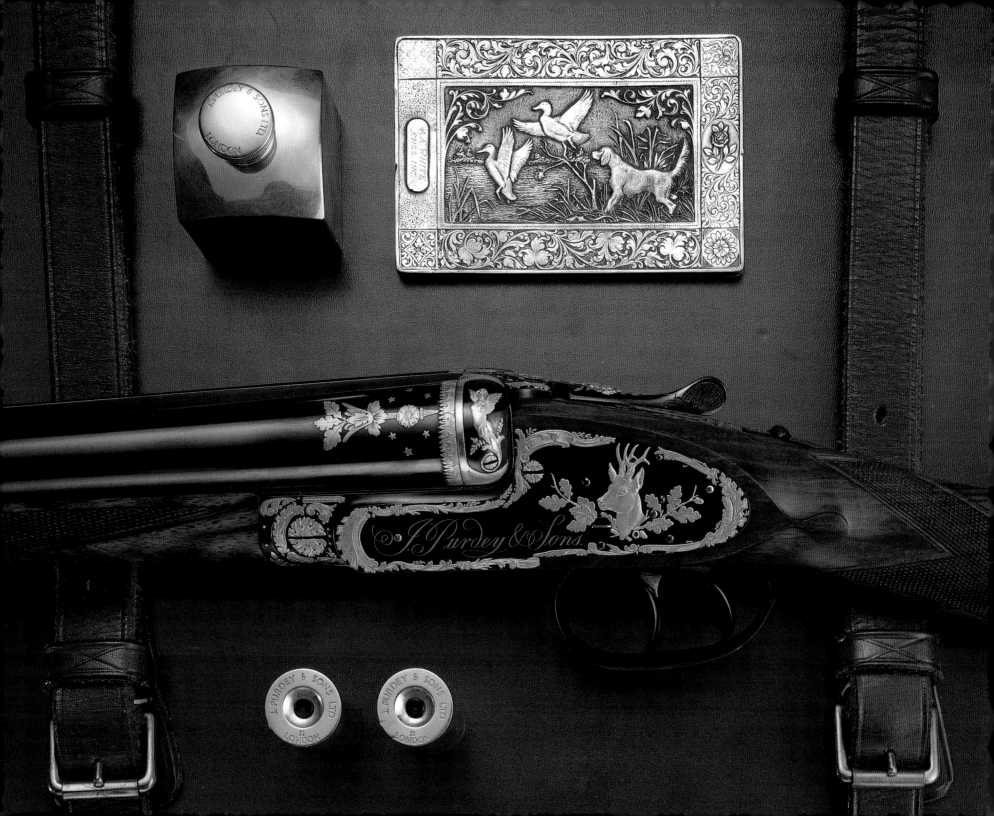

The Saurian, a 4-bore shotgun by Holland & Holland, Ltd., London, in celebration of their sesquicentennial, 1985. Engraved and sculpted with dinosaur scenes and related creatures and vegetation, by the Brown brothers, Alan and Paul. Gun is accompanied by an elaborate case and an array of accessories. Note interplay of figural scenes with decorative motifs of scales, as evidenced on the metal and wood.

decorated, this ceased to be an indispensable feature...."

The Kentucky Rifle

Perhaps the first display of indigenous American art was the Kentucky rifle. After the Revolutionary War, Kentucky rifles became increasingly fancy. Engraved and pierced patchboxes were usually rendered in brass and sometimes in silver, or with silver accents. Though the quality of engraving was usually somewhat primitive, the motifs evolved from Pennsylvania-, Maryland-, and Virginia-area folk art to include scrolls, borders, floral patterns, cross-hatching, horse heads, eagles and other birds, snakes, fishes, Indian weapons, sailing ships, zigzag lines, and geometric patterns.

At the end of the Kentucky period, Simeon North, a Connecticut gunmaker and a pioneer in mass production, produced a tour de force in two superb pairs of flintlock pistols that rivaled the finest guns of British and French masters. Engraved and mounted in gold and silver gilt, the pistols were commissioned by the State of Connecticut for presentation to Commodores Thomas McDonough and Thomas Hull, naval heroes of the War of 1812. One of the stipulations of the commission was that both pairs of pistols be produced entirely within the state of Connecticut. Equally exquisite swords were also commissioned, from the shops of Nathan Starr, also of Connecticut. The war had ushered in a new era of American craftsmanship in arms.

As an individual trade in America, gun engraving was a by-product of the machine age. Mass-produced "pepperbox" multibarreled pistols of the 1830s and 1840s

Twelve-bore shotgun by the Rizzini brothers of Brescia, with bulino engraving in Art Nouveau style by Firmo Fracassi, c. 1980. The minute detailing required to execute bulino with perfection makes it the most demanding technique in the art of the arms engraver. Note the imaginative rendering, with eagle flying out of the cartouche, wings overlapping the border.

The bulino style by American engraver Winston Churchill; the shotgun an over and under by Ivo Fabbri of Brescia. Game scenes inlaid in gold; the scroll and borderwork line engraved.

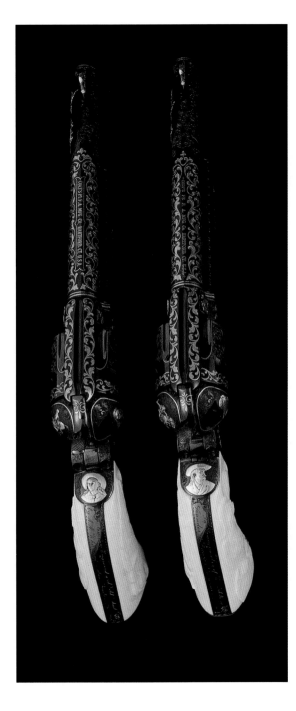

often sported hand engraving as standard, and the demand for specialist gun engravers was immediate. When Samuel Colt's first revolving hand- and long guns issued from the short-lived Paterson, New Jersey, plant, most were plain except for engraving on the cylinders, which Colt cleverly executed with roll dies. But even the few Paterson Colts that were hand engraved served to bolster the demand for craftsmen able to execute such work.

American Arms and the Machine

By about 1850, most manufacturers had stopped offering engraving as a standard feature of their arms, but at the same time, deluxe-grade guns were being maintained in inventory and produced on the special order of military and civilian clients. Sam Colt was in the forefront of this development, promoting his business and seeking government contracts both here and abroad with the help of carefully calculated presentations of fancy revolvers to heads of state and military officers. Deluxe guns were being made in Colt's new Hartford factory almost as soon as the doors opened in 1847, and Sharps, Volcanic, and Smith & Wesson followed his lead within a few years.

The western migration, the Mexican War, and the continuous battles with the Indians, as well as events in Europe, South Africa, and Australia, fed the rapidly expanding arms industry. The Victorian taste for garish and profuse decoration in art and architecture profoundly influenced weapons embellishment. What quickly evolved was a golden age of arms decoration in America.

Hundreds of Germans and Austrians responded to the demand for expert gunmakers, most of them settling in New England. The immigrations began in force in the 1840s and continued in diminishing quantities into the

Matched pair of gold-inlaid, engraved, ivory-gripped, and steel-buttcapped Colt Peacemaker revolvers, embellished by Alvin A. White and Andrew Bourbon, of American Master Engravers, Inc., 1984–88. Casing of ebony, with ivory-mounted accessories. Extra cylinders feature the Capitol Building (Washington, D.C.), the Colt factory, and battle-scene motifs, inlaid and sculpted in gold.

Bolt-action sporting rifles by the David Miller Co., Tucson, Arizona. Rifles of this type—combining precision machining and handwork with modern materials—have reached the zenith of perfection and are a particular speciality of American custom gunmakers. *Bottom view* reveals engraving, gold inlaying, and special finishing by Leonard Francolini, on .300 Weatherby, *at top.*

(*opposite*) The patriotic eagle has been dominant in American arms since the Revolutionary War. Numerous gold inlays in minute detail, with equally fine engraving, are hallmarks of this Smith & Wesson revolver, embellished by Winston Churchill c. 1980. An American who learned his art from the Austrian master Joseph Fugger, Churchill is also a master gunsmith, stockmaker, and metalsmith. Absolute perfection in every decorative detail is the goal of this modern artisan in every firearm.

twentieth century. Several master gun engravers came to America as well in this period, among them Louis Daniel Nimschke, Gustave Young, and the first of the Ulrichs—men who were destined to become the most influential style setters and taste makers in the evolution of American arms engraving. The Young and Ulrich families spawned dynasties, with descendants of the latter active in the craft as late as 1950.

The rich, strong style of these engravers has continued to dominate American arms engraving to the present. Among the better-known examples of their distinctive artistry are a Colt Single Action Army revolver done for Theodore Roosevelt and a Model 1876 Winchester rifle presented to General Philip Sheridan. Gold-inlaid Colt percussion revolvers were presented to Czar Nicholas I of Russia (displayed, in 1979, at The Metropolitan Museum of Art). Equally lavish Colts were presented to the Sultan of Turkey and the kings of Sweden and Denmark; and a Remington Army Model revolver was presented to Lt. Colonel George Armstrong Custer.

Twentieth-Century Arms

The dawn of the twentieth century saw a decline in the commercial arms trade. Most of the Wild West had been tamed and the great era of big-game hunting was suspended until conservation and game management would later restore many species in large quantities. World War I largely interrupted civilian arms production, and afterward, a shortage of craftsmen and the ravages of the Depression saw the engraving of arms almost die out. Of equal significance were the advances in metallurgy that resulted in harder steels, many of which attained such a degree of hardness that engraving tools often broke and lines were difficult to cut neatly or to the desired depth. As a consequence, the times required to complete an engraving assignment often increased.

Prominent during this period were R. J. Kornbrath, George Ulrich of Winchester, Wilbur Glahn of Colt, William McGraw of Ithaca, and Harry Jarvis of Smith & Wesson. Probably not more than twenty persons in America made their living from gun engraving between

Browning Highpower automatic pistol embellished by American Raymond Wielgus, 1976. Influenced by Art Nouveau and Art Deco styles, Wielgus has introduced his own distinctive style into the 500-year history of arms decoration. The forms and mechanical designs of the firearms he embellishes are accentuated by his use of gold and other materials. A major sampling of Wielgus-decorated arms is collected at The Art Institute of Chicago.

Tiffany & Co. designed and made decorations for Colt, Winchester, and Smith & Wesson firearms in the Art Nouveau style, from the mid-1880s to the early twentieth century. The firm is also credited with cast bronze, silver, and gold grips for Colt arms in the period c. 1860–70. In 1983 the firm returned to firearms embellishment, and the illustrated Colt revolver was made on commission for the U.S. Historical Society (begun 1991). Gold-damascened and -inlaid grips mounted in gold, the gripstraps gold-plated, the buttcap of gold and silver-inlaid steel. The fresh approach of Tiffany's designers has created an entirely new chapter in arms decoration.

1914 and 1945. The most influential was Kornbrath, an Austrian whose reputation has become almost legendary in America. In general, these engravers held much more closely to the German style than their predecessors had, and not a few American engraved arms from this period differ little from their European counterparts.

A Modern Arms Renaissance

A renaissance in engraving interest began after World War II, accompanied by an increase in the number of craftsmen, some returning from wartime service. A renewed interest in shooting sports, a generally favorable economy, and the realization among buyers that quality decorative firearms represent good investments have been strong influences. Today there are more than 175 engravers at work in the United States, and they enjoy a wider than ever range of pictorial subjects to work from as well as the ability to share knowledge and techniques with each other. The Education and Training Division of the National Rifle Association has been instrumental in inaugurating engraving schools, spearheaded by H. Wayne Sheets and master engraver Neil Hartliep.

About twenty-five of the contemporary American craftsmen are masters, rivaling the best of Europe. Of European arms engravers, there are probably over 350. The best of both continents rival, and sometimes surpass, the wonderful skills and artistry of the finest master engravers of the past.

While the buyers of modern engraved firearms are more likely to be businessmen or oil tycoons, bankers or show business personalities, there are still aristocratic patrons as well, and they are keen to have examples of functional, modern-made artistry, for they recognize the strong ties of these exquisite objects with an uninterrupted 500 years of magnificence in the production of "best-quality" arms. The fact that Tiffany & Co. has returned to the decoration of arms is indication that the field has new life, and a future as brilliant as its past.

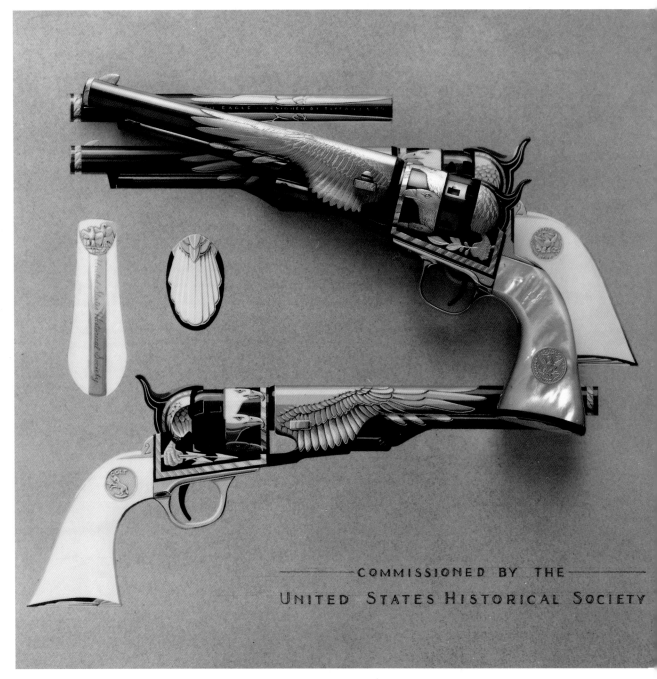

—————COMMISSIONED BY THE—————
UNITED STATES HISTORICAL SOCIETY

23

Chapter 2
From Colonial Arms to the Kentucky Rifle

How and why New England became America's gunmaking focal point is a subject for historical and technical speculation. In considering arms as decorative art objects, the Yankee psyche must surely be taken into account: plain, functional, and simple was the rule of thumb at the beginning. It would be makers of the Kentucky rifle who introduced rich embellishments to native-made arms, and then subsequent makers, particularly Samuel Colt, who would create objects rivaling, and sometimes bettering, the arms of contemporary European makers.

The first New England guns to offer any artistic interest were copies of, or improvements on, European and British fowling pieces. Long fowlers of French, English, and Dutch manufacture were known in America as early as the 1600s. Distinctly American long fowlers evolved in

Treasures of Colonial and Federal America. Besides their practical role in the colonization of North America, the quality, craftsmanship, and beauty of arms were part of the evolution of American culture and civilization. Wooden patchbox covers (at butt of stock) are indicative of early rifles; beneath lid was compartment for small accoutrements, including patches, in which bullets were wrapped for loading.

time, probably by 1725, serving to harvest quantities of wild fowl, usually on the ground and on the water. The long fowler, which began as a somewhat cumbersome contraption with a thick breech and stock to absorb recoil, gradually evolved into a graceful arm, likely influenced by French and English designs. A major inspiration for improvement was the importance of streamlining, to make the guns lighter for carrying over long distances.

Gunsmithing was a craft in demand from the very beginning, although the early artisans dealt mainly with repairs. Restocking was one such task, as may be evidenced by the numerous surviving guns with non-American locks, mounts, and barrels but stocked in such native woods as cherry, black walnut, and maple. Parts were also imported as spares, or to be used for building guns.

Sometimes replacement parts were crudely made, forged, filed, and fitted—as well as time, and cost, would permit. On the other hand, there were colonists who appreciated quality in a gun, and long fowlers of handsome design and high-quality workmanship are known, some with raised carving, as well as artistically formed

mounts, often engraved. The essentially plain New England guns were, in contrast to Hudson Valley fowlers, likely to have raised carving and engraving, reflecting the Dutch heritage of many who resided in that area.

Partly due to improvements in black powder that diminished the need for long barrels, long fowlers fell out of fashion by the early nineteenth century.

For versatility in hunting varied game, another type of gun was developed known as the buck-and-ball, which fired shot or bullets. These differed from rifles by the lack of rear sights (other than a possible groove on the breech) and the absence of rifling and patchboxes. Thickness of the barrel wall was greater than in the long fowlers, but not as thick as in rifles, a subject covered on the following pages.

The New England Rifle
New England rifles were a later development than the fowlers, the buck-and-ball guns, military arms—and the early Kentucky rifles. But their relationship to colonial gunmaking, and the mass-produced arms to follow, warrant their consideration here. These flintlock (and later, percussion) rifles, like their predecessor arms, reflected

From the manual of arms by Jacob de Gheyn, Amsterdam, 1607–08. Musketeer with matchlock, musket rest, and bandolier with cartridges.

New England tastes and sensibilities. Makers such as Silas Allen, Thomas Holbrook, Welcome Mathewson, Alvan and Henry Pratt, Hiram Slocomb, Martin Smith, and R. Perkins rivaled in precision and performance their more recognized fellow gunmakers from the leading centers of Pennsylvania, Maryland, and Virginia.

Present scholarship puts the New England rifle in production as early as 1773. An example by Thomas Tileston (Duxbury, Massachusetts) is both marked and dated 1773. These distinctive arms are easily identifiable as coming from New England by their sparse style, limited embellishments, plain, straight stocks, and overall good quality. Raised carving (other than some molding along forestocks) was not present, but silver wire was a popular and prevalent decorative device, an influence from English gunmaking. Also present might be sheet silver or brass inlays, bone, ivory, or horn as thumb or cheek inlays and as barrel wedge escutcheons. Forends and ramrod tips might also be of bone, horn, or ivory.

Stocks of cherry were common, but black walnut and (rarely) maple were also used. Mounts were usually of brass, but occasionally of silver or iron. Checkered wrists will sometimes be encountered. Patchboxes were simple, and if engraved, normally had designs of an urn, sunflower, or horse head (though this last is scarce). A daisy decor, also found on Lancaster, Pennsylvania, rifles, has been identified with Maine rifles. It is likely a traveling artisan may have engraved a number of New England mountings, judging from consistent details of style and quality on guns made in varying towns and cities.

The majority of New England rifles were built in Worcester County, Massachusetts. Names of gunsmiths from Sutton, a center of barrel production, will sometimes be found stamped under the breech. The best known and most respected of New England riflemakers was Silas Allen, of Shrewsbury, Massachusetts. An engraved motif believed to identify his work is found on the wristplate: two long bow-tie devices, pointed at the ends, with four vertical hash marks at the center of each.

The market for guns of quality grew with the accumulation of wealth in the colonies. Although this market was still largely served by importation of fine guns, local gunsmiths of talent were already established by 1730. An iron industry was developing in America around this time, enabling sourcing of native parts, rather than relying on imports.

Colonial gunmaking centers were in Boston, Worcester, Sutton, Springfield, and Greenfield in Massachusetts; New Haven, Middletown, Hartford, Goshen, New London, and Norwich in Connecticut; Providence, Burrillville, and Smithfield in Rhode Island; and Windsor in Vermont. The Connecticut River Valley was the leading cluster of such gunmakers, an important group of craftsmen well established by the time of the Revolutionary War.

Several hundred native gunsmiths made arms for the revolutionists during the war, often relying on salvaged parts from European-made guns. Wartime demand gave a spur to native gunmaking, and ultimately contributed to the evolution of the fine gun trade, which was largely put on hold during the conflict.

Even with the establishment of the Springfield Armory (1795) and the armory at Harpers Ferry (1796), the vast majority of American arms were still produced by private gunmakers in small, often one-man shops. Contemporary authorities, most of them earnest arms collectors, have researched makers through surviving guns, documents, and other sources, hoping to ferret out these hand craftsmen, not a few of whom failed to sign their guns.

While the aesthetics of American arms without embellishment is too broad a subject for the present book, it is important to recognize that until modern manufacturing shortcuts were adopted, in the twentieth century, the workmanship and overall appearance of the vast majority of American arms was quite pleasing to the eye. This visual appeal is part of the reason why Americans have what might be termed a birthright fascination with firearms. The way a gun handled, its balance, and feel were also important.

Militia groups, target clubs, sportsmen, pioneers, frontiersmen, adventurers, and gun enthusiasts com-

Selections from the Requa Collection of Hudson Valley fowlers. *From top left,* the rare doglock, c. 1680, *above* the historic Anthony Van Schaick gun. The gun *at bottom* is the carved, two-toned, maple-stocked fowler, c. 1760. *Next,* the Cornelis Wynkoop cherry-stocked gun dated 1738. *To its right,* the Requa family fowler, exhibiting profusely carved stock and decorative brass triggerguard. Muzzle *at left* is of a c. 1760 maple-stocked fowler; that *at bottom* a walnut-stocked gun c. 1740. The brass powder flask was found with a c. 1720 fowler (*second from left* in the photographs on pages 28 and 29). Decorative canteen shows Hudson Valley scene, oil painted on wood, c. 1830.

27

Unrivaled collection of Hudson Valley fowlers. *From the left,* the earliest known example, a doglock c. 1680; maple stock with a matchlock-era barrel; overall length 7 feet, 4 inches. Next, with maple stock, c. 1720; and another of like era, with walnut stock, the barrel breech inscribed with the owner's name, ANTHONY VAN SCHAICK. *Fourth from left,* a maple-stocked gun from Kingston, New York, c. 1740; the next gun, with walnut stock, found in western New York, is of the same period; next two guns also stocked in maple, and of like date. *Eighth gun from left,* dated 1738 on wood, with cherry stock, CWK monogram on thumbpiece, and CORNELIS WYNKOOP engraved on barrel breech; owner from a distinguished family of silversmiths. *Fourth gun from right,* with maple stock, c. 1740, next to a rare two-tone maple-stocked fowler, 1760. *Second gun from right,* from family of the present owner, Glode M. Requa, stocked in maple, c. 1770. *Final gun, at right,* of like date, and also stocked in maple.

The opposite sides of the Requa collection of Hudson Valley fowlers; beginning *at left* with the doglock gun, c. 1680. Note earlier guns having pierced sideplates and more substantial butts, barrel breeches, locks, and overall configurations.

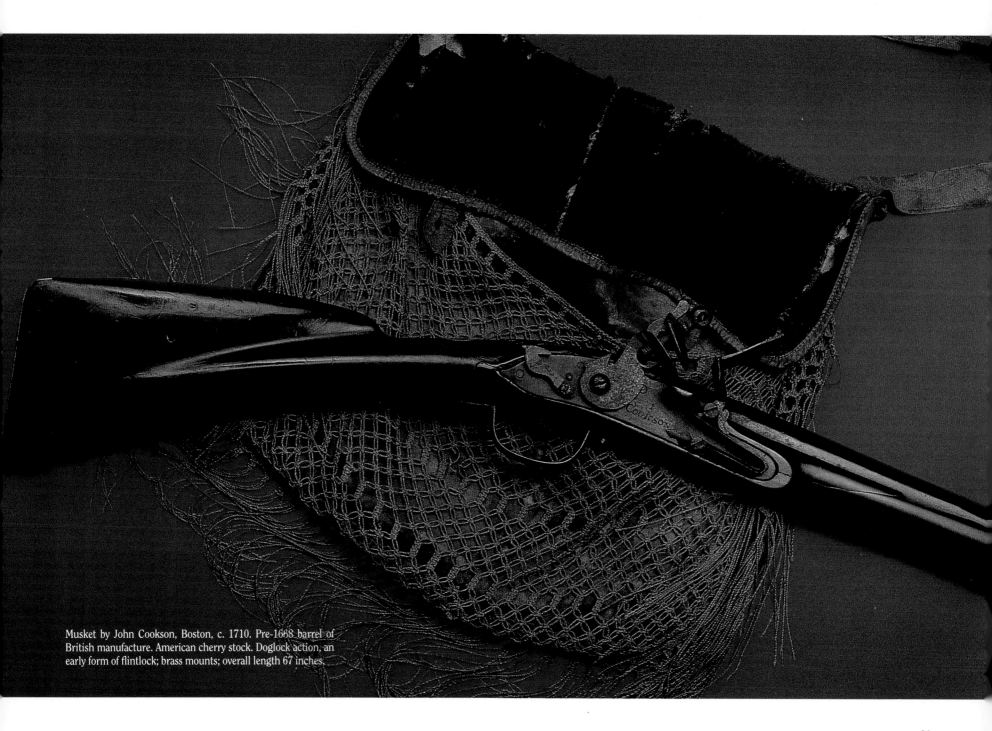

Musket by John Cookson, Boston, c. 1710. Pre-1688 barrel of British manufacture. American cherry stock. Doglock action, an early form of flintlock; brass mounts; overall length 67 inches.

prised a market that inspired craftsmen to create objects that not only functioned, but had aesthetic appeal.

The Kentucky Rifle

But Jackson he was wide awake
and wasn't scar'd at trifles
for well he knew what aim we take,
with our Kentucky rifles,
so he led us down to Cypress Swamp,
the ground was low and mucky,
there stood John Bull in martial pomp
but here was old Kentucky.

Fifth stanza of "The Hunters of Kentucky," a ballad (c. 1814) celebrating the American victory at the Battle of New Orleans.

Since the might of Great Britain had been defeated at New Orleans by American military imagination, a secure defensive position, and regular troops boosted by 2,000 American frontier riflemen—with their deadly fire over long ranges—it was logical that this world-shaking feat would be celebrated in song. "The Hunters of Kentucky" establishes the early use of the name "Kentucky rifle" for what is arguably America's first indigenous art form. An American legend had come of age. (Although it has also been termed, variously, the Pennsylvania rifle, the Pennsylvania-Kentucky rifle, the American rifle, and the American longrifle, the author prefers "Kentucky rifle," the name by which this hallowed arm has been known since at least the early nineteenth century.)

Expert Joe K. Kindig III has stated that

the Kentucky rifle is the artistic bridge between the rural, homespun, Germanic cultures of middle Europe and the carefully integrated technology and design concepts of the English and German colonists in Pennsylvania, resulting quite possibly in the creation of our only native American art form. The gunsmiths who made the rifle bridged the English and German cultures in the province of Pennsylvania in a way that no other artisans did.

For over a century in America's westward expansion,

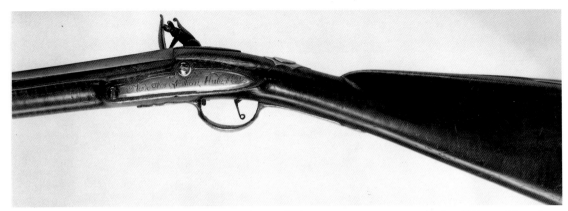

Long fowler by Benoni Hills, Goshen, Connecticut, c. 1741. Inscribed MADE FOR NATHAN HUBELL on sideplate. Hills was father of gunsmiths Medad and John Hills.

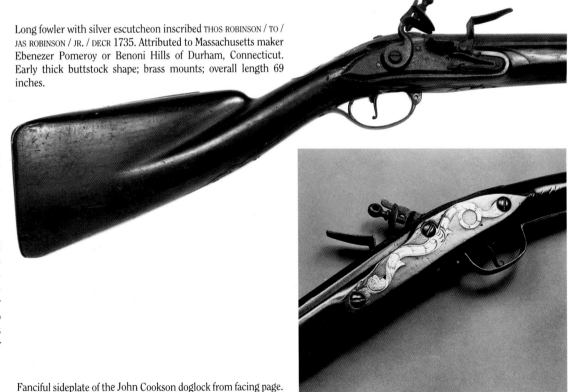

Long fowler with silver escutcheon inscribed THOS ROBINSON / TO / JAS ROBINSON / JR. / DECR 1735. Attributed to Massachusetts maker Ebenezer Pomeroy or Benoni Hills of Durham, Connecticut. Early thick buttstock shape; brass mounts; overall length 69 inches.

Fanciful sideplate of the John Cookson doglock from facing page.

Fowler with club stock of cherry, late eighteenth century. Imported French military lock and mix of iron and brass mounts. Some fowlers used as muskets by colonists in Revolutionary War. Overall length 64½ inches.

NO SLAVERY, believed to be a rejection of George III and Great Britain during Revolutionary War. Fowler altered to military musket. Stocked in maple; overall length 64 inches.

Long fowler by Thomas Earl, Leicester, Massachusetts, c. 1760, overall length 71½ inches. Earl, active c. 1760–1810, was maker of several muskets and long fowlers; one of latter built for George Washington.

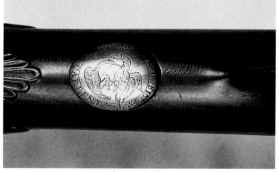

Musket by Ambrose Peck of Swansea, Massachusetts, inscribed with patriotic, Revolutionary War devices. Escutcheon motif taken from $3 currency, issued in 1776, shows eagle fighting a heron. Bayonet in stock rarely observed.

gunmakers created these often beautiful and always deadly accurate rifles, whose design and decoration evolved primarily from Germanic and Swiss origins with an admixture of English influence. The European models were generally shorter and heavier, larger in caliber, and more suited to short-range shooting. Frontier America required a lighter, longer rifle, of smaller caliber, one capable of accuracy at ranges of 150 yards and sometimes beyond. The Kentucky rifle is the result of a process of trial and error, but the traditions of European gunmaking served to guide its craftsmanship and decoration.

The best of the Kentucky rifles were masterpieces of mechanical excellence, artistic style, and elegant craftsmanship. These qualities made the Kentucky a legend in its own time. It is also among the most American of all firearms, and the subject of intense artistic and historical fascination.

To the American pioneer rifleman, often alone in the wilderness and totally self-reliant, no possession had greater importance or meaning than his Kentucky rifle. It was the necessary implement for providing meat for his table and protection against Indians (and at times against the British, French, and Spanish), as well as a source of great aesthetic pleasure owing to its intrinsic beauty: a magnificent reminder of the civilization the rifleman left behind to hunt or explore and open up new territory.

A fine Kentucky is a masterwork created with primitive tools on the frontier. Although it has roots in its European predecessor arms, the Kentucky rifle is distinctly and uniquely American. The greatest Kentucky riflemakers were masters of many skills and crafts: silversmiths, lockmakers, barrelmakers, polishers, finishers, ironmongers, furniture makers, brass makers, jewelers, engravers, and designers. And the Kentucky is the one artifact from pioneer America that required these combined skills in a single craftsman.

The first half of the eighteenth century constitutes a developmental period, in which the Germanic and Swiss styles of rifles were adapted to American needs. The

New England rifle with signed barrel by Ware & Morse, Worcester; attributed to James Jennison of Southbridge. Patchbox typical, in profile and decoration, of central Massachusetts. Overall length 60 inches; c. 1800. The traditional shape of the patchbox is a rectangular panel, hinged to a decorative plate inlaid on the stock. The opening panel is often surmounted by decorative inlays, sometimes pierced, and often scalloped. Materials used included brass, and sometimes silver, German silver, or iron. After c. 1775, decorative embellishments appear with increasing profusion.

Patchbox from silver-inlaid, half-stock smoothbore New England rifle, c. 1825; barrel marked COTTON, and lock marked LANE AND READ—BOSTON.

evolving design was also influenced by English and French smoothbore fowling pieces—long, graceful, and light, with beautiful architecture. The early Kentuckys retained an overall heavy look, large in caliber, the stocks thick, often carved on the butts, and with patchboxes of wood (later of brass). Barrels were generally octagonal, swamped, rifled, and long. These pioneer American rifles were largely utilitarian. Only a handful of such early pieces have survived to modern times.

In the second half of the eighteenth century, the rifles attained their zenith, the best of them combining finely executed lock and barrel work, handsome inlays of brass and/or silver, rich carvings, and a combination of line and form that qualified them to be recognized as masterful and original works of decorative art. In studying contemporary silver, one finds that the piercing on silver

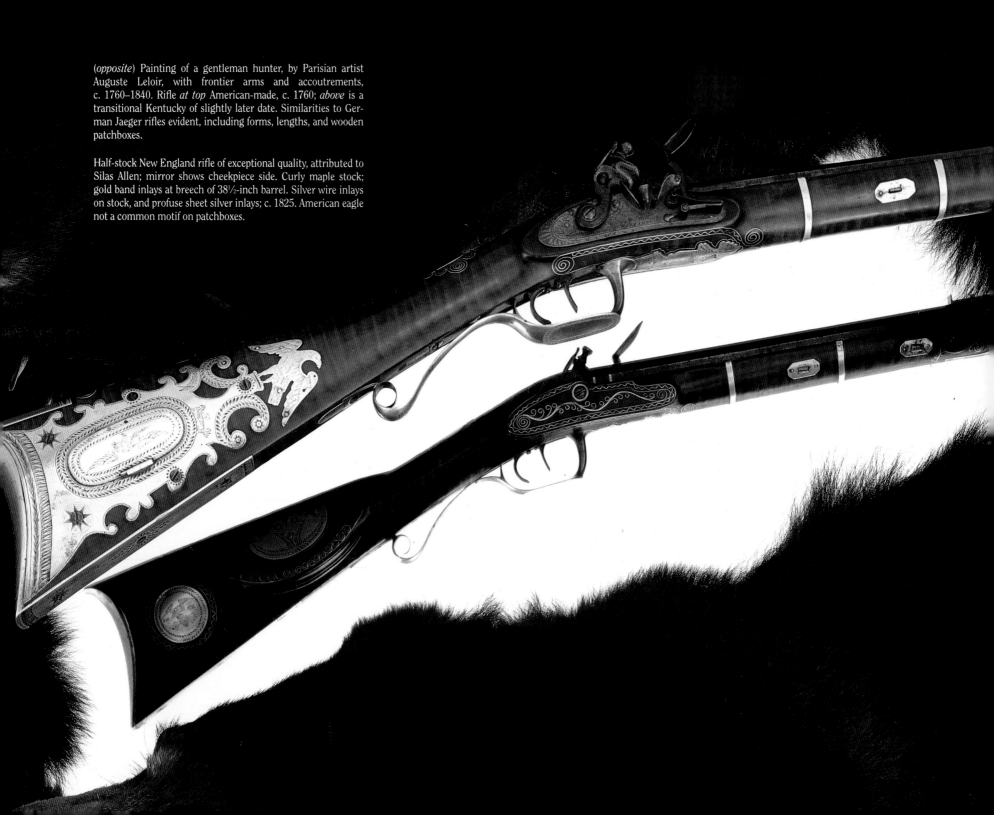

(*opposite*) Painting of a gentleman hunter, by Parisian artist Auguste Leloir, with frontier arms and accoutrements, c. 1760–1840. Rifle *at top* American-made, c. 1760; *above* is a transitional Kentucky of slightly later date. Similarities to German Jaeger rifles evident, including forms, lengths, and wooden patchboxes.

Half-stock New England rifle of exceptional quality, attributed to Silas Allen; mirror shows cheekpiece side. Curly maple stock; gold band inlays at breech of 38½-inch barrel. Silver wire inlays on stock, and profuse sheet silver inlays; c. 1825. American eagle not a common motif on patchboxes.

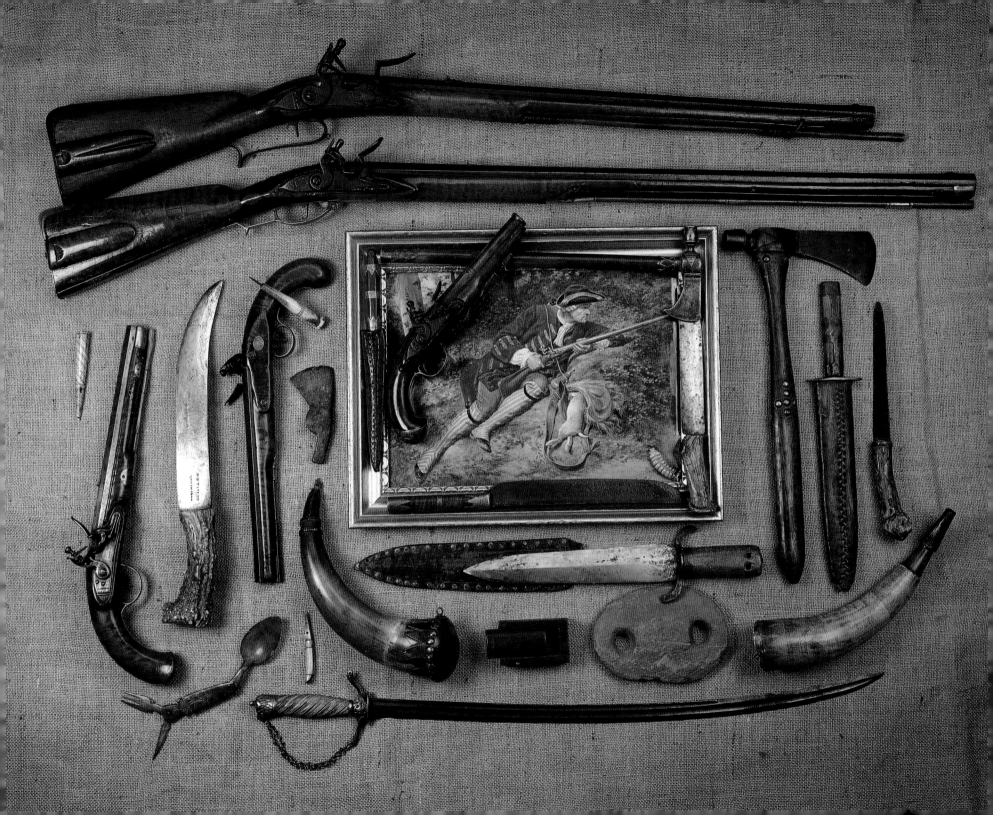

Oil painting of frontiersman shooting with Kentucky rifle at American Indian adversaries, by C. I. Kingsley, 1888. Kentucky rifles with wooden patchboxes, of 1770s, the *top* made in England and marked GRICE, likely copied from captured rifle; others American, of Reading or Lancaster make (its wood patchbox replaced with brass); *bottom,* possibly by Virginia gunsmith. Powder horn from Fort Trumbull, Connecticut, dated 1777, IN SUPPORT OF INDEPENDENCE. (N.B. Unless noted otherwise, in this chapter, place names without reference to state are in Pennsylvania.)

porringer handles is comparable to piercing on patchboxes. Further, there are many similarities in engraving between contemporary silver and engraved Kentucky rifles and pistols, and similarities in carving between the rifles and furniture of the period.

Schools of Makers

The Kentucky being a prized possession, decorative motifs were in order. Styles evolved in various regions that are recognized by today's authorities as schools. These regional groups of makers range from the most influential and important—Lancaster—to such centers as Bethlehem, Reading, Lebanon, Dauphin, York, Littlestown, Emmitsburg, Chambersburg, Bedford (all in Pennsylvania), and various centers in Maryland, Virginia, and North Carolina. At its peak, around 1800, Lancaster boasted some one hundred riflemakers. However, although modern scholarship credits Lancaster as the center during its golden age, the birthplace of the Kentucky could well have been the Bucks County area.

The schools of makers were not confined to rigid centers, and overlaps existed. Journeymen, and sometimes masters themselves, moved about. And some rifles will demonstrate a mixture of skill and style identified with more than one craftsman. Grouping surviving rifles by schools of makers is the evolving, collective achievement of experts like the Kindigs (Joe Jr. and his son, Joe K. Kindig III), and hundreds of other devotees of the Kentucky.

Engravers and Carvers

Although manufacture was largely in frontier communities, some of the craftsmen excelled in carving and engraving, producing work comparable to that of the finest shops in such refined cities as Philadelphia, New York, Charleston, and Boston. Among the most distinguished such gunmakers were Jacob Kuntz, Martin Frey, John Noll, Isaac Haines, Abraham Schweitzer, George Eyster, Henry Lechler, John Philip Beck, Jacob Lowmaster, Conrad Welshans, and Peter Berry. The achievement of these artisans is all the more remarkable when one

36

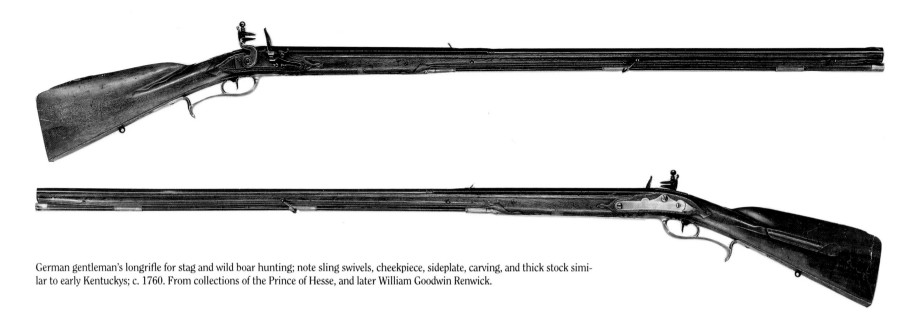

German gentleman's longrifle for stag and wild boar hunting; note sling swivels, cheekpiece, sideplate, carving, and thick stock similar to early Kentuckys; c. 1760. From collections of the Prince of Hesse, and later William Goodwin Renwick.

considers the fact that many worked alone, or with no more than one or two assistants, whereas contemporary continental and British shops usually employed a half-dozen or more craftsmen, most of them specializing in a specific task.

However, expert Siro Toffolon, himself a professional designer and artist, has observed that

> in many cases the man who signed the barrel did not make the complete gun. For example, John Rupp rifles were sometimes engraved by Jacob Kuntz. There is no documentation to support this, rather this is based on the observation of engraving style, layout, and execution. The same is sometimes true with carving, in which a particularly skilled carver might assist by applying his art to another craftsman's rifle.

Toffolon has also commented on the intermingling of gunsmiths with silversmiths. Among the North Carolina silversmiths he identified who were also gunsmiths were John Vogler, of Salem, Martin Noxon, of Edmonton, and John B. Mills, of Fayetteville. Jacob Kuntz and John Noll were gunsmiths who were well qualified as silversmiths. At least two rifles by John Rupp have the crude signature of that maker but bear silver mounts and engraving of

impressive quality. Toffolon attributes the engraving to Jacob Kuntz, based on ornament, style, and quality. It follows that a craftsman in a particular locale, aware of the availability of other craftsmen with superior skills, might call on them for an assignment, such as engraving, or even carving.

Toffolon has listed no less than forty-two silversmiths known from the Lancaster, Pennsylvania, area (eighteenth and nineteenth centuries), many of whom would have been qualified to assist at least in the embellishments of a Kentucky rifle. Ten silversmiths from York County are also noted.

The Golden Age
Joe Kindig, Jr., dean of Kentucky rifle authorities and author of the classic work *Thoughts on the Kentucky Rifle in Its Golden Age,* identified the period of the most striking and beautiful of these rifles as "The Golden Age." This includes the arms built in the period following the Revolutionary War through about 1825 that featured patchboxes of striking elegance and beauty. To quote Kindig: "During this period . . . the patchbox began to acquire a beauty through rococo design which made it

the outstanding element of the Kentucky rifle and a purely American innovation worthy of being considered a work of art."

Joe K. Kindig III, further considering the artistic factors, has observed:

> The whole story of the artistry of gunsmithing in Pennsylvania revolved around a common interest in the rococo vocabulary and infinite individualistic interpretations of it, from early academic efforts on the part of the Lancaster and York makers, to late, provincial, statements long after the style in the artistic centers had gone out of fashion.

Kentucky rifles were built as late as the mid-nineteenth century.* The percussion rifles soon had to compete with the mass-produced, oft times repeating, arms of the industrial revolution. The day of the Kentucky was soon over. The late production guns of c. 1830–50 were of a flatter, thinner configuration, with incised, sometimes relief, or no stock carving whatever, having flat

---

*In modern times the rifle has been revived to the extent that nearly as many Kentuckys are in production today as during its peak period, from the end of the Revolutionary War till the dawn of the percussion era.

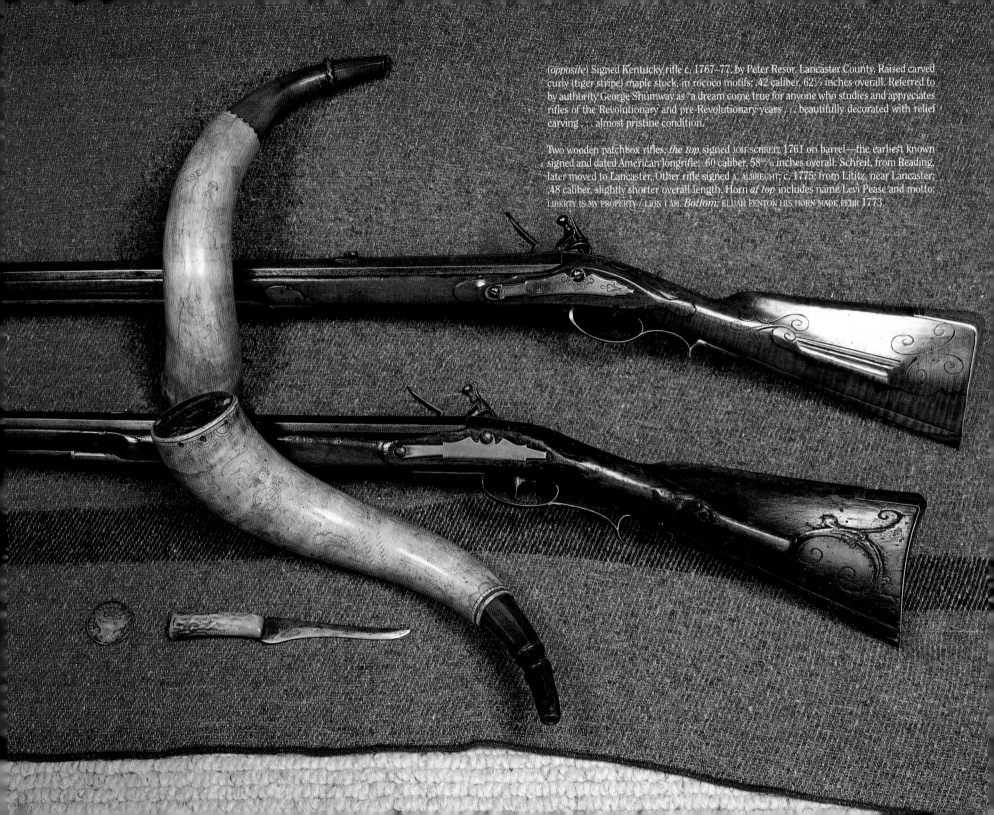

(*opposite*) Signed Kentucky rifle c. 1767–77, by Peter Resor, Lancaster County. Raised carved curly (tiger stripe) maple stock, in rococo motifs; .42 caliber; 62½ inches overall. Referred to by authority George Shumway as "a dream come true for anyone who studies and appreciates rifles of the Revolutionary and pre-Revolutionary years . . . beautifully decorated with relief carving . . . almost pristine condition."

Two wooden patchbox rifles, *the top*, signed JOH SCHREIT 1761 on barrel—the earliest known signed and dated American longrifle; .60 caliber; 58⅞ inches overall. Schreit, from Reading, later moved to Lancaster. Other rifle signed A. ALBRECHT, c. 1775, from Lititz, near Lancaster; .48 caliber, slightly shorter overall length. Horn *at top* includes name Levi Pease and motto: LIBERTY IS MY PROPERTY / LION I AM. *Bottom:* ELIJAH FENTON HIS HORN MADE FEBR 1773.

Ornamentation of the Kentucky Rifle*

Gunsmiths of Pennsylvania and their clients were quite religious, and embraced rather strong and somewhat superstitious views. Marks and symbols, commonly known today as hex marks, became part of everyday life and in decorative demand.

The X mark, or symbol, represents Christ, the crescent moon the Virgin Mary. The fifth wound of Christ is depicted by an ancient Christian symbol of a heart with the lower point curved to one side. In many cases a bird symbolized the human soul.

Following the Revolutionary War, the eagle came to represent freedom. The double-headed eagle was a German motif. Most frequently found as inlays on the cheekpiece is the eight-pointed birth, or Bethlehem, star. The most primitive Christian symbol representing Christ is the fish, found on forestocks of some guns, in brass or silver. Such motifs and decorations on Kentucky rifles served as talismans to ward off evil spirits.

Few of the Pennsylvania Dutch motifs can be said to have been strictly American in origin. Usually the source was in nature, history, or religion. By and large, the immigrant copied in America what had already been done in his European homeland, adding here and there personal touches of his own. The art of Fraktur or illuminative writing, for instance, came from pious German descendants.

However, at times designs were influenced by the new surroundings and the culture of the New World.

The tulip, brought to Europe from Asia Minor about the sixteenth century, was one of the most frequently used motifs. Immediately it gained popularity, spreading farther north to the gardens of England as well as Germany and the Low Countries.

The tulip, widely known in Pennsylvania, must have been a constant reminder of its European use in peasant design, and the simple outline made it suitable for untrained as well as trained hands to execute. Most authorities believe the presence of a three-petaled tulip symbolized the Trinity. It was accepted in Germany as a variation of the Holy Lily. This being the case, it is easy to understand its prominence in the art of so strongly a religious people as the Pennsylvania Dutch.

Inspirations came from many sources, including textile pattern books published in Switzerland, Germany, France, Italy, and England in the years 1580–1750. Decorative birds, parrots, peacocks, doves, chickens, and eagles—and particularly the "distelfink," or goldfinch—were favorite motifs.

Animals included lambs, lions, and deer. The unicorn and other motifs were borrowed from heraldic sources. Strangely enough, these aristocratic symbols represented the very classes from which the freedom-loving Germans had escaped. On occasion, stags and other animal motifs appeared, but the human figure was rare since a higher degree of skill was required for its delineation.

The Pennsylvania gunsmith, being influenced by this folk art, developed his own repertoire of symbols and patterns, so that one can sometimes recognize his work by their presence. Nicholas Beyer was one of these craftsmen, as were Johanes Neff and Peter Angstadt.

Rococo Style

When a Kentucky has elements of rococo design, it exhibits characteristics as follows: S-curves, C-scrolls, and naturalistic motifs inspired by plants, shells, and rocks. The gunsmiths utilized this style in outlining and engraving metal parts and in carving the stocks. The rococo is considered the highest order of decoration in the vocabulary of these craftsmen.

The age of any object made prior to this century can be determined to a great extent by the style of its design and ornamentation: artisans were thoroughly schooled in a single style for long periods of time. The rococo style of decoration, so popular in the sophisticated centers of cultured Europe and America, was also the style utilized by backwoods gunsmiths to enhance their rifles. It constituted a good percentage of the decoration of these guns. Therefore, the most artistic and capable gunsmiths were familiar with good pieces of furniture, silver, china, clocks, pottery, and porcelain.

America continued to look to England for its cultural models and standards. Even while Washington was leading the cause for political independence on the battlefield, his workmen at home were using English architectural manuals for reference in the renovation of Mount Vernon.

Furniture makers relied heavily on various pattern books compiled by English designers—notably *Chippendale's Director,* and several others—to produce their most stylish pieces. The sofa, tables, chairs, and other forms illustrated as samples on the trade card of Benjamin Randolph are derived from models pictured in three different English books that had been brought to Philadelphia shortly after their publication.

Philadelphia had become the most progressive city in America, and the largest. Its population had tripled during the twenty-five years preceding the Declaration of Independence, and its craftsmen had attained an admirable degree of competence.

Philadelphia Chippendale furniture represented the most ambitious achievement of colonial craftsmanship. There, the prevailing style was executed with the greatest exuberance and vigor. The carved woodwork and the stucco ceiling decorations of the Samuel Powell house in Philadelphia were largely copied or adapted from Abraham Swan's *Designs in Architecture,* an English sourcebook that was subsequently republished in America.

Many riflemakers were primitive and amateurish in their engraving, despite the high level of their other skills at making a fine gun. John Noll, however, may have been trained by a silversmith or an engraver, as his execution and flow of engraving is superb, masterful for his time and area. John Philip Beck was a creative gunsmith whose carving shows knowledge of the true and high form of ornament. Some of his carvings are in the folk-art category, and some guns by him combine both extremes.

---

*Condensed from Siro Toffolon's "The Kentucky Rifle and Its Ornamentations," in *The Kentucky Rifle Association,* winter 1980.

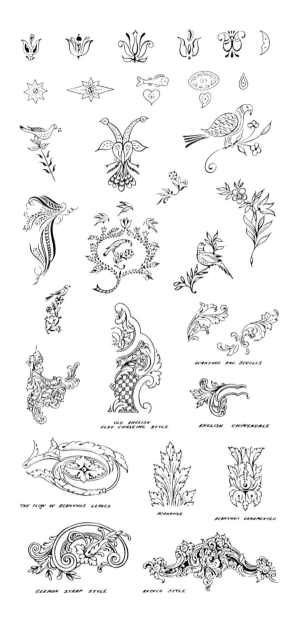

Drawings by Siro Toffolon of Pennsylvania Dutch motifs and various styles of ornamentation that influenced American gunsmiths in the eighteenth and nineteenth centuries.

Labels within drawing:

ACANTHUS AND SCROLLS

OLD ENGLISH FLAT CHASING STYLE

ENGLISH CHIPPENDALE

THE FLOW OF ACANTHUS LEAVES

ACANTHUS

ACANTHUS ORNAMENTED

GERMAN STRAP STYLE

ROCOCO STYLE

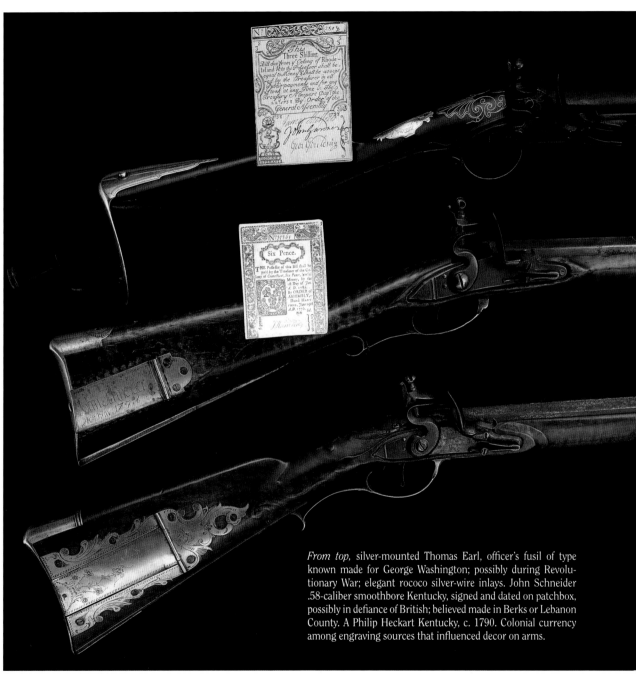

From top, silver-mounted Thomas Earl, officer's fusil of type known made for George Washington; possibly during Revolutionary War; elegant rococo silver-wire inlays. John Schneider .58-caliber smoothbore Kentucky, signed and dated on patchbox, possibly in defiance of British; believed made in Berks or Lebanon County. A Philip Heckart Kentucky, c. 1790. Colonial currency among engraving sources that influenced decor on arms.

Bethlehem school. *From top,* one rifle by Peter Neihart, and two by Herman Rupp. All three signed, and dated 1787, 1793, and 1809, respectively. Note brass-wire stock inlays. Bethlehem makers known for Roman nose stock profile, thin and flat, oval-contoured wrist, and two-part patchbox.

Carved cheekpieces in rococo style from golden-age Kentuckys by, *from top,* Nicholas Beyer, John Noll, and Jacob Sell.

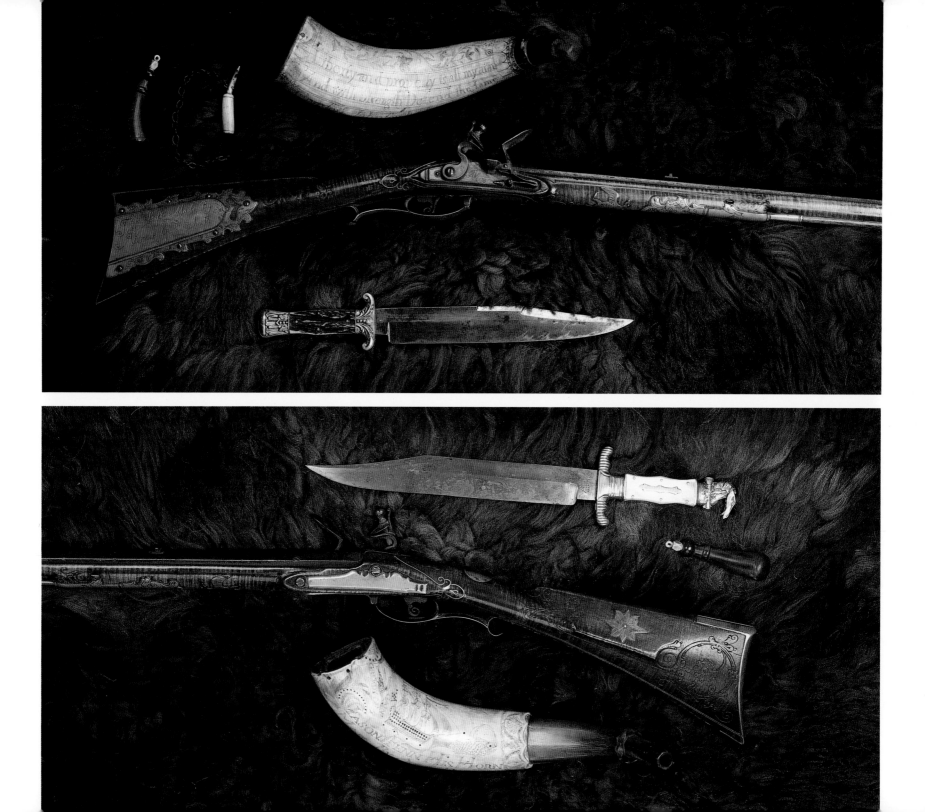

Lebanon school. *At top,* by John Philip Beck (signed with initials on thumbpiece); underside of barrel inscribed: INRI (*Iesus Nazarenus Rex Iudaeorum*—Jesus of Nazareth, King of the Jews); classic Kentucky maker. Rifle observed by author has half-horse, half-alligator motif engraved on breech. Nicholas Beyer rifle signed with name on barrel; Beyer a student of Beck. Folk-art quality to relief-carved bird on stock, as well as to circular cheekpiece inlay. School recognized for attractive patchboxes, light and restrained engraving, variety of patchbox finials, longwrist, high stock comb, and fine relief carving.

Kentucky rifle by A. VERNER, believed to be Andrew Verner, gunsmith and blacksmith at juncture of western Bucks County and northern Montgomery County. Profusely decorated, with dropdown patchbox lid, elegantly inscribed. Double-headed silver eagle on bottom of forestock. Wire inlays of brass. Powder horn made for Jason Fenn by Amos Dunbar, dated March 4, 1777; knives of Sheffield (England) make, c. 1840s.

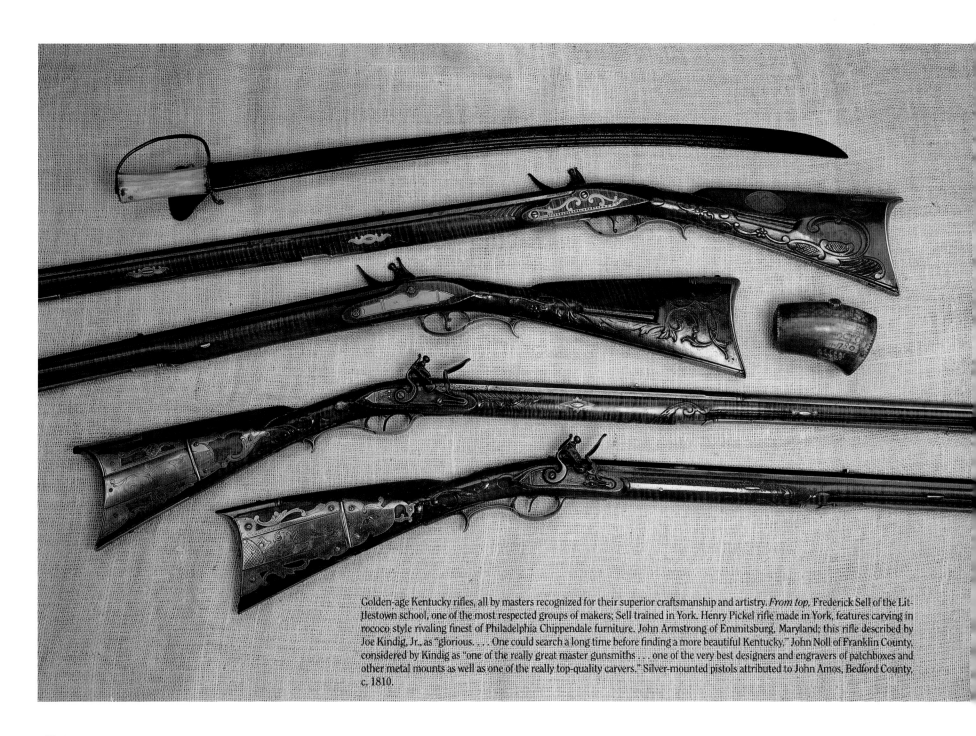

Golden-age Kentucky rifles, all by masters recognized for their superior craftsmanship and artistry. *From top,* Frederick Sell of the Littlestown school, one of the most respected groups of makers; Sell trained in York. Henry Pickel rifle made in York, features carving in rococo style rivaling finest of Philadelphia Chippendale furniture. John Armstrong of Emmitsburg, Maryland; this rifle described by Joe Kindig, Jr., as "glorious. . . . One could search a long time before finding a more beautiful Kentucky." John Noll of Franklin County, considered by Kindig as "one of the really great master gunsmiths . . . one of the very best designers and engravers of patchboxes and other metal mounts as well as one of the really top-quality carvers." Silver-mounted pistols attributed to John Amos, Bedford County, c. 1810.

Kentuckys of the golden age. *From top,* by Reading school's John Bonewitz, rare signed example (ɪʙ with lion stamped on breech). J. Dickert rifle, important example of Lancaster school, signed on barrel and includes his touchmark of crossed arrow and tomahawk within sunken oval; c. Revolutionary War; lock believed made in Dickert's own shop. Peter Neihart rifle, signed, with date 1787 on patchbox; maker lived and worked near Allentown. Important powder horn *at right* with silver bands and applied silver inlays, engraved FREDERICK WILLIAM HECHT, LAKE GEORGE, ANNO 1758. Map shows Hudson River and New York environs, with eastern woodland Indian beaded sash. Pistols by J. Troxell, Ohio, c. 1815. Silver armband engraved with U.S. arms, by J. Richardson, for Indian treaty presentation. Horn *at left* engraved with view of Philadelphia.

brass and/or German silver inlays. Artistically they were expressions of the end of the Federal and the beginning of the Victorian periods. Functionally they were relics of a past era.

Nothing symbolizes the contributions of firearms to American history and culture better than the Kentucky rifle. And no species of firearm or other object better exemplifies the pioneer spirit or our native creative impulses.

American Flintlock Pistols

Whereas the artistry of most Kentucky rifles is centered on the buttstock and breech, the pistol offers a smaller area, easier for the eye to comprehend and enjoy. Relatively few flintlock colonial or Kentucky pistols have survived, and they represent an area of continuing research. The late Samuel E. Dyke categorized these arms in three groups, based on period of manufacture: those made before and during the Revolutionary War, those made before and during the War of 1812, and those made at the dawn of expansion to the West.

Discoveries in this area have proven that the best of the colonial gunmakers were skilled at a level rivaling their English and continental European contemporaries—and that the ratio of Kentucky rifles to pistols is about 250 to 1!

Powder Horns

The publication in 1993 of William H. Guthman's *Drums A'beating, Trumpets Sounding: Artistically Carved Powder Horns in the Provincial Manner, 1746–1781* marks a milestone in a field in which study has reached a quite advanced stage in recent years. This work removes much of the speculation about these objects as unsophisticated folk art and identifies numerous engravers and schools of engravers (whom Guthman and some other specialists prefer to call "carvers"). Loan exhibitions at the Her-

Rifles of beauty even from bottom view. *From left,* by A. Verner, Herman Rupp, Frederick Sell, Christian Beck III, John Rupp, Jacob Ruslin, and John Clark. Each rifle shown in greater detail elsewhere in chapter.

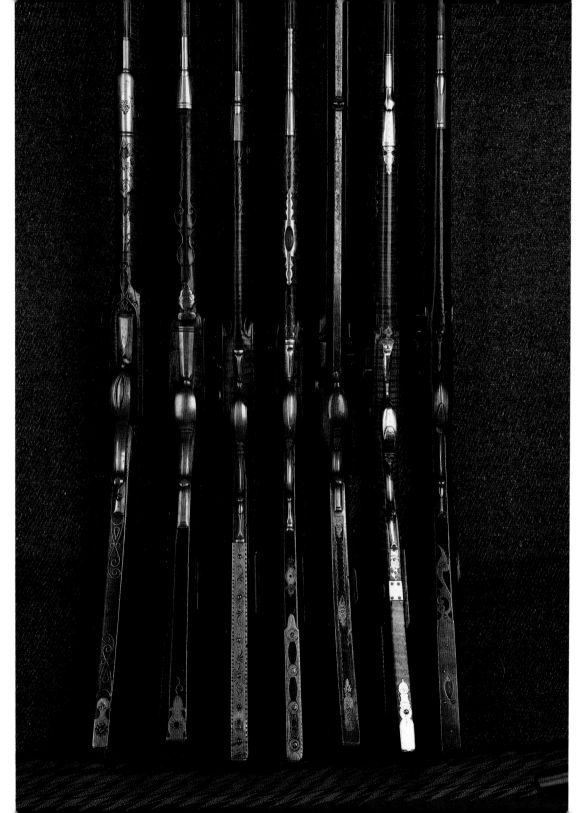

Only known Kentucky rifle chest, c. 1810–25; found in estate sale at the Willows, near Moorefield, West Virginia, May 1989. Rifles on lid, *from top,* signed examples by J. Dickert, John Bonewitz, and Peter Neihart. Among accoutrements, *clockwise from left,* engraved pipe made from antler; silk-embroidered buckskin coat; beaverskin hunting bag; horn and knife; c. 1790 belt axe with leather scabbard; beaver top hat as used by American riflemen; and horn-handled, silver-mounted Bowie knife.

Rupp family homestead sign, with guns by members of family. *From top,* J.R.-signed pistol (by John); rifle signed and dated by Herman; rifle by John (only known swivel-breech rifle by him), with state seal of Pennsylvania on patchbox; and another rifle by John, with basket-weave checkering. Detail photograph of house with sign beneath tip of American silver-mounted sword.

Federal period arms and memorabilia: Kentucky rifle with exceptional brass and silver inlays and engraving; cheekpiece side with rare folk-art griffin. Flintlock pistol with rare brass forend. Gilt eagle spurs. Baltimore silver dirk with eagle quillons. Northampton, Pennsylvania, light dragoon cross belt plate. U.S. Artillery gilt buckle and metallic-thread-decorated morocco belt. Call to arms broadside for War of 1812, from New York.

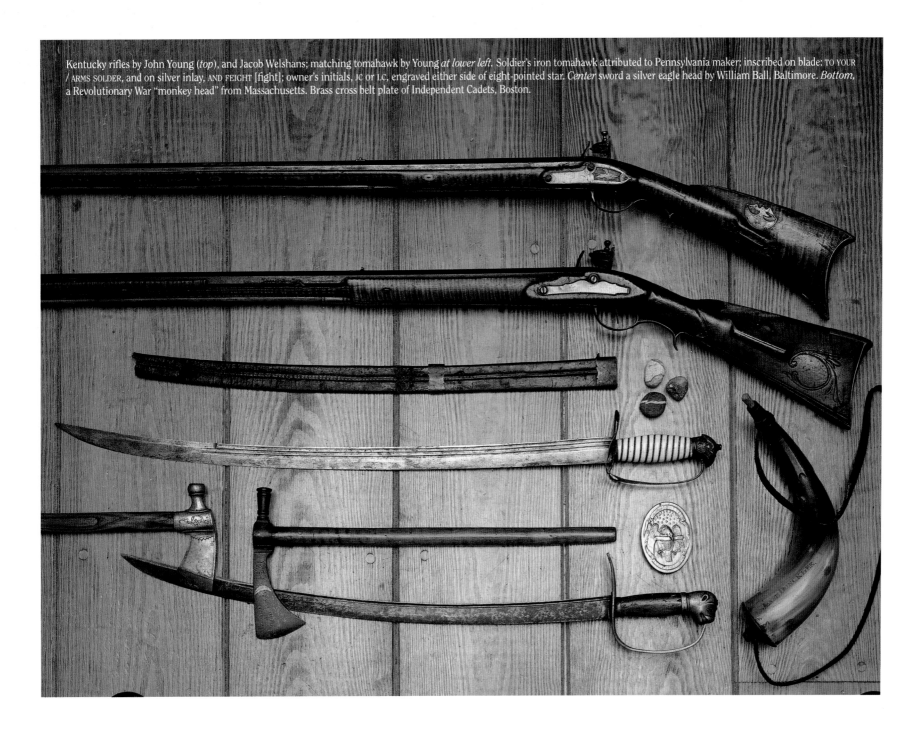

Kentucky rifles by John Young (*top*), and Jacob Welshans; matching tomahawk by Young *at lower left*. Soldier's iron tomahawk attributed to Pennsylvania maker; inscribed on blade: TO YOUR / ARMS SOLDER, and on silver inlay, AND FEIGHT [fight]; owner's initials, JC or LC, engraved either side of eight-pointed star. *Center* sword a silver eagle head by William Ball, Baltimore. *Bottom*, a Revolutionary War "monkey head" from Massachusetts. Brass cross belt plate of Independent Cadets, Boston.

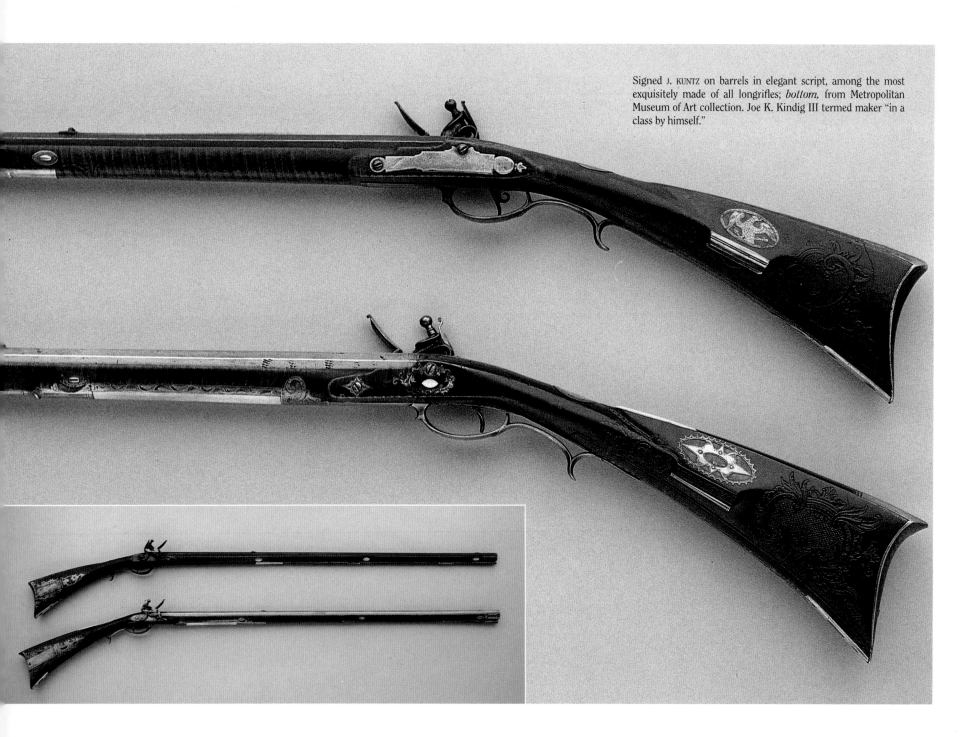

Signed J. KUNTZ on barrels in elegant script, among the most exquisitely made of all longrifles; *bottom*, from Metropolitan Museum of Art collection. Joe K. Kindig III termed maker "in a class by himself."

Rifles by John Armstrong, whose workmanship was described by Joe Kindig, Jr., as "magnificent . . . his designs are just about perfection. I cannot overemphasize the beauty of his rifles." On *top* rifle, silver eagle encircled with brass on cheekpiece, accompanied by elegant simplified rococo-style carving, c. 1820. Engraved brass militia button with similar primitive eagle. *Bottom,* rare rifle, heavily mounted in sheet silver instead of carved, with resulting simplified designs, c. 1835. Armstrong active c. 1793–1841, Emmitsburg, Maryland.

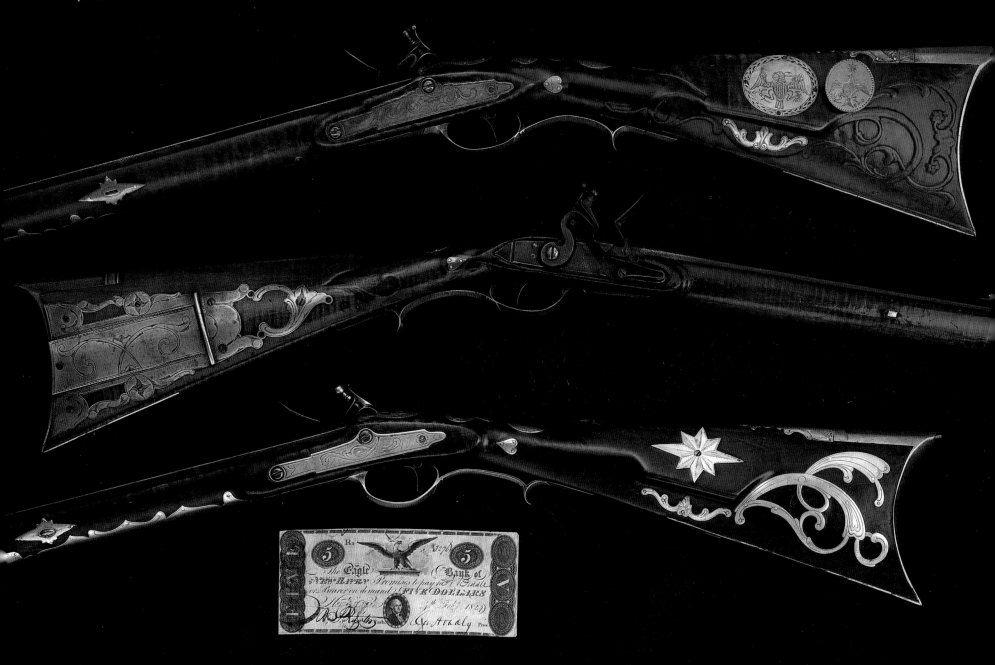

(*above and opposite*) *Top:* Chambersburg school's Christian Beck III (nephew of J. P. Beck) built and signed this elaborate rifle; features of the school incorporated in fancy silver inlays (often pierced), long, slender profile, straight comb, rich relief carving, and symmetrical S-scroll patchbox lids and sideplates. S.SPANGLER signature on lockplate, of Bedford-Somerset region; made profusely silver-inlaid and engraved rifle for iron merchant Jacob Ruslin. Latter's name gold-inlaid on barrel breech, surrounded with feathery scrolls in gold. Rare Bedford County flintlock. Tomahawk by longrifle maker, mounted in brass, silver, and pewter. American knife mounted in silver and gold; spear-point knife with horn handle by Congreve. Rifles date between knives, which are c. 1790–1810 and 1835, respectively.

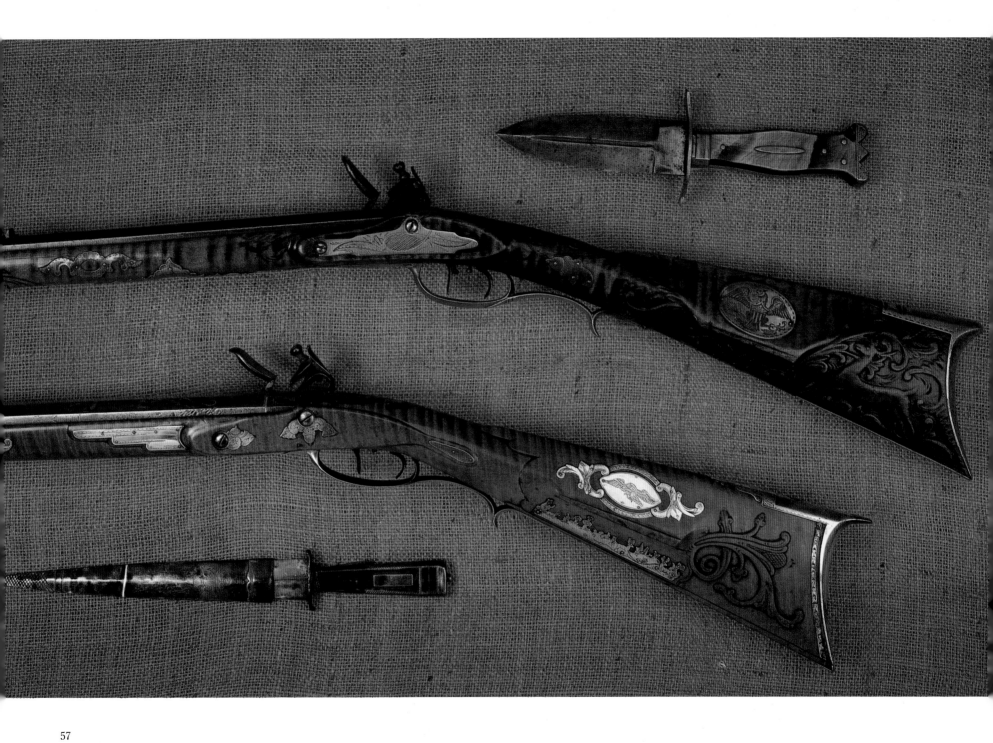

itage Plantation of Sandwich (Massachusetts), The Connecticut Historical Society (Hartford), and The Concord Museum, featuring horns from the above-mentioned study, placed focus on these objects and further spurred their research and appreciation. In Guthman's words, "For the first time . . . powder horns are being treated as art objects and not as military accoutrements."

Like the Kentucky riflemakers, the powder-horn makers were evolving a uniquely American craft and art form. The fact that most engravers were centered in well-populated areas of Connecticut and Massachusetts suggests in itself a greater degree of sophistication in their creation than traditionally thought by previous generations of students and collectors. Guthman has observed that there existed a community of engravers who drew upon one another for ideas and inspiration.

The geographic region of these engravers ranged from northern New England to the eastern Great Lakes and Canada and upper New York State. Guthman sums up the engraved themes on horns as "the rigors of frontier living, the brutal effect of frontier warfare, the impact of Indians the soldiers faced in combat, and the homesickness that each soldier felt while serving at a remote frontier fort." Provincial troops often had to sup-

Considered finest *silver-inlaid* Bedford County rifle, with thirty-two inlays, including one on the barrel, engraved with maker's name, J. STOUDENOUR, in script. Distinctive Bedford County styling, including hammer, finely grained curly maple wood, long and slender profile, small caliber, and high-quality decorative details; c. 1820; 59 inches overall.

Finest Bedford County rifle known, and the ultimate in achievement of maker Peter White, who was considered dean of this school of gunmaking. Made for Moses Wright, whose name is marked on barrel near breech. Thirty silver inlays; c. 1810; 58 inches overall.

Swivel-breech Kentucky by P. Smith, believed of Franklin County. Elaborate brass patchbox, with doves joined on finial and dove motif continued on side panels. Extensive brass and silver inlays and mountings. Both barrels of .45 caliber, rifled; c. 1840; overall length 53 inches.

58

ply their own accoutrements, and cartridge boxes not being readily available, cow and steer horns were an ideal and handy substitute.

No less than eighteen New England engravers have been identified (either by name or by style), and most of the New England soldiers who carried horns have themselves been identified. Studying the horns has revealed schools of craftsmen as well as an important evolution from English and continental influence to a style uniquely American. This new artistic vocabulary was evident during the French and Indian War (1754–63), and became more pronounced soon thereafter.

Guthman's carefully organized research further determined that the best of the engraved horns date from the French and Indian War and that the year 1758 was the most productive. The level of scholarship devoted to these horns at present is summed up by author Guthman:

> An obsession with historical events and topography is out of the question for today's informed collector or curator, who must exercise judgment with respect to talent, skill, and creativity. Studying powder horns for evidence of these latter qualities will lead, eventually, to connoisseurship and an informed appreciation of these objects as works of art, albeit of an extremely specific type.

American Swords Deluxe

Swords are an intriguing subject, associating the decorative arts with martial and naval interests during the course of American history through the early twentieth century.

The era of the American silver-mounted sword spans the period 1700 to 1815. The craftsmanship and design of these swords were heavily influenced by British swordmakers and the silversmiths of London. These

Virginia rifles, *from left*, signed J.B. (believed Beeton) on barrel; maple stock includes silver wire inlay, as does quite similar rifle attributed to John Sheetz, considered finest Virginia-made Kentucky known; twenty-seven sheet silver inlays. Silver-mounted pistol attributed to Silas Allen, one of finest New England flintlock pistols known.

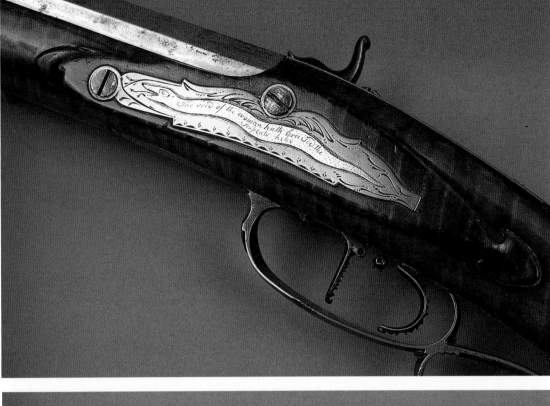

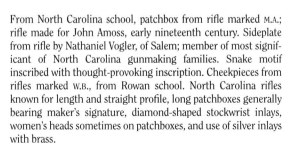

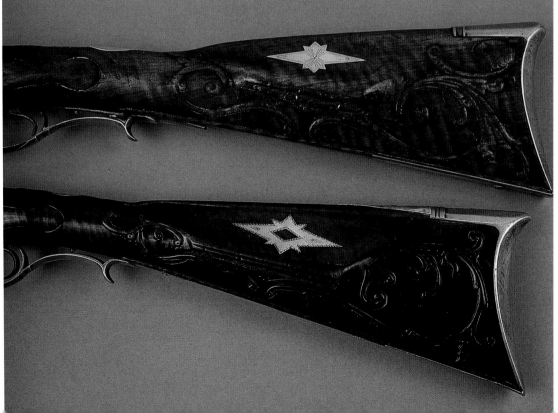

From North Carolina school, patchbox from rifle marked M.A.; rifle made for John Amoss, early nineteenth century. Sideplate from rifle by Nathaniel Vogler, of Salem; member of most significant of North Carolina gunmaking families. Snake motif inscribed with thought-provoking inscription. Cheekpieces from rifles marked W.B., from Rowan school. North Carolina rifles known for length and straight profile, long patchboxes generally bearing maker's signature, diamond-shaped stockwrist inlays, women's heads sometimes on patchboxes, and use of silver inlays with brass.

61

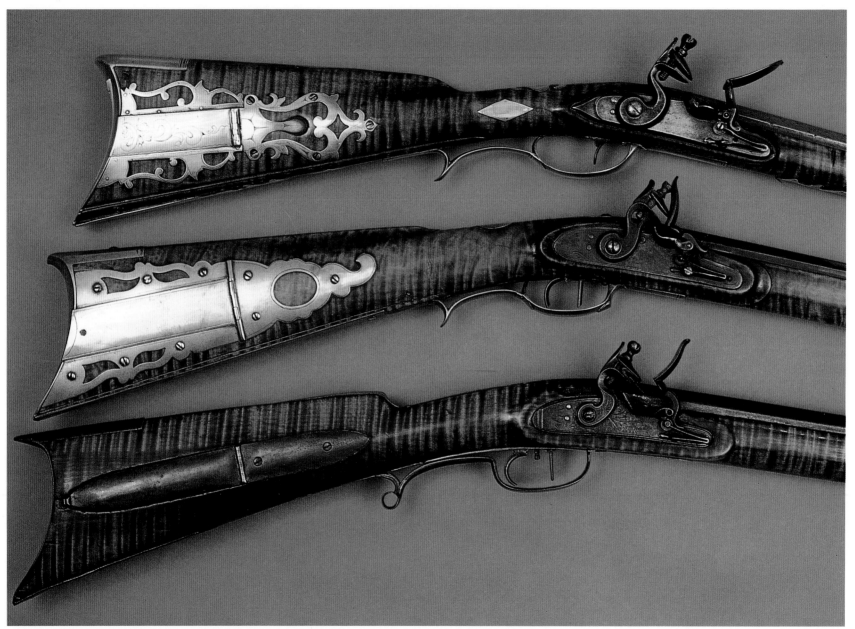

Regional rifles, each with individual styling, and each signed on barrel. *From top,* by J. N. Small, Vincennes, Indiana; began career in North Carolina and West Augusta, Virginia; moved west after Revolutionary War. By J. Lautzenheiser, from Bedford County area; moved to Ohio following Revolutionary War, settling in Louisville. By J. G. Gross, a native Tennessee gunsmith, from Sullivan County; iron mounts an east Tennessee trademark.

Georgia-made silver-mounted longrifle, described by Joe Kindig, Jr., as having "the most beautiful patchbox that I have ever seen on any Kentucky rifle . . . over thirty piercings . . . more piercings than I have ever seen on any other patchbox and each one is formed by the engraved design. . . . The mounts and inlays have over a hundred piercings in all! . . . the engraving is by an extremely masterful hand with every detail beautifully designed and executed." Buttplate and triggerguard of silver-plated brass; balance of silver. By Wiley Grover Higgins, of Monroe County, later Macon County, Georgia; made for Dr. Joe A. Davis. Both names inscribed on rifle; c. 1830.

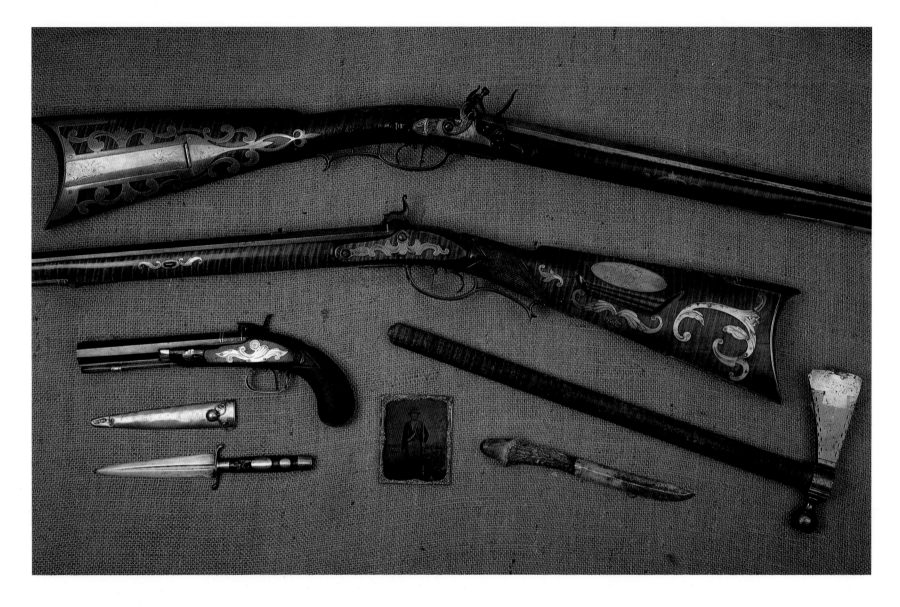

Ohio gunmakers, c. 1820–45. *From top,* by J. Clark, Lebanon, this is considered finest known Ohio rifle, and among best silver- and brass-inlaid rifles. Pistol and rifle by Valentine Libeau, Cincinnati, c. 1825–29. Tomahawk signed by J. Snevely, of Piqua. Knife *at left* by Ohio silversmith, and antler-handled knife marked D. B. Neal, of Morrow County.

Ohio arms in unequaled array, dating from 1777 to c. 1840. *From top,* incised carved and silver-inlaid rifle by James Teaff, Steubenville; curly maple underhammer cane gun; J. Clark of Lebanon, silver-mounted rifle; Valentine Libeau of Cincinnati, rifle: Silver-mounted and wire-inlaid pistols *at left* by D. Searles of Cincinnati (famous Bowie knifemaker); pistols *at right* by J. Troxell; pistol *at bottom* attributed to Valentine Libeau.

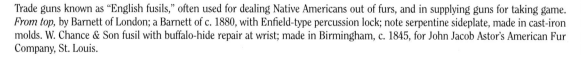

Trade guns known as "English fusils," often used for dealing Native Americans out of furs, and in supplying guns for taking game. *From top,* by Barnett of London; a Barnett of c. 1880, with Enfield-type percussion lock; note serpentine sideplate, made in cast-iron molds. W. Chance & Son fusil with buffalo-hide repair at wrist; made in Birmingham, c. 1845, for John Jacob Astor's American Fur Company, St. Louis.

J. P. Beck pistol, important evidence that colonial American gunmakers were capable of producing guns of fine quality and sophisticated design equal to Old World contemporaries. Mountings of silver, with part-round, part-octagonal iron barrel. Curly maple stock. Signed J.P. BECK on barrel; the R.C. on silver thumbpiece probably for Robert Coleman, a wealthy Lancaster County ironmaster.

objects, especially those bearing makers' names, are among the most rare of all American swords and are generally considered among the most rare of American silver work.

The American presentation sword was born when the Continental Congress voted that several be made in recognition of officers who served with distinction in the War for Independence—a vote taken while the conflict was still in progress. Revolutionary War presentations are customarily the small sword, with superb decorations by European artisans.

In time, a number of towns, cities, states, and organizations followed suit, and the presentation sword became a tradition that lasted until after World War I. These gifts were tied to an act of heroism, recognition of service, or an indication of respect.

Tomahawks

Whether weapon or tool, pipe or symbol of rank, tomahawks were instruments of war and of peace, as well as important decorative, ceremonial, and social objects. Besides lavishing fine craftsmanship on his Kentucky rifles and pistols, the frontiersman saw fit to extend those amenities to tomahawks. Those few surviving examples rank among the most glamorous and intriguing of weapons from pioneer America.

The Colonial and Federal periods offer some remarkable examples, and a limited number have been identified as the work of specific Kentucky riflemakers. Heads are normally of forged iron, some with brass, silver, or German silver inlays. Hafts were of hickory or maple,

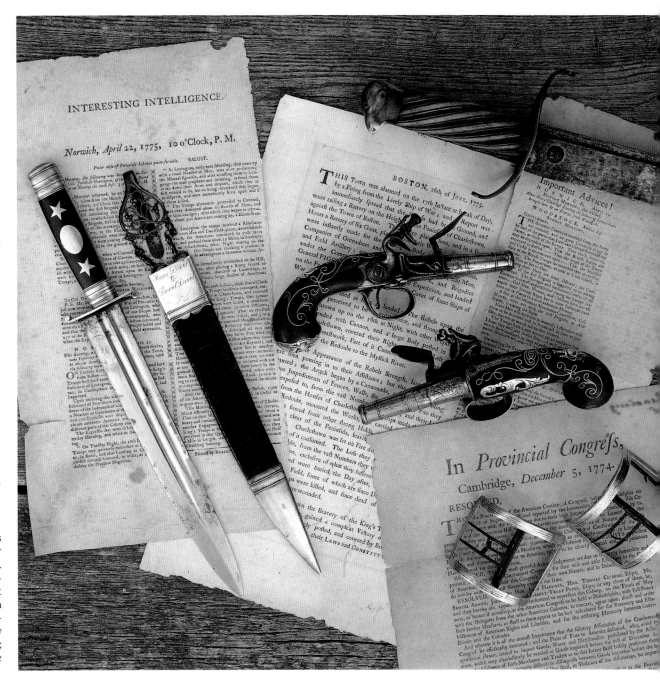

American silver-mounted pistols, c. 1760–70, measuring 7 inches overall, with screw barrels of .44 caliber. Marked: PERKIN, FECIT N.YORK. Sophisticated styling, based on English pistols of period. Gentleman's hunting knife of somewhat later date, silver-mounted; signed A.O. at base of swordlike blade; inscribed throat of silver-mounted scabbard; pierced iron belt clip. David David, a prominent citizen of Montreal and a founder of the Bank of Montreal. Sword of Revolutionary War era, with green-tinted ivory handle, attempting at sophistication but retaining quaint charm; signed EB, possibly Elisha Buel of Hebron, Connecticut. Rare broadsheets of Revolutionary War significance.

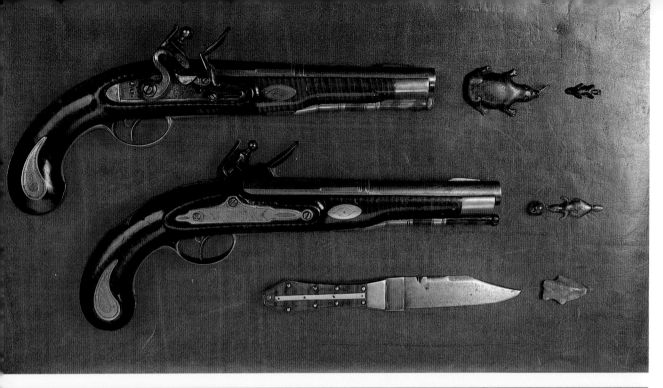

often with inlays of silver, German silver, or pewter. A standard feature was the pipe bowl, smokeable by drawing strongly on the mouthpiece at the opposite end of the haft. Most of these early frontiersmen tomahawks were made in Pennsylvania, Virginia, or Maryland, but they are also known from New York and New England: the King Philip pipe tomahawk (c. 1670) is the earliest pipe tomahawk known. Though a few known rifleman tomahawks are inscribed with Indian names (and some were presented to them), most were made for and used by frontiersmen.

War hammers and hatchets had been used in European warfare for centuries. However, the tomahawk in American culture evolved in a tradeoff of tactics, know-how, and experience between the Indians and their frontier adversaries. Hand-to-hand combat called on tomahawks, and scalping and hunting knives. The result, aided by the decorative wizardry of the Kentucky riflemaker, was still another indigenous decorative art form; no American tomahawk might be confused with a European war hammer or hatchet.

Unusual pair of Peter White, Bedford County, pistols, with left- and right-hand locks. To accentuate mirror image, maker's signature reversed on sideplate. Knife a silver-mounted coffin-hilt, American-made, c. 1835. Silver trade beaver marked R.C., for Robert Cruickshank.

Bedford County styling of Peter White silver-mounted pistols; c. 1835; signed P.W. on locks and barrels.

By Kuntz; this is the premier of all known Kentucky pistols and among the finest of known Federal period American flintlock pistols. Silver sideplates engraved PHILADA on one, and LIBERTY on the other.

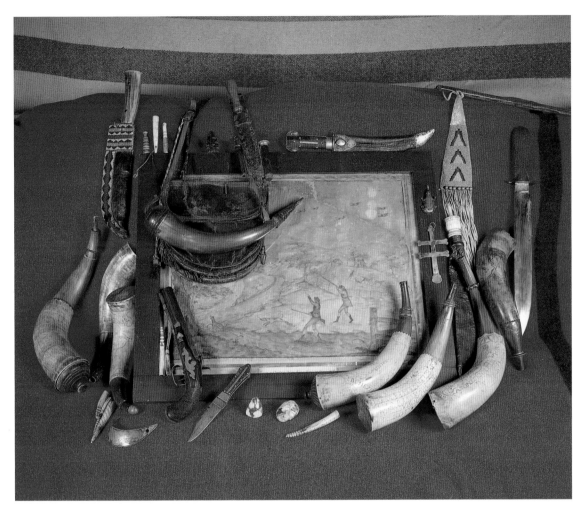

(*above*) *From top,* horns of Aaron Page, Nathaniel Selkrig, and David Hamilton (shortened from original length), examples of the Lake George school of engravers, influenced by artisan John Bush and the Boston school's phalanxes-of-soldiers motifs. All c. 1757–58.

(*above*) Horns dated 1758, 1759, 1762, and 1777, including one, *at left,* signed by artisan "Jacob Gay Hand," meaning made by Jacob Gay, and another by Amos Dunbar *at bottom right.* Hunting scene drawn and painted by William Philips, Philadelphia, 1800. Silver-mounted pistol attributed to Valentine Libeau, active in Cincinnati 1825–29.

(*opposite*) Believed made in Snyder or Union County (Pennsylvania), Kentucky pistol *at bottom* with violin-finished maple stock, brass mountings, and nine silver inlays; 10⅛-inch barrel, c. 1820. Contemporary Connecticut-made pistols by Simeon North, Middletown. Single barrel an unfinished dueling pistol, from North Estate; lighter and more elegant than contemporary English duelers. Over-and-under unique, with locks on each side. Claims that North relied on gunmakers in England for these arms remain unproven at this writing. Silver hilt and scabbard on Bowie knife by Rose of New York; cannon-and-flag motif etched on spear-point blade.

(*right*) *From top,* horns of Robert Baird, Isaac Whelpley, and David Wheeler; c. 1757–58. By Lake George school engraver J.W., who signed the Baird and Whelpley horns.

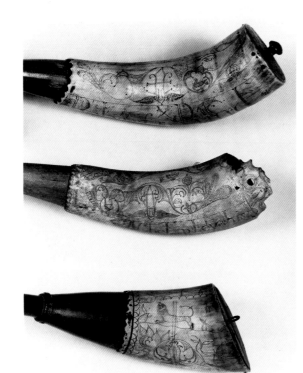

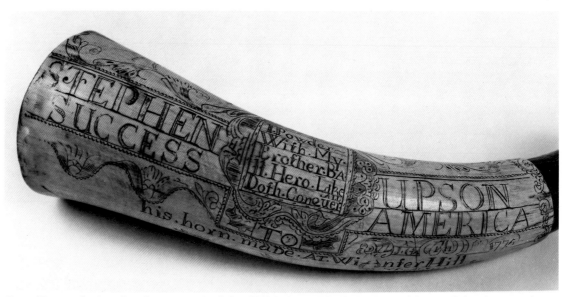

Siege of Boston school, attributed to engraver Jacob Gay, 1775. Active c. 1758–87, Gay is one of the period's best-known craftsmen. Identified by such features as the broken-scroll cartouche around the inscription, he was also known for monkeylike faces, and highly stylized animals. "Siege of Boston" refers to a common theme used by Gay and certain other carvers.

Reverse sides of the Baird, Whelpley, and Wheeler horns, revealing J.W.'s trademark stylized geometric fantasies.

The Lieutenant Christopher Palmer horn, also of the Lake George school, 1758. Note quality of lettering. Palmer was from Stonington, Connecticut.

From the Lake George school, the William Patterson horn, c. 1759, with ship motif and profuse geometric designs.

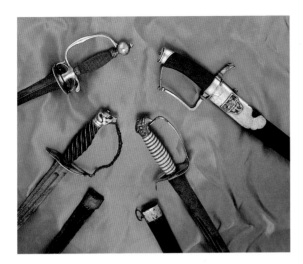

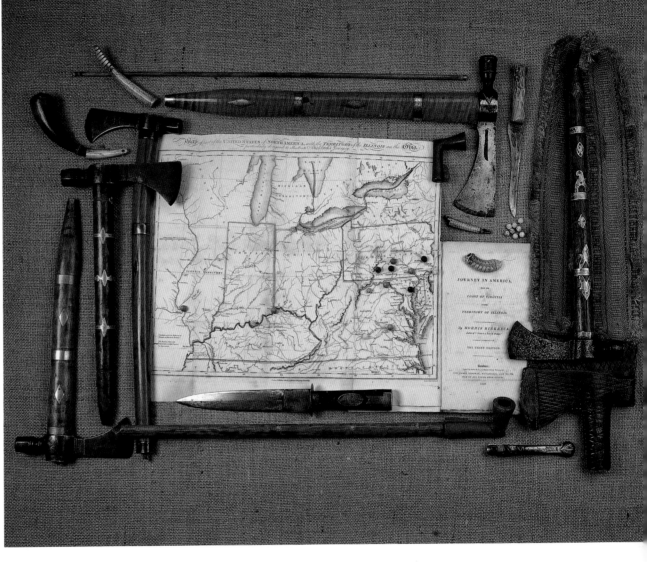

Examples of some of the best native swordmaking of the eighteenth and early nineteenth centuries, all silver-mounted. *From top left:* classic American simplicity in a piece based on English gentleman's small sword of the period; touchmark attributed to Francis Richardson of Philadelphia, c. 1718; 27-inch blade; grip formed of braided silver wire closely wrapped. Dog's-head pommel on sword attributed to Ephraim Brasher (maker of "Brasher Doubloon" of coin collecting fame), New York, c. 1760–70; green-tinted carved ivory grips; mounts bear inscription I.M. for General Jonathan Moulton, York, Maine, a Revolutionary War figure; 27-inch curved blade. Foot officer's sword, c. 1805, with Baltimore-type eagle-head pommel, attributed to William Ball, Jr., silversmith of that city; hilt of spiral-carved ivory grips wrapped in twisted silver; important patriotic blade detail engraved on each side: rattlesnake over flowing riband with motto DONT TREAD ON ME; 25½-inch curved blade. Naval officer's sword, c. 1815, marked T. C & H, for silversmiths Thomas, Chadwick & Heims, Albany, New York (not visible: center mount with large spread-winged eagle and U.S. shield beneath cluster of stars); 34-inch curved blade engraved with Goddess of Liberty, liberty cap, American eagle and shield, riband with E PLURIBUS UNUM, and floral and scroll designs.

With important gunmaking and related trading centers marked by bullets, map shows areas of intense activity in early westward expansion. Pipe tomahawks of period, c. 1790–1820, some with silver inlays. Note knife silver-inlaid on head *at top right*. British scout Alexander McKenzie's *at left* with curved cherry handle head gold-inlaid AM., sash and carrier *at lower right*. McKenzie preceded Lewis and Clark expedition by sixteen years.

Largely from the David Currie Collection (with some material from William Myers and Thomas Parker), this amazing array is the finest group privately assembled of American Colonial and Federal tomahawks. From c. 1750 to 1874, several are dated; the one to *left* of photograph of Pacer's Son, Kiowa Apache, built by Kentucky riflemaker Peter Angstadt (c. 1800–15). Spontoon tomahawk across photo actually being held by subject.

Revolutionary War hero and victorious Indian fighter "Mad Anthony" Wayne strikes Washingtonian pose in portrait from life by John Pierre Henri Elouis. Among personal mementos (*clockwise from top*), journal (1793), epaulet, silver saddle cups used on campaigns, gorget (a gift from George Washington), and shoe buckles. Rare tomahawk inlaid in silver and bronze; J.H.K. on blade, believed mark of silversmith John H. Kinzie; inscribed CHAS. DUKE 1793, for a British soldier stationed in North America. Haft carved by Indians. Kentucky rifle by Bernard Hauck, York County.

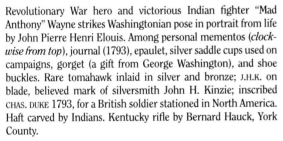

Tomahawk and rifle attributed to John Young, Easton, active c. 1775–1800. Steel edge dovetailed onto brass head. HY engraved on head, and may allude to Henry Young, the maker's brother, another local gunsmith. Overall length of tomahawk, 13¼ inches.

York gunmaker Jacob Welshans, active 1779–1807, made both rifle and tomahawk, and each bears stamp from the same die, visible on brass head. Pipe bowl made to unscrew, for more efficient fighting use; brass loop allowed attaching tomahawk to belt with thong. Tomahawk's overall length, 15½ inches.

Chapter 3
Handcraftsmanship and the Industrial Revolution

The nineteenth century comprised a significant era in the decoration of firearms. The first fifty years continued the tradition in which any gun not constructed for military purposes was likely to be engraved. At this time, the assembly-line production of arms was still in its infancy. In the second fifty years, gun engraving was at an all-time peak in popularity and practice; and in this time span, the mass produc-

Elegant silver-mounted rifle made for Major Robert Anderson, Union Civil War hero, by Daniel Searles, Baton Rouge, Louisiana. Searles is best known for knives he made for Jim Bowie. Gold and silver band inlays on 41-inch, .36-caliber barrel. Sideplate richly engraved and inscribed: R. ANDERSON, U.S. ARMY. Silver mounts attributed to Rees Fitzpatrick, a Baton Rouge silversmith, considered the finest weapons artisan of his day in the South (though it may have been by C. Moore, also of Baton Rouge). American silver-mounted Bowie knives *at top left* (15½ inches overall) and *center left* show marks indicating they were made for F. C. Goergen, New Orleans; possibly by Schively of Philadelphia. *Center* knife of Sheffield (England) make, by S. C. Wragg; cutlery handle with patriotic motifs. Gambler's push dagger with silver hilt, marked by Dufilho, New Orleans. Henry Deringer pistol with gold mounts; agent marking on barrel indicates made for Hyde & Goodrich, New Orleans; c. late 1830s, early 1840s.

tion of firearms on an assembly-line basis became widespread. Nevertheless, most manufacturers had hand-engraved weapons available as stock items, or at least they were prepared to respond to demand.

What would quickly evolve in the 1850s from an influx of German immigrant engravers and the rapidly increasing demand for machine-made arms was nothing less than a golden age of arms engraving in America. For the period 1800–1850, the total number of gun engravers active in America was probably less than fifty, and very few of them have been identified by name. In the years 1850–1900, the number exceeded at least 275; a number of them are now known by name, and several have been identified by the style and quality of their work.

The German Masters
This was the period when masters like Young, Nimschke, and the first of the Ulrichs lent their influence and artistic expertise to American armsmaking. These were artist-craftsmen who had been trained in the European traditions of guilds and brought with them their tools, their European pattern books, and varying degrees of

experience. Of these artisans, the most thoroughly studied to date has been L. D. Nimschke, whose scrapbook record was published in this author's *L. D. Nimschke, Firearms Engraver* (1964).

Collector and antiquarian Glode Requa owned the Nimschke papers for many years, the collection having been discovered by his aunt and saved from destruction at a time when descendants of Nimschke, frightened by New York's Sullivan Law, were pitching gun parts off a bridge and were about to consign the master's scrapbook and remaining records to the fireplace! Excerpts from the scrapbook were initially published in this author's first book on American arms engraving, *Samuel Colt Presents* (1961).

The tradition of engraving—and of fine metal and stock work—begun by the Kentucky riflemakers was continued by their successor craftsmen who devoted their skills to the so-called Plains rifle and such arms as the Henry Deringer pistols. However, relatively few American firearms masterpieces have survived from the first half of the nineteenth century.

The Industrial Revolution, which reduced the amount of handwork, ironically spurred the demand for

Dueling pistols by James Haslett of Baltimore; early nineteenth century, signed in gold on the barrel breeches and on lockplates, with flush gold lightning bolts and gold bands at barrel breeches, gold-lined rainproof pans, gold-inlaid top jaws of hammers, and some gold inlays on steel mounts; forend caps of silver; set in fitted mahogany case, lined in velvet, with accessories; 15½ inches overall length. Haslett trained under the well-known Irish gunsmith Robert McCormick and first opened his own gunshop in Baltimore, at the "Sign of the Golden Gun," in 1803. Styling of his guns was heavily influenced by English and Irish makers.

Harpers Ferry Armory Model 1803 U.S. flintlock rifles, revealing the handsome beauty to be found in several American military arms.

hand engraving. Machine-made pepperbox handguns were made in some quantity in the 1830s and 1840s, and hand engraving was standard on many of these. The tradition of hand embellishments dating from the Kentucky and its nonmilitary contemporaries was carried over into these new mass-produced weapons almost as a necessary part of gunmaking.

This new demand for engravers in steel was augmented by the introduction of the Colt revolver, a development of such significance that Colt and his creations occupy a chapter of their own in this book, as do the Winchester arms and their predecessors.

Ironically, the engraver was now in demand for the embellishment of deluxe-grade factory-built guns, which were maintained in inventory or produced to the special order of clients. Mass production increased the number of native-made firearms, and the traditional affinity of man for embellishing his arms continued, and actually increased.

The new style of engraving that these pioneers fostered was rich and fancy, crisply executed, and usually included a beaded (also called punched dot) or matte background. Sizes of scrolls varied, but on handguns (for example, Colts) were generally tight and small, and on longarms (for example, Winchesters) generally large and flamboyant. Animal-head finials were sometimes present; of these, the wolf head is popular with collectors.

For many years the Sharps factory, established first in Philadelphia, then in Hartford, and later in Bridgeport, Connecticut, enjoyed a thriving demand for deluxe rifles. Some of the engravers of Hartford-made Sharps arms were simultaneously decorating Colts. These were first done in the "doughnut" scroll. When the contractor responsible for that work was replaced, c. 1852, by Gus-

Presentation set of flintlock pistols by Simeon North, c. 1818. One of the two pairs commissioned as gifts by the state of Connecticut for War of 1812 heroes Thomas McDonough and Isaac Hull (see also page 8). This pair presented to Captain Isaac Hull; displayed in the USS *Constitution* Museum, Boston, along with a gold-hilted dress sword and scabbard by Nathan Starr, another gift from the state of Connecticut. A watercolor design drawing for these pistols may be found in the Connecticut Historical Society collection. Sideplate engravings by W. H. Bassett, banknote engraver from Hartford, Connecticut, as determined by gunmaker's pull and accompanying letter, discovered by William H. Guthman.

Silver-mounted sporting rifle by James Haslett, c. 1820. Barrel marking, flush gold inlaid: HASLETT, BALTIMORE. Cornucopia motif on the patchbox symbolic of prosperity.

tave Young, both Sharps and Colt arms adopted the Young style—and both then relied primarily on Young's shop for their engraving needs. Besides the Colt and Sharps work, Young took in engraving from other factories in the area as well.

A rare and historic engraved Sharps is the Model 1853 Carbine that was property of Dr. John Day, of Lawrence, Kansas. On its patchbox is the inscription: SUCCESSFUL AGENT OF THE IRREPRESSIBLE CONFLICT. The gun's barrel band bore Day's name, city, and state. This was one of the "Beecher's Bibles," sent to keep the Kansas territory from becoming a slave state. Other Sharps carbines from the shipments are also known with inscriptions, though some were marked later to document their capture from John Brown at Harpers Ferry.

Louis D. Nimschke

From the golden age of American gunmaking, L. D. Nimschke left the most extraordinary documentation. His personal work record, a scrapbook totaling one hundred pages, is composed of impressions taken from the actual engraved surfaces. Over one hundred different makers and manufacturers of firearms are represented, as well as all of the contemporary engraving styles. This unique record is an archive of gun engraving at near its best for the period it covers.

L. D. Nimschke was born in Germany in 1832 and emigrated to the United States around 1850. He died on April 9, 1904. Little is known of him personally, but it is obvious from his engraving record that he was a dedicated, serious craftsman with an active imagination. Judging from the tremendous number of guns he engraved (estimated in excess of 5,000), he was extremely industrious.

Most of Nimschke's active years in America were spent in New York City, then a preferred place of business for many individuals in the firearms trade.

Among indications of Nimschke's significance is the substantial number of his customers, as well as the stature of many of these. Still another indicator is the nature of work he did for the many factories who

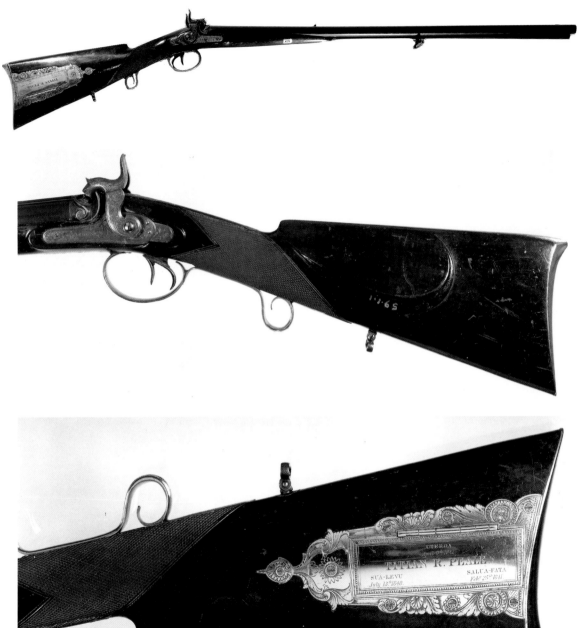

Engraved J. KUNZ on the right lockplate and PHILAD on the left, this finely made, silver-mounted, side-by-side, double-barrel sporting rifle belonged to Titian Peale, of the distinguished family of artists. Dates on the patchbox reference the Wilkes Expedition to the South Seas (1838–42) of which Peale was a member. Peale had also accompanied the Stephen H. Long expedition to the upper Missouri (1819–20); in 1821 was appointed assistant manager of the Philadelphia Museum. From the Carl Otto Kretzschmar von Kienbusch Collection, Philadelphia Museum of Art.

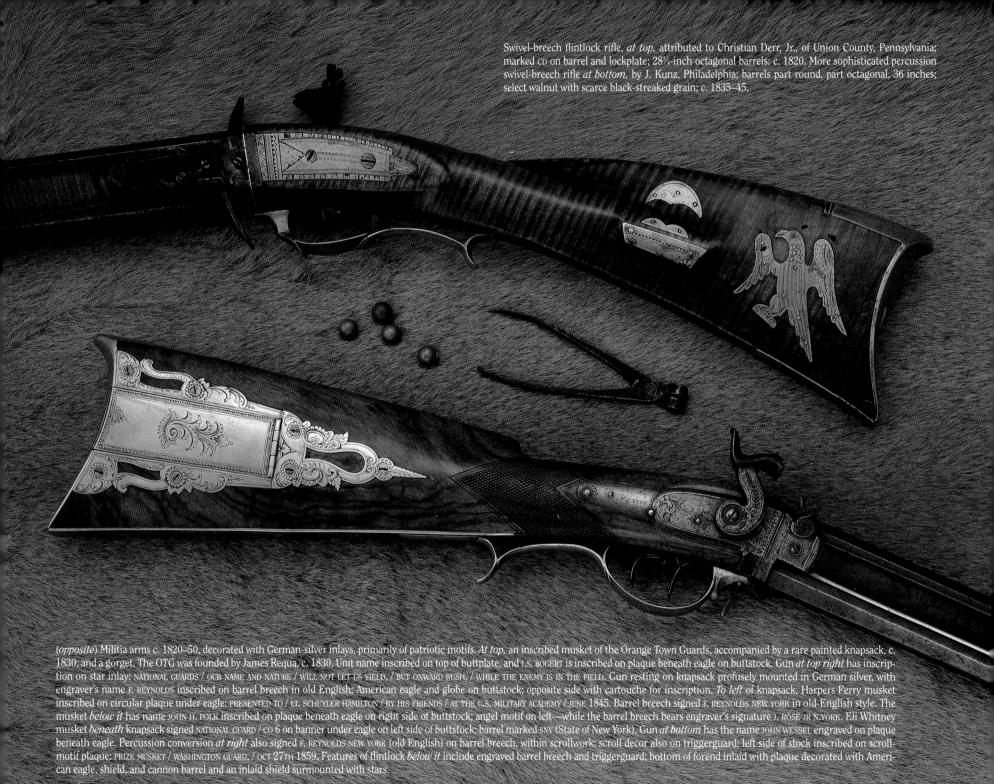

Swivel-breech flintlock rifle, *at top*, attributed to Christian Derr, Jr., of Union County, Pennsylvania; marked CD on barrel and lockplate; 28¾-inch octagonal barrels; c. 1820. More sophisticated percussion swivel-breech rifle *at bottom*, by J. Kunz, Philadelphia; barrels part round, part octagonal, 36 inches; select walnut with scarce black-streaked grain; c. 1835–45.

(*opposite*) Militia arms c. 1820–50, decorated with German-silver inlays, primarily of patriotic motifs. *At top*, an inscribed musket of the Orange Town Guards, accompanied by a rare painted knapsack, c. 1830, and a gorget. The OTG was founded by James Requa, c. 1830. Unit name inscribed on top of buttplate, and J.S. BOGERT is inscribed on plaque beneath eagle on buttstock. Gun *at top right* has inscription on star inlay: NATIONAL GUARDS / OUR NAME AND NATURE / WILL NOT LET US YIELD, / BUT ONWARD RUSH, / WHILE THE ENEMY IS IN THE FIELD. Gun resting on knapsack profusely mounted in German silver, with engraver's name F. REYNOLDS inscribed on barrel breech in old English; American eagle and globe on buttstock; opposite side with cartouche for inscription. *To left* of knapsack, Harpers Ferry musket inscribed on circular plaque under eagle: PRESENTED TO / LT. SCHUYLER HAMILTON / BY HIS FRIENDS / AT THE U.S. MILITARY ACADEMY / JUNE 1845. Barrel breech signed F. REYNOLDS NEW YORK in old-English style. The musket *below it* has name JOHN H. POLK inscribed on plaque beneath eagle on right side of buttstock; angel motif on left—while the barrel breech bears engraver's signature J. ROSE JR N.YORK. Eli Whitney musket *beneath* knapsack signed NATIONAL GUARD / CO 6 on banner under eagle on left side of buttstock; barrel marked SNY (State of New York). Gun *at bottom* has the name JOHN WESSEL engraved on plaque beneath eagle. Percussion conversion *at right* also signed F. REYNOLDS NEW YORK (old English) on barrel breech, within scrollwork; scroll decor also on triggerguard; left side of stock inscribed on scroll-motif plaque: PRIZE MUSKET / WASHINGTON GUARD, / OCT 27TH 1859. Features of flintlock *below it* include engraved barrel breech and triggerguard; bottom of forend inlaid with plaque decorated with American eagle, shield, and cannon barrel and an inlaid shield surmounted with stars.

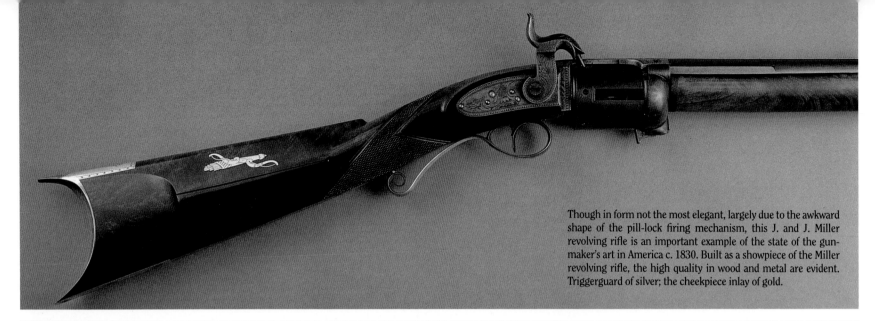

Though in form not the most elegant, largely due to the awkward shape of the pill-lock firing mechanism, this J. and J. Miller revolving rifle is an important example of the state of the gunmaker's art in America c. 1830. Built as a showpiece of the Miller revolving rifle, the high quality in wood and metal are evident. Triggerguard of silver; the cheekpiece inlay of gold.

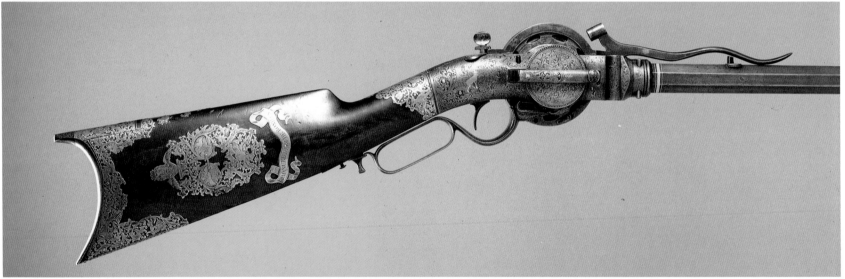

Presentation engraved, gold- and silver-inlaid, and silver-sheathed P. W. Porter revolving sporting rifle, no. 405. Among motifs on gun are stag, deer, wolf, and wild boar being pursued by hunter and hounds, a stag and hunting horn, and seated hunter with gun and dog. Silver-inlaid plaque on top of barrel inscribed: AGRADECIMIENTO ("with appreciation"). On silver plaque on right side of stock: MANUEL DIEZ DE BONILLA. Among details on silver stock decor are floral, bird, animal, human, and mythological motifs, including griffins, lambs and lions, a medieval huntsman, a wild man with snake encircling his neck and swallowing its tail. Medieval huntsman also on silver plaque encircling stock at wrist; stock of select American walnut. Some motifs taken from mid-nineteenth-century engraver's pattern books, notably those of G. Ernst, Zella. Identities of engraver and inlayer presently unknown, but embellishments American in origin. Most elaborate Porter firearm known, and among the most richly decorated nineteenth-century arms of any American gunmaker. Exhibited at the Crystal Palace, New York, 1853, and documented in the official publication of the event: *The World of Science, Art and Industry Illustrated for Examples in the New York Exhibition of 1853–1854,* edited by Prof. B. Stillman, Jr., and C. R. Goodrich, Esq. Page 49 of the book pictures this exact gun, captioned: "The adjoining engraving represents the repeating rifle invented by Col. T. W. Porter, of Tennessee. It is an excellent example of the beauty and good workmanship of American firearms. The engraving also shows to a considerable extent, the mechanical peculiarities which render this so efficient and formidable a weapon. . . ."

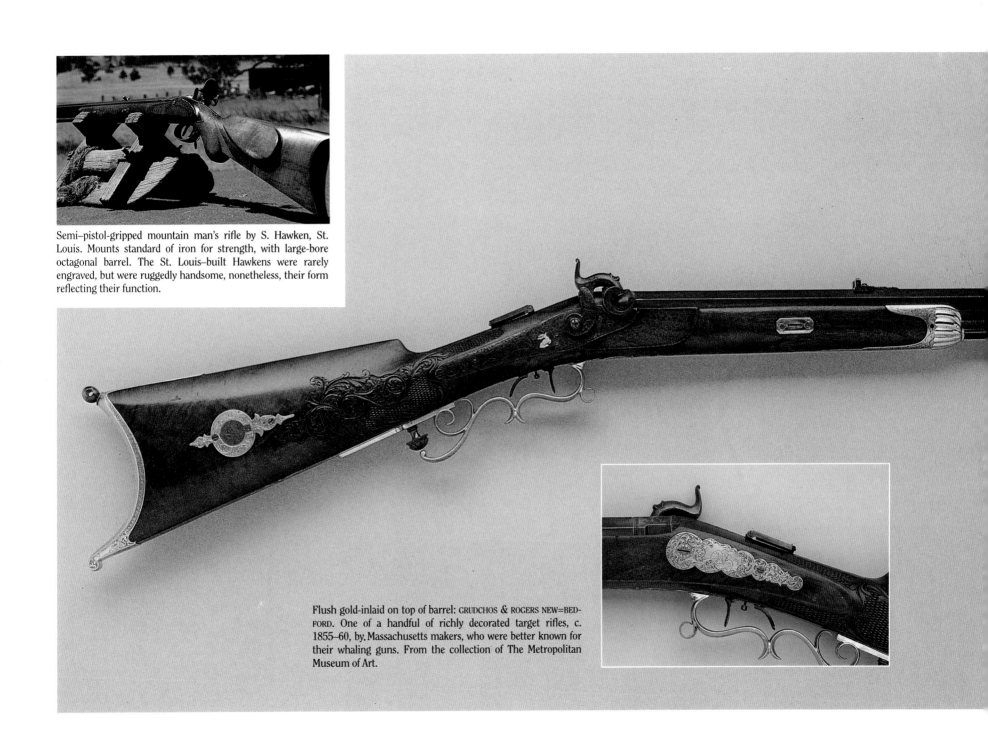

Semi–pistol-gripped mountain man's rifle by S. Hawken, St. Louis. Mounts standard of iron for strength, with large-bore octagonal barrel. The St. Louis–built Hawkens were rarely engraved, but were ruggedly handsome, nonetheless, their form reflecting their function.

Flush gold-inlaid on top of barrel: GRUDCHOS & ROGERS NEW=BED-FORD. One of a handful of richly decorated target rifles, c. 1855–60, by, Massachusetts makers, who were better known for their whaling guns. From the collection of The Metropolitan Museum of Art.

The distinctive scroll and border engraving of L. D. Nimschke is found on this halfstock, German-silver-mounted sporting rifle, attributed to New Haven gunmaker Samuel Miller, c. 1850–55. One of the earliest known examples of Nimschke engraving.

Trade card for A. J. Plate, one of San Francisco's leading dealers in firearms during the years 1850–78. Adolphus J. Plate testified in the trademark infringement trial of *Deringer vs. Plate.* In his own words: "I am not a practical mechanic, but keep them in my employment and make arms to order. . . . [Among them are] Charles Schlotterbeck [who] has not a superior as a workman in California in any branch of his business. . . . Schlotterbeck [who formerly worked for Henry Deringer] informed me of his right to use Deringer's name on pistols, shortly after his arrival here." Those pistols, normally marked SLOTTER & CO., were usually of workmanship superior to Henry Deringer's originals.

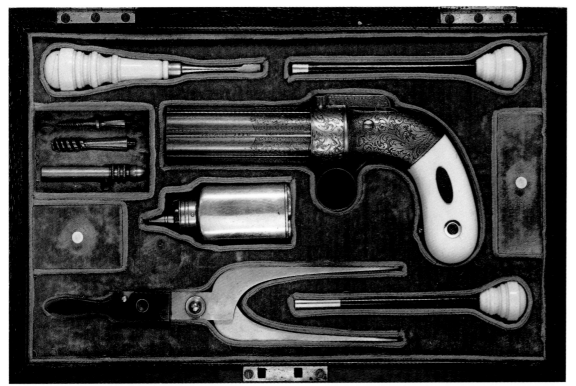

Pepperbox pistol by Ethan Allen and Charles T. Thurber, Norwich, Connecticut, c. 1842–47. Engraved with floral scrollwork; nipple shield of silver, engraved to match. Grips of gold-mounted ivory; rosewood case lined in velvet, and mounted in German silver; accessories including ivory- and silver-mounted tools. Comparison should be made with the cased pair of deringer pistols, made by John Mullin (of New York) for Henry G. Freeman, and the cased Second Model Colt Dragoon revolvers, made for James Janeway van Syckel (see page 117); both clients from Philadelphia. All three cased sets and accessories appear to have been supplied by the same maker.

Aphonso, controlled the Spanish monarchy for many years after her husband's death. A Frank Wesson rifle engraved for her is recorded in Nimschke's scrapbook (pictured on page 95). The fanciest Winchester in his book was done for a client in Peru. In Nimschke's own description, the frame for this gun was "solid silver." A survey of the many owners noted in the record book shows better than 20 percent to be Mexican, South American, or Spanish. Engraved, plated, and pearl- or ivory-gripped guns were highly prized by the Spanish-speaking clients. The decoration of this type gun was a Nimschke speciality.

Nimschke was skilled in many styles of engraving. However, his two mainstays were the American and English styles. The principal differentiation between them was the treatment of scrollwork. It was in scrollwork, particularly, that Nimschke excelled. He could execute the rich, bold scrolls of the American style and, with equal skill, the fine and delicate English scrolls. Much of the engraving done in the United States during Nimschke's years of activity (1850–1904) was in the American style.

The prints in Nimschke's record book also encompass silverware, watch cases, jewelry, stamps, seals, nameplates, and even dog collars. Though the major share of his work was on firearms, he obviously did not limit himself to them for his livelihood.

Much of His Work Was Signed

Not less than 35 percent of the arms in Nimschke's scrapbook bear some form of his signature. The usual form was initialing, particularly N, LN, or LDN. As a rule, the larger the signature, the more important and fancy the gun. Approximately 85 percent of his signatures were on longarms. Nimschke rarely signed a handgun, and when he did, it was seldom more than initials only.

It was not common practice for an engraver in Nimschke's era to sign a firearm. During the nineteenth century in the United States, only Nimschke and some of the Ulrichs are known to have done so to any noticeable extent.

already had engravers in their employ. For tasks requiring the finest quality, they often turned to Nimschke.

As a custom engraver, Nimschke worked on individual order, executing virtually anything the customer wanted; thus the high proportion of extras in his work: monograms, inscriptions, coats of arms, and other personal symbols. The weapons to be engraved were brought to him, generally, "in the white." Bluing, case hardening, or plating were done after completion of the engraving (standard practice to this day).

Nimschke engraved guns for more than a hundred leading manufacturers, and most of his commissions

came through them, though some came through dealers or from individual owners. Nimschke's customers also included gunsmiths, shooting clubs, and various persons and firms outside the sphere of firearms. The sources of these projects were primarily in and around New York City, but with such notable exceptions as Nashville, Tennessee (Bitterlich & Legler), Kansas City, Missouri (E. Masuch), and Houston, Texas (E. Schmidt & Co.). Those cities also had capable gun engravers, but in these instances the work was sent to Nimschke.

Among his international clientele Nimschke could boast Maria Cristina of Austria, who, as widow of King

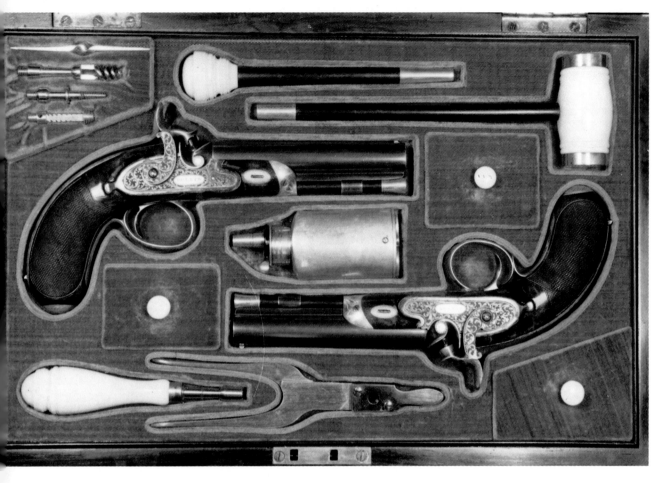

The John Mullin deringers, .36 caliber, each measuring 7¾ inches overall. Mounts of engraved silver; Mullin marking on locks in gold. Owner Henry G. Freeman was a prominent Philadelphia lawyer.

Various styles of percussion Deringer engraving, beginning with earlier at left, and standard Henry Deringer decor in first three pistols *at top.* To their *right,* a Slotter-made pistol marked DERINGER / PHILADELA, and engraved in the popular Henry Deringer style. *Right center,* a Butterfield (no. 16) with its customary engraving. *Bottom left,* a pair of A. Wurfflein's, with light scrolls. *At center,* one of the finest of all deringer pistols, an A. G. Genez of New York, exhibiting the masterful work of L. D. Nimschke; mountings of silver, with gold thumbpiece. Largest deringer is a Gillespie, measuring 7¹³⁄₁₆ inches overall, also a product of New York City. The Williamson, a standard example, with the 1724 marking on stock of the U.S. Cartridge Company collection. The minute handmade revolver, like a fine pocket watch, engraved on topstrap ORRIN SMITH / MAKER; in .17 caliber, of delicately engraved steel, with rosewood grips.

Nimschke, like many of his contemporaries, made use of pattern books. There were, in fact, four books of gun-engraving patterns found with his records. Their value is clear on comparison with his work. A careful tabulation indicates that several motifs in Nimschke's record were copied directly from these sources. The four books are all of German origin, and two are the work of G. Ernst of Zella. Although none is actually dated, they were published c. 1840. Lockplates, hammers, triggerguards, buttplates, and various other gun mountings comprise most of the designs. None of the four books exhibit scrollwork in the American style.

Sources of Ideas

These pattern books were Nimschke's main source of animal figures, but he found inspiration and ideas from a variety of supplementary sources, including the 1864 Schuyler, Hartley & Graham military goods catalogue (state seals and coats of arms), newspaper cuts, American coins, currency, stamps, and a Spencer gun catalogue of 1866.

Most of Nimschke's scroll motifs were bold and rich, with lining and shading in strength. Nearly all his scrolls were intertwining and, space permitting, often had small hairlike frills. His backgrounds were mostly punched-dot matting (beading); second to this in frequency was fine hatching. Sometimes little or no background was present.

Characteristic L. D. Nimschke engraving motifs are shown in several of the arms illustrated; nevertheless, the mere presence of some of these on a firearm does not positively identify the arm as having been engraved by Nimschke. For such an identification, the quality, skill, design, and "feeling" must be considered, because many of the same motifs were employed by other arms engravers.

The use of animal and animal-head motifs in American gun engraving of the 1850–1900 period was not uncommon. The best example—and one often seen—is the wolf head in profile on the hammers of Colt percussion revolvers. In Nimchke's work, the use of animal

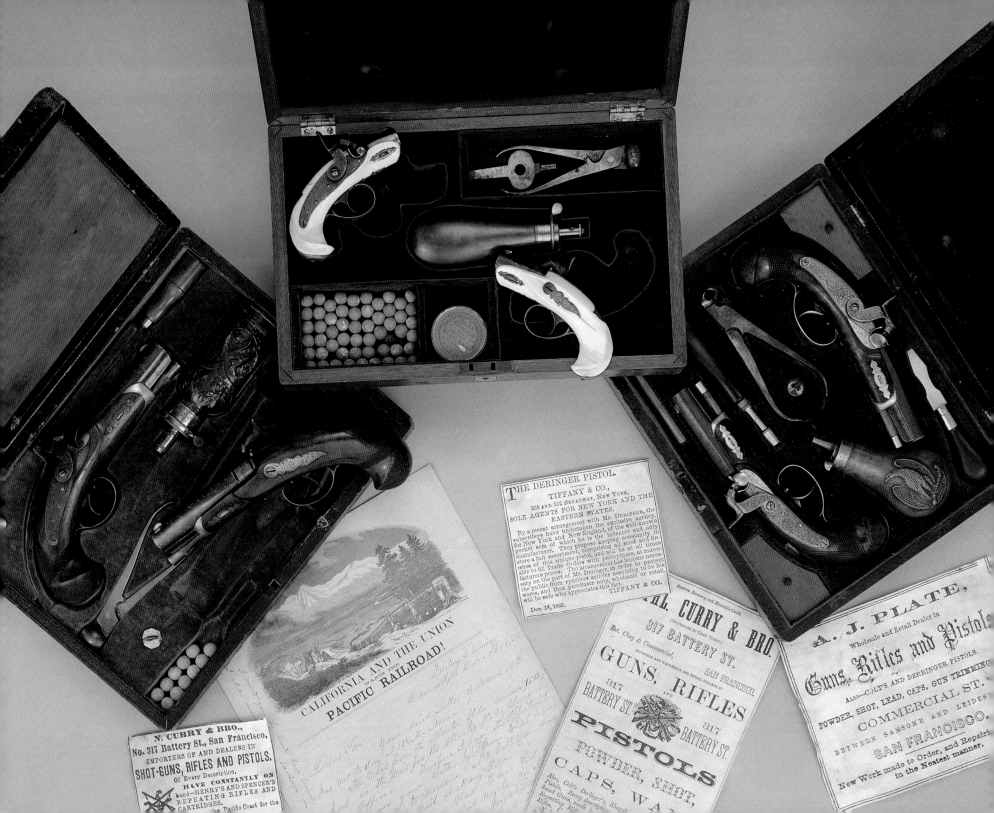

THE DERINGER PISTOL.

TIFFANY & CO.,
550 AND 552 Broadway, New York,
SOLE AGENTS FOR NEW YORK AND THE
EASTERN STATES.

By a recent arrangement with Mr. DERINGER, the
subscribers have undertaken the exclusive agency
for New York and New England, of the well-known
pocket arm of which he is the inventor and only
manufacturer. They propose keeping constantly in
store a full assortment, comprising all sizes and finishes of this unique pistol, and will be at all times
able to fill Trade Orders with promptness, at manufacturers prices. The arrangement has become necessary on the part of Mr. Deringer, in order to protect
the public from spurious articles assuming to be his
wares, and that purchaser only, wholesale or retail,
will be safe who appreciates this fact.
                              TIFFANY & CO.

Dec. 18, 1863.

CALIFORNIA AND THE UNION
WANTS THE
PACIFIC RAILROAD!

N. CURRY & BRO.,
No. 317 Battery St., San Francisco,
IMPORTERS OF AND DEALERS IN
SHOT-GUNS, RIFLES AND PISTOLS.
Of Every Description.
HAVE CONSTANTLY ON
hand—HENRY'S AND SPENCER'S
REPEATING RIFLES AND
CARTRIDGES.
Pacific Coast for the

Eastern Directory and Mercantile Guide.

N. CURRY & BRO.
(Successors to Chas. Curry.)
317 BATTERY ST.
SAN FRANCISCO.
Bet. Clay & Commercial
IMPORTERS AND WHOLESALE AND RETAIL DEALERS IN
GUNS, RIFLES
317 AND 317
BATTERY ST. BATTERY ST.
PISTOLS
POWDER, SHOT,
CAPS, WA

A. J. PLATE,
Wholesale and Retail Dealer in
Guns, Rifles and Pistols
ALSO—COLT'S AND DERRINGER PISTOLS.
POWDER, SHOT, LEAD, CAPS, GUN TRIMMING
COMMERCIAL ST.
BETWEEN SANSOME AND LEIDES
SAN FRANCISCO.
New Work made to Order, and Repairing
in the Neatest manner.

The superb large-size Henry Deringer pistols, a cased set with each pistol having 9½-inch barrels. Made for A. Millspaugh, Washington, Louisiana, who evidently was quite fond of Deringers, having ordered at least three pairs. Mountings in gold and silver; barrels with streaked special finish, a pride of the genuine Deringer.

(*bottom left and right*) Factory-inscribed Deringer pistol belonging to President Lincoln's assassin, the actor and activist John Wilkes Booth. Booth lost it as he landed on the stage of Ford's Theater, after his dramatic leap from the president's box following the shooting. Engraving typical of most such pistols by Henry Deringer, which were in production by c. 1830, and remained so through the Civil War era.

Deringers by Henry Deringer. Each pistol 8 inches overall, with agent markings of Wolf & Durringer, Louisville, Kentucky; silver mounts; casing covered in leather, with recessed brass handle on lid. Ivory-stocked pair attributed to casing by Tiffany & Co.; silver mounts; mahogany case lid with German-silver ribbon plaque inlay, engraved O.W. TURK. Pistols *at right* mounted in gold with silver triggerguards.

motifs was strongly in evidence, more so than in the work of most of his contemporaries. The Nimschke scrapbook depicts numerous examples of the artist's reliance on these themes.

American-Style Engraving

In discussing L. D. Nimschke's work, reference has been made to the American style of gun engraving. This engraving style was an outgrowth of German techniques of the mid-nineteenth century, and nearly all engravers who developed it were immigrants from Germany. In use from about 1850 to the present, it was especially prevalent up to about 1900. Largely peculiar to this country, it featured smoothly flowing foliate scrollwork, with occasional animal motifs, of which the wolf head is best known. The background was commonly beaded, but sometimes hatched.

Coverage varied according to the amount of engraving desired by the client as well as the shapes and sizes of surfaces. Handguns often had little nonengraved surface remaining.

Major variations in the distinctive American engraving styles are: (a) tight, close, fine scrolls; (b) heavy, bold scrolls; (c) intermediate scrolls.

In addition to variations on American- and English-style engraving, Nimschke's records illustrated the arabesque, consisting of geometric scrolls with plain or finely hatched background.

The Nimschke scrapbook yields rich rewards for the historian, for the master engraver also recorded the work of his contemporaries—specifically Gustave Young, Jacob Glahn, Mathias Grunewald, E. A. Coleman, and Colt factory engravers (collectively identified by him as "Htfd"). Their work was recorded by prints pulled by Nimschke. Notably in the case of Gustave Young, Nimschke's references served to identify whole groups of guns by one engraver. Prints from a gold-inlaid Manhattan (thought at the time the book was written to have been a Model 1849 Colt Pocket revolver), with the notation "*by G. Jung*" matched in style gold-inlaid percussion Colt revolvers, and were instrumental in positively

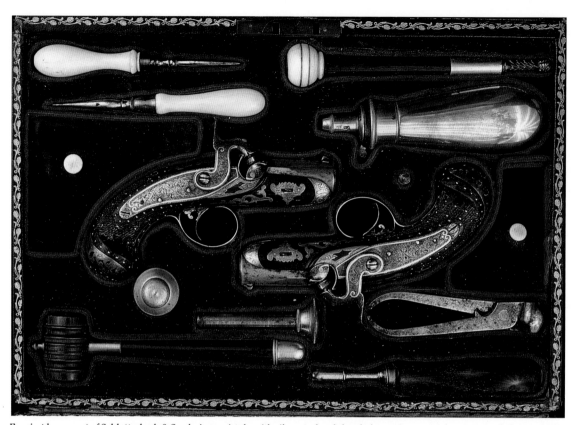

Fanciest known set of Schlotterbeck & Co. deringer pistols, with silver stud and sheath decoration on stocks, mounts of silver, and gold inlays on major steel parts (other than barrels). Research has proven original recipient, Mme H. De Laurencel, was respectable lady, not madam of bordello as previously conjectured. Presented in 1860. See the author's *The Peacemakers*, pages 131 and 165, for exceptional gold-mounted deringer pairs from mid-nineteenth century.

Target rifle by John S. Dutton, of Jaffrey, New Hampshire, made in the 1850s for George F. Ellsworth, whose name appears engraved on an eagle inlay on left side of the butt. The .42-caliber barrel is 31 inches; its false muzzle pictured *at top*. Accompanied by rare original manuscript notebooks (dated 1858–78) on how to make and decorate rifles. The double patchbox was a trademark of Dutton. Engraving and inlays with folk-art style and quality.

attributing the style to Gustave Young.

Further, Nimschke's numerous prints of wolf-head motifs, especially on percussion Colt revolver hammers by Nimschke and others, were important in dispelling the myth that an engraver named Joseph Wolf had used that motif as a signature to identify guns that he had engraved.

Swordmakers Excelled

Rivaling, and sometimes surpassing, the gunmakers were the swordmakers. Swords from the War of 1812, used by American servicemen, are usually American-made, and they reveal the degree of craftsmanship and design developed by native craftsmen. The eagle pommel, with origins dating back to Roman times, was pop-

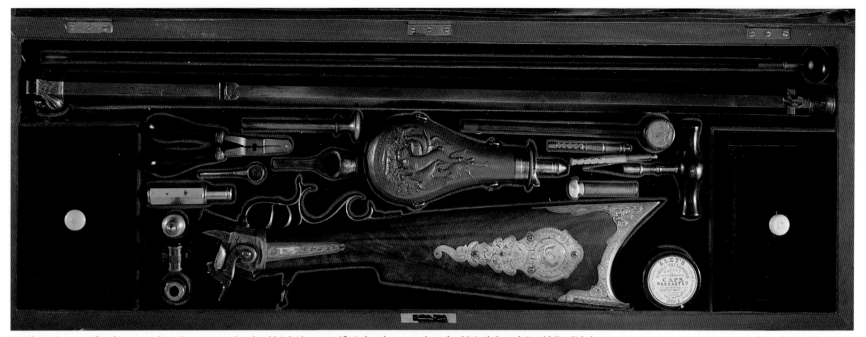

The finest known rifle of its type, this silver-mounted and gold-inlaid target rifle is hand-engraved on the 30-inch barrel, in old English letters: D.B. WESSON, HARTFORD, CT. Brassbound case lid plaque inscribed C.W. STOUGHTON, a shareholder in the Smith & Wesson and Sharps Rifle companies. In .31 caliber, with brown-finished barrel. Engraving of the doughnut-style scroll, and a masterwork by this craftsman, c. 1848–50.

Selection of large-size pepperboxes, c. 1840s and 1850s, whose engraving tended to be open scrolls, without backgrounds.

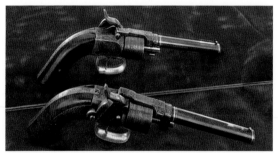

Massachusetts Arms Company .31-caliber pocket revolver, with rare gold-inlaid arrow, barrel bands, and initials CR, for Cadwalader Ringgold, a distinguished naval officer who retired as a rear admiral in 1866. Massachusetts seal engraved on Maynard tape primer door. Cylinder with etched scene. Gold-plated brass triggerguard. Ringgold was involved in various expeditions, including the Wilkes South Seas Expedition, the surveying of the California coast (1849–50), and the North Pacific Exploring and Surveying Expedition, which charted numerous Pacific islands, reaching China in March 1854.

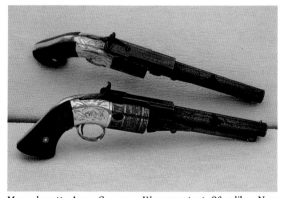

Massachusetts Arms Company Warner patent .36-caliber Navy revolver, one of only 125 made. Etched decoration on barrel and cylinder, in leaf and floral designs, with name SHELDON LEAVITT on cylinder periphery; frame plated in silver. In the mid-nineteenth century, etching appears occasionally as a substitute for hand engraving or (on cylinders) the roll-engraving that was a feature of most percussion Colt firearms.

ular with army officers, while the naval style—with nautical motifs—had its own characteristics.

Some of the most spectacular presentation swords were ordered by state legislatures. New York metalsmith John Targee was commissioned by his state legislature to create swords for army and naval officers worthy of recognition for their service in New York State during the War of 1812. These swords had gold four-sided hilts, with eagle pommels, rococo-style knuckle bows, and a counterguard on the obverse side with three neoclassical designs: two from classical mythology and the third an American eagle motif. All are credited to Moritz Furst, considered America's foremost die sinker and engraver of the day. One of the classical scenes, Hercules wrestling the Nemean lion, has been traced to the *Herculean Labours* created by the English sculptor John Flaxman for bas relief ceramic plaques by Josiah Wedgwood. The Flaxman design was also used on sword scabbards produced by Richard Tweed for Lloyd's Patriotic Fund. Author John D. Hamilton further identifies the design as used on Mexican War presentation swords by Nathan P. Ames and on presentation Civil War swords by Tiffany & Co. Another counterguard motif depicts a kneeling male figure on whose back rests a female figure holding a trumpet to announce victory. The third motif is of an American eagle on a panoply of war trophies. The blades were etched with patriotic motifs, E PLURIBUS UNUM, and the ever-present eagle.

When Connecticut's legislature voted a presentation sword for Captain Isaac Hull, the commission was given to Nathan Starr. He also received commissions for elaborate, and expensive, sabers for Generals Andrew Jackson and Edmund P. Gaines (for Seminole War service), and for Colonel Richard M. Johnson. These three had been voted by the legislature of Tennessee. All four swords were of gold.

Another group of spectacular presentations are the classically elegant swords ordered by the state of Maryland in recognition of native naval heroes of the War of 1812. These were made under the aegis of metalsmith Harvey Lewis, along with etcher John Meer and mem-

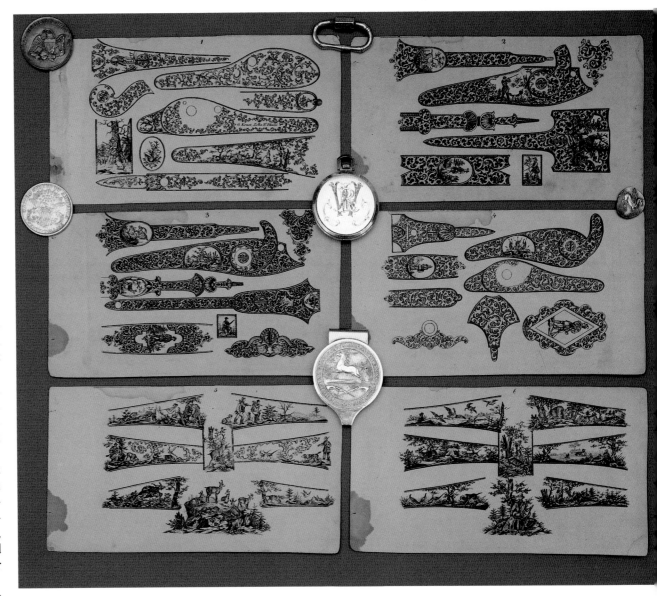

Pattern book from the L. D. Nimschke archives, signed by G. Ernst, Zella. Comparison with prints in the Nimschke record book and with engraved arms of the period occasionally locates examples having specific scenes taken from this and other pattern sources. The L. D. Nimschke scrapbook, along with pattern books and other materials, rests in the collection of Richard C. Marohn, M.D.

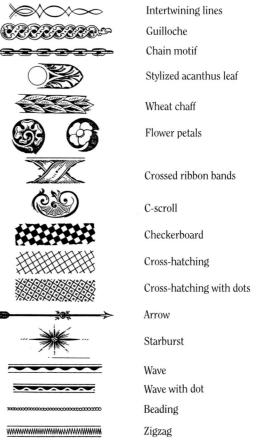

Intertwining lines

Guilloche

Chain motif

Stylized acanthus leaf

Wheat chaff

Flower petals

Crossed ribbon bands

C-scroll

Checkerboard

Cross-hatching

Cross-hatching with dots

Arrow

Starburst

Wave

Wave with dot

Beading

Zigzag

These decorative motifs are so much a part of Nimschke's repertoire that they often, along with the quality and style of the scrolls, quickly serve to identify his work. Drawings by Eduardo T. Coelho.

(*top left*) Another pattern book from the Nimschke archive. Deringer engraved by Cuno Helfricht, and used as pattern, c. 1870s. Very likely Helfricht was familiar with pattern books.

(*bottom left*) Nimschke marked this set of patterns with his name, probably a die stamp from his own hand. Careful examination reveals marking of G. Ernst, of Zella, on some lockplates. Some of these scenes have been traced to existing firearms decorated by Nimschke, Gustave Young, and other engravers of the period.

The fourth of the Nimschke pattern books, every page stamped with L. D. Nimschke's name.

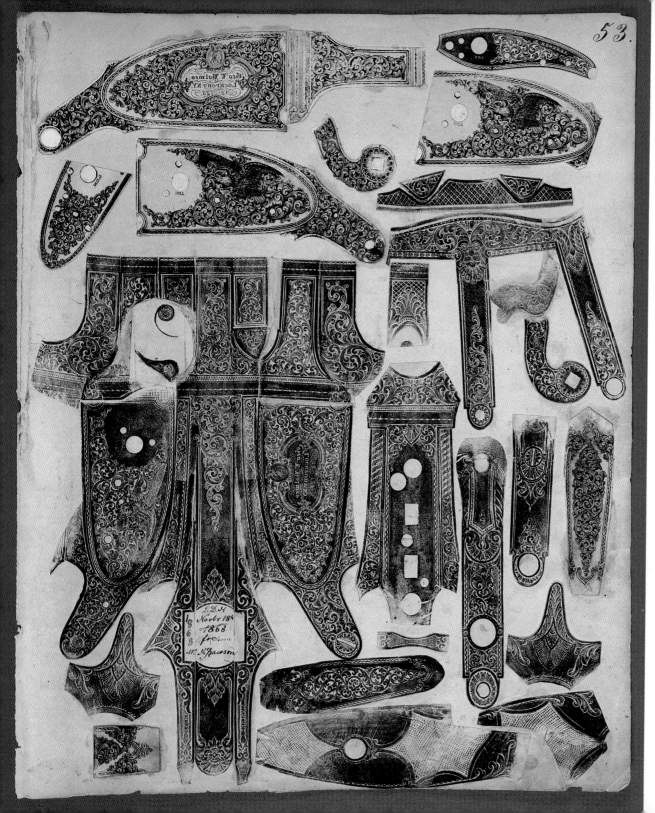

bers of the blade-making Rose family, all of Philadelphia. Meer is credited by authority E. Andrew Mowbray as the source of the "very best American blade decoration of the period 1815–1830."

Still another maker of superb presentation swords of the post–War of 1812 period was Fletcher & Gardner, of Philadelphia (formerly of Boston). The state of Georgia was a prominent client of this firm. Another sword-making craftsman is known through his marking, J. HUB, on the bottom surface of the quillon of a sword by Harvey Lewis.

The Mexican War provided another occasion for presentation swords, and among the products of Nathan Ames alone we find a gold design for Brigadier General Franklin Pierce from the state of New Hampshire, a silver gift for Colonel John C. Hays from the state of Texas, a silver for Major General William O. Butler from the state of Kentucky, another silver to Colonel George Washington Morgan from citizens of Ohio, still another silver to Captain George A. McCall from citizens of Philadelphia, and many, many more. John D. Hamilton's study of Ames (*The Ames Sword Company, 1829–1935*) lists over 120 orders, dating from June of 1846 through January 1851. Six gold swords were ordered by Congress for Generals Quitman, Twiggs, Worth, Henderson, Hamer, and Butler. Among the most deluxe of presentations was a state of Virginia sword to General Zachary Taylor (fifth sword by Ames for Taylor, honoring his Mexican War exploits), with 300 pennyweight of gold and a value of $1,000. On the scabbard were pictured the Goddess of Liberty, the American eagle, and the storming of Monterey; the hilt was of solid gold.

War of 1812 and Mexican War presentation swords (as well as those of the Civil War) were of such elaborate decoration that they lost all usefulness as weapons, being too heavy to carry comfortably. Makers the likes of Nathan Starr, Thomas Fletcher, Harvey Lewis, George Jackson, Frederick Widmann, Ames Manufacturing

Impressions from Nimschke's scrapbook, taken from the Holmes target pistol, with attachable stock. Nimschke saw fit to sign the grip spur and the lockplates (in both cases, on both sides).

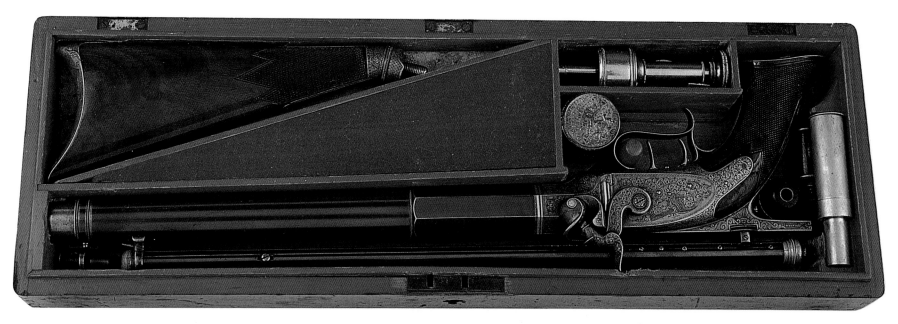

George L. Holmes target pistol, represented in Nimschke's scrapbook (on page 53). Metal parts case-hardened and blued, with gold-inlaid bands. One of Nimschke's finest decorative creations.

Probably the finest deringer maker in America, A. G. Genez appears to have relied on Nimschke to embellish his best arms. This superb set is marked on each barrel, tapering from breech to muzzle: A.G. GENEZ, MAKER, NO. 9 CHAMBERS ST., N.Y. Silver triggerguards and buttcaps, each of the latter with grotesque mask and intertwined monogram S.W.W. Overall length of each pistol is 6 inches; in .44 caliber; casing of velvet-lined leather; c. 1855–60. Prints from Genez arms appear in the Nimschke record book.

Company, Horstmann, and Tiffany & Co. created some of the most elaborate arms of any period.

American artists and designers were influenced by the publication of George Richardson's *Iconology; Or a Collection of Emblematical Figures* (London, 1779). To quote author John D. Hamilton (from *The Ames Sword Company*),

[Richardson's book] had a lasting effect on American artists who became acutely sensitive to creating, through the veil of allegory, poetic images addressed to the mind rather than the eye. Allegory was subtly used to define feelings of nationalism in aesthetic terms, and kindle the fires of patriotic emotion. . . . Not all allegorical decoration was subtle. Since adoption in 1782 as the principal device on our nation's seal of state, the eagle and shield, emblazoned with stars and stripes of the national colors, generated instant recognition as symbols of national pride. Early in the 19th century, a revived interest in classicism inspired artistic expression through Greco-Roman themes such as imperial emblems, medallions of heroes, Gods and Goddesses, ornamentation suggesting leaves of the acanthus, and

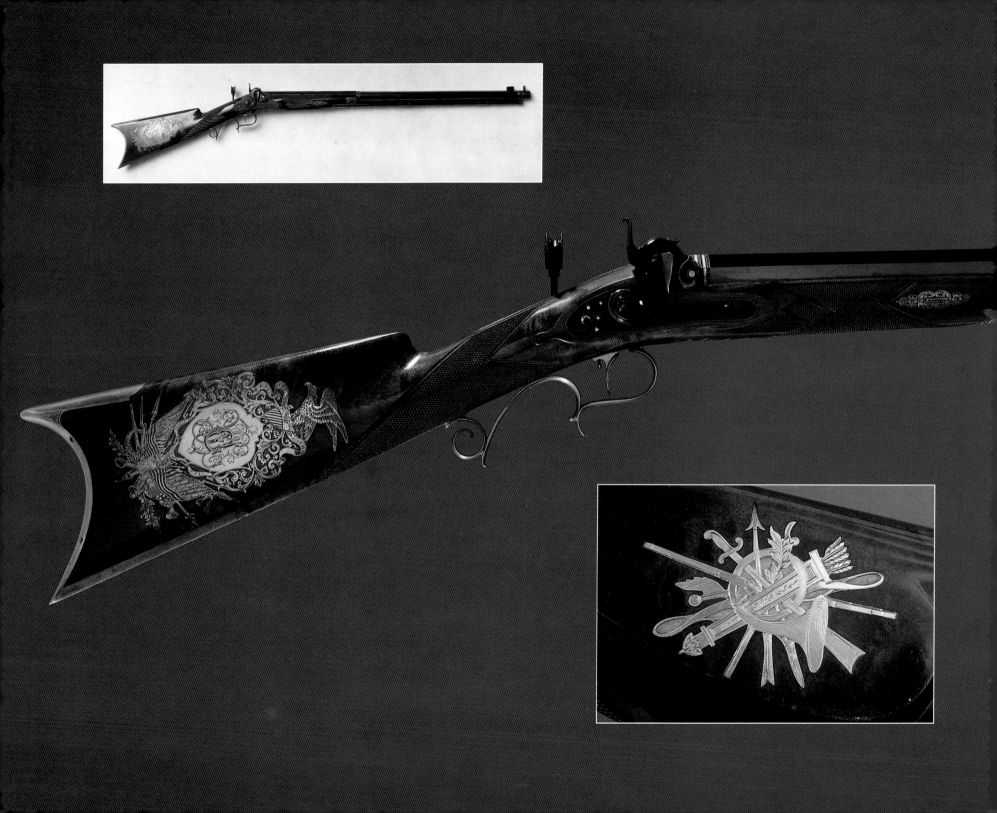

A gift from the citizens of Rhode Island to General Ulysses S. Grant, in recognition of his Civil War service. Makers of this silver-mounted percussion sporting rifle were N. and N. G. Whitmore. Engraving in a Germanic style, though patriotic eagle and shield, stand of flags, and E PLURIBUS UNUM are strongly American details. Note symbolism on cheekpiece inlay. Soon after presentation of this rifle, Grant was elected president of the United States; in 1883–84 he was president of the National Rifle Association.

EY monogram at *top left,* a die engraved for use by engraver Eugene Young. Wax impressions from Gustave Young family collection, made from seals, signet rings, and other devices, done by the master while still in Germany (pre-1948). Note Hercules and lion figures, in brown wax at *left center,* a motif known on American and British presentation swords of the early nineteenth century. Photographs from family archives, of a bearded Gustave and sons.

Model 1853 exhibition-grade Sharps Shotgun, no. 18220. Attributed to Gustave Young, or his shop. See also page 363, for top view of barrel, which is flush gold-inlaid with scrolls, and the old-English marking: SHARPS RIFLE MANUFG CO. HARTFORD CONN. Stylized dogs and rabbit scene on left side of frame. Deep brown color of barrel, a popular finish also seen on some military arms, and not infrequently observed on rifled longarms.

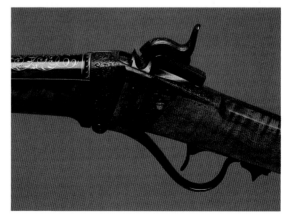

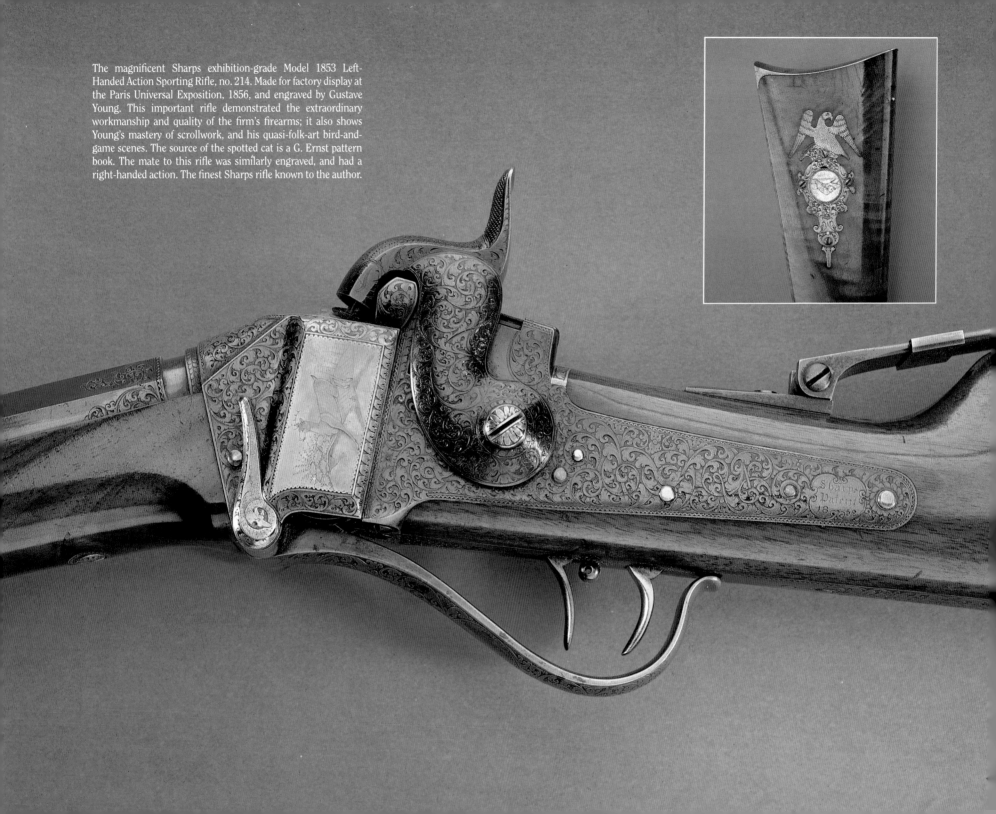

The magnificent Sharps exhibition-grade Model 1853 Left-Handed Action Sporting Rifle, no. 214. Made for factory display at the Paris Universal Exposition, 1856, and engraved by Gustave Young. This important rifle demonstrated the extraordinary workmanship and quality of the firm's firearms; it also shows Young's mastery of scrollwork, and his quasi-folk-art bird-and-game scenes. The source of the spotted cat is a G. Ernst pattern book. The mate to this rifle was similarly engraved, and had a right-handed action. The finest Sharps rifle known to the author.

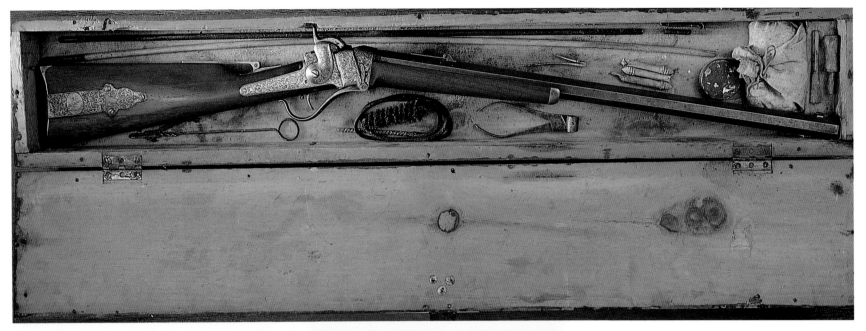

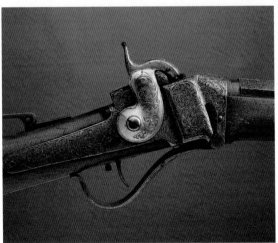

Sharps Model 1853 Sporting Rifle, no. 8421, with shipping box and accessories. Engraved in a larger scroll than the left-handed rifle, and probably executed by a worker in Young's shop rather than by Young himself. Case lid stamped with owner's name in large letters: FERDINAND RHOADS / SHAMOKIN / NORTHUMBERLAND CO PENNA.

swags. . . . Minerva, Goddess of Wisdom . . . reflected the wisdom of charting a Republican course for our national destiny. . . . Concurrently and with increased usage, the image of Columbia, Goddess of Liberty, eventually supplanted Minerva as the primary icon of nationalism. She was often represented bearing a staff or pole, atop which was displayed the Phrygian-style cap of liberty or manumission.

In 1837 Nathan Ames went to England to perfect his swordmaking. There he learned the process of silverplating with electricity. His techniques remained largely unknown in the United States until around 1856. Ames relied on his own designer, Silas Mosman, to draw the majority of the designs he used in presentation pieces.

Ames had a feeling for promotions and public relations, like his contemporary Samuel Colt, and saw fit to make a special sword for the "Kentucky Giant" of sideshow fame, James D. Porter. The 56-inch blade was mounted on a substantial hilt of ebony inlaid with mother-of-pearl. P. T. Barnum paid for the sword and made the presentation to the seven-foot-nine-inch

celebrity. Mounted on the crossguard, whose quillons terminated in eagle heads, was an American shield.

The Etching of Sword Blades

The etching and gilding of sword blades was an occupation that would rouse the ire of the most tolerant of OSHA inspectors. The gilding process yielded mercury fumes, which were fatal if inhaled. Etching was much safer, but still could lead to painful burns. The visual fruits of these hazardous professions, however, were often beautiful and varied combinations of decorative motifs and contrasting finishes of gold and blue and bright steel.

Early in the nineteenth century, sword blades, most of which were imported from Germany or France, were decorated in the fashion popular in those countries. The decoration combined etching and gilding with fire-blu-

Though the engraving was done in England, the gold inlaying on this Webley revolver was by an American craftsman, for military goods dealers Evans & Hassall. Right side of barrel bears flush gold-inlaid inscription, in matching old-English letters: CAPT'N D.D. PORTER, FROM CAPT'N D.G. FARRAGUT—1862. The .44-caliber cylinder periphery has three flush gold-inlaid American soldiers and naval officers of the Civil War period, and the numbers 1 through 5, denoting each chamber. Case lid inlaid with silver plaque, also inscribed. Believed presented to commemorate the Union's capture of New Orleans, March 1862.

War of 1812 and Mexican War presentation swords, from the federal or state governments, honoring heroism and gallantry in action; such presentations much more scarce than those from cities, towns, or organizations. *From left*, silver-hilted eagle-head pommel from state of Georgia to U.S. officer; ivory grips; made by Thomas Fletcher and Sidney Gardner, Boston; blade by W. Rose, etching signed by William John Meer; 1814. Gilt bronze-hilted sword with helmeted female pommel and grip motif of mermaid holding urn, from U.S. Congress; Rose blade signed by etcher John Meer; c. 1813. *Center*, solid gold by Ames, presentation from president of the United States to Captain James Hunter, a hero of Battle of Fort Stephenson, 1813, but made and presented in 1835. Mexican War presentation voted by state of Vermont; awarded posthumously, to son of hero Truman Bishop Ransom; by Ames; silver grips and scabbard. Silver-hilted, gilt-finished sword from state of Delaware to Brevet Captain C. P. Evans, 1849; by Wm. Horstmann & Sons.

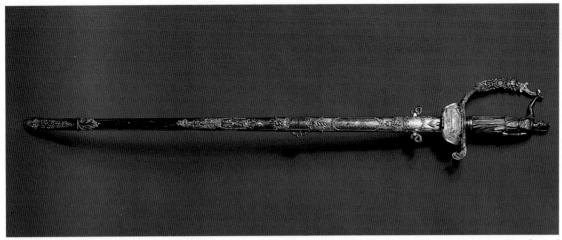

From the state of New Hampshire to Brigadier General Franklin Pierce, 1849. By the Ames Manufacturing Company. Hilt in form of Columbia, Goddess of Liberty, extending laurel wreath. Gilt scabbard engraved with New Hampshire state seal, list of battles, and inscription; mounts of gold. The counterguard scene is that of the attack on Contreras (Mexico), wherein Pierce led his brigade in a bold charge. Walnut case not illustrated.

Made in France for the American trade, presentation set for a South Carolina officer of French descent. Embossed in French on the case lid and engraved on scabbard (translated as follows): PRESENTED TO CAPT. V. DURAND BY THE FRENCH ARTILLERISTS CHARLESTON 3 JAN 1839, along with names of five members of the committee of presentors. Silver-gilt hilt and scabbard, with French silversmith's hallmarks. Swords of this style generally found in gilt bronze; this is the only example known to author in silver. Note American motifs, including Indians and Liberty cap and American eagle and shield. Blade measures 30½ inches.

ing. As the century progressed, blades became more elaborate, and by the period c. 1830–40 could have as many as three panels within a blued background of floral and scroll designs as well as patriotic symbolism. At about the same time an etching technique that left a scene with the background frosted and of a grayish cast gained currency. John D. Hamilton credits F. W. Widmann (active c. 1822–47) as being among the first in America to use this system.

Widmann, who was succeeded by William Horstmann, produced a quality of etching superior to the work of Ames and other competitors. In time, Ames and others would again be competitive. The etching of sword blades was brought to new heights as the nineteenth century developed. The best of blades proved wor-

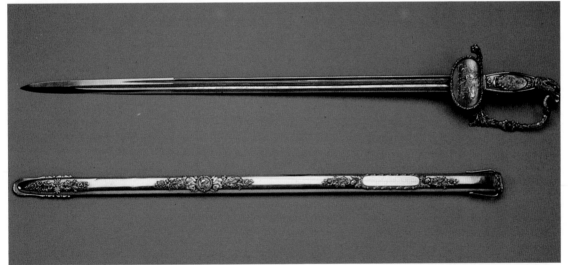

Nathan Starr, Middletown, Connecticut, was selected to make this commission sword, voted by the General Assembly of the state of Connecticut, October 1817, for War of 1812 hero Captain Isaac Hull. This magnificent expression of nationalism also embodied the pride of Connecticut as the cradle of armsmaking in the United States at the time. Gold mounts and styling were the ultimate expression of Starr's craftsmanship and artistry; cost of the sword was $1,000, making it one of the two most expensive sword presentations in America at that time (the other being a gift from the U.S. government to Colonel R. M. Johnson, also made by Starr). Hull blade believed made in Solingen, Germany. Simeon North, maker of the Hull and McDonough presentation pistols, occupied shops near Starr's in Middletown.

Naval dirks made for American market, c. 1800–20, with one rare specimen of the Regulation Pattern, adopted, U.S. Navy midshipman's dirk of 1869 (*fourth* eagle head *up from bottom left*); most of English or French manufacture, with patriotic devices specific to America, particularly eagle heads. In the early nineteenth century, the United States lacked facilities for making dirks of this quality in any quantity, thus those made in America are quite rare. Largest dirk measures 21 inches overall.

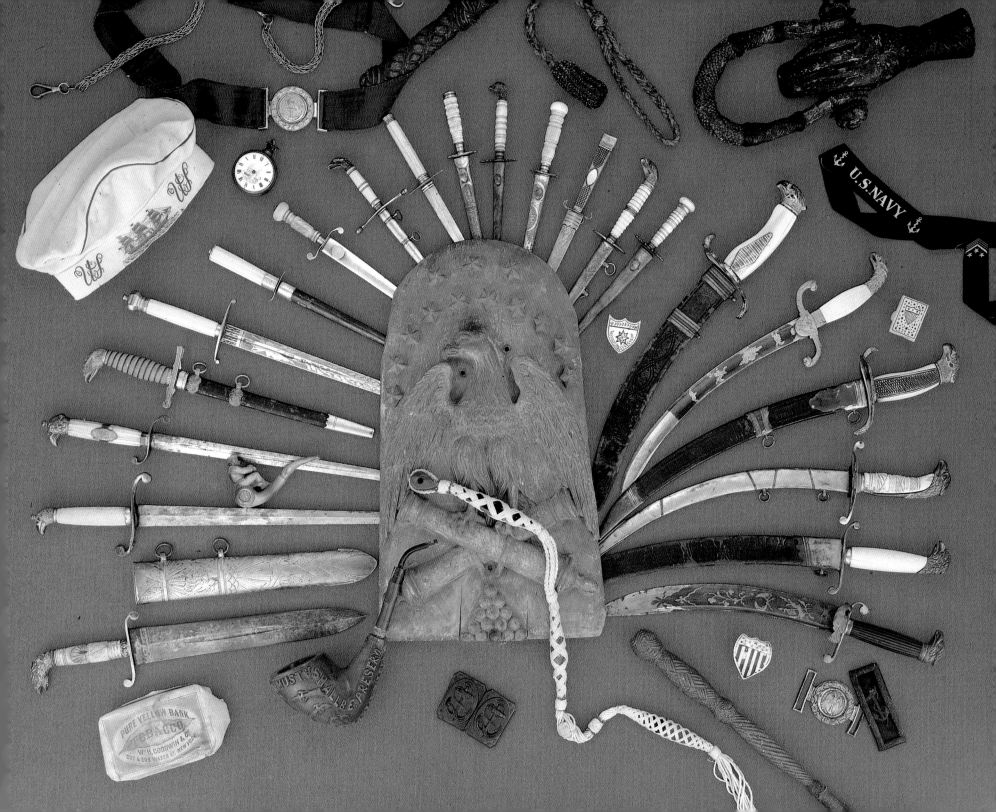

thy accompaniments to the intricate and elaborate hilts and scabbards to come.

Gun-Engraving Tradition

The immigrant German craftsmen set a high standard of arms embellishment, but as the twentieth century unfolded, the standard began a downhill slide. The demand for engraved arms would level off, and most of the younger generation of craftsmen would not have the benefit of the thorough training of their predecessors.

The golden age of American gunmaking, which begins with the Industrial Age and continues into the early twentieth century, is of such significance to the *Steel Canvas* story that the period is also covered in chapters 4 through 7 and in much of chapter 9.

An early silver-mounted Bowie knife inscribed on throat of scabbard from Rezin P. Bowie to H. W. Fowler, U.S. Dragoons. By Searles, and signed on inlaid silver plate on top flat of blade, adjacent to crossguard. Further development of the classic Bowie knife, from the Jim Bowie–Edwin Forrest original.

Assortment of Elgin Cutlass pistols, the *center* pistol with sharply etched blade. Overall length of *second pistol from top,* 17$\frac{1}{8}$ inches; c. 1837–38; made by C. B. Allen and Morrill, Mosman and Blair.

(*opposite*) *At center,* the silver-mounted, hand-forged knife (with sheath) presented by Jim Bowie to one of the nineteenth century's leading thespians, Edwin Forrest. Considered to be the original "Bowie knife," this massive weapon measures 17 inches overall. Both legends in their own right, Bowie and Forrest became friends in the 1820s, in New Orleans. *At left and top center,* portraits of Forrest; *at right,* Bowie himself. Also pictured: the seal of the Edwin Forrest Home for infirm and needy actors (where the guns and knives were kept until 1989); a silver-mounted Henry Deringer rifle and Deringer dueling pistols of Forrest, as well as his Robbins & Lawrence pepperbox cased set; a theater ticket to the actor's final performance; a stag-handled American primitive knife and U.S.-military John Miles–marked Model 1798 musket used by the actor in the Indian play *Metamora* (Currier & Ives print depicts Forrest costumed for that role); and several biographies of Forrest. An elaborate case in the actors' home exhibited arms from his collection, among them the rifle, the musket, and—most significantly—the Bowie knife. Extensively documented, the knife was given to Forrest c. February 1829, most likely in Natchez, Mississippi.

NO. 5 ON MODEL P.

CHARLES J. HELFRICHT HARTFORD CONN.

NO. 1½ ON ALL MODELS

NO. 2½ ON MODEL P.

NO. 2½ ON ALL MODELS

NO. 5 ON ALL MODELS.

NO. 5 ON ALL MO

COLT'S PATENT FIREARMS MFG. CO.,
HARTFORD, CONN.

Del. E.R.L.	Tr. E.R.L.	Ch'k,	App.
1-21-1915	1-23.1915	____ 1915	____ 1915

No. C-4200   SUPERCEDES
SUPERCEDED BY

Some sixty years of Colt engraving. Shotgun *at top* believed decorated by Charles J. Helfricht, or his son Cuno, c. 1870. Early 1870s Deringer by Cuno as pattern for piece work. Model 1895 Colt revolver attributed to Cuno, and part of elaborately inlaid presentation pair. Graver, stamps, dies and proofplate from Helfricht workbench. Rare blueprint from set made by Helfricht to guide successor engraver, Wilbur A. Glahn, 1915.

Chapter 4
Colonel Colt's Deluxe Revolvers

No individual had a more profound impact on American arms engraving and embellishment than Samuel Colt. Recognizing that the decoration of his arms would add to their appeal, he ordered engraving and silver and German-silver-mounted select walnut stocks on many of his prototypes preceding the Paterson, New Jersey, period. By the time Colt began manufacturing at Paterson, roll-engraved scenes on the cylinders were standard, and a few of the production arms were hand-engraved, some fitted with ivory or mother-of-pearl grips, and some with German-silver band inlays. Even silver-plating was employed, and the youthful Colt also introduced his clever promotional practice of presentation revolvers. Some of these arms were quite elaborately decorated, among them a Holster Model revolver prepared for and presented to the Russian czar Alexander II.

The pre-Paterson and Paterson-era Colts had a primitive style of scrollwork, in keeping with the common scrolls of the time. Only a few deluxe revolvers were made. Besides the czar's presentation piece, a magnificent set of ivory-gripped Holster Models was apparently employed by young Colt as sample and display guns. One

of these (serial number 984) ranks among the finest of Colt revolvers, and was maintained by the Colonel in his private arms collection. During the Paterson period, 1836–42, Colt was still exploring new ideas in gun decoration. Better business and more elaborate decorative times would come later.

Not until the early 1850s would Colt start turning out decorated arms of the highest grade of mass-produced weaponry, even though he reentered gunmaking in 1847, with the Walker Model, after a five-year hiatus. A magnificent set of Whitneyville-Hartford Dragoon revolvers was prepared on order of Moore & Baker of New York for presentation to Mexican War hero Colonel George Washington Morgan. These are the earliest known Hartford Colt production firearms with engraving. The sterling silver grips were inscribed with an elaborate presentation, and the scrollwork was present only on the butts. The engraving should be attributed, however, to a craftsman normally working in silver and gold.

Colt's attention to arms embellishment had started anew with the Walker, whose cylinders were roll-engraved with a Texas Ranger–and-Indian battle scene, the die executed by New York engraver W. L. Ormsby.

The same roll was used on the cylinders of the transition Dragoon pistols of Colonel Morgan. Various roll-cylinder scenes would remain a standard feature of all production Colt firearms of the period, at least on guns having round cylinders. Who could predict that from the rather simple scroll decor on the Morgan pistols there would quickly evolve some of the most elaborate of firearms decoration produced in nineteenth-century America?

The Early Vine, the Doughnut, and Exhibition-Grade Scrolls

A few early Dragoon Models were hand-embellished with a scroll customarily identified as the Early Vine style, a simple decor of open scrolls, lightly shaded and without punched dot or beaded background. The first revolvers so embellished were quite similar to the more plain of the engraved Patersons, and were likely to have coverage only on the gripstraps, hammers, and frames. Soon scrolls were also cut on the barrels and loading levers.

For his dramatic and smashingly successful panorama of arms at London's Great Exhibition of 1851, Colt had special presentation-grade cases of "Buhl" work made in Austria, and Dragoon, Navy, and Pocket

Holster Model Paterson revolver presentation made for Czar Nicholas I, in promotion of Colt arms; serial no. 346. Contrasting early scroll decor to the refined artistry of Gustave Young, as on shoulder-stocked Third Model Dragoon, inscribed to Grand Duke Constantine from the inventor, Colonel Colt; serial no. 16481. Gifts made c. 1839 and 1858, respectively.

Historic Model 1839 Paterson Revolving carbine, serial no. 711, with elegantly inscribed silver plaque inlaid on stock to document presentation from the governor of Rhode Island to Henry C. Clark, Orderly Sergeant R.I. Carbineers: AS A SLIGHT MEMENTO OF THE GRATITUDE OF THE STATE FOR SERVICES RENDERED DURING THE LATE DORR INSURRECTION, July 4, 1842. Brass plate *below* reveals roll-engraved cylinder scene, made for Colt by W. L. Ormsby. Handsome cased set, a Holster Model revolver above the most imposing of cutlass pistols, that invented by Elgin, and made by C. B. Allen. Indian trade musket *at right* is of London manufacture.

revolvers elaborately engraved in an exhibition-grade scroll. These arms are of such rarity that only a handful are known, and the cases have survived in an equally scarce number. The best examples of these show guns are in the Windsor Castle Armoury, presented by a grateful Colonel Colt (he had received this honorary rank from the state of Connecticut in time for his London appearance) to Prince Albert and Edward, Prince of Wales.

The next step in decoration adopted by Colt was a scroll known to modern-day collectors as the "doughnut," due to its roundish and puffy appearance. The identity of the engraver remains unknown, and his reign at Colt spanned only 1851–52. This easily recognizable style has also been observed on Sharps and Massachusetts Arms Company revolvers, the latter bitter competitors of Colt who were successfully sued by him for patent infringement in 1851.

Gustave Young, Master Engraver

On his return from the Great Exhibition of 1851, Colt's mind was teeming with the extraordinary firearms he saw in displays by the continental and British makers. The Colonel knew he would have to employ the finest European artistry to showcase the exquisite quality of his machine-made repeaters, and it was at about this time that he learned of the artist-engraver Gustave Young, a recent immigrant from Germany.

Young had a background in the highest European standards of craftsmanship, and had even executed projects destined for the czar of Russia. Having remarkable technical abilities, Young must be recognized as indisputably America's premier arms engraver in the nineteenth century. Hired by the Colonel in 1852—six years after his arrival in the United States—Young was put to work immediately on establishing styles and patterns of production engraving, while creating the most exquisite show guns built in America to that time. Soon after the start of Young's association with Colt, the firm abandoned its thick, somewhat primitive scrollwork for the

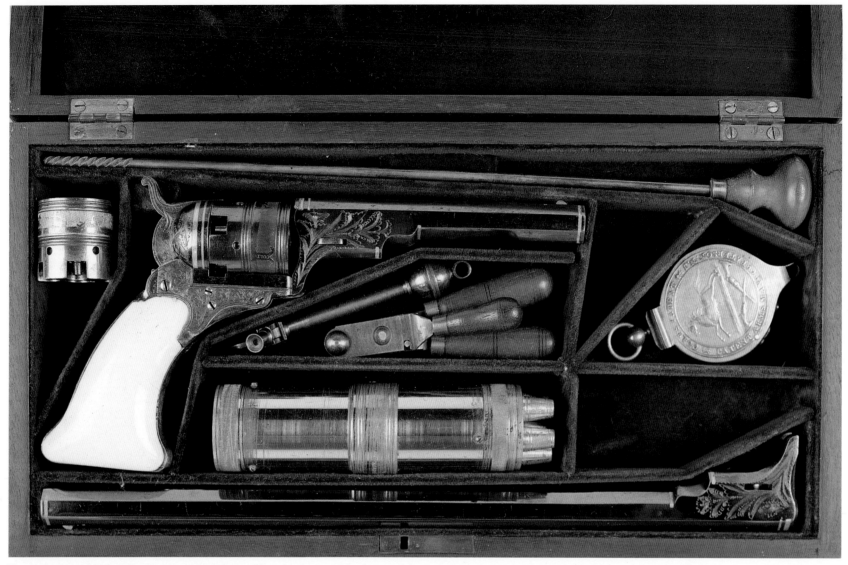

The simple vine-and-leaf scroll, as present on the majority of those few Paterson Colts that were factory-engraved; sometimes accompanied by German-silver band inlays. Rare ivory grips. Nontypical Paterson case of mahogany, with partitions; serial no. 548; c. 1839.

Several styles of Colt engraving, 1848–90. *From top left,* the most primitive of Hartford types, the Early Vine on a First Model Dragoon (coverage only on the frame, hammer, and gripstraps). *Beneath,* an 1849 Pocket and 1851 Navy in the Gustave Young scroll, both *above* an 1851 Navy with doughnut scroll. *Top center,* a presentation Model 1855 Sidehammer cased set (from Colonel Colt to Willis Thrall), also with Gustave Young scroll. The 1860 Army and Open Top .22 revolvers *below* exhibit distinctive L. D. Nimschke scrollwork. The cased New Line .22, Model 1877 Lightning, and the gold-plated Thuer deringer *at right* are variants of Helfricht scrolls. The Single Action Army, *right center,* was shipped in the "soft state," and was engraved in New York, probably by Nimschke's shop.

One of the series of six lithographs commissioned by Samuel Colt from artist George Catlin, depicting Colt firearms in wilderness conditions. Colt is believed to be the first American industrialist to commission works of art in promotion of his products. The Colonel became a keen art collector, as did his wife, the former Elizabeth Hart Jarvis. Most Bowie knives of English manufacture were for U.S. market. Rifle *at left* by Libeau of New Orleans; pair of pistols *at left* by Daniel Searles. American knives *at right center* by Rees Fitzpatrick; those *at top left* by Rose.

very forceful German-influenced American-style scroll with beaded background.

Young quickly organized a shop that took on Colt factory work plus some guns from Sharps and other factories. He would also do a few Winchesters at a later date, as well as miscellaneous arms by other makers. As a contractor to Colt, the company would supply work and quarters. The contractor supervised his craftsmen and billed on a piecework basis. A rare period photograph of a view of State Street, Hartford, shows a second-story shop with a simple sign that says either G. YOUNG, GUN ENGRAVER or G. YOUNG, GEN'L ENGRAVER.

His years with Colt (first onsite, then in his own shop) were productive ones for Young. A published list of the serial numbers of 108 Colt Pocket and Navy revolvers, dated September 23, 1854, bears Young's name. The list specifies delivery in four weeks. The size of the order indicates that Young must have had at least four engravers working under him; the pistols on the list also reveal the engraving style Young developed for Colt.

From this and two other such lists of pistols, as well as from Colt factory ledger data and from the Nimschke scrapbook, the author established that Young was responsible for the superb engraving and gold inlaying on the Colt Model 1860 Army revolvers President Abraham Lincoln presented in 1863 to King Frederick VII of Denmark and to King Charles XV of Sweden and Norway. These magnificent revolvers represent the ultimate in firearms decoration in nineteenth-century America.

Among Gustave Young's other masterworks for Colt were the gold-inlaid show guns and presentations of Third Model Dragoons, 1851 and 1861 Navys, 1860 Armys, and 1849 Pocket models, executed in the period c. 1853–67. Chief among the known recipients of presentations were Czar Nicholas I and the Sultan of Turkey. All of these aristocratic recipients seemed delighted to have received such truly regal gifts of state. (King Charles XV is known to have fired his Armys, carefully keeping the wrappers from the opened cartridge packets in the luxurious rosewood case!) The Gustave Young gold-inlaid revolvers are the most deluxe and exclusive of

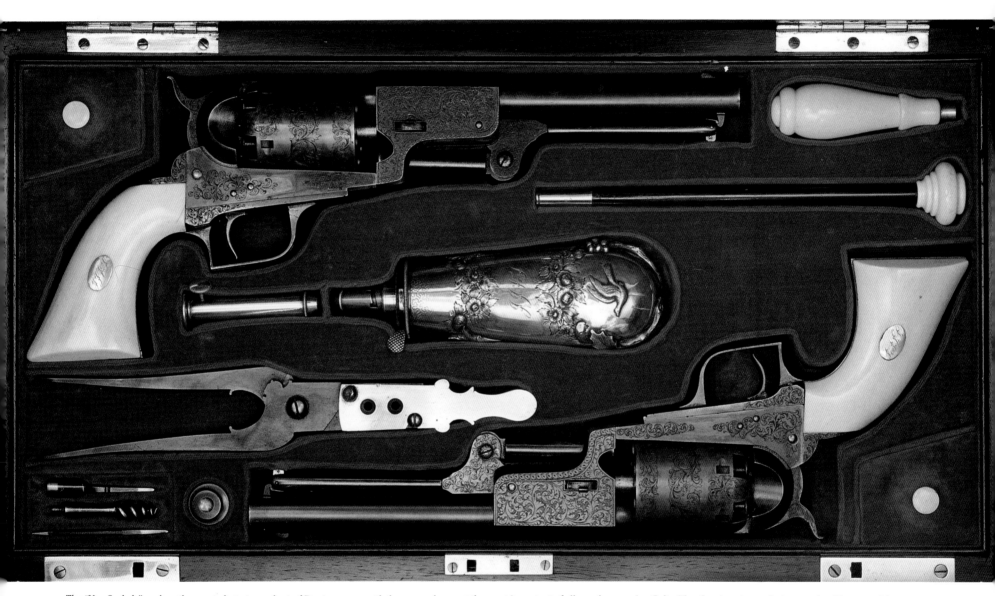

The "Van Syckels" rank as the most elegant cased set of Dragoons presently known and among the most important of all cased percussion Colts. They boast custom gripstraps and gold-mounted ivory grips, special scroll and border engraving, and a combination of browned, blued, and case-hardened finishes. Set ordered by Philadelphia gentleman of wealth, James Janeway Van Syckel. Elaborate rosewood casing bound in German silver. Serial nos. 8154 and 8913; c. 1852. See pages 87 and 88 for similarly cased special-order sets.

Generally regarded as the most important set of Colt firearms in existence, these doughnut-scroll pistols were a gift from a grateful Colonel Colt to his patent attorney, Edward N. Dickerson, after winning the landmark case of *Colt vs. Massachusetts Arms Co.* (1851). The casing is one of a group of the so-called Buhl style, made on the Colonel's order in Austria, in 1849. Pistol sets in similar cases were presented by the inventor to the Prince of Wales, and to his father, Prince Albert, consort to Queen Victoria.

Watercolor depicting the classic confrontation between the noble Native American and the determined frontiersman, tomahawk versus Colt revolver. Dragoon Colt with doughnut scroll. Issued as print, "The Last Shot," by Currier & Ives.

all Colt firearms, and probably not more than about thirty-five in all were made, out of approximately one million Colts dating from the percussion period.

Presentation sets of pistols and rifles given to Secretary of War John B. Floyd by the Colt factory workmen in 1857 were engraved at Young's shop, as was a similar set presented by Samuel Colt to his chief engineer, E. K. Root, in the same year. Still other recipients were the Chinese emperor at Peking, the Japanese emperor (who received revolvers from Colt's friend Commodore Perry), Secretary of War Jefferson Davis, journalist Horace Greeley, philanthropist George Peabody, and the first and second kings of Siam. The three gold-inlaid revolvers presented by the Colonel to Czar Nicholas I were later joined by more than a dozen engraved and/or inscribed handguns and longarms, specially cased, for Czar Alexander II and his brothers, the Grand Dukes Michael and Constantine. An estimated total of more than 1,300 presentations were made by Colt during the Gustave Young years, the majority of them engraved, and most emanating from the Young shop.

The two pairs of magnificent President Lincoln Model 1860 Army revolvers were done in 1862–63, and the engraving for each pistol was billed to Colt for the

Cylinder scene broadside by W. L. Ormsby of New York; published by Colt, c. 1850. Ovals *left* and *right* are scenes from cylinder roll die for Model 1839 Paterson carbine. Scene *at left* based on John Trumbull painting depicting the Battle of Bunker Hill. Ormsby was a leading practioner of the engraver's art and executor of special assignments for Samuel Colt since the Paterson years. Signed several cylinder scene rolls by cutting his name in reverse on the die.

seemingly reasonable figure of $225! But considering that a workman's salary at the time was about five dollars a week, the sum was quite substantial. In March of 1867, "3 Pistols for the Fair in Paris" were billed by Young to Colt. The engraving was listed as "fine," which is interpreted as meaning extra work beyond standard patterns.

The demanding style and execution of nearly all factory gold-inlaid and engraved percussion factory Colts made in the period 1853–69 indicates the gifted hand of Gustave Young. Yet not a single specimen of these ultimate Colt rarities has been noted to bear a signature by the artist. Not signing work was the general rule of the day among artisans in other fields of decorative art at that time.

Young is also known to have done die-cutting work for the Colt firm. Impressions in his pattern book include certain barrel-roll dies for the Model 1849 Pocket, the Model 1855 Sidehammer rifles and revolvers, the First and Second Model Deringers, and the London Model 1851 Navy. In addition, dies were cut for the Russian barrel markings on Colt Berdan rifles.

Records in Young's account book also show that in April–July 1868 he cut one full alphabet and a total of 173 letters and numbers for the Colt firm. Judging from surviving records, it is probable that work as a die cutter paid better than gun engraving and that gradually Young devoted more time to the die-cutting aspects of his business.

Despite the demands of contract work for Colt, Young's shop was still capable of handiing additional work, and account records show that his other clients, at least in the 1860s, included the Sharps Rifle Company, Smith & Wesson, the Connecticut Arms and Manufacturing Company, the Wesson Arms Company, Charles Parker, and the Meriden Arms Company.

In 1869, Young moved his business and his family (his wife, Marie, and their three young sons, Eugene, Oscar, and Alfred) to Springfield, Massachusetts. They lived at 39 and 41 Broad Street, and Gustave had his shop at the same address. There he took in work mainly from Smith & Wesson, while continuing to serve many of his previous clients—among them Colt, who still called on him to execute special orders, and Tiffany & Co., for whom he and his sons cut dies.

Young's relationship with Colt did not end with his departure for Springfield, however, and occasional special orders were executed. Further, his sons Eugene and Oscar served apprenticeships under their father.

Other styles of engraving found on Colt percussion firearms are the Vine style used on the London-made Dragoon, Navy, and Pocket revolvers, the Late Vine and Heavy Leaf scrolls, and embellishments by nonfactory engravers like L. D. Nimschke.

Cuno A. Helfricht and the Gustave Young Tradition

In 1871, a new artisan took over the reins as engraving contractor at Colt, the youthful Cuno A. Helfricht. In that year, Helfricht launched a career that would prove unmatched in longevity (fifty years) for Colt engravers, a career that would span an era as exciting and colorful as any in American history. The profusion of guns he and his staff engraved were enthusiastically admired throughout the world. Their quality helped advance the image of Colt arms as among the finest made anywhere, a tradition begun by Samuel Colt and resoundingly augmented by Gustave Young's artistry.

Daguerreotype known as "The Mechanic," symbolic of the craftsmen who made the steel canvas for engravers and stockmakers. *At top,* an 1851 Navy with doughnut scroll, its backstrap inscribed W.H. MORRIS U.S.A. A note from U.S. Ordnance Inspector William A. Thornton requesting the inscribed revolver directly from Colonel Colt. *At bottom,* 1849 Pocket, inscribed on backstrap: NATHAN HALE / FROM THE INVENTOR.

Among the many thousands of Colt guns orna-mented by Helfricht and his team of assistants were a presentation-engraved and silver-inlaid rifle for Buffalo Bill Cody, a fancy Peacemaker revolver for Bat Master-son, and a pair of engraved and pearl-handled double action revolvers for the president of Mexico.

Helfricht and his father, Colt stockmaker and gun-maker Charles J. Helfricht, had much in common with the Youngs of Hartford and Springfield, and such other engraving dynasties in America as the Ulrichs of Hart-ford and New Haven, and the Glahns of Hartford and New York State. Certainly at least the working members of contemporary generations of these families were known to one another; and geographically Springfield, Hartford, New Haven, and New York were mutually con-venient, even with the relatively long travel times of that period. Between them, the Helfrichts, the Youngs, the Ulrichs, and the Glahns boasted a total of sixteen or more engravers, all master craftsmen.

Charles Helfricht served his apprenticeship in gun-making in Germany, and was capable of fancy stockwork, gold inlaying and engraving, and any other gunmaking skill. As contractor to Colt for hand- and long-gun stocks, Charles and his workmen played an important role in filling government and commercial orders dur-ing the turbulent period of the Civil and Indian wars.

Cuno Helfricht was born in Thuringen, Germany, on January 26, 1851, and resided in Hartford from 1860. It is believed that Cuno was trained as an arms engraver while apprenticed to his father from c. 1860 through 1869.

Cuno's only client throughout his career was the Colt firm. For almost the entire fifty years with them he was a contractor, as was his father from about 1860 through

Selection of ivory, mother-of-pearl, and carved walnut grips on Model 1849 Pocket revolvers. Plain ivory was priced higher ($5) than the standard grade of Gustave Young–style scroll engraving ($4) for the Pocket pistols. All pistols engraved in the Gustave Young style. Rare double casings of rosewood and mahogany. Colt broadside touted scroll engraving. Mother-of-pearl grip c. 1852 represents an early use of this substance in American deco-rative arts.

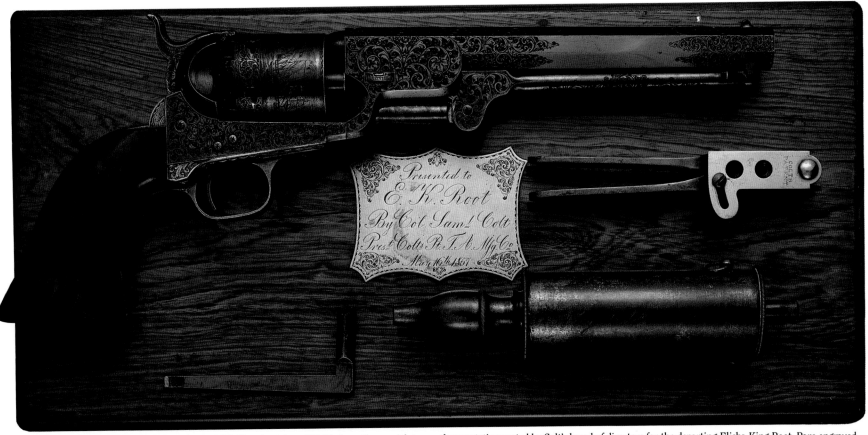

Profuse scroll engraving by Gustave Young on 1851 Navy (serial no. 55447), from the special group of presentations voted by Colt's board of directors for the departing Elisha King Root. Rare engraved loading lever. Rosewood case had interior glass lid and mirror; plunger-style flask inscribed NAVY PISTOL.

1900. Long-term working relationships were traditional with the Colt firm, as was customary with contemporary manufacturers.

When Gustave Young decided to move his shop to Springfield, a highly skilled successor was required as engraving contractor to Colt. Most likely to groom him for this position, Cuno had been sent to Berlin, Germany, to study engraving more formally. In 1871, young Helfricht, now twenty years old, returned to America to Colt's engraving and stockmaking departments. Within five years he would be Colt's chief engraver, a position he

was destined to hold until retiring in 1921.

From 1871 through 1921 Colt's production included the last of the percussion revolvers and longarms, and the beginnings of their single action cartridge arms (1871), the double action revolvers (1877–78 and 1889), the automatic pistols (1900), plus their shotgun lines (1878–1900), and the Lightning rifles (1885–c. 1910). Until the turn of the century, engraving on Colt arms was in such demand that an engraved supply of the more popular models was kept in stock. The rapidly developing market created by the settlement of the western United

States accounted for a large share of sales. Cattlemen and lawmen were enthusiastic admirers of fancy Colt handguns—particularly the classic Single Action Army—and hunters held the Colt shotguns in high regard. The Lightning and Frontier double action revolvers, the New Line single actions, and the Colt deringers were other popular engraved Colt firearms during this period. In longarms, the shotguns were the only models engraved in any noteworthy quantity. Any other hand-engraved rifle, carbine, or musket made by Colt from 1836 to the present is a rarity. Only three of

The equally richly appointed rosewood case for the E. K. Root Dragoon, with suede lining and silver-plated flask; also engraved by Gustave Young.

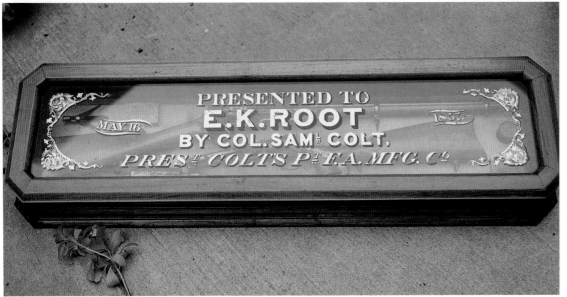

Most elaborate of all known percussion Colt casings, this glass-topped, carved mahogany case was lined in red, white, and blue velvet, and had a special fixture to secure the shoulder-stocked revolver in place. Still another Gustave Young engraving project, with an elegant maiden engraved on the Navy's barrel lug, and a leopard on the shoulder-stock yoke, both copied from a G. Ernst pattern book.

the Burgess Model lever-action rifles are known to have been factory-engraved out of the total production of 6,403.

Demand Declines

A decline in demand for engraving on Colt and other makes of firearms was not evident until the late 1890s. At that time, Cuno Helfricht reduced his engraving staff from as many as six regulars (c. 1875–85) to as few as two. By 1900, firearms were usually engraved only on special order.

Some significant information is available on the force employed by Cuno Helfricht as Colt's engraving contractor. Helfricht's records from August 1875 through August 1886 provide a clear picture of the demand for Colt engraving during this period. These account books list six regulars of long-term service, seven of shorter service, and no less than seven apprentices.

With so many engravers having worked on Colt arms at various times during Helfricht's career, how can one hope to identify which artisan engraved a specific gun? For the years 1871 through 1900 this is extremely difficult. Some pieces can be identified by their degree of excellence and by strong stylistic features. However, working from predetermined patterns restricted the craftsman's individuality. If they had worked without patterns, it would be relatively easy, as the identity of a workman's engraving can be likened to the uniqueness of his fingerprints. In a few cases, identities can be determined by engraver's records. A notebook kept by Eugene Young, from August 1879 through October 1880 and from February through April 1881, lists a total of 300 serial numbers of Colt shotguns engraved by him. All are the Model 1878 hammer type; and the serial numbers range from 902 through 10553.

Young Brothers, Engravers

Eugene Young's initial work, after his apprenticeship for his father, was under Colt engraver Cuno Helfricht, during the period c. 1879–83. To quote Helfricht (Hartford, September 16, 1882), "Eugene Young has been in my

Set inscribed from Colonel Colt to H.A.G. Pomeroy: Navy, serial no. 69640, Sidehammer no. 4473. Coverage referred to by Gustave Young as "extra," rated above standard pattern, known as Style No. 2.

Only known double cased set of 1851 Navys with matching shoulder stock, serial nos. 88066 and 88067; from the Gustave Young shop, made for President J. M. Salamanca of Bolivia, believed to have toured the Colt factory, 1858. Initials J.M.S. engraved on oval lid plaque and on backstraps.

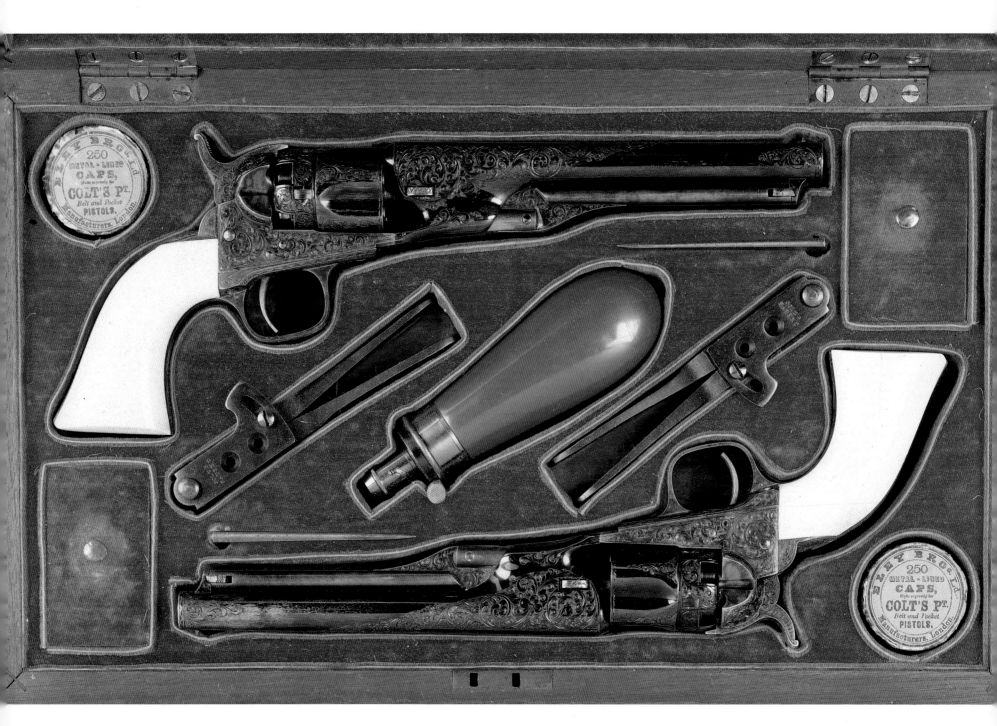

Rare ink impression from author's discovery of Gustave Young engraving treasure trove. From an as yet undiscovered Third Model Dragoon; print helped to identify Gustave Young as craftsman who embellished most of the best-grade Colt factory arms c. 1852–69.

Plate from W. L. Ormsby's 1852 book *A Description of the Present System of Bank Note Engraving, Showing Its Tendency to Facilitate Counterfeiting: To Which is Added a New Method of Constructing Bank Notes to Prevent Forgery.* Illustrations such as herein published by Ormsby, as well as postage stamps, picture books, coins, and paper money all number among the pictorial sources useful to arms engravers. Ormsby presented this copy of book to Colonel Colt.

Cased identically to a pair of 1861 Navy revolvers presented to General James B. McPherson, Model 1862 Police revolvers nos. 15859/I and 15860/I rest in velvet-lined mahogany. The "I" stamped in the serial marking referenced ivory, c. 1861 to early 1870s; "P" stood for plating or special polish, and "E" for engraved, from same period. Other symbols used at factory included punched dot similarly placed, c. 1849–61, indicating special finish and handling; and apostrophe from c. 1854–61 for ivory *and* engraving.

Exquisite Third Model Dragoon, gift to the Sultan of Turkey from Colonel Colt, c. 1854. Gripstraps heavily gold-plated. One of Gustave Young's most distinguished creations, with patriotic tributes to George Washington (portrait based on period art or currency) and the American eagle and shield; yet Young's Germanic roots evident in game scenes and scrolls; serial no. 12406.

Magnificent set of deluxe Colt Navy revolvers, custom-made on order of Colonel Colt for presentation and display at world's fairs and expositions. Pistol *at top,* no. 20133, mate to presentation Navy from Colonel Colt to Czar Nicholas I. *Bottom* pistol, no. 23477, less profusely embellished but still a superbly executed showpiece.

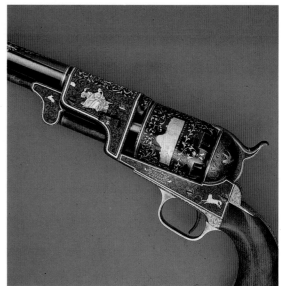

(*above and left*) Showpieces built for the Colonel, c. 1853, and subsequently presented personally by him to Czar Nicholas I, in Russia, in 1854. Mate to Dragoon *at top and above* was the previously pictured gift to the Sultan of Turkey. Some of the more involved motifs on gold-embellished arms by Gustave Young appear to be applied or damascened rather than true inlay.

Inscribed presentation from Alexander Thuer to Prince Louis of Bentheim. This finest known set of Model 1855 revolvers, nos. 6662 and 6663, has rare German inscription; was hand carried to His Highness by inventor Thuer. Prince's coat of arms and portrait carved on ivory grips. Walnut case with silver lid plaque, engraved with initials L.B. and crown. Late Vine scroll, which does not employ beaded background.

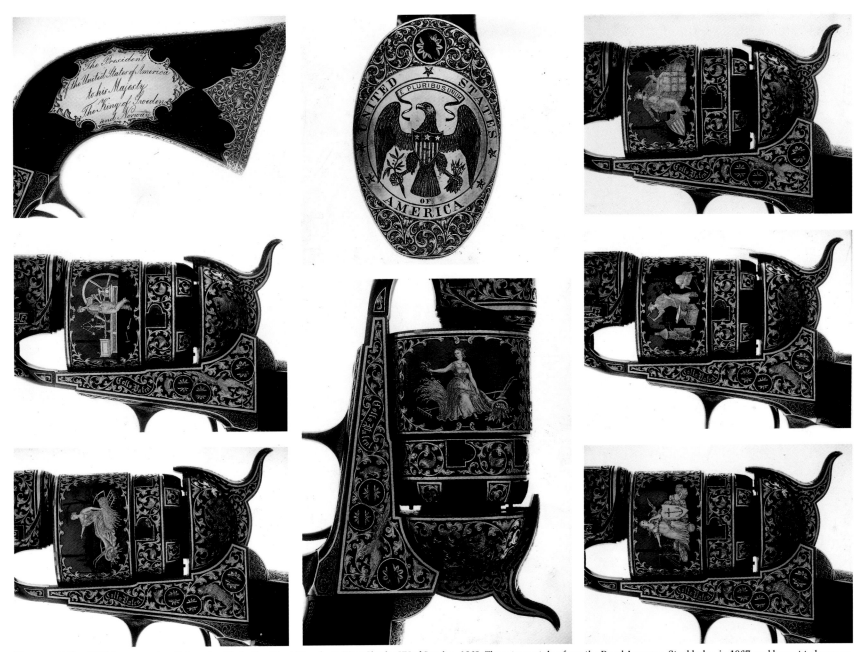

The presentation 1860 Armys used as diplomatic gifts by President Lincoln to King Charles XV of Sweden, 1863. The set was stolen from the Royal Armoury, Stockholm, in 1967, and has yet to be recovered. Serial nos. 31906 and 31907. An equally extraordinary set, nos. 31904 and 31905, given by Lincoln to King Frederick VII of Denmark. Casings, in velvet-lined rosewood, by William Milton, Hartford.

Maj. General Joseph R. Hawley's 1860 Armys, Late Vine engraved, with ebony grips. Hawley, a distinguished Civil War officer, was governor of Connecticut, a U.S. senator, and president of the U.S. Centennial Commission. Serial nos. 151388 and 151389.

Schuyler, Hartley & Graham and Cooper & Pond displays at a benefit fair, New York City, during Civil War. Several of the percussion arms *at left* later assembled into display board of Colts for former firm's New York emporium.

From the pair of Model 1861 Navy pistols, nos. 17239 and 17240, inscribed FROM / E.K. ROOT PREST COLTS PT F.A. MFG. CO / TO / LEWIS LIPPOLD. Gold-inlaid and engraved by Young, with profuse scrollwork and precise borders in flush gold. Soldier panel scene, symbolic of role Lippold played in Colt's production efforts during Civil War.

Colt Navy, no. 17509, inscribed on backstrap to the Hon. D.P. Holloway from the president of Colt, May 1865. One of the finest examples of the Late Vine scroll, honored commissioner of patents and was rare gift from E. K. Root. Bullet mold given extra polish and blue.

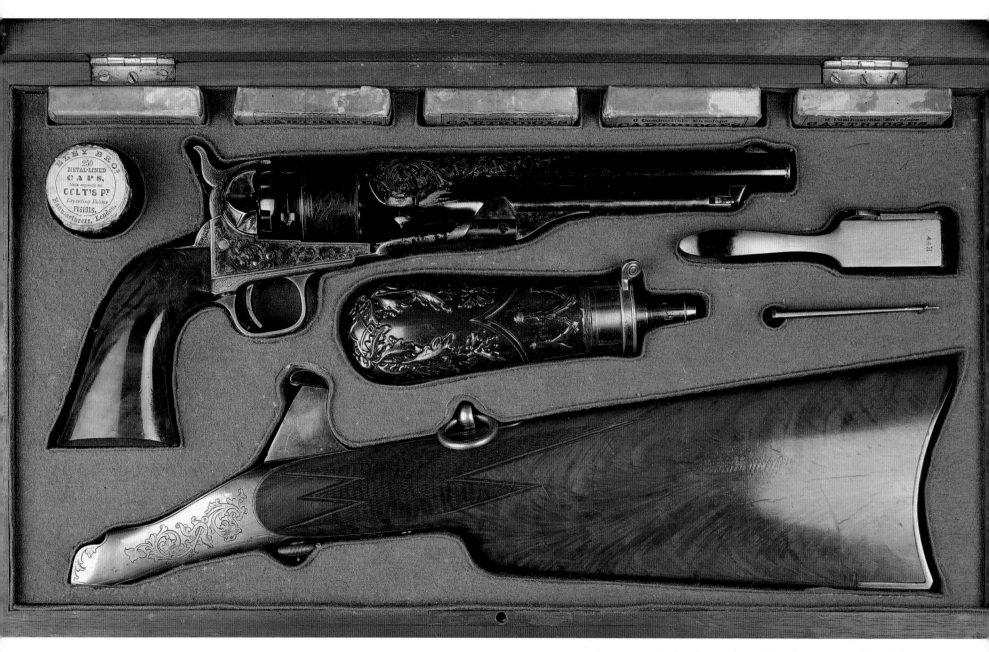

No. 183226, this 1860 Army was the finest known example of the Heavy Leaf scroll pattern, observed only c. 1870. No serial number on cylinder, a feature observed from time to time on deluxe Colt arms of the 1860s and early 1870s.

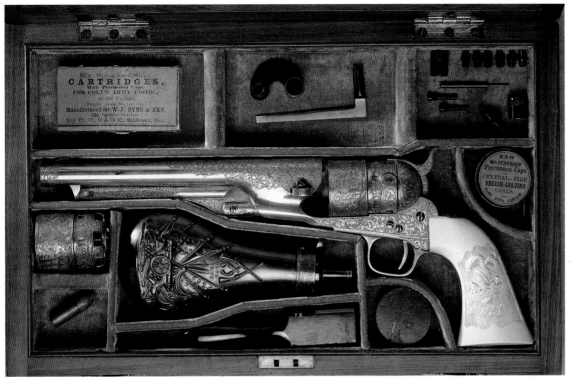

Rosewood cased 1860 Army Thuer conversion, serial 185326/I.E., made for Don Louis Laureano Sanz, the Marquis de San Juan, and Governor General of Puerto Rico. Complex and interlocking scrolls, mixing German and arabesque styles. Probably by Gustave Young, the Thuer cylinder attributed to an assistant. Plated in gold and silver.

employ for over two years, on Gun Engraving, Stamp Cutting, etc., and I recommend him as a steady, honest young man." A notebook kept by Eugene while at Colt identifies his work as including some pistols, but most of his assignments were the Model 1878 hammer shotgun. Interestingly, Eugene's notebook indicates an average week of six ten-hour days. When he joined Helfricht in 1879, Eugene was only sixteen years of age.

Sometime in 1883, the firm of Young Brothers, Engravers, was established in Chicago. Eugene and Oscar were partners in this endeavor, with Oscar apparently being on hand at the Chicago address (107 Randolph Street), Eugene doing work after hours in Elgin and Aurora. Their advertising during this period

included the legend: "Engraving on Wood and All Kinds of Metal." Probably the amount of work done on firearms during their operation in Chicago was limited.

However, about five years later, the Young brothers returned to Springfield, Massachusetts, and rejoined their father at his Broad Street address. The firm was obviously quite versatile and prepared to accept virtually any type of work, including, according to their notice, "Gun and Pistol Engraving, Wood Cutting, Fine Steel Stamps and Dies." (Further discussion of the careers of Gustave Young and his sons appears in chapter 6.)

Signatures

No Colt firearms engraved by the factory contractors are known to this writer with engravers' signatures openly evident until the twentieth century (although a hidden signature may be discerned on the Colt Lightning rifle, number 5164, engraved for Porfirio Díaz by Herman L. Ulrich). Even the fancy presentation pistols went unsigned. The practice of adding engravers' signatures did not become popular in the United States until after World War II. With the surge of interest in collectors' firearms, clients began to encourage artisans to sign their work. In Europe the old custom of rarely signing work didn't change until the 1970s and 1980s, as the international prominence and demand for engraving skyrocketed and clients wanted to see signatures, particularly on deluxe pieces. In America most private engravers, and several company craftsmen, now sign their work as a matter of course, even when the decoration is quite limited.

In January 1885, a total of 1,142 hours of engraving was done by Helfricht's six-man workforce. Production was so hectic that the contractor employed a delivery form that listed standard work and left blank spaces for tabulations for completed arms.

Interesting Items

The items listed under "Miscellaneous" on Helfricht's work records are of interest because they show the versatility of his craftsmen. Their skills included die and stamp cutting, pearl and ivory carving, barrel and rib matting, and trigger checkering. Colt also commissioned hand-engraved markings for some of their Gatling guns, plus special engraving on their railway ticket punches (a little-known Colt product), and the engraving of a marking plate for one of the Colt Armory's printing presses (another Colt product).

Like his predecessors, Cuno Helfricht determined standard patterns for engravings and drew up many of these himself. For example, his role in developing styles for Colt double-barrel shotguns is documented by a set of pencil sketches showing different degrees of engraving coverage. These testify to Helfricht's artistic skill as well as to his expert knowledge of the English style of

On its leather-covered wood casing, this exhibition-grade Single Action Army, no. 50932, exhibits Special Scroll style, dating c. 1873–79. Only a few hundred Colts believed made in this style, of various models, of which this specimen ranks at the pinnacle. Style and quality point to Gustave Young or Herman L. Ulrich, but Helfricht and his shop may have done these arms, or at least some of them.

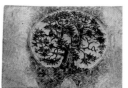

Letterhead, *top*, and trade card from two shops of the Young brothers.

Gunmaker's pulls from Young family papers. Lockplate from Model 1878 Colt shotgun; *top* prints appear to be from a Model 1855 Sidehammer revolver cylinder, and attributed to Gustave Young; *bottom* by either Oscar or Eugene. Samuel Colt, friend of I. W. Stuart, on whose property stood the Charter Oak, made pistols with oak grips from the tree. Colt also commissioned two lamp-and-screen devices (see page 339), and acquired such high kitsch artifacts as the carved Charter Oak Chair.

Cuno A. Helfricht.

Important pattern pieces from the Helfricht family collection: 1860 Army, no. 167676, and Thuer deringer, both engraved by Cuno Helfricht himself, c. 1871 and 1873 respectively. They remain "in the white." Extra coverage on both, with the style heavily influenced by Gustave Young. Cylinder with Late Vine style, without beaded background. Business card was printed in various colors, with name only. Graver and stamps from Helfricht's workshop. Over twenty stamps were found that bore scrollwork designs; these used by such engravers as Helfricht and the Ulrichs to speed up arms decoration. The "250" marks on deringer indicate $2.50 price paid to engraver for each piece embellished in this pattern and degree of coverage. This is the most deluxe Thuer deringer yet observed by author.

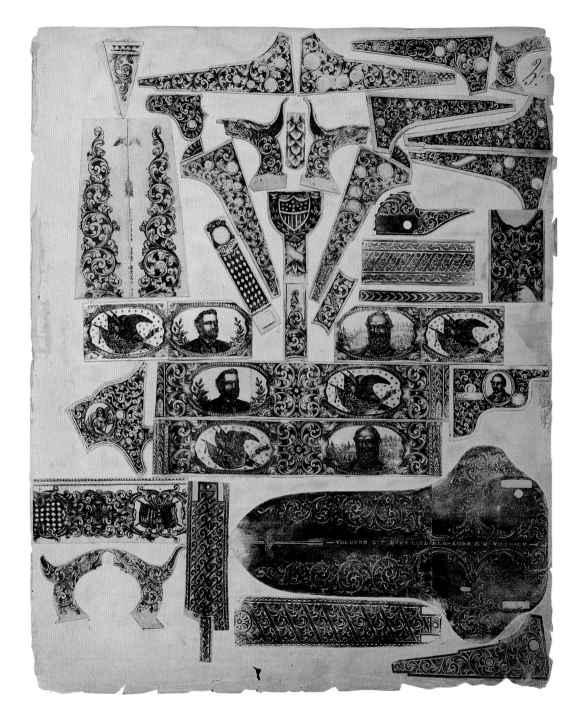

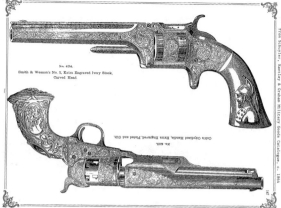

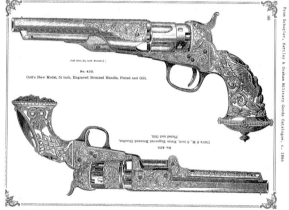

From Schuyler, Hartley & Graham's military goods catalogue of 1864, three patterns of Tiffany-style grips; scrollwork rendered in Nimschke style.

(*opposite and left*) Civil War scenes and scrollwork cover "Tiffany-gripped" 1860 Armys, nos. 156567 and 156633. Page from record book indicates L. D. Nimschke as probable source of engraving, although not the engraver of this pair of revolvers. Battle-scene grips of silver-plated bronze, with American-eagle buttcaps. Napoleon III Manhattan revolver pulls *at upper right* and *lower left;* see page 180.

scrollwork, which, with rich Germanic influences, was standard on Colt doubles.

Basic engraving styles changed with changes in shop leadership. Young's staff had engraved according to patterns meeting with his approval and presumably of his own design. Helfricht's patterns included some that were strongly Germanic, but already in the early 1870s, definite style changes are obvious. Variations of patterns for the Single Action Army revolver are graphic examples of handgun designs during the Helfricht period. The basic American scroll was adapted, with border motifs (and rare panel scenes), for the several models of Colt handguns of the 1871–1921 period, among them the automatic pistols introduced in 1900. The Third Model Deringers are an exception to this change, in that they are regularly found with the Gustave Young scroll.

Shotguns and rifles are a different matter. Rifles show

Young-style scrollwork on a pair of New Lines inscribed to El Conte Del Donadio from J. R. Hawley. Equally fancy, the rosewood casing lined in silk and velvet.

Deringers from the Helfricht shop, *at center right* and *bottom*. All-metal pistols similarly embellished, but from Moore and National, pre-Colt era.

The Sears Roebuck & Co. "Cow Boy" revolver, one of Cuno Helfricht's most inspired Colts. A display piece built in 1897, and featured in Sears' 1901 catalogue. Goddess of Liberty, seated, on carved mother-of-pearl grips.

145

Pioneer arms collector and Wild West buff Captain John R. Hegeman, Jr., commissioned the pair of Bisley-triggerguard Single Actions, from the Helfricht shop, with rare browned finish. *Top* set by R. J. Kornbrath; shipped to South America on order of Colt jobber Don Alfredo Gottling, who had a penchant for gold-inlaid Colts.

From the Putnam Phalanx of Hartford to the Washington Continentals, Model 1877 Lightning, serial no. 48165, the most prized of early double action Colts. Engraved mother-of-pearl grip bears portrait of General Israel Putnam.

little regularity, since so few were engraved (estimated at an average of ten per year, from 1885 through c. 1910), and probably few were ever done as stock items. Patterns vary, as confirmed by examination of factory-authenticated examples. Shotguns show greater conformity, and basic styles were identified by the Colt factory as numbers 1 and 2 for the Model 1883 hammerless, and numbers 1, 3, 4, 6, and 7 for the hammer Model of 1878. All of these patterns were what can best be described as a British scroll with Germanic influences. Since the Colt shipping ledgers are complete for both models of shotgun, the engraving on any piece can be identified as to grade by an inquiry to the factory's Historical Department (by serial number).

Colt Pride

The Colt firm took great pride in its talented artisans and regularly displayed engraved arms at expositions and sportsmen's shows. An impressive array of such arms was shown at the Philadelphia Centennial Exposition of 1876. A total of eighteen engraved and ivory- and pearl-gripped Single Action Army revolvers was in that display, plus about 325 other Colt handguns and longarms.

Another treasure from the Helfricht shop, attributed to the master himself. Model 1895 nos. 88566 and 88567 boast hand-engraved serial numbers, gold and silver inlays, state of Pennsylvania coat-of-arms sideplate motifs, and walnut casing. Shipped in October 1897 to a Colonel Asher Miner.

Colt Double Rifles, Caldwell Hart Colt's own serial no. 1, *bottom*, and Anson George McCook's no. 13, with engraving artifacts from the Helfricht workshop. Several of punches, with face showing, cut to allow stamping small scrolls. Lettering page from previously unpublished engraving pattern book by G. Ernst.

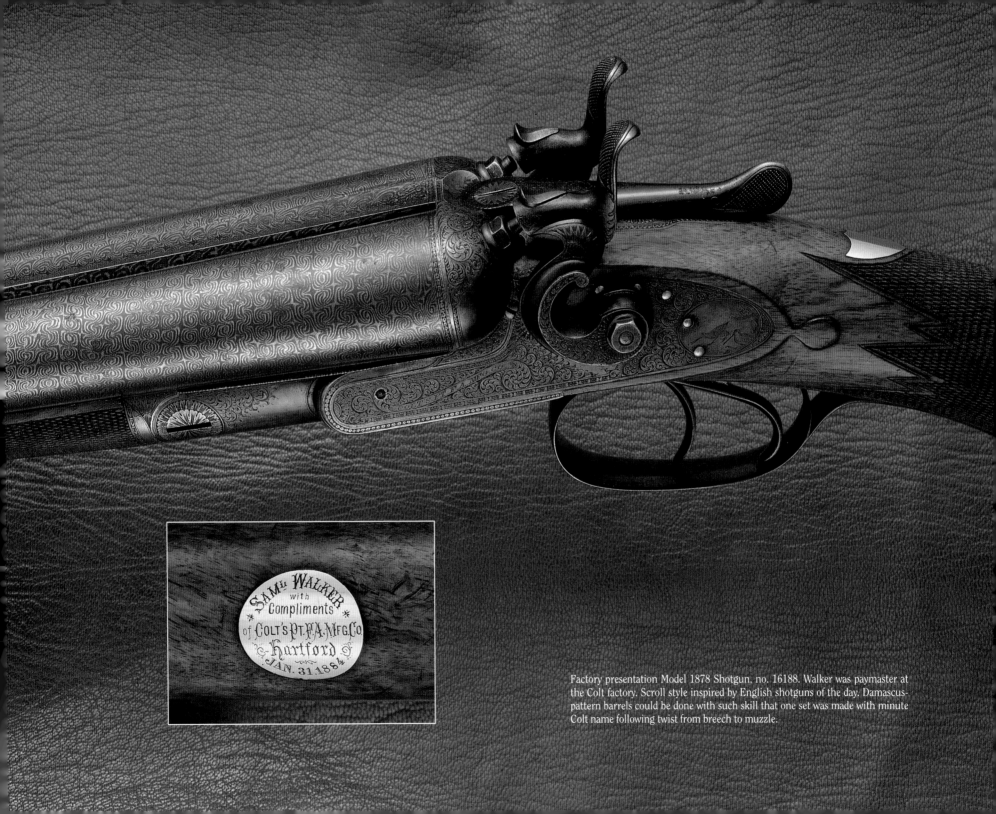

Factory presentation Model 1878 Shotgun, no. 16188. Walker was paymaster at the Colt factory. Scroll style inspired by English shotguns of the day. Damascus-pattern barrels could be done with such skill that one set was made with minute Colt name following twist from breech to muzzle.

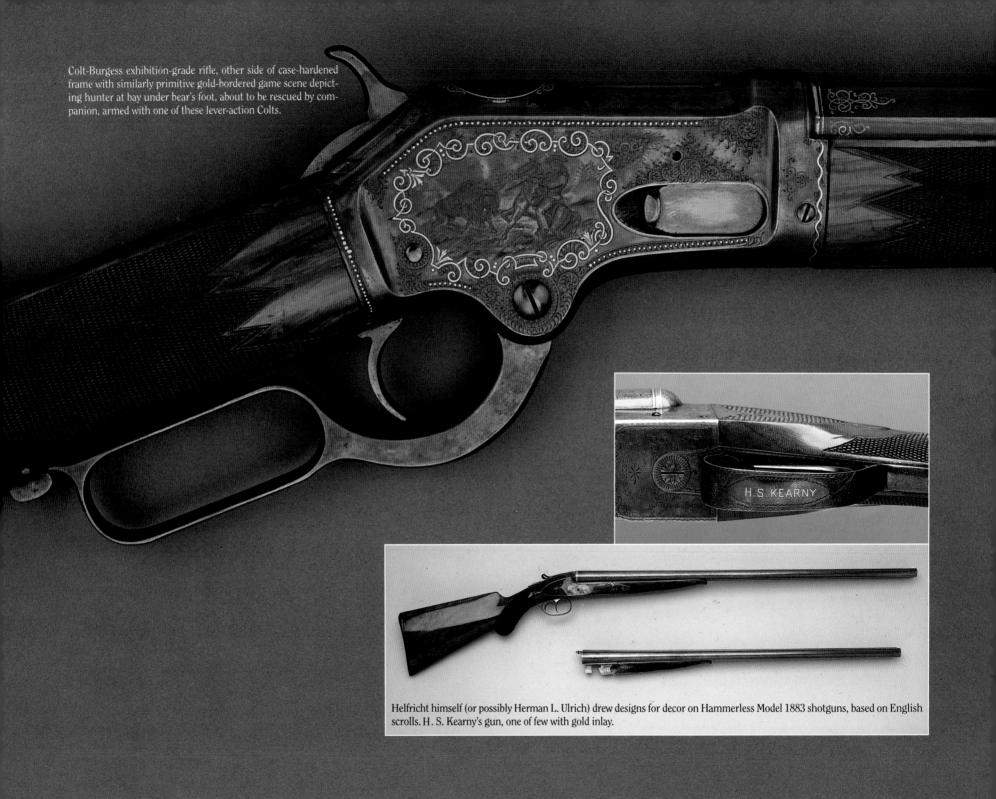

Colt-Burgess exhibition-grade rifle, other side of case-hardened frame with similarly primitive gold-bordered game scene depicting hunter at bay under bear's foot, about to be rescued by companion, armed with one of these lever-action Colts.

Helfricht himself (or possibly Herman L. Ulrich) drew designs for decor on Hammerless Model 1883 shotguns, based on English scrolls. H. S. Kearny's gun, one of few with gold inlay.

Fancy Colt arms are also known to have been displayed at the sportsmen's shows at Madison Square Garden, in New York City, in 1895 and 1896. *Shooting and Fishing* magazine's issue of May 19, 1896, said this about the engraved arms in the Colt display at the 1896 show:

> The familiar business-like Frontier models, .44 and .45 caliber, some of them elaborately and beautifully engraved and inlaid with gold [and] fitted with ivory and pearl handles, finished in outline carving showing heads of Texas steers [are exhibited], and also 2 . . . old models [percussion] are there, both very heavy, and both finished in bright and blued steel, silver, and gold inlaid work, while figures of solid gold are embossed in relief.

Such fancy arms have been part of Colt displays since Samuel Colt's first demonstrations of his new repeating firearms in the 1830s. This tradition continues into modern times, a featured part of the Colt repertoire.

Into the Twentieth Century

After the turn of the century, with the decline in demand for engraved firearms, Cuno Helfricht is believed to have done much of the Colt work himself, with the help of one regular assistant. In 1910, R. J. Kornbrath came to Hartford, but he is not known to have engraved for the Colt firm until after Helfricht's retirement in 1921. Kornbrath is discussed further in chapter 8.

Helfricht's chosen successor was Wilbur A. Glahn (active for Colt c. 1919–50); his career is discussed in chapter 8, as are the careers of subsequent craftsmen A. F. Herbert, factory engraver c. 1956–68, and outside contractor A. A. White.

This .22-caliber Lightning Rifle is unsurpassed for engraving coverage; with nine-line inscribed silver presentation plaque on select walnut buttstock. Similar game scene found on contemporary Winchesters, suggesting possible engraving by Herman L. Ulrich.

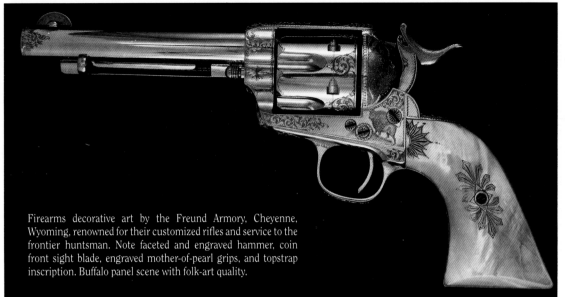

Firearms decorative art by the Freund Armory, Cheyenne, Wyoming, renowned for their customized rifles and service to the frontier huntsman. Note faceted and engraved hammer, coin front sight blade, engraved mother-of-pearl grips, and topstrap inscription. Buffalo panel scene with folk-art quality.

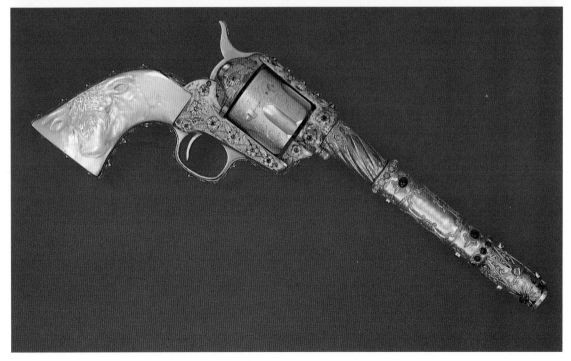

(*above*) Most deluxe and historic of large-frame Lightning Express rifles, cased set made for Mexican leader Porfirio Díaz, keen arms collector. Case lid interior gold-embossed HARTLEY & GRAHAM / NEW YORK. Among stylized panel scenes: Mexican eagle and snake, "Monarch of the Glen" stag, pointer dog, dog head, quail, prairie chicken, rampant colt trademark, and buffalo hunt on horseback. Buffalo hunting scenes commonly used in the fine and decorative arts of the period, including those by Tiffany & Co. and Albert Bierstadt. Signed by Herman L. Ulrich within monogram panel on right side of frame: HLU with reclining E, and HLU monogram. From the Díaz Collection, at the Royal Military College, Kingston, Ontario. Gold- and silver-plated; the select walnut stocks checkered.

Another non-Colt factory creation, one of a pair (with matching baton) built for Dodge City Cowboy Band leader Jack Sinclair, c. 1892. Colored gemstones dominate this rather garish, yet charming, semi–Rube Goldberg jewelry original. Barrel and frame sheathed in plated metal, onto which the gemstones—turquoise, rubies, tourmalines, and garnets—and other decorative devices were mounted.

Bearing special serial no. 00, this Model 1903 Automatic was a commission of C.L.F. Robinson, company president 1911–16. Helfricht's design drawing depicted the scrolls in some detail, and indicated "Head of Washington" and "Head of Lincoln" on top of slide. Grant's bust at rear of slide. Changes were made to drawing before Helfricht finished the pistol, the most deluxe of this model known, factory-made.

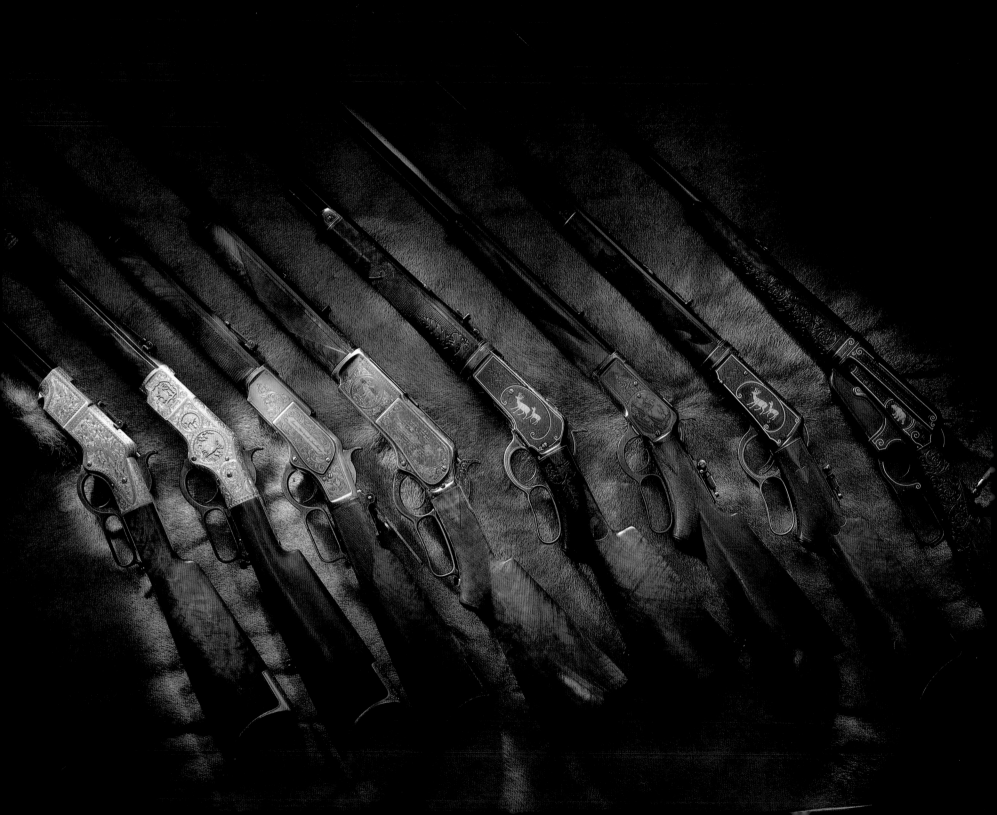

Chapter 5
Winchester's Repeating Masterpieces

The pioneer years of Winchester engraving run concurrently with those of Smith & Wesson, since both firms can trace their ancestry back to 1852, when D. B. Wesson and Horace Smith began manufacture of lever-action repeating magazine arms (and Winchester even further, to the non-engraved Hunt rocket ball repeater). The S&W Norwich, Connecticut, operation relied on the Early Vine scrolls almost exclusively for the first few years, while Samuel Colt was much more advanced with his dough-

Evolution of the lever-action Winchester and various examples of their embellishments. From left to right, the Henry repeating rifle, a special triple presentation begun by B. Tyler Henry himself; the Model 1866, a sculpted and relief-engraved, gold-plated factory show gun, serial no. 112272; the Model 1873, custom-built by the factory for the Colorado ranching empire of Essington & Lackburg, no. 8956; Model 1876, the renowned Colonel Gzowski presentation set (bird's-eye maple case not shown), no. 53072; the Model 1886, a takedown rifle, no. 125176; the Model 1892, no. 881840; the Model 1894 with special scheutzen buttplate, no. 303492; the Model 1895 with rare Monte Carlo stock and barrel threaded for silencer, in .405 caliber, no. 81851. The Models 1866, 1886, 1894, and 1895 (the latter three with gold and platinum inlays) are all signed by or attributed to John Ulrich.

nut scroll and the masterful artistry of the Gustave Young style.

With establishment of the New Haven Arms Company, and introduction of the Henry Rifle (c. 1860), the embellishments graduated to a more florid scroll, with punched or beaded background. Some of the more important rifles, such as the presentation Henry for President Abraham Lincoln, and the O. F. Winchester Henry for Captain J. R. Burton, are profusely embellished, with distinctive styles: the first possibly by New Haven engraver Samuel J. Hoggson, and the second by a craftsman influenced by Gustave Young. Gustave Young's influence on Winchester would prove substantial, however, since the three Ulrich brothers, John, Conrad F., and Herman, all studied and worked under Young at Colt.

Comparisons between Colt and Winchester indicate that in sheer numbers, more Colts were embellished. But in complexity and coverage, Winchesters tended to have been more extensive productions, particularly in that their stockwork was more elaborate. A possible explanation is that more changes in personnel, and thus in styles, took place at Colt.

The Ulrich Dynasty

In the mid-1860s a migration of sorts took place when the three Ulrich brothers went to work at the Winchester factory engraving shop. Considering the quality and quantity of their collective work, the Ulrichs—John, Conrad F., and Herman, and their various sons and grandsons—reign supreme in the genealogy of American arms engraving.

The Conrad Ulrich family emigrated to the U.S. from Germany in 1849; the first gun-engraving Ulrich dates from late in the 1850s, and the last Ulrich engraver died in 1949. Within the period of that near century of continuity, Winchester employed six engraving members of the family: Conrad F., John, Herman L., Alden George, Rudolph E., and Leslie Borden. Two of the six engraved at various times for Marlin (Conrad F. and Alden George), and three of the six engraved for Colt (Conrad F., John, and Herman L.). A seventh member of the family, Augustus F., worked only for Colt, and is also on record for at least a few years as an engraver. The patriarch of the family, Conrad, was a general gunsmith.

There were still other members of the family who were Winchester and Marlin employees, but not in

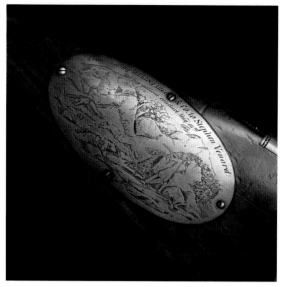

Serial no. 1228 presentation Henry, with German-silver plaque by factory engraver. Rare Wells Fargo & Co. presentation includes engraved frame and buttplate, silver-plated. The most prized arm in the Wells Fargo Bank's San Francisco museum. Engraver appears to have had artistic training, the scene rendered with spatial depth, much like a landscape painting with a foreground, middle ground, and background.

Milestones in the evolution of Winchester engraving. *From top,* standard Volcanic scroll, with silver-plated frame; standard Henry pattern, on silver-plated, brass-frame rifle; Model 1866 has gold-plated frame, Ulrich engraving, factory-inscribed H. REYNOLDS on left side of frame.

In new condition, President Lincoln's Henry rifle, serial no. 6, has gold-plated frame and buttplate, rosewood buttstock. The scroll style as attributed to J. Hoggson. Other dignitaries receiving fancy Henrys were Secretary of War Edwin M. Stanton, Secretary of the Navy Gideon Welles, and Tennessee governor William G. Brownlow.

Historic presentation from inventor, gunmaker B. Tyler Henry. The buttplate inscribed in script, FROM B. TYLER HENRY / AS A TOKEN / OF / FRIENDSHIP / TO JAMES H. CONKLIN / AUGUST / 1864. Balance of inscription as illustrated. Unusually profuse floral decoration, and the most profuse sequence of inscriptions known on a Henry rifle.

(*bottom right*) Besides rare presentation from O. F. Winchester, Captain Burton's rifle has scrollwork with beaded background, differing from the majority of Henrys. Other side of frame has Civil War camp scene and artillery piece. Silver-plated frame and buttplate.

157

The Porfirio Díaz ivory-stock Model 1866, no. 21921, with Mexican eagle carved in butt; engraving attributed to Nimschke shop. A classic in American antique arms.

Only recently discovered, ivory-stock Model 1866 rifle, no. 83904, engraved by Nimschke on frame and hammer; built for client south of the border. J.A.P. on right side of frame, initials of Juan Antonio Pezet, president of Peru. Gold-plated hammer (rare engraved), frame, and lever; blued barrel and tube, remaining parts silver-plated. Carving on left side of stock polished off; appears to have been initials.

Model 1866, serial no. 103675, a signed work of C. F. Ulrich, has no less than ten sculpted game scenes, barrel inscription GREGORIO ROZAS PHILADA PA SEPT 1876, gold-plated frame, buttplate, and forend, and was probably displayed by the factory at the Philadelphia Centennial Exhibition. Rare C. F. Ulrich business card, silver-plaque inlaid John Ulrich engraving handle, engraving tools, and rare copy of Ormsby's book on banknote engraving, inscribed by author to Colonel Samuel Colt.

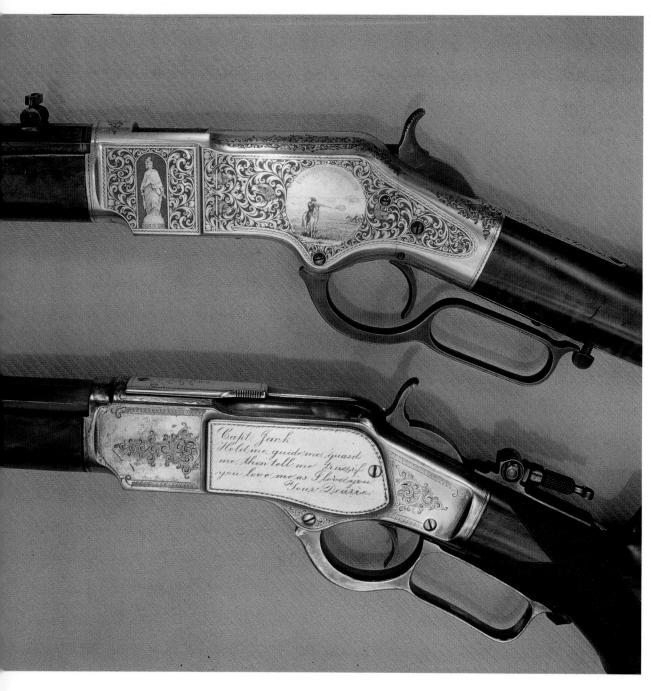

engraving capacities. A composite collection of engraved firearms by the Ulrich dynasty would dazzle the most experienced and jaded of arms collectors or museum specialists. On behalf of their employers at Colt, Winchester, and Marlin, the Ulrichs created and executed some of the great masterpieces in the decoration of American firearms. Most of their pieces were done in the standard styles of factory embellishments. But whether it was an extra-deluxe rifle for a European aristocrat or a five-dollar order for a midwestern farmhand, the Ulrichs consistently gave their best. It is a family whose tradition of hard work and quality craftsmanship represents a high standard in the annals of American art and industry.

Conrad was a citizen of Mansbach, Germany, where he was born in 1815; as a young man, he received training as a tradesman, general mechanic, blacksmith, and locksmith. Around 1840 he married Anna Margarette Viel, and the couple had seven children, all but one born in Mansbach: Augustus F. (1841), Jane (1842), Conrad F. (1844), Herman L. (1846), John (1850), George (1851), and Mary (born in Hartford, 1852). The family moved to Hartford from New York City in 1852. Conrad's first listing in Hartford city directories was in the edition of 1857–58: "Ullrich Conrad, pistol maker, h. 15 Wells st."

As a Colt employee, Conrad was not a gun engraver but a machinist. According to family history, he served as an assembler, barrel straightener, and general mechanic. However, it is also likely that Conrad learned the rudiments of gun engraving and was able to do at least the simpler work of basic borders and scrolls.

Hartford directory listings indicate a steady employ-

Model 1866, serial no. 26283, a masterpiece and likely a factory showpiece; its banknote-quality decoration attributed to Gustave Young or Herman L. Ulrich; gold-plated frame, forend cap and buttplate. Goddess of Liberty from U.S. fractional currency of the day. Other side of frame with mounted Civil War officer and female nude similar to Hiram Powers's *Greek Slave,* a popular sculpture of the period. Captain Jack Crawford's Model 1873 .22 with inscription from Jack's flowery poetry; other sideplate with factory presentation legend; silver-, gold- and nickel-plating; Ulrich engraving.

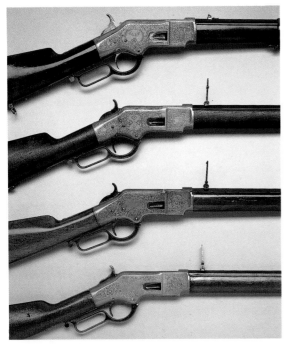

(*top left*) *From top,* 1866 carbine signed C.F. ULRICH (no. 38051); rifle no. 38055, also from Ulrich shop; rifle no. 16114 by L. D. Nimschke; and rifle no. 35383, signed LDN, also by Nimschke.

(*bottom left*) Author recently discovered script initial signature of Herman L. Ulrich (H.L.U.) on Model 1866 rifle, no. 38524; engraving quite similar to work of brothers John and C.F., so much so that telling one from another is difficult in the absence of a signature.

(*top and bottom right*) Likely factory showpiece, with somewhat primitive game and huntsman scenes, yet crisply cut and attractive; Young-style scroll and border work. Signed C.F. ULRICH on lower tang, behind trigger; gold-plated frame, forend cap, and buttplate.

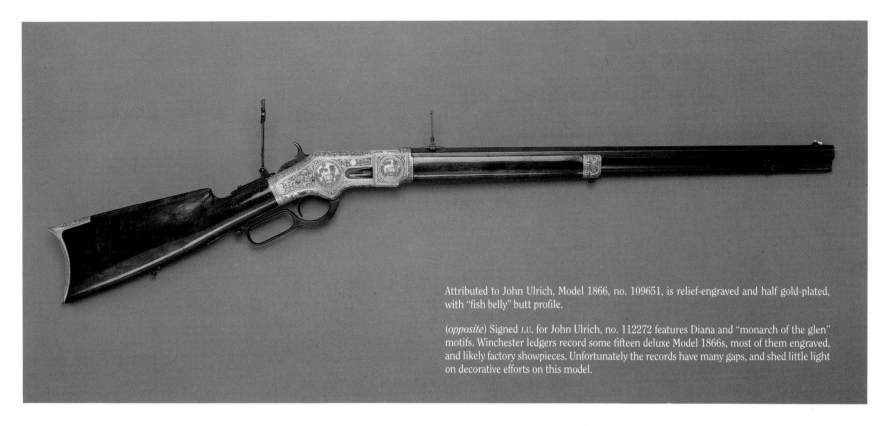

Attributed to John Ulrich, Model 1866, no. 109651, is relief-engraved and half gold-plated, with "fish belly" butt profile.

(*opposite*) Signed J.U. for John Ulrich, no. 112272 features Diana and "monarch of the glen" motifs. Winchester ledgers record some fifteen deluxe Model 1866s, most of them engraved, and likely factory showpieces. Unfortunately the records have many gaps, and shed little light on decorative efforts on this model.

ment and an unremarkable existence throughout Conrad's life in Hartford. It was three of his sons who, through their excellence in the engraving craft, would make the name Ulrich one of the most famous and respected in the history of American gunmaking.

Augustus Friedrich Ulrich, the eldest son, became a Colt factory employee, and is listed in Hartford directories as a toolmaker and (for the years 1872–85) as an engraver. Augustus worked variously as a toolmaker, a machinist (operating rifling machines), and a barrel straightener. He and his father were the only gunsmith-engraver-stockmaker Ulrichs who did not work for Winchester.

Although the Hartford city directories first list Augustus F. in 1863, it is likely that his employment (or apprenticeship) at Colt began in the mid or late 1850s.

Judging from the city directory information, he continued with the company almost up to the time of his death in 1916. Until well into the twentieth century, Colt allowed their employees to remain on the job as long as their work was judged within inspection standards. In 1915, Augustus was seventy-four years of age.

Conrad F. Ulrich

The second-oldest brother, Conrad Friedrich, proved to have a remarkable gift for engraving and gold inlaying, and along with brother John became best known of all the Ulrichs. Conrad learned the trade at Colt in the early and mid-1860s, and brothers John and Herman came on board soon after. It is believed that Conrad began his training at Colt under his father but soon leaned toward engraving, so that his apprenticeship was primarily

under Young or a successor.

Conrad appeared in Hartford city directories from 1865 through 1871, but it is likely no listing was made during his apprentice years at Colt. It also appears that his name continued in the directories after his departure to New Haven. Demand at Colt for engraving was on a temporary decline at this time, and thus the brothers left because there would be more work for them in New Haven, primarily with Winchester. Factory records indicate Herman was employed at Winchester from July 1870 to May 1875. C.F. was employed at Winchester from April 1871 to March 1874, and John from April 1871 to c. 1910 (holding various positions of gun assembler, engraver, and stockmaker and carver).

The brothers first appeared in the New Haven directory of 1873–74, John and Herman both listed as

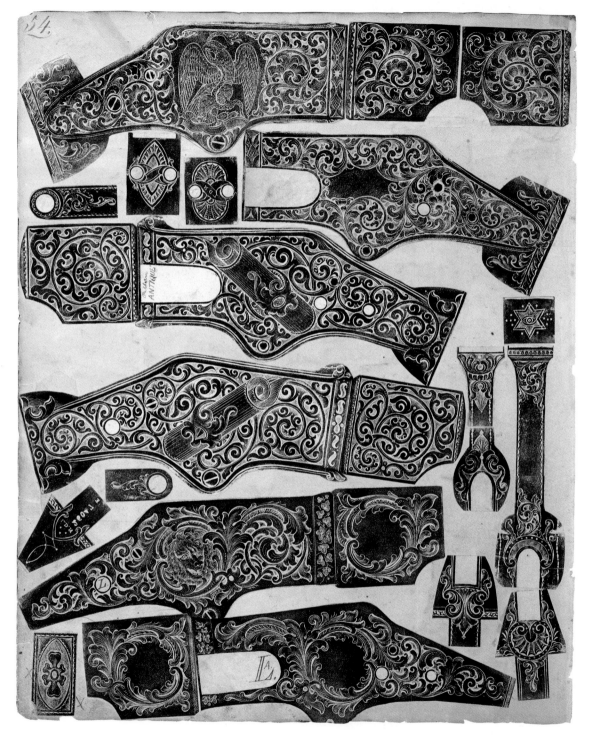

Looking very much like panel scenes for Winchester frames, details on factory cartridge board of c. 1874 reveal promotional acumen of company. For display by jobbers and dealers. First of several decorated boards and (from c. 1887) calendars and posters, some of which relied on artists the likes of Frederic Remington. Alexander Pope, N. C. Wyeth, Philip R. Goodwin, A. B. Frost, and W. R. Leigh also received commissions for calendar art from Winchester.

Page 54 from the L. D. Nimschke record book, a clear expression of the strongly stylized American scrolls and borders of this master craftsman. Note his reference to "Antique" pattern on center rifle, done in an arabesque style. Two guns bore his L.D.N. signature, and one bore Masonic symbolism. See also page 13, the "Solid Silver" Winchester.

General William E. Strong's Model 1873, no. 2681, has sculpted panel scenes, gold plating, and XXX-grade checkered walnut stocks. This superb ⅔ magazine rifle inspired a magnificent Model 1876 presentation, by General Strong to his friend General Philip H. Sheridan. The monogram, executed in Gothic style, is typical of the period. Though rifle bears signature of J. Ulrich, engraving has been attributed to Herman L. Ulrich.

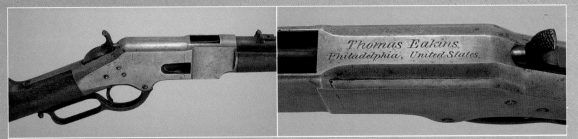

(*left*) Thomas Eakins' Winchester Model 1866 saddle-ring carbine, number 167417, owned and used by the renowned artist from c. 1873. Eakins (1844–1916), a distinguished realist painter, sculptor, and teacher of art, enjoyed hunting and fishing, some of which he was able to pursue at the Avondale (Chester County), Pennsylvania farm of his brother-in-law, William J. Crowell. Eakins also traveled in the West, and had a keen interest in shooting. Inscription on top of frame, by the Winchester factory. Appropriately, one of America's leading artists saw fit to own one of America's most esthetic of firearms.

Gold-inlaid, engraved and cased Model 1873 Winchester rifle, with annotated page from the Highly Finished Arms catalogue of 1897. Rifle signed J. ULRICH., in reverse italics behind trigger. Gold-inlaid buck deer and tiger on left side of frame; gold lion and roe deer on right; serial no. 127953A; .44-40 caliber; 24-inch round barrel. Shotgun buttplate of horn, checkered. Lid of case embossed with name of General J. Roca, Argentinian dignitary and friend of Theodore Roosevelt. Made in 1883.

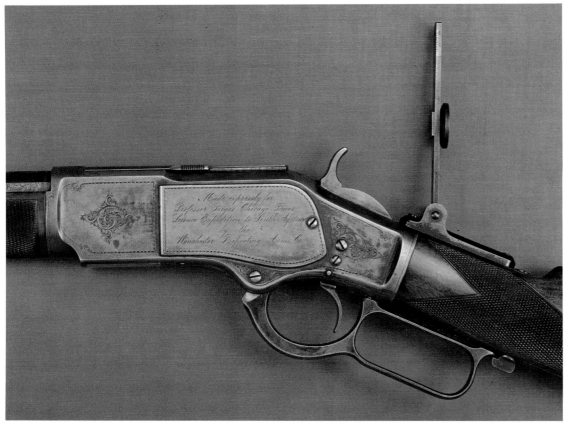

When exploring Africa was the rage, Winchester made up this deluxe Model 1873 rifle for Professor Paige's *Chicago Times* Scientific Expedition to South Africa. The handsome condition suggests this arm saw little or no service on the Dark Continent.

Conrad and Catherine Eagan (of Newport, Rhode Island) were married in 1879. They had four children: Alden George, John (who died in infancy), John C., and Rudolph E. The first of these, better known as George Ulrich, was the last member of the family to carry on the engraving tradition. John C. and Rudolph E. were both expert stockmakers, and the latter is also on record as an engraver.

Conrad was somewhat eccentric, and some humorous stories have come down through the family. While separated from his wife (their marriage was a rather tempestuous one, eventually ending in divorce), he was not a tidy housekeeper. When the coal man made his deliveries, he was told to dump the supply on the kitchen floor! A notebook Conrad kept in copious detail recorded expenses, income, stock transactions, and calculations down to the penny. He even estimated his daily income from investments. One of Conrad's own favorite stories was about Samuel Colt at Christmastime. On Christmas Eve, Colt would go through his factory telling all the "crazy Germans with their Christmas trees" that they were expected to report to work on Christmas Day!

Conrad was an admirer of William F. "Buffalo Bill" Cody, which becomes apparent in a perusal of the family photographs. He sported a goatee in the style of Cody, and is likely to have met the hunter-adventurer-showman during visits of Cody's Wild West show to New Haven. According to family tradition, Conrad presented an engraved gun to Cody. Another family story tells of John or Conrad visiting O. F. Winchester's home with key members of Buffalo Bill's stage-show troupe. One of the Indian chiefs is said to have guzzled down a container of alcoholic beverage and promptly pitched the empty into one of Winchester's fireplaces!

Signatures by Conrad were almost always C.F. ULRICH, in a quite small stamp, but the hand-engraved C.F.U. and C.ULRICH are also known.

Conrad died April 22, 1925. Despite their remarkable skills in engraving and stockwork, none of the engraving members of the family, other than Alden George (who died in 1949), was properly eulogized in an obituary.

engravers for the Winchester Arms Company, Conrad recorded simply as "engraver, rooms 114 Grove." Conrad was never listed in the city directories as an employee of Winchester, though he did appear as an employee of the Marlin Fire Arms Company, from 1895 through 1907. These are considered to be only approximate dates for Conrad's work for that firm on a full-time basis, though undoubtedly he continued to do outside work on his own. During his other active years in New Haven, it appears that he maintained a home workshop and took in a wide variety of assignments. Work for Marlin probably first began c. 1875–76, on the Ballard rifles, and continued as late as World War I. His business card emphasized, above all other types of work, his skill as a die sinker. Also advertised was "Shot Gun & Rifle Engr, Sculptor & Wood-carver, and Portrait & Landscape Painter."

A few paintings by Conrad have survived, in the family collection, all done in oils, in a relatively small size and with substantial detail. Grandson George Ulrich remembered a larger painting, equally detailed and precise, depicting Wild Bill Hickok and Calamity Jane. The picture was done around 1908 and disappeared in later years.

Model 1873, no. 40633, a 26-inch rifle in as-new condition, the finest 1 of 1000 Winchester known. A perfect example of the spelled-out factory inscription, accompanied by scroll and border engraving; matching decor on muzzle, but of less coverage.

One of two historic Model 1873s from the arms collection of Porfirio Díaz, both attributed to John Ulrich. No. 222286 plated in gold and nickel; other rifle, no. 206057, gold-plated with blued barrel and tube.

A selection of 1 of 100 and 1 of 1000 sporting rifles. *From top,* no. 711, 1 of 100, and no. 455, 1 of 1000 (both Model 1876s); no. 18443, 1 of 100, and no. 37944, 1 of 1000 (both Model 1873s); *at left,* no. 470, 1 of 100 Model 1876, and *at right,* no. 4113, 1 of 1000 Model 1873 with sideplate inscription of original owner. Insets show inscriptions for rifles *at center.*

VARIETY OF ARMS.

It is the purpose of the manufacturers of these arms to introduce a greater variety than has heretofore been made, to meet the different purposes and uses to which they are applicable, whether for sporting or war. Among these the demands of the amateur sportsman are the most exacting, for an arm that will shoot with unerring accuracy.

With the perfect machinery and great skill of the men we employ in boring, rifling, straightening, polishing, and finishing our barrels, we can always count with confidence upon any barrel shooting with accuracy; but in this, as in all other cases, the degree of accuracy will vary. The barrel of every sporting rifle we make will be proved and shot at a target, and the target will be numbered to correspond with the barrel and be attached to it.

All of those barrels that are found to make targets of **extra merit** will be made up into guns with set-triggers and extra finish, and marked as a designating name "one of a thousand," and sold at $100. The next grade of barrels, not quite so fine, will be **marked** "one of a hundred," and set up to order in any style at $20 **advance** over the list price of the corresponding style of gun as shown in price list.

The 1875 factory catalogue promoting the 1 of 100 and 1 of 1000 rifles.

Notices were brief and no mention was made of their skills or accomplishments.

John Ulrich

In the period c. 1869–c. 1920, the majority of signed, engraved Winchesters will bear the stamp J. ULRICH. John was six years younger than his brother Conrad, and his professional career seems to have been that much shorter, but he was a full-fledged employee at the Winchester factory rather than a freelance. By far the greater number of signed Winchester arms noted by this writer have been by John.

Although brothers John, Herman, and Conrad arrived in New Haven as early as 1870, city directories did not begin to list their names until the edition of 1873–74. John was recorded as an "engraver, Winchester Arms Co." He died August 9, 1924, and continued to be listed through 1924–25.

John married Esther Munsill and the couple had three children: John M., Leslie B., and Anna. Son John became a stockmaker, and Leslie did both engraving and stockwork; both were Winchester employees.

Old-timers among the Winchester employees related to the author in the 1970s that John Ulrich used sharp and tough nails for laying out designs on gunmetal. A can of nails stood by his vise, and he would draw the basic lines on the gun's surface with one of them, his legs wrapped around a high stool. Should the nail drop from his hand or go dull, he would take another from the can, never looking away from the pattern in progress.

Another story they tell about John Ulrich concerns the peephole in his workroom door. While at work he would keep the door locked; should someone knock, John peered through the hole. If he didn't want to interrupt his work to admit the visitor, he would simply close the sliding peephole cover and go back to his vise. Sometimes, when he wanted to work completely undisturbed, John would refuse entry to even high-ranking company officials.

Considerable similarity exists between the engraving styles, designs, and quality of John and Conrad, and of

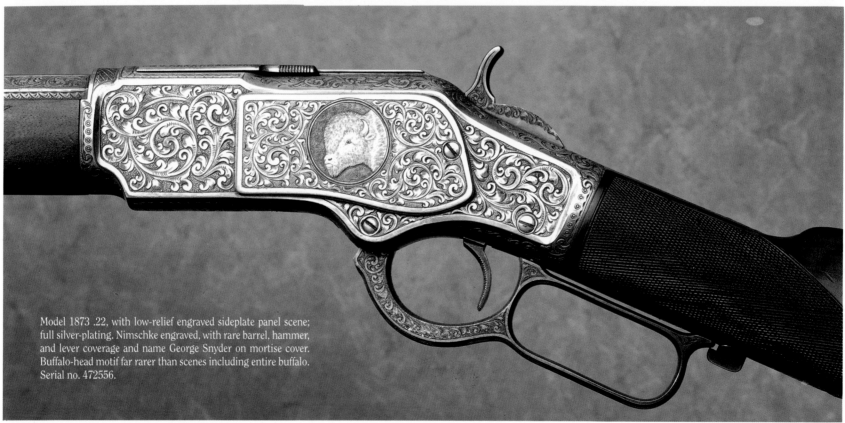

Model 1873 .22, with low-relief engraved sideplate panel scene; full silver-plating. Nimschke engraved, with rare barrel, hammer, and lever coverage and name George Snyder on mortise cover. Buffalo-head motif far rarer than scenes including entire buffalo. Serial no. 472556.

Showing an increased sophistication in panel-scene motifs, Model 1876, no. 14327, a presentation to General Philip Sheridan from his friend General William E. Strong, is considered one of the masterpieces of nineteenth-century Winchesters. John Ulrich was so proud of this commission that he signed his initials in each panel.

(*right*) Custom-built for "Little Miss Sure Shot" (Annie Oakley), Model 1873, serial no. 256170B, was a .44-40 smoothbore with 20-inch round barrel, fancy XX stock of short and distinct configuration; no aperture in butt for cleaning rod; its sliding brass buttplate panel, spring and screw purposely not used; expressly adapted front and rear sights (latter possibly done for Annie on the road), case-hardened and blued, shipped February 14, 1888. Clarke was son of a prosperous estate owner in Shropshire, England, who befriended Annie and husband Frank Butler. The couple vacationed with the Clarkes, enjoying the countryside and local game shooting.

PRESENTED
BY
Annie Oakley
~ TO ~
Col. R. C. Clark
1891

(*opposite*) Another John Ulrich masterpiece (signed on lower tang), the Colonel Gzowski Model 1876 no. 53072, a presentation to Queen Victoria's aide-de-camp for Canada. In rare bird's-eye maple case, lined in velvet.

One of Theodore Roosevelt's favorite Winchesters, Model 1876, no. 38647, signed J. ULRICH on lower tang. Special-order stocks with cheekpiece; gold oval with bear inlaid on right buttstock. Custom order reflects exotic tastes of hunter-conservationist T.R., who ordered several deluxe lever-action arms, beginning with Model 1873 and continuing through Model 1895.

Herman as well. At times attributions to one or the other prove difficult. Fortunately, John tended to sign his work, and the forms of signature will vary from the simple initials J.U., engraved or stamped, to the stamp J. ULRICH. The size was almost always extremely small, the location generally on the lower tang, beneath the lever. Earlier marks, engraved, have been observed on the side of the tang, requiring the stock to be removed for examination.

Herman Leslie Ulrich

Not as famous as his brothers Conrad and John, Herman is nevertheless known to have been a supremely talented engraver. A limited number of firearms signed by him are known: among these are Model 1866 rifles, nos. 28549 and 38524, with H.L.U. engraved in script on the left side of the upper tang. The quality of engraving on these rifles is certainly in the same league as that of his brothers. In fact, Herbert G. Houze has recently suggested (in his 1993 article "The Appearance of Evidence: A Brief Examination of the Life and Work of Herman Leslie Ulrich") that Herman may well have been the most talented of the three engraving brothers.

Herman's engraving career was divided between Colt and Winchester. Although first listed in Hartford city directories in 1867, Herman began his apprenticeship around 1860, at Colt, and he remained with the company through 1870. Though he moved to New Haven in that year, the first directory listing there for Herman was in 1873–74: "engraver Winchester Arms Co." In 1880 he moved to Brooklyn, New York, to pursue a career as a stockbroker. Failing health caused him to retire from that endeavor in 1889, and in that year he returned to his native Hartford. He appeared in the Hartford city directory of 1890 as: "engraver at Colts." He is known to have continued working with Colt into 1899, but is also known to have returned to an association with Winchester as early as 1897.

From 1905 through 1925 he was listed in most New Haven directories, which noted his employment at the Winchester Repeating Arms Company. One reason Her-

172

Presented to
Colonel Gzowski.
A.D.C. to the Queen.
through the Council of the
Dominion of Canada Rifle Association
on his retirement in 1884 from the
Presidency of the Association
in recognition of the valuable
services rendered by him to the
Riflemen and Rifle Associations
of the Dominion.

man returned to New Haven was because he did not get along well with Cuno Helfricht, whom he referred to as a "sore-ass." Herman died in 1937, in Hartford, but had retired from engraving long before, probably around the end of World War I.

Signatures by John Ulrich

A little-known practice by John Ulrich presents a challenge for the student of Winchesters that bear his signature in the period about 1871 to the mid-1880s. As evidenced by a May 1884 letter from Herman L. Ulrich to a California Winchester customer, John Ulrich "has adopted the fashion of stamping Winchester Repeating Arms Company rifles &c with his touch mark when they are sent to that company's works for any reason." A rifle attributed to Herman L. Ulrich but bearing the J. ULRICH signature stamp is pictured on page 165.

Other Engravers at Winchester

Though overshadowed by the renowned Ulrich dynasty, there were other engravers on staff at Winchester. In particular, William H. Gough and Angelo J. Stokes stand out, and they are recorded in a collection of factory photographs of rifles and shotguns dating c. 1905–10. These pictures clearly identify, by model, serial number, and other features, lever- and pump-action Winchesters, even giving the costs of engraving. Two pictures identify an engraver named Phil Clundt showing examples of "Deep Etching" done with acid on the frame of a Model 12 shotgun and a Model 1907 semiautomatic rifle.

Stokes was from a family in which several members were Winchester employees. Angelo appeared in New Haven city directories in 1905, listed as an engraver at Winchester. In 1917 he moved to Meriden, Connecticut, where he continued his work as an engraver through 1936, but for another company apparently. He died in 1951, at age eighty-three; his work is seldom observed by collectors.

Very little is known of Gough, Stokes, and Clundt, though it appears Gough is the same W. H. Gough who engraved several arms for the Colt factory in the period

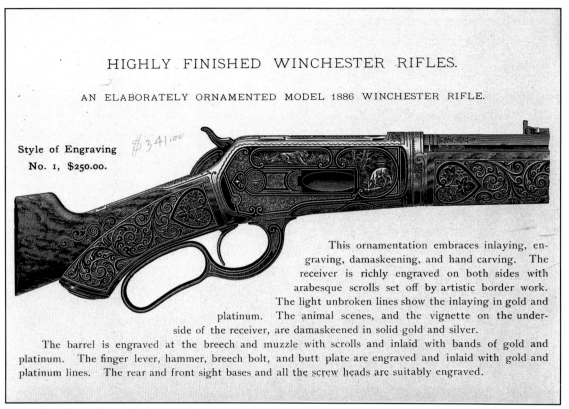

HIGHLY FINISHED WINCHESTER RIFLES.

AN ELABORATELY ORNAMENTED MODEL 1886 WINCHESTER RIFLE.

Style of Engraving
No. 1, $250.00.

This ornamentation embraces inlaying, engraving, damaskeening, and hand carving. The receiver is richly engraved on both sides with arabesque scrolls set off by artistic border work. The light unbroken lines show the inlaying in gold and platinum. The animal scenes, and the vignette on the underside of the receiver, are damaskeened in solid gold and silver.
The barrel is engraved at the breech and muzzle with scrolls and inlaid with bands of gold and platinum. The finger lever, hammer, breech bolt, and butt plate are engraved and inlaid with gold and platinum lines. The rear and front sight bases and all the screw heads are suitably engraved.

Page 4 from the Highly Finished Arms catalogue, with Model 1886, similar to rifle no. 129666, pictured at *top* of page 177.

1910–40. Though not a craftsman with the skills of a Helfricht, an Ulrich, or even a Stokes, Gough's work is highly prized by collectors due to its rarity in comparison with most other Winchester engravers. His career is also of interest because he took on assignments from several other firms—Winchester, Savage, Colt, Remington, Marlin, and even Auto Ordnance.

Landmark catalogue of 1897 that defined Winchester's commitment to engraving excellence; also, collected illustrations based on special-order and show guns by the Ulrichs. Notations by factory regarding special orders.

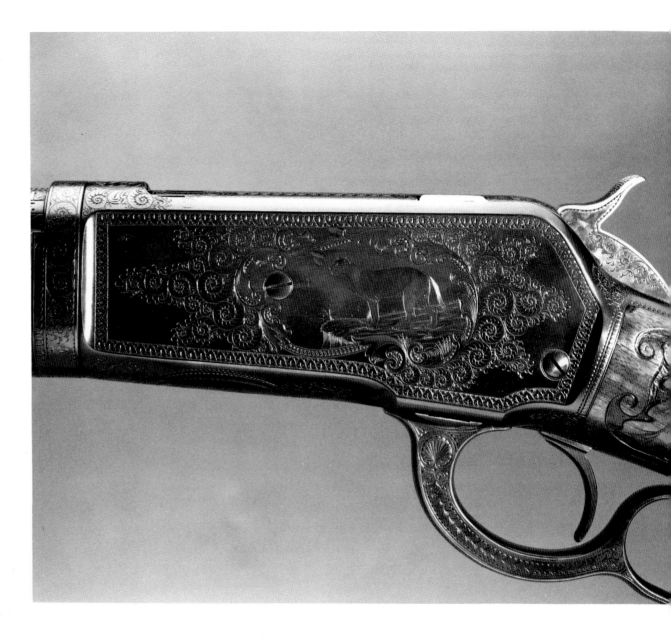

Angelo Stokes–engraved Model 1886 Takedown Rifle, no. 145592. Factory notation, c. 1905–10, indicates *"Stokes Design D/Lab $80/Mod. 92."* Likely new pattern for revised and updated Highly Finished Arms catalogue.

Most exquisite of known Model 1892s, no. 11009 has traditionally been identified as made for the Emperor of Japan. Signed J. ULRICH on lower tang. Grecian-key motif gold-inlaid front and back of frame, with matching motif on stocks.

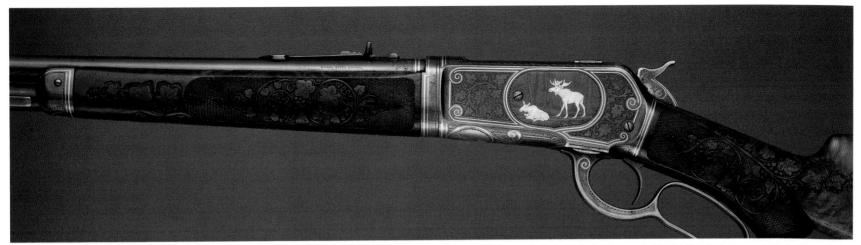

Model 1886 sporting rifle, signed J. ULRICH on lower tang. Gold- and platinum-inlaid in catalogue Style No. 1, with deluxe stocks in Style A. Documented in detail in factory records, including notation "New design by Mr. Ulrich"; frequently shipped for sample use during years 1904–06. One of the finest Model 1886 Winchesters, and distinguished by its maple-leaf engraving and matching carved stocks. Platinum (platina) began to be used in jewelry at turn of century; however, it was used at Tiffany & Co. as early as the 1870s as inlays on silver and occasionally in jewelry and exhibition pieces.

Factory-engraved and cased Model 1892 Carbine, no. 60909, plated in gold and nickel and showing evidence of use of stamp for some scroll details. Factory No. 10 engraved, with Style H stocks. Another factory sample piece.

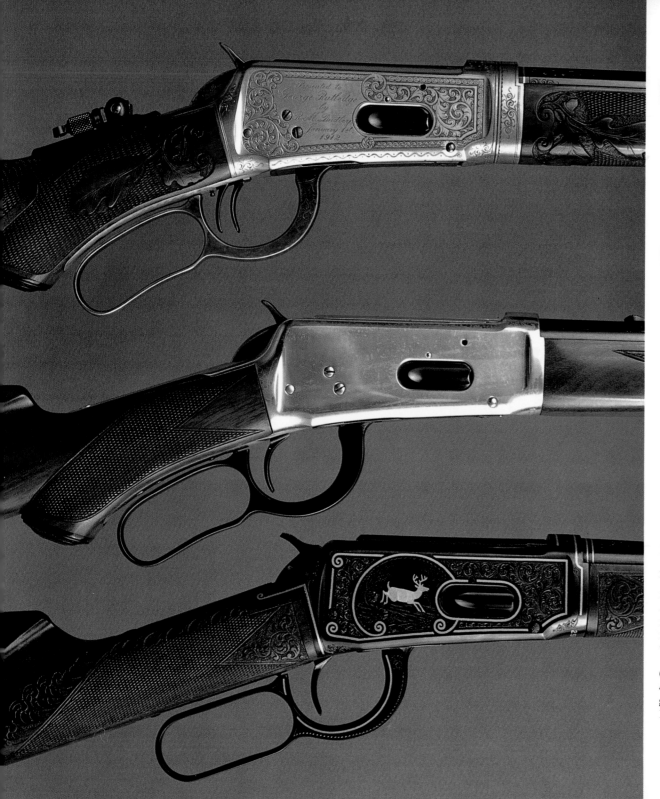

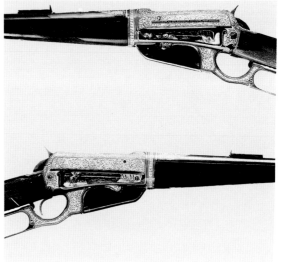

Back of early factory photograph bears penciled marking "John Gough Design A/Lab $110.00/106 grains of gold/Mod 95." Another print of same picture marked on front, "Mod. 1895/405 W.C.F.T.D. No. 73916 S.B./List $160.00/Fancy checked stock oil finished/Engraved by Gough $110.00 106 grs. gold/Lyman front and four leaf express rear sight/without 97 tangent." Approximately thirty similar photographs discovered that describe work, most identified in the notations as by Stokes and Gough, with varying degrees of information.

George Rutledge Model 1894 Takedown Rifle, engraved Style No. 4, with Style D stocks; attributed to John Ulrich. *Center,* rifle half-gold deluxe Model 1894; *bottom,* a 94 from the 1960s, based on 1897 Highly Finished Arms.

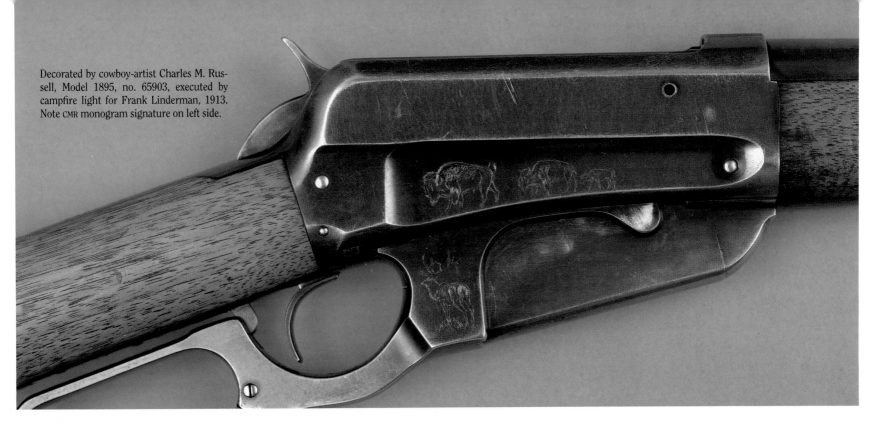

Decorated by cowboy-artist Charles M. Russell, Model 1895, no. 65903, executed by campfire light for Frank Linderman, 1913. Note CMR monogram signature on left side.

This Manhattan Navy is one of the few Nimschke arms known with gold and silver inlaying. Page 17 of his scrapbook presents major details, with gold details lined in yellow. Ivory carving also by Nim-schke. Presentation made for Napoleon III, whose portrait is in the rondelle; casing is of rosewood.

Chapter 6
Handguns Supreme:
c. 1860–1914

Although Colt and Winchester took the lead in arms decoration and have held on to it into modern times, engraving continued as a popular feature on guns by other makers through the end of the nineteenth century and up to World War I. In handguns, Remington, Smith & Wesson, Sharps, and a myriad of other firms, many of them deringer manufacturers, kept engravers busily engaged with varied degrees of handgun decor.

Of the some seventy-five cartridge deringer makers active at various times during this era, most offered hand embellishments. With some, like Williamson, Moore, and National, the entire production was engraved. Occasionally special showpieces or presentations were created, such as General Abner Doubleday's exquisite First Model Moore, replete with a cannon motif, an American eagle, the general's name, and full gold plating.

L. D. Nimschke's scrapbook records over 150 handguns from this period, custom engraved for the makers, for dealers, or for private clientele. The makes are as varied as Bitterlich & Legler, Colt, Connecticut Arms, A. G. Genez, George L. Holmes, C. Keller, Manhattan, Marlin,

Marston, Merrimack, Merwin & Bray, Merwin Hulbert & Company, Moore, Newbury, Prescott, Reid, Remington, Sharps, Slocum (by Brooklyn Arms Company), Smith & Wesson, Starr, Stevens, Tranter, Webley, Westervelt, Rollin White, and the Whitney Armory. It is tantalizing to speculate how many more makers were documented in the pulls and other records that were trashed by the fearful descendants.

Among Nimschke's masterpiece handguns is the Manhattan Navy revolver built as a presentation for Napoleon III, with gold-inlaid portrait of the recipient, gold borders, finely detailed scrollwork, relief-carved ivory grips, and an extraordinary pattern on the normally roll-engraved cylinder. The revolver was presented in a German-silver, bound, velvet-lined, rosewood box, and is the most elaborate known of any Manhattan.

A historic Remington New Model Army revolver for the near-legendary Lt. Colonel George Armstrong Custer is recorded in the scrapbook with prints from various parts, including the presentation-inscribed backstrap: TO GENERAL G.A. CUSTER / FROM E. REMINGTON & SONS. The revolver bore relief-carved ivory grips, the portrait of

Custer most likely carved by Nimschke. The rosewood-cased set ranks among the most historic and captivating Remingtons from any period.

Remingtons
Remington handguns are seldom found engraved, other than deringers and pocket pepperboxes. The factory workmen followed two patterns of scroll and border embellishments. A leafy scroll with minimum shading was likely to be found on percussion handguns, some models accompanied with acid-etched cylinder scenes. The more elaborate coverage was a scroll with punched-dot or beaded background, much like the work commonly associated with Colts done by Gustave Young's shop.

Some of the most impressive show-quality handguns of any U.S. gunmaker were the matched, cased pairs of Remington Rolling Block pistols, prepared on order of the Remington family for displays in Europe. The embellishments were executed in Belgium, which is evidenced by Belgian proofmarks visible on some of the sets. Three such deluxe pairs are known at this writing,

and individual pistols have also been found. One of these was discovered in the hands of a Remington family descendant; another was owned by Captain Jack Crawford.

However, unlike Samuel Colt and his staff, the Remingtons seldom presented any deluxe firearms. Displaying at fairs and expositions, however, was an effective promotional tool. The firm was well represented in Europe at such events, and had a grand display at the Philadelphia Centennial Exposition of 1876. No photographs are known of the Remington Arms display at the Philadelphia Centennial, nor has an inventory or detailed description survived. The Remington Gun Museum has a gold- and platinum-inlaid Rolling Block pistol, which was one of the firm's showpieces. An American eagle and shield device was inlaid on the breech of the frame (similar to the inlays in the Belgian-embellished European showpieces) and the grips were also of ivory.

Remington was another of the makers that, like Colt, gave some projects over to nonfactory craftsmen. Nimschke-engraved Remingtons have been observed in several models, among them Remington Army Model revolvers. One exotic pair has elaborate scroll and border engraving, gold and silver plating, and finely relief-carved ivory grips; the set is cased in a German-silver-bound rosewood box lined in velvet. These guns once had an inscription on their backstraps, but it was carefully removed at some distant time. Had this set been presented to a renowned figure of the day? The paucity of Remington shipping ledgers suggests that we may never know for sure. Whoever they were made for, the outfit ranks as the best of all known deluxe Remingtons from the percussion period.

Known to have engraved at the Remington factory in Ilion, New York, from 1880 through 1910 was Owen De Lange. From 1894 through 1940, Joe Loy worked his own bench there.

Smith & Wesson

Like Colt, Smith & Wesson recognized and responded to the public demand for deluxe arms. From the beginning,

Somewhat varied scroll treatment found on these Southerner deringer pistols, made in Newburyport, Massachusetts, c. 1869–73.

National First and Second Model deringers, with standard factory engraving; decoration carried over into Colt production, 1870.

Comparison of Remingtons, *at left,* and Colts reveals closeness of American scroll styles.

engraving was offered, and it is a matter of irony that these longtime competitors both employed the nineteenth century's premier arms engraver: Gustave Young. This gifted artisan did not move to Springfield or become an S&W contractor until a few years after the Colt factory fire of February 1864. Prior to Young's move, S&W relied on a variety of other craftsmen, one of whom was Richard Bates Inshaw, who had contracted with the firm as early as 1858. Still earlier, simple vine-like scroll embellishments were done by unknown craftsmen on the lever-action magazine pistols.

Other identified S&W engravers who were contemporaries of Gustave Young were S. T. Merritt, F. W. Martin, E. A. Timme, and P. S. Yendell. Nimschke engraved S&Ws for jobbers throughout most of his career. The type of engraving he usually employed on these guns is often called the "New York Style." Several S&Ws of varying coverages and patterns appear in the Nimschke scrapbook.

Gustave Young's efforts on behalf of S&W have been documented in substantial detail. In 1967, the author had the good fortune to discover, through Young's grandson, Robert, a store of valuable documents in the family home, in Springfield, Massachusetts. The attic was bulging with records, samples of engraving, and three carloads of memorabilia. The ledgers and notebooks recorded several jobs done for the S&W factory.

A few years later hundreds of pulls and other material turned up in the hands of other Gustave Young descendants.

Although Young's engraving of the best quality is easily identified, he seldom signed his work. To date, only a handful of S&W handguns with his signature are known, and factory and other records document several guns from his bench. His masterpiece, a gold-inlaid New Model No. 3, was done on order for S&W for the 1893 World's Columbian Exposition, in Chicago, and required nearly a year to complete. The topstrap bore the simple signature: G. YOUNG ENGRAVER. As the predominant arms engraver in America in the nineteenth century, Young was a master of his craft, and could engrave in any style.

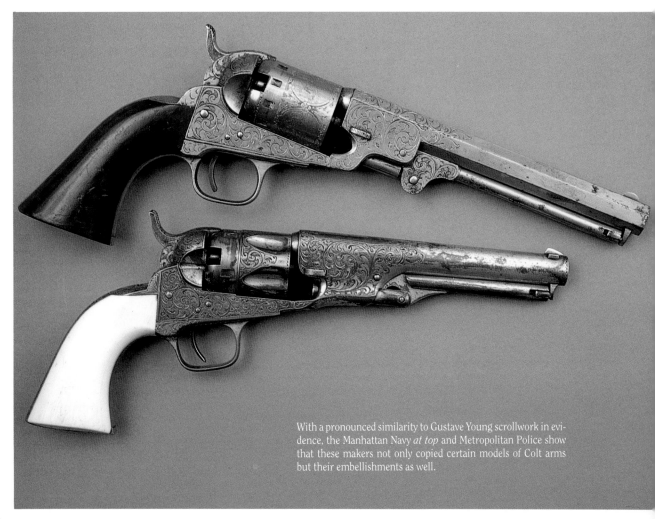

With a pronounced similarity to Gustave Young scrollwork in evidence, the Manhattan Navy *at top* and Metropolitan Police show that these makers not only copied certain models of Colt arms but their embellishments as well.

His Columbian Exposition creation was scroll-engraved in high relief, the recesses within each scroll roughened and then gold-overlaid for contrast. The final effect of engraved and polished steel against bright gold was spectacular. S&W was awarded a medal in honor of the revolver's beauty and workmanship. To this day the piece is a pride of the firm and is customarily displayed in the rotunda at the factory.

Only a few American arms have been decorated in the involved fashion of Young's Columbian Exposition show gun. Such complex interlocking of scrolls, the extra-deep cuts, the gold background, and the crispness of detail would tax the most able craftsman. Not a single animal motif appears on the pistol, so that Young apparently had decided to create the last word in intertwined scrollwork accentuated by the richness of gold.

Two years later, in 1895, Young was dead, but sons Oscar and Eugene carried on in their father's footsteps,

both of them accomplished craftsmen, with styles nearly identical to their father's.

Oscar Young was a S&W engraver during the period 1891–1911, while Eugene Young (primarily a die cutter) engraved S&Ws for some ten years, around the turn of the century. A number of dies were made by the Youngs for Tiffany & Co. The association of S&W with Tiffany remains a highlight in the histories of both firms and is presented in detail in chapter 9.

Harrington & Richardson

An American manufacturer much less inclined toward engraving was Harrington & Richardson, of Worcester, Massachusetts. However, for the Philadelphia Centennial the company created an impressive display featuring twenty-four deluxe revolvers. This elaborate exhibit is the only one from the Centennial gala to have survived intact. The relief-carved display cabinet was bedecked with four clusters of six revolvers each. All were single action spur-trigger pocket models fitted with selected grips of rosewood, walnut, ivory, or pearl. Two pairs of pearl grips and two of ivory were relief-carved, while twelve of the revolvers were engraved, with plated finishes. Serial numbers ran from 1 to 6, 8 to 15, and 17 to 26.

The craftsmen responsible for the H&R Centennial engraving have yet to be positively identified. The scrolls are in the style of L. D. Nimschke, who might have been the source—but he was often imitated. Nimschke was also a talented carver of ivory and pearl, and worked in the style as pictured. The Goddess of Liberty ivory stock shares the same design source as the panel motif on the

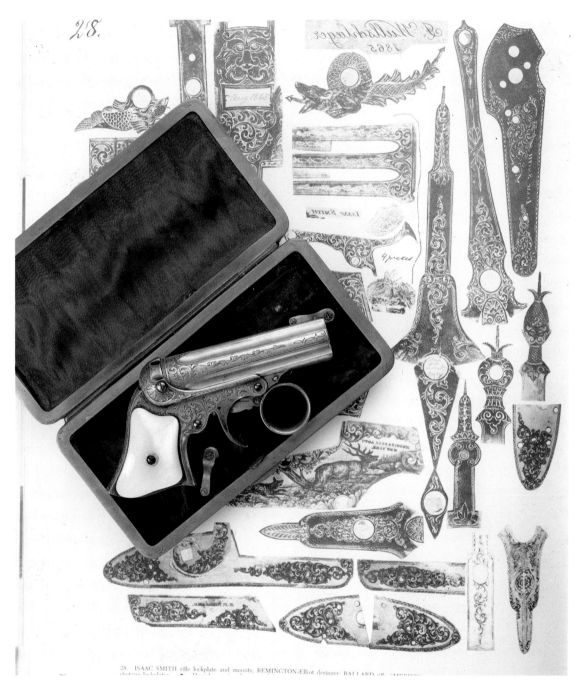

Remington-Elliot deringer of exhibition grade, featured on page 28 of Nimschke's record book; serial no. 4; gold- and silver-plated.

E. Remington & Sons commissioned Nimschke to decorate New Model Army .44, including backstrap inscription and carved ivory grips. Page 13 of record book has ample prints pulled by the engraver from various parts. Some of the Custer arms collection visible in album photo *at left;* extraordinary selection of arms, accessories, and memorabilia.

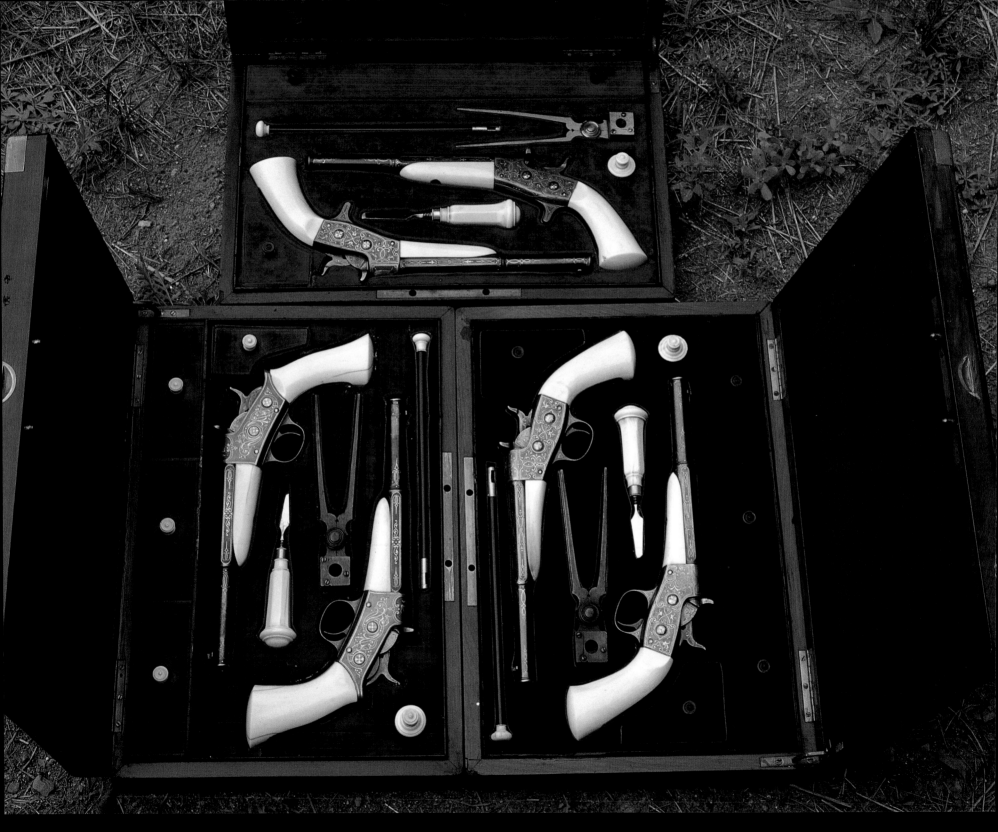

Young-engraved Model 1866 Winchester number 26283 (see page 198).

Merwin & Hulbert, and Others

Among the most distinctive and bizarre of engravings from American handguns of the period were on Merwin & Hulberts, especially some presentation-grade revolvers made to impress Mexican dictator Porfirio Díaz. Of the two sensational gold-embellished Merwin & Hulberts from the Díaz Collection, the more deluxe is pictured: encrusted with gold, it is likely to have been decorated in Spain, where such damascene designs have been a tradition for centuries. The grips are of carved and engraved mother-of-pearl. Another Merwin & Hulbert revolver, this one cased, has a combination of engraved scrolls, game scenes, a PD monogram, punched motifs, nickel and gold plating, and deluxe mother-of-pearl grips. Some of the engraving was accented by enamel. A handful of similarly decorated Merwin & Hulbert handguns have been observed, but the identity of the engraver remains unknown at this writing.

Other handgun firms of the period that offered engraving, but whose styles duplicated those pictured herein, include the various Ethan Allen associates; Bacon; Chicago Firearms Co. (palm pistols); Connecticut Arms & Manufacturing Company; Cooper; Forehand & Wadsworth; Lindsay; Marston; National; Pond; Reid; Rupertus; Starr; Walch; Warner; and a myriad of makers of inexpensive cartridge revolvers. In *The Peacemakers* (page 233) a selection of these is collected in an illustra-

Remington New Model Pockets. *From top,* factory display piece from the Philadelphia Centennial, no. 3436, with special half-nickel finish and engraved hammer; nickel-plated revolver with profuse factory engraving; gold and silver pistol with another factory style of decor.

At top, presentation- and exhibition-grade Remington Rolling Block pistols, Model 1866 Navy, nos. 3 and 4; *bottom right,* Model 1867 Navy, nos. 1 and 2; and Model 1871 Army, nos. 2 and 3. Breechtops of pairs inlaid, respectively, with crest of King Alfonso XII of Spain, royal cipher of King Charles XV of Sweden, and American eagle and shield.

187

High points in the evolution of Smith & Wesson engraving, from c. 1861 to 1880. Represented are styles associated with Gustave Young, Richard Bates Inshaw, and L. D. Nimschke and the New York school of engravers. *At upper right,* daguerreotype cases and similarly styled pistol cases of thermoplastic. *Top right,* Goddess of Industry motif. Plate inscribed W.B. WETMORE from now missing cased set, for an Indian fighter who had penchant for fine guns.

Thermoplastic (often termed "gutta-percha") pistol cases by Littlefield, Parsons & Co. (two *at left*, stand of flags *at top center*, and two floral and scroll *at right center*), date from 1858–66. Daguerreotype cases by that firm and others date from as early as 1854. Gunmakers marketing pistols in this style case included Smith & Wesson, Warner, Sharps, and Allen & Wheelock. Popular themes of patriotism, floral bouquets, and scrollwork. Note hand-cut steel production dies *at top left*.

S&W pocket revolvers by factory engravers (*top* and *bottom*), and by L. D. Nimschke; the latter exhibits what is often termed New York Style, since dealers and jobbers not infrequently had guns engraved by craftsmen, like Nimschke, working in New York City. These and several other pieces pictured on these pages were featured in S&W's widely viewed and admired traveling exhibition "Artistry in Arms," the catalogue for which was authored by factory historian Roy G. Jinks.

Believed cased and etched by Tiffany & Co., Custer's S&W Model No. 2 commemorated a hunting expedition in which J. B. Sutherland and friends had been hosted, under heavy guard, by Custer and his troops, 1869. Silver-plated; same pistols appearing in Custer album photo, from Fort Lincoln, Nebraska (page 184). See also similar cases, on pages 90 and 273.

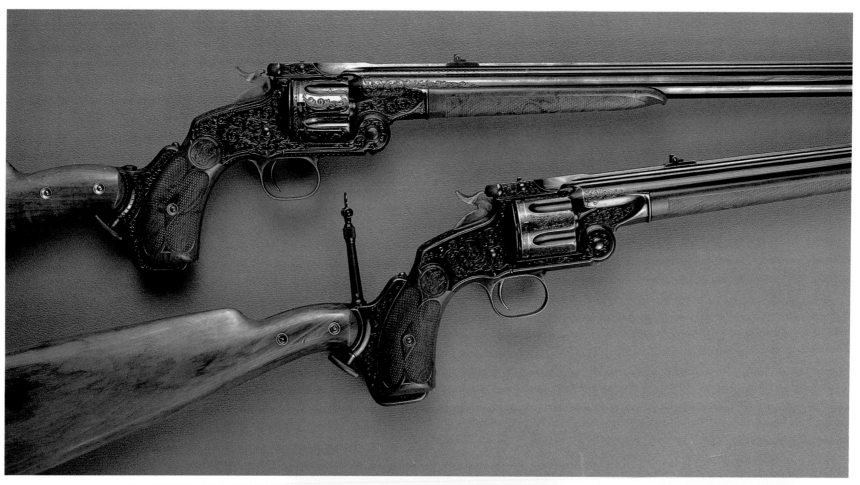

S&W's equivalent of the Colt Buntline Special, the Model 320 revolving rifle was seldom engraved. Note molded hard-rubber grips and forends, molded from dies cut by Gustave Young.

Signed L.D.N. / N.Y., Second Model topbreak shows Nimschke at his best, with the scrolls thick and flowing, and fitting forms perfectly. Case lid embossed with long inscription, noting gift from New York Rifle Club to L. V. Sone on occasion of his visit to Europe.

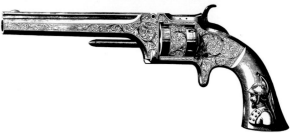

From the Schuyler, Hartley & Graham Military Goods catalogue of 1864, S&W Model No. 2 with carved ivory grips and factory or Nimschke scroll and borderwork.

Cased S&W Model No. 3 American Second Model, an exhibition piece shown by the factory in Moscow (1872), Vienna (1873), and Philadelphia (1876). Gold-inlaid Second Model also factory display piece; both pieces later sold through New York dealer M. W. Robinson. Gold inlaying and engraving by Gustave Young.

Masterpiece by Gustave Young, made for factory's ambitious display at Columbian Exposition and exhibited with Tiffany-mounted revolvers and other deluxe arms.

Gustave Young gold inlays. Single Action Third Model in .38 caliber (*top*) and .32 Single Action, both part of factory's exhibit at the Chicago World's Fair.

Single-Shot First Model in .22 caliber (*top*), by Eugene Young (1897); .32 Hand-Ejector First Model (*center*) and .38 Single Action Third Model, both by brother Oscar. Though difficult to detect Oscar Young's work in comparison with his father, Eugene's can be identified by the very delicate, light hand.

From Frank Butler to his wife, Annie Oakley, c. 1900. S&W at *center* inscribed with name, and case lid so embossed. Oscar Young engraved the S&Ws; the Stevens by another artisan, and in noticeably contrasting style—one observed on arms by this maker occasionally. Gold-plating made guns glisten in sun during daytime shows outdoors.

Exhibition-grade Allen & Wheelock .44-caliber Army revolver, its decoration attributed to Gustave Young. Hand-engraved cylinder depicting farm scene, including dogs, birds, rabbits, men, and haystacks. Finished in gold and silver plating and case-hardened; serial no. 2322. Checkered ivory grips inscribed on left side E. ALLEN & CO. MAKERS, and on right side WORCESTER, MASS.

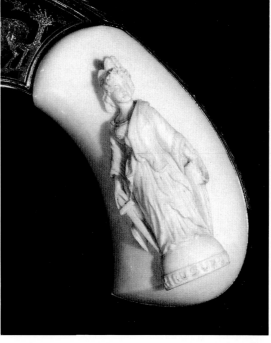

Goddess of Liberty carved on ivory grip of one of Harrington & Richardson Centennial Exhibition display-board revolvers. Panel scene and scrollwork on frame; one of most deluxe revolvers from display.

A treasure of fine guns from the Philadelphia Centennial Exhibition.

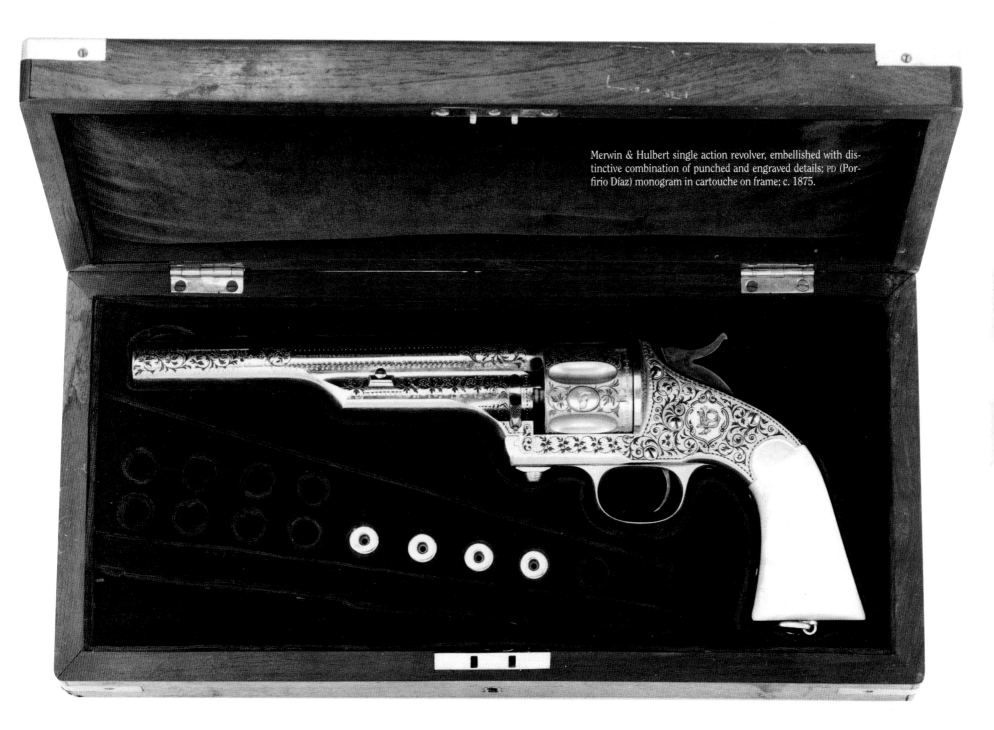

Merwin & Hulbert single action revolver, embellished with distinctive combination of punched and engraved details; PD (Porfirio Díaz) monogram in cartouche on frame; c. 1875.

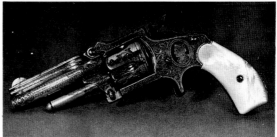

Marlin revolver, engraved by Ulrich or Nimschke, c. 1880–81. Goddess of Liberty or Columbia within rondelle.

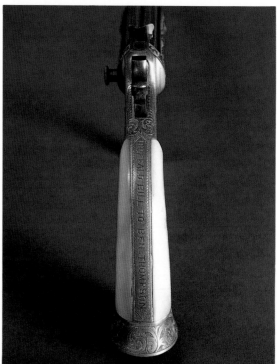

Historic Stevens-Lord Model No. 36 Target Pistol, serial no. 32, a gift from showman Buffalo Bill Cody to gunfighter-gambler–peace officer Ben Thompson. Engraved by L. D. Nimschke; gold-plated frame, nickel-plated barrel. Presented June 1881 while Thompson was city marshal and chief of police of Austin, Texas. Thompson was killed in 1884, in a hail of bullets at San Antonio's Variety Theater. Was veteran of at least fourteen gunfights. See also page 216.

Even more elaborate Merwin & Hulbert, also custom-made for Díaz, in Toledo, Spain. Note Spanish-style damascene and inlay; style best known on sword decorations. Right grip relief carved with Mexican eagle.

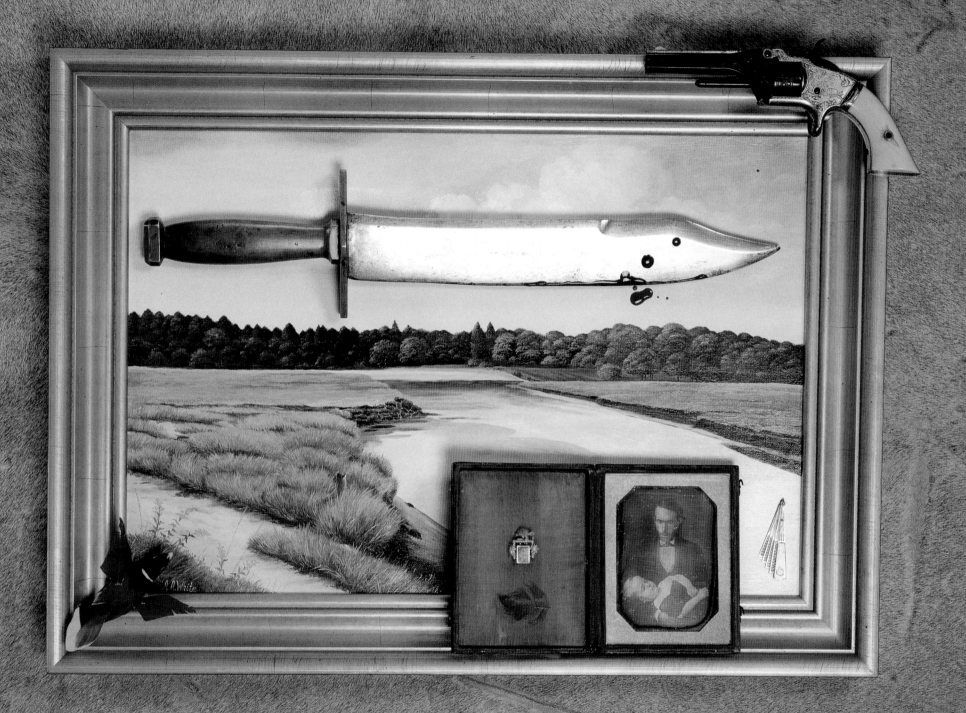

Confederate Bowie knife, its forged iron blade etched: DEATH TO YANKEES / CROSKEYS MAKER. Made near Charlottesville, Virginia, likely at beginning of Civil War; 16¼ inches overall length. A menacing and lethal weapon, with strikingly handsome proportions and admirable quality. Painting by A. A. White. c. 1985.

Extraordinary array of Bowie knives, of American and English manufacture. 1, Silver-mounted American knife, c. 1790–1810; horn grips, 7-inch blade. 2, Silver-mounted American knife, c. 1800–10; horn grips. 3, Silver-hilted and -mounted American dagger, c. 1790–1810; horn grips, with initials WM; sheath inscribed CAPT. C. QUARY TO LIEUT. COL. MCMILLON / 17'TH U.S.I. 4, Bowie knife, marked SCHIVELY / CHESTNUT STREET / PHILAD; c. 1835; German-silver mountings; maker of knife for Rezin Bowie and one attributed to use by Davey Crockett. 5, Bowie, marked MARKS & REES / CIN'AT with similar marking on gold-embossed sheath; wood grips, silver-mounted, c. 1835. 6, Large Bowie, marked SAMUEL BELL / KNOXVILLE TENNESSEE; c. 1840, silver- and German-silver mounted ivory grips. 7, M. P. Ames, Springfield and Chicopee, Massachusetts, c. 1840 knife with elaborately etched frontiersman and Native American–motif blade; rosewood grips; deluxe sheath. 8, Ames knife of c. 1852, for California trade; note bear on pommel; sharkskin grips with wire wrapping; etched blade with patriotic motifs, including eagles. 9, Marked REINHARDT / BAL, renowned Baltimore maker of knives and surgical instruments, c. 1845. 10, By ROSE / NEW YORK; SELF PRESERVATION etched on blade panel; reverse with etched American eagle; brass handle. 11, Also by Rose, and of same period, with silver-mounted ivory handle, obverse of blade etched: A TIGER IN WAR BUT IN PEACE A LAMB; German-silver mounting engraved T.H. MCCLELLAN / CAPTURED AT GETTYSBURG 1863. 12, Also by Rose and of same period, with ivory grips and German-silver mounts. 13, Rose, with ivory grips, German-silver mounts. 14, Ivory-handled Bowie with silver studs; German-silver mounts; made in Philadelphia by J. English & Huber, c. 1840, trying to simulate Sheffield manufacture. 15, Marked CHEVALIER / NEW YORK, with coffin-shaped pommel; half-pearl grips; c. 1835–40. 16, Chevalier-marked Bowie, c. 1840s–50s; German-silver mounts, ivory plaque grips. 17, Michael Price, San Francisco, noted California maker of 1850s, early 1860s; ivory grip studded in German silver; scabbard of elegant, engraved sterling silver. 18, One-piece relief-carved ivory grips on Price knife with 5¼-inch blade. 19, Price knife with silver handle paneled in abalone shell. 20, Gambler's push dagger by Price. 21, Marked WILL & FINCK / S.F., spear-point push dagger. 22, Black ebony handle on Will & Finck push dagger. 23, California knife, unmarked; its silver handle with abalone-shell panels. 24, By Boston maker KINGMAN & HASSAM, and so marked; stag-antler handle, c. 1856–60. 25, Rare Civil War Bowie by Connecticut maker Collins & Co., with blade etched: THE UNION NOW AND FOREVER and S.M. TATRO / COLLINSVILLE. Tatro was inspector of grinding at the Collins Company, major sword and bayonet makers. 26, Attributed to Ames Manufacturing Co., inscribed Civil War soldier's knife; etched on blade: SERG'T SAM'L MORSE CO. G / 27 REGIMENT. Killed in action at Cold Harbor, June 3, 1864; similar knives believed issued to 27th Regiment from Chicopee area, as was Morse. 27, Civil War soldier's knife, marked by C. Roby, West Chelmsford, Massachusetts; blade etched with patriotic and Civil War motifs; wood grips. Most knives with sheaths, generally not shown.

California Bowie, c. 1855; unmarked. German-silver mounted hilt, with gold inlay and abalone. Gold shield on silver sheath.

Half-horse, half-alligator hilted Bowie knife, by Thomas Short, Sheffield; c. 1850; 8¼-inch blade. Imposing buffalo-head cross-guard; German-silver mounts.

Bowie knives made in Sheffield or vicinity for the American trade, c. 1840–60, with large oversize manufacturers' display knives; vertical knife measures 24½ inches overall. Clipped-point blades were intended for American market. Knife *at bottom* by R. Smith, York, with elegant sheath in embossed leather, probably by maker of oversize sheath *above.* Makers, *counterclockwise from top left:* Woodhead & Hartley; J. Nicholson & Sons; J. Walters & Co. Globe Works; unmarked; J. Nicholson & Sons; J. Walters & Co. Globe Works; C. Barnes & Sons; G. Woodhead; Tillotson; and Thomas Short, Jr. Several blades with etched patriotic and/or hunting and mining motifs.

Sheffield Bowies for the American trade, with variety of shapes, pommels and grips; quotations indicate etched-blade markings. Vertical knives, c. 1850, *from left:* with rare German-silver and velvet sheath, James Rodgers & Co. knife measures 14 inches overall; bone grips. W. Broadhurst massive knife with 2-inch, wide clipped point. John Yeomans "California Knife" with horse-head pommel. *At left, from top:* "Texas Ranger" by S. C. Wragg, with German-silver cutlery handle. James Rodgers & Co. horse-head pommel knife. Rare "The Hunter's Companion/My Horse Knife and Rifle," made for and sold by "Graveley & Wreaks/New York" and so marked on blade; hand-engraved German-silver mounts; c. 1840. "Alabama Hunting Knife" deep-stamped with running stag, hounds, and hunter motif, and with various inscriptions, by W. F. Jackson. Mexican War motifs and legends etched on blade, by S. C. Wragg. American eagle motif on crossguard of W. Broadhurst knife. *At right, from top:* "American Bowie Knife" by Woodhead, c. 1840. "Hunter's Companion" by R. Bunting & Son; state of Louisiana imagery on hilt; tortoiseshell plaque grips. "Arkansas Toothpick" by James Rodgers. "A Real Mississippian" by Ibbotson, Peace & Co.; ebony grips. "Cast Steel Bowie knife" by S. C. Wragg. "Bowie Knife/Sheffield" by Enoch Drabble; horse head over cannon, and artillery and patriotic motifs.

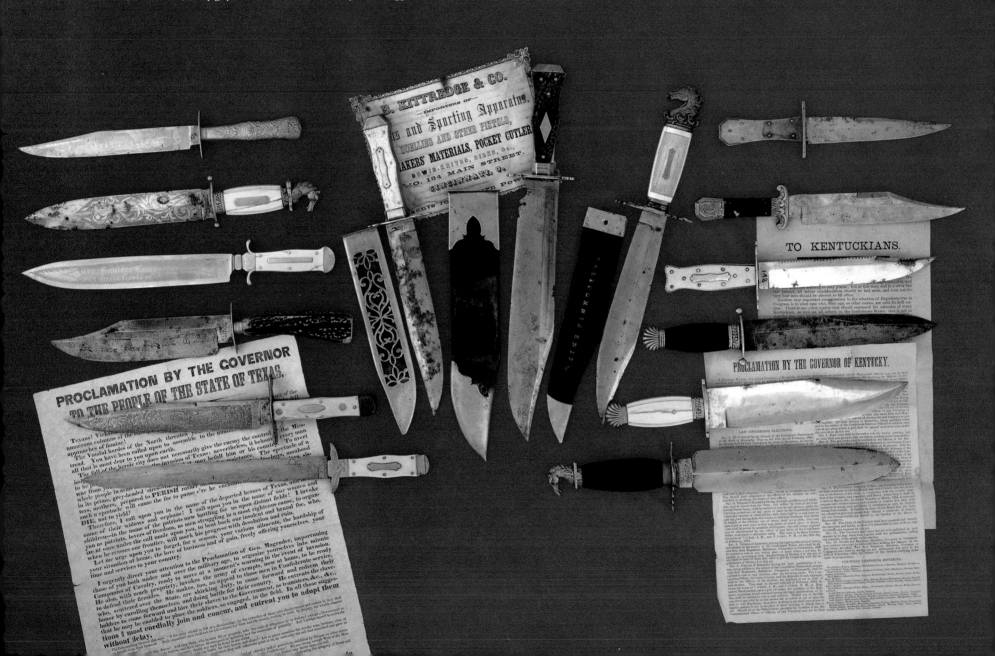

tion that indicates their broad spectrum of style, quality, and design. Some of the less expensive arms bore crude embellishments, an embarrassment to the trade. The Colt factory's view of these sublevel gunmakers appeared in a cartoon depicting the makers of these "suicide special" goods holding on to reins attached to a running colt, dragging it down; the caption read: " 'Our Colt,' and how we drove him."

Bowie Knives

Part of the romance and lore of the California Gold Rush, the Civil War, and the American West—occupying the same league in the popular imagination as the Colt and the Winchester—are Bowie knives. They hold an additional fascination for their design and craftsmanship, the oftimes flamboyantly etched blades, and their not infrequent use as vehicles for patriotic, military, or outdoor themes. The credited originator of the knife, though his role remains obscure, is part of the sizzle: Jim Bowie, the American adventurer who died at the Alamo, at the hands of overwhelming numbers of Santa Anna's troops.

The knives considered in the present volume are either of domestic manufacture or were made for the American market; the foreign-made knives are almost entirely the work of the talented artisans of Sheffield, England. In form, embellishment, materials, styles, themes and quality, these knives (foreign and domestic) are a worthy study for any student of decorative arts. The high period of Bowie-knife production continued through the end of the nineteenth century, coinciding

Remarkable California knives. *From top:* inscribed PRESD TO M J BURKE CHIEF OF POLICE (San Francisco) BY SOME GERMAN FRIENDS, 1861; gold- and silver-mounted with ivory hilt; overall length of knife 10⅜ inches; by I. H. Schintz. Badge of gold and enamel, engraved on back PRESENTED TO / CHIEF BURKE / BY / THOMAS CODY. Accompanied by early set of mug books with index. Michael Price gold and silver knife signed twice, including in tiny script on both sides of silver mount near ricasso; monogram HJB and 1865 date on gold grip plaques, and J.H. BRADFORD on scabbard. Large Bowie *at bottom* silver-mounted, inscribed on silver sheath PRESENTED BY / MR. J. THOMAR WHITING. / TO / CAPT. JEREMIAH S. SILVA, / WHILE IN COMMAND OF SLOOP VELOS, / ON THE SACRAMENTO RIVER, / CALIFORNIA. On butt, the initials J.S.S.

207

Folding knives of Sheffield make, for the American trade, with Metropolitan Police, *top left,* and Moore tit-fire revolvers. Large knife *at top* possibly for maker's display rather than use, due to size; 22½ inches when fully opened; etched blade with patriotic and California motifs, by Unwin & Rodgers; note half-horse, half-alligator symbolism. *Center,* by J. Fenton; *bottom,* made for New York's J. Curley & Brothers, with rare knucklebow of silver. *From top left:* "Liberty and Union" by George Wostenholm; Civil War era. Eagle and shield crossguard on W. & S. Butcher knife. Pearl and German-silver grip mounts, with Native American crossguard motif, by J. Lingard. Horse-head folder, by unknown maker, owner's name "A.W. Master" on brass plate of stag grip. Horse-head pommel, ivory-gripped knife by S. C. Wragg. Stained ivory grips with cross inlaid in silver; by W. F. Mills, London. *At right, from top;* small horse-head pommel, with rosewood grips, by A. Davy. Scales of Justice and liberty cap with American eagle and shield motifs on pommel; by A. Davy & Sons. Unmarked with patriotic and leaf grip mounts, by G. Crookes. Horn grips with American-eagle mounts, by Ruff. Horse head and cannon with ivory grips, by W. & S. Butcher. Pearl-gripped folder by Unwin & Rodgers. "Alabama Hunting Knife," "A. Davy's Celebrated American Hunting Knife" with half-horse, half-alligator decor, and horn grips. The Metropolitan, with inscription on barrel top in place of maker's marking: PRESENTED TO HON. E.C. STACEY / BY CO. C 2'D REG'T MINN CAV'Y JANUARY 1, 1864. The gold-plated Moore etched on cylinder and barrel, including American-eagle and shield motif on cylinder; scroll-engraved in a Nimschke style on brass frame.

Silver-mounted presentation Bowie knife, to Colonel Thomas G. Stevenson, from his Boston friends. Representing height of American elegance in Civil War–era knifemaking. By Hassam Brothers, Boston. Patriotic eagle-head terminals to quillons. High-relief carved ivory grip of Union soldier with U.S. flag in one hand, and Bowie knife in other. Massachusetts State seal near base of handle. Silver-mounted, velvet-covered scabbard, inscribed on throat; 13½ inches overall; c. 1861–62. Leather-covered, silk and velvet lined storage case not illustrated.

(*top left*) Display of George Wostenholm at Chicago World's Columbian Exposition. *Center of lower case* exhibits gold medals firm won in earlier exhibits. The American market was a crucial one to this respected English firm.

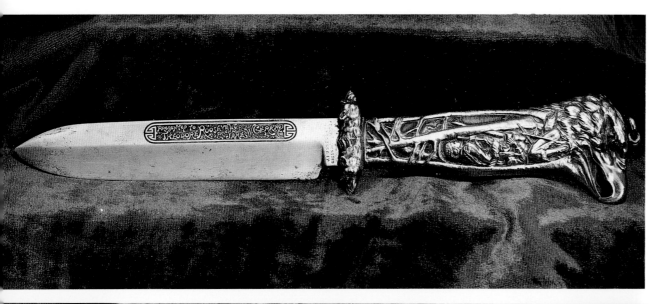

with the great period of the Wild West. A spirited revival, which coincided with that in best-quality gunmaking, would take place beginning in the 1960s and 1970s—not only of Bowies, but of a broad variety of knives.

The Presentation Sword, Civil War to World War I

The Civil War saw a veritable avalanche of patriotic sentiment and virtuoso productions. Here the sword as male jewelry reached its apotheosis, with some designs precisely detailed miniature statues, dripping with ornament, precious metals, and not a few with precious and semiprecious stones. The use of symbols was equally profligate, with the Goddess of Liberty, a variety of classical figures, and the popular American eagle and shield the most common.

A list of Tiffany's more sensational commissions of the period reads like a who's who of the Civil War: General Ulysses S. Grant, General William Tecumseh Sherman, Major General Winfield Scott Hancock, Major General John McAllister Schofield, Major General John C. Robinson, Brigadier General William A. Pile, and Admiral David G. Farragut. The firm could rightly boast of the design brilliance of Edward C. Moore, and a number of his design drawings of presentation swords are in the firm's archives.

John Quincy Adams Ward, recognized as the dean of nineteenth-century American sculptors, was commissioned to design presentation swords for the Ames firm, and for gifts to such luminaries as General Ulysses S. Grant, Admiral Andrew Hull Foote, and General James

On his last day in the White House, March 4, 1909, Theodore Roosevelt was given this superb custom-made hunting knife, inscription etched in panel on blade from his friend James W. Gerard. Made by J. Russell & Co., Green River Works, Turners Falls, Massachusetts. The hilt of gold, silver, and bronze by Dreicer & Co., prominent New York City jewelers. (Dreicer's collection of paintings donated to The Metropolitan Museum of Art.) Pommel set with ruby eyes, and one side of hilt cast with Boone & Crockett motif in forest setting; other side with gold and silver TR monogram in relief, with American eagle and wishbone. Blade 6 inches in length.

210

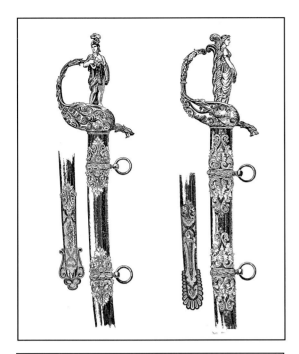

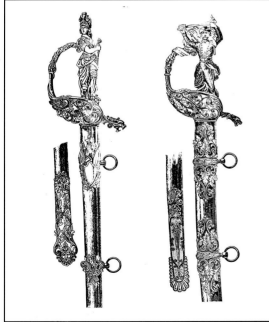

On a silk patriotic banner made in London for the American market, array of Civil War–period presentation officers' swords. *From left:* gilt bronze and silver hilt, presented to Brevete Brigadier General D. H. Vinton. General Joshua Owen sword of gilt brass and silver, with elegantly engraved grip; made by W. H. Horstmann & Sons, Philadelphia. Tiffany & Co. mounts of silver gilt, the blade by Collins & Co., source of many blades on Tiffany production; presented to Brigadier General T.E.G. Ransom. Lavish Victorian composition of gilt bronze and silver, by Schuyler, Hartley & Graham, presented to General Selden E. Marvin. Gilt-bronze hilt with silver grips wrapped in gilt wire; by W. H. Horstmann & Sons; presented to Colonel Isaac C. Bassett; inscription on gold panel on scabbard, with delicately engraved silver panel motifs. Unusual design Navy presentation with high-relief cast silver grips and profusion of decorative motifs and themes, including mermaid and dolphin on sharkskin scabbard. Generous use of symbols evident in elaborate embellishments. Customarily deluxe casings (not shown), often of velvet-lined rosewood or walnut, accompanied such elaborate presentations.

Promoting "Rich Presentation Swords" in the Schuyler, Hartley & Graham Military Goods catalogue, 1864. The firm was a major source of elaborate arms, with deluxe swords a speciality. Statuary hilts were one of the prevalent decorative motifs on the more elaborate Civil War presentation swords.

Oglesby. This latter sword, at $2,200, was the most expensive ever produced by the Ames firm. It was destroyed in a fire at the recipient's home in 1893, but is preserved in illustrations in company promotional literature.

Even the Confederacy got caught up in presentation and deluxe swords, although domestic production in the South was unable to rival in quality and style the output of the North. The most splendid Confederate sword would appear to be a jeweled and enameled masterpiece of gold and silver presented to Captain Raphael Semmes as an honorific replacement for the sword he lost in the sinking of the CSS *Alabama,* by the USS *Kearsage.* The maker of the sword was an English firm.

In the years following the war, a few standout presentation orders were completed by Tiffany & Co. and other firms. Although sword presentations continued into the World War I period, the practice subsided soon after. Firearms had displaced swords as ceremonial objects worthy of embellishment—just as they had on the battlefield as practical tools of warfare.

Civil War presentation officers' swords, with carved ivory grips. *From left:* to Colonel Louis D. Watkins, gold- and silver-mounted, made or sold by H. H. Hirschbuhl, Louisville, Kentucky. To Colonel Peter Lyle from the Old Guard of Philadelphia; gilt-bronze hilt; pierced gilt-bronze overlays on scabbard. To 1st Lt. L. C. Fowler; gilt-bronze hilt; coiled snakes form carrying-ring mounts on scabbard. To Captain Lawrence H. Thompson, grips depicting Goddess of Liberty; made or sold by military outfitters G. W. Simons & Bro., Philadelphia. Important gift to prominent leader Brigadier General George Gordon Meade; gilt-bronze hilt, the scabbard of silver mounted in gilt brass, with eight-line inscription. To Captain H.E.W. Clark, captain of black 5th Massachusetts Cavalry regiment; gilt-bronze hilt, made by G. W. Simons & Bro.; scabbard of silver, with gilt-bronze mounts. To Colonel William Forbes; elegant half basket guard on gilt-bronze hilt. Similarities in style and quality suggest carvers probably also executed revolver grips; relief carved ivory grips rarely encountered on Civil War swords, and these specimens represent majority of known examples.

Diamond- and amethyst-inlaid presentation to General George H. Thomas, "The Rock of Chickamauga," with statuary-style grip of silver gilt; by Ball, Black & Co., New York, jewelers and military outfitters. Important presentation honoring the first victory of the Union in the Civil War, the obverse of the blade etched: MILL SPRINGS, KT: JAN: 19, 1862/THE FIRST VICTORY WON BY THE UNION ARMY. Shown with memorabilia of this highly underrated leader.

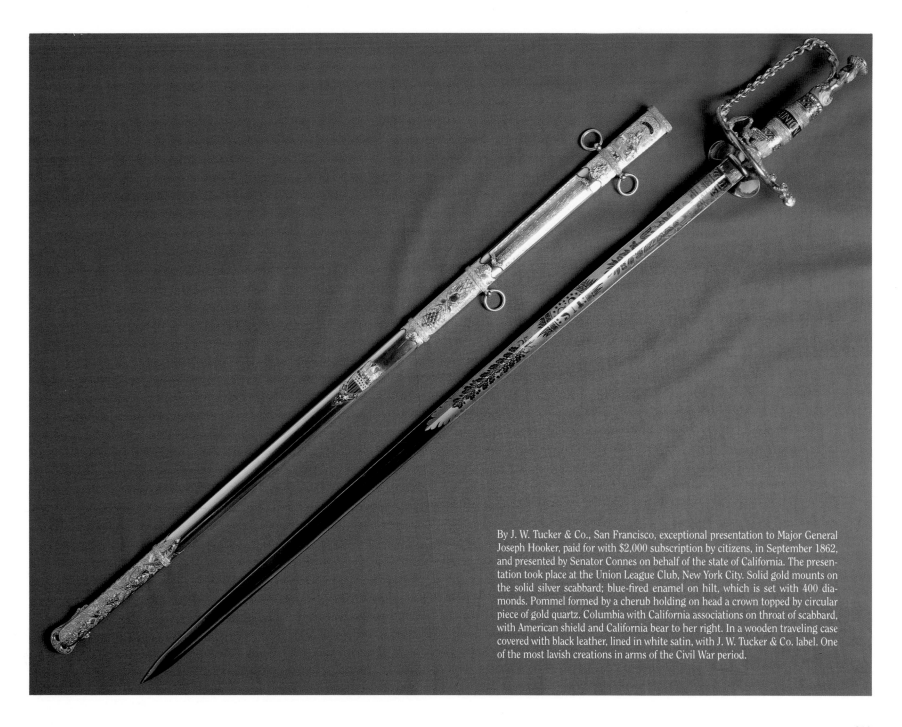

By J. W. Tucker & Co., San Francisco, exceptional presentation to Major General Joseph Hooker, paid for with $2,000 subscription by citizens, in September 1862, and presented by Senator Connes on behalf of the state of California. The presentation took place at the Union League Club, New York City. Solid gold mounts on the solid silver scabbard; blue-fired enamel on hilt, which is set with 400 diamonds. Pommel formed by a cherub holding on head a crown topped by circular piece of gold quartz. Columbia with California associations on throat of scabbard, with American shield and California bear to her right. In a wooden traveling case covered with black leather, lined in white satin, with J. W. Tucker & Co. label. One of the most lavish creations in arms of the Civil War period.

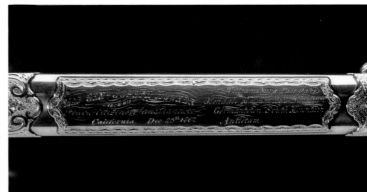

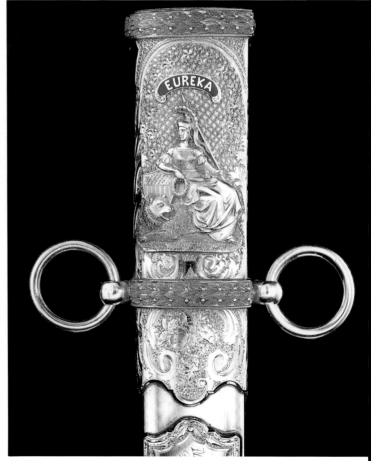

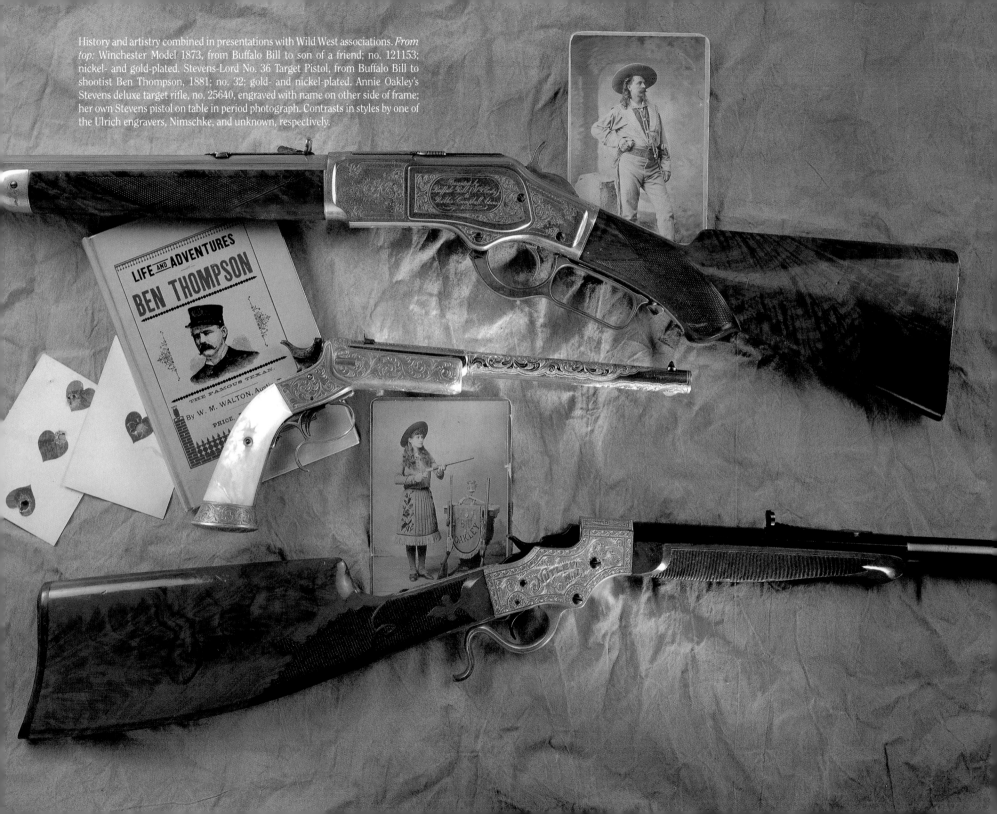

History and artistry combined in presentations with Wild West associations. *From top:* Winchester Model 1873, from Buffalo Bill to son of a friend; no. 121153; nickel- and gold-plated. Stevens-Lord No. 36 Target Pistol, from Buffalo Bill to shootist Ben Thompson, 1881; no. 32; gold- and nickel-plated. Annie Oakley's Stevens deluxe target rifle, no. 25640, engraved with name on other side of frame; her own Stevens pistol on table in period photograph. Contrasts in styles by one of the Ulrich engravers, Nimschke, and unknown, respectively.

LIFE AND ADVENTURES
OF
BEN THOMPSON
THE FAMOUS TEXAN.
By W. M. WALTON, Austin.
PRICE,

Chapter 7
Best-Quality Longarms:
c. 1860–1914

In the period 1860–1914, shoulder arms attained a level of elaborate decorative indulgence that would rival the work done on handguns and not be equaled until the last quarter of the twentieth century. Although most target shooters were satisfied with well-made arms, especially when they were capable of deadly accuracy at extreme ranges, not a few marksmen, as well as sportsmen-hunters, yearned for beautiful appointments, and the practice of presenting gifts of fine guns gained in popularity. Whoever the client, the temptation was always there to order rifles or shotguns that were as beautifully decorated as they were capable of straight shooting. The best of these arms played a significant role in making this period the golden age of American gunmaking.

Single-Shot Rifles

Single-shot rifles such as the Sharps, Marlin, Remington, Stevens, Winchester, Frank Wesson, Wurfflein, Peabody, Peabody-Martini, Maynard, Whitney & Phoenix, Hopkins & Allen, Farrow, and Bullard are relics of the great days of formal and informal target shooting from the second half of the nineteenth century. A major

shooting match then would win the sort of attention shown today to a World Series baseball game.

As a theme of collector passion, the single shots attract enthusiasts whose interests cross the boundaries of makers, calibers, or other differentiations likely to be evident in other collecting categories. Many single-shot specialists pursue all makes, or particular types of actions, or only customized rifles, and so on. Because of the breadth of regions in which these rifles were made, their engraving styles are often quite distinctive.

Sharps

The demand for arms during the Civil War meant that engraving at the Sharps factory, Hartford, Connecticut, took a backseat to regular production. Surprisingly, although the firm did produce an occasional engraved arm in wartime, the Confederacy created a fine Sharps of its own; and certainly among the most rare of embellished arms are Southern-made guns for the Confederate States of America, which bore engraving. An example of this luxury is a copy of a Sharps rifle made by S. C. Robinson, of Richmond, number 1642, embellished with Gustave Young–style scrollwork, though executed with a

lower level of artistry. Nevertheless, the embellishments, checkered stocks included, demonstrate the desire and spirit of the newly formed nation.

Some years following the war, advertised models of Sharps rifles with engraving as a standard feature began to appear. In the 1876 company catalogue the Long Range Rifle No. 1 was offered with "solid sterling silver inscription plate, engraved to order." The January 1877 catalogue alerted the public with a generalized reference: "Special arms of either calibre .40, .44, .45 or .50, of any weight or length, made and engraved to order." The Long Range Rifle No. 1 continued to be offered with the sterling silver inscription plate, and under the notation "Orders, Etc." ran a paragraph encouraging deluxe embellishments:

> Monograms, animals and other designs elegantly engraved on our arms, the price for which is governed by the time occupied in its execution. Customers can order engraving to the amount of $5, $10, $15, $20, or more, as desired. Engraving can be done only on new work, and before the parts are case-hardened.

The 1878 catalogue announced the forthcoming Sharps

Only a handful of Spencer repeating rifles were engraved, and this one, by L. D. Nimschke, for presentation to company president Frank Cheney, 1868, is the finest known example. Other side of frame depicted Union soldier confronting five Confederates, and defeating them, with his Spencer rifle—a scene used by company in several catalogues. Bearing no serial number, Cheney's prize is one of three cased Spencers known. Prints on page 52 of Nimschke record book.

double-barrel shotgun, and went on to specifically list engraving for the Model 1878 (Sharps-Borchardt) Mid-Range Rifle and Long Range Rifle, and repeated the paragraph as above. Under "Orders, etc." the catalogue stated: "If extras are wanted, state them in detail." The June 1879 Sharps catalogue continued the listing as above, and for the Hunter's Rifle, the Business Rifle, and the Sporting Rifle (all Model 1878) indicated: "Special arms of any weight or length made and engraved to order." The Mid-Range Rifle, Model 1878, "In extra finish, fancy wood stock, engraving, etc.," was listed at $150. Finally, the Long Range Rifle, Model 1878, was available at the highest price in the catalogue: "... to order, with extra fancy Italian stock, engraving, and extra finish ... $125.00 to 300.00."

L. D. Nimschke was a frequent source of engraving for the Sharps Rifle Company. His record book illustrates prints from Sharps longarms on pages 24, 70–71, and 93. Correspondence and other documentation concerning Nimschke and the company has survived. Some of his most inspired artistry appears on the Sharps-Borchardt and the Model 1877 rifles. On the former, the hard rubber sideplates might be embellished as well.

Customized Sharps-Borchardts by A. A. Kellogg of New Haven offered another steel canvas; some of these fine guns have gold sideplates, and some steel. In contrast, a rustic decoration on Sharps arms, and on a variety of other makes, was accomplished by Native Americans, who often hammered brass or iron tacks onto the stocks.

Due to the competition from makers of large-caliber lever-action repeaters—particularly Winchester—the Sharps Rifle Company went out of business in 1881. A move from Hartford to Bridgeport in 1876 had failed to save the company, just thirty-one years old when the end came.

Sharps Customized by the Freunds and Others

The Freund brothers, Frank and Joseph, rank high in the annals of American fine guns. Their customizing of rifles

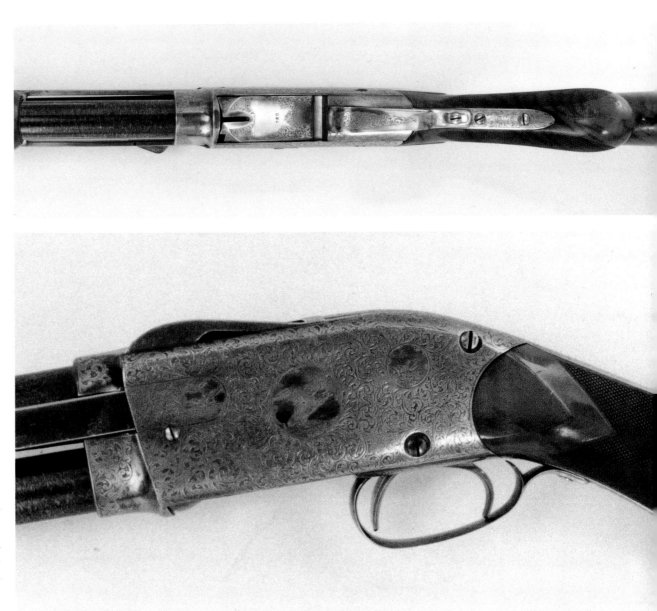

Spencer pump shotgun, c. 1884, made for Porfirio Díaz; serial no. 280. Plated in gold and with damascus-twist barrel. Panel scenes appear to be plated or inlaid in silver. Hartford engraver Robert Steel is credited by Spencer authority Roy Marcot as having embellished a similar shotgun in the early 1880s. Still another such gun was made for Spencer himself, and another for his wife; both were engraved.

Sharps Model 1874 Long Range Target Rifle No. 1, special order; engraved by L. D. Nimschke for factory. Shipping records indicate "special order," and tested for perfection by factory superintendent. Won as a shooting prize by W. L. Ellison, Kansas City, Missouri, February 1879.

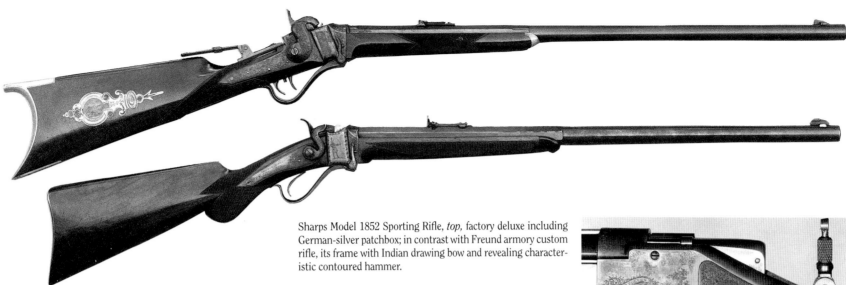

Sharps Model 1852 Sporting Rifle, *top,* factory deluxe including German-silver patchbox; in contrast with Freund armory custom rifle, its frame with Indian drawing bow and revealing characteristic contoured hammer.

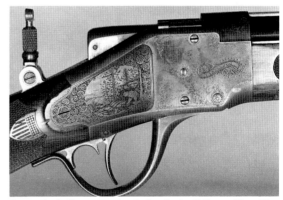

Customized Sharps-Borchardt by A. A. Kellogg; Nimschke-engraved, with blued-steel sideplates. Fancy stocks of Winchester quality, brass-inlaid horn buttplate, escutcheon inlay on stock bottom of gold and silver, and engraved brass pistol-grip cap; c. 1880.

was a specialty part of their larger operation of selling guns and ammunition. Freund armories were located in Denver and Cheyenne, and a relatively few guns were custom-made in Jersey City, New Jersey. Grades of Sharps rifles with engraving were the Famous American Frontier, the Boss Gun, the Model 1877, and the Wyoming Saddle Gun. The latter was a special rifle entirely built by Freund, whereas the others were customized Sharps. Two Model 1877 rifles were made for Theodore Roosevelt by F. W. Freund in Jersey City, and engraved by L. D. Nimschke. Prints from these rifles appear on pages 83–85 of the Nimschke record.

Another gunmaker who customized Sharps rifles and other factory-made arms was Charles Schlotterbeck, of Philadelphia (where he was employed by Henry Deringer) and later California. A trademark of his work was a bow-and-arrow motif inlaid on the buttstock. His brother Henry was also known to have customized Sharps arms.

J. Stevens and Frank Wesson

Stevens factory production was centered in Chicopee Falls, Massachusetts, beginning in 1864. As the location was somewhat remote, embellishments tended to be provincial. Those few engraved J. Stevens arms usually present a rather naïve vine scroll (with or without beaded background), or a scroll appearing similar to a student's exercise book for penmanship. The latter style is represented on a deluxe .22 target rifle made for Annie Oakley. Some scrolls included floral motifs. The game scenes appear unsophisticated.

On the other hand, Stevens arms were occasionally engraved by the omnipresent Nimschke. Examples appear in his record book on pages 21, 27, and 68. A Stevens target pistol he embellished for presentation by Buffalo Bill Cody to shootist Ben Thompson is pictured, along with the Oakley .22, on page 216.

Frank Wesson rifles, produced in both Worcester and Springfield, Massachusetts, have been observed with Nimschke engraving, or similar beaded background American-style scroll and border decor. A Wesson rifle in the Royal Armoury in Madrid bears Nimschke scrolls, borders, and decorative devices, and a monogram of Maria Cristina of Austria, second wife of Alfonso XII,

Annie Oakley's Stevens presentation rifle, with distinctive factory scroll style; see also page 216.

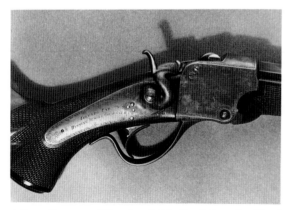

A Freund's armory "Wyoming Saddle Gun." Opposite side of frame gold-inlaid with CK monogram.

Nimschke-engraved Frank Wesson rifle, for Queen Maria Cristina of Spain. Note signature on left side of frame; also royal cipher and three-dimensional scrolls.

King of Spain (who reigned 1874–85). Nimschke's record book, page 2, recorded that rifle with the simple note: "*Aug. 1882 Queen of Spain.*"

Ballard Rifles

In the thirty years of Ballard production, which commenced in about 1861, hundreds of handsomely engraved rifles were built. Not a few of the grades of sporting rifles were advertised with engraving as standard: among these were the No. 6 Scheutzen Rifle (scrollwork, borders, and game scenes), the No. 6½ Rigby Off-Hand Mid Range (scrollwork, borders, and game scenes), the No. 6½ Off-Hand (scrolls), the No. 7 Long Range (scroll and game scenes), the No. 7 Creedmoor A-1 Long Range (scrollwork with inscribed BALLARD A-1 on the left side and LONG RANGE on right), the No. 7 A-1 Long Range (scrolls with inscribed BALLARD A-1 on left side and LONG RANGE on right), and the No. 7 A-1 Extra Long Range (deluxe, profuse scroll and game motifs). Stocks for the engraved rifles were in degrees of deluxe according to the rifle's grade.

Judging from style and quality of engraving, some of America's finest craftsmen decorated Ballard arms. L. D. Nimschke's record book features Ballards on pages 26, 28, 76, 77, and 86, showing differing coverages, styles, game scenes, and inscriptions. A signed Ballard rifle of c. 1872, made by Brown Manufacturing Company, Newburyport, Massachusetts, bore the signature L.D.N. on the frame bottom. Some of the large lettering on the frames is quite decorative. One might speculate that Nimschke's vivid imagination in design could well have contributed to the use of the large lettered inscriptions on the frame sides of some models.

Since the J. M. Marlin and (later) the Marlin Firearms Company took over manufacture of the Ballard rifles beginning in 1870, it is reasonable to attribute their engraving to Marlin engravers the likes of C. F. Ulrich. Scrolls, borders, lettering, and game scenes are often related to contemporary decoration on Winchester firearms.

Battle of Bunker Hill on Peabody-Martini single-shot, a display piece at Philadelphia Centennial Exposition. Note: some Peabody-Martini engraved rifles are known signed on the cocking indicator by an N. J. Wolcott; details as yet are sketchy. However, the style and quality of the Bunker Hill rifle appear to be distinctly Gustave Young.

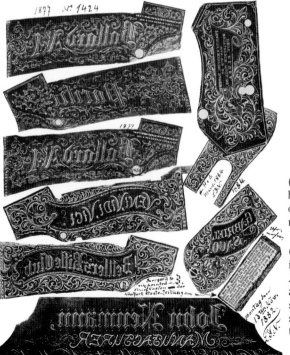

(*above*) Allen & Wheelock rifle, from page 8 of Nimschke record book. Dog-and-stag scene repeated by Nimschke on other makes of arms, including Henry, Winchester Model 1866, and Ballard rifles.

(*left*) Page 76 from Nimschke record, one of five presenting impressions from Ballard rifles. Such regional gunmakers as John Meunier, of Milwaukee, often had German roots and were active in Schutzenfests and Schutzenvereins, continuing target-shooting traditions from homeland. Meunier's rifles retained a strong flavor of Germany, including heavy stock-carving, though their engraving had American flavor.

The Philadelphia Centennial Exposition

In their concerted efforts to impress the millions of Centennial visitors, gunmakers often featured deluxe engraved firearms. One of the surprises of the exhibition was that what was perhaps the most dramatic and striking of the displays came not from a major manufacturer—such as Colt, Winchester, Remington, Sharps, or Smith & Wesson—but from the Providence Tool Company, of Providence, Rhode Island. Their major rifle was the Peabody-Martini breechloader, first made in the 1860s, which, to the engraver's advantage, offered large and flat panels on each side of the frame.

Providence Tool had at least two sporting rifles decorated by the master engraver Gustave Young, and these guns were finished with such perfection that they must be ranked among the true masterpieces of the engraver's art in America. The premier specimen was cut with a miniature banknote-quality copy of John Trumbull's well-known panoramic painting *The Battle of Bunker Hill.* Young's detail included every single segment of the original, down to coat buttons and tricornered hats.

Young created a masterwork from what would otherwise have been a rather ordinary, even unattractive, firearm. In this panel scene the proud immigrant proved his mastery of steel and his patriotism to America. The superb detail, reduced from the wall-sized original to approximately a two-by-three-inch rectangle, required a sure eye and a steady hand, and the utmost of concentration. Each line was cut with a handheld burin, carefully scrutinized through the eyepiece magnifier worn by the patient craftsman. Probably over 120 hours were required to complete the battle scene alone.

Young's "Battle of Bunker Hill," with its rich scroll and curved-line borders, is indisputably a masterpiece of the arms engraver's craft. Few, if any, of his contemporaries could have equaled this accomplishment. Those hundreds of thousands of persons who saw the rifle at

Springfield Armory engraved Trapdoor Officer's Models *at top and bottom.* Note superior finesse and crisper detail in C. F. Ulrich scroll and game scene on Marlin Model 1881 rifle. Running buffalo with folk-art style.

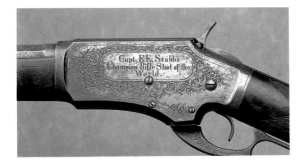

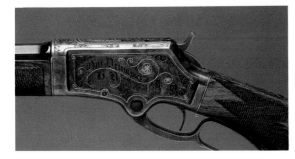

(*top left*) Factory presentation to Captain Stubbs, one of several professional shooters of the day who contributed to national rage for guns and shooting. The C.F. probably engraved by C. F. Ulrich.

(*center and bottom left*) Early example of gold inlaying and engraving by C. F. Ulrich, on Marlin Model 1881. Drummer modeled on an employee—believed to be either Cyrus McCormick or William Deering—who was probably an accomplished salesman.

(*right*) Factory-engraved, gold-inlaid Marlins. Clearly in evidence is the style and influence of C. F. Ulrich, who was, in turn, inspired by Gustave Young. Guns verify role Marlin deserves in American tradition of excellence in gunmaking. Among clients of deluxe Marlins: Porfirio Díaz.

Special High Grade
MARLIN REPEATERS

Manufactured by
THE MARLIN FIRE ARMS CO.
NEW HAVEN, CONN. U.S.A.

CUT OF : : :
MODEL 1894 RIFLE
ILLUSTRATING OUR NO. 2 ENGRAVING

Receiver, barrel, forearm tip and butt plate engraved with scroll engraving.
Reverse side as illustrated on opposite page.

Extra list for No. 2 engraving : : : $10.00

The stock illustrates in part our No. D checking. This is one of our styles of checking for extra selected stocks and forearms with special checking.

Extra list for pistol grip stock and forearm of extra selected walnut, extra finely finished with this checking : : : $20.00

NO. 5 ENGRAVING

CUT OF : : :
MODEL 1893 TAKE DOWN
ILLUSTRATING OUR NO. 5 ENGRAVING

Receiver elaborately engraved with scrolls and figures in relief.
Barrel, forearm tip and butt plate engraved.

Extra list for No. 5 engraving : : : $25.00

On the opposite page will be observed the reverse side, showing a slightly different type of engraving of this grade.

The checking is as previously illustrated—our No. B checking.

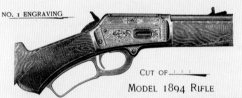

CUT OF : : :
MODEL 1894 RIFLE

Illustrating rifle with plain walnut pistol grip stock, checked on grip and fore-end. Our No. A checking.

A pistol grip stock is considered by most people as a distinct addition to the rifle as regards facility and convenience in handling, while adding to the beauty. The extra expense of a pistol grip stock has been too great for the average purchaser, as it is in many cases made up with selected wood only. This grade of rifle is put at such a slight extra cost that it is within reach of everybody desiring a pistol grip stock.

As in all cases we offer stocks with rubber shot-gun butt plates at the same prices as these with metal rifle butt plates.

Extra list for pistol grip stock and forearm of plain walnut, with this checking : : : $5.00

NO. 2 ENGRAVING

For description see opposite page.

These pictures illustrate some of the variations in center pictures.

21   22   23

If any particular picture is preferred please mention the special number in addition to the number of engraving.

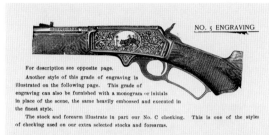

NO. 5 ENGRAVING

For description see opposite page.

Another style of this grade of engraving is illustrated on the following page. This style of engraving can also be furnished with a monogram or initials in place of the scene, the same heavily embossed and executed in the finest style.

The stock and forearm illustrate in part our No. C checking. This is one of the styles of checking used on our extra selected stocks and forearms.

Extra list for pistol grip stock and forearm of extra selected walnut, extra finely finished, with this checking : : : $20.00

NO. 1 ENGRAVING

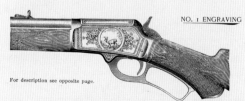

CUT OF ____
MODEL 1894 RIFLE
ILLUSTRATING OUR NO. 1 ENGRAVING

Receiver engraved with scroll engraving.
Reverse side as illustrated on opposite page.

Extra list for No. 1 engraving : : : $5.00

The rifle illustrated is with round barrel. This is one of our regular rifles, not take-down. The stock and forearm illustrate in part of our No. B checking.

NO. 3 ENGRAVING

CUT OF ____
MODEL 1893 TAKE DOWN
ILLUSTRATING OUR NO. 3 ENGRAVING

Receiver embossed; barrel, forearm tip and butt plate engraved.
Reverse side as illustrated on opposite page.

Extra list for No. 3 engraving : : : $15.00

The stock and forearm illustrate in part our No. B checking. This is our regular style of checking for stocks and forearms of selected walnut.

Extra list for pistol grip stock and forearm of selected walnut, with this checking, $15.00

NO. 5 ENGRAVING

CUT OF : : :
MODEL 1894 RIFLE
ILLUSTRATING OUR NO. 5 ENGRAVING

Receiver elaborately engraved with scrolls in relief.
Barrel, forearm tip and butt plate engraved.

Extra list for No. 5 engraving : : : $25.00

This represents our full scroll engraving of this grade. In all grades full scroll engraving will be furnished if preferred.

The checking illustrated is our No. G checking.

NO. 1 ENGRAVING

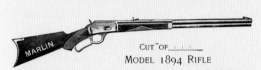

For description see opposite page.

For a person desiring an engraved rifle at a moderate extra expense we can recommend this grade very highly. The engraving is neat and adds greatly to the appearance of the rifle. Variations are of course made in center pictures and style of scrolls but these illustrations give a good idea of the engraving of this grade. In case any particular animal is desired we can in most cases substitute it.

NO. 3 ENGRAVING

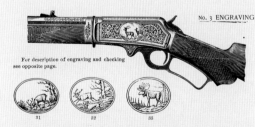

For description of engraving and checking see opposite page.

31   32   33

These pictures illustrate some of the variations in center pictures. In case any particular center picture is desired, please designate by the numbers under the special pictures.

NO. 5 ENGRAVING

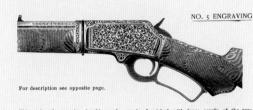

For description see opposite page.

This style of engraving in this grade can be furnished with large scrolls of the type illustrated or with smaller as may be preferred.

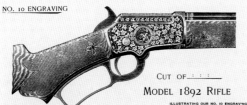

NO. 10 ENGRAVING

CUT OF ———

MODEL 1892 RIFLE

ILLUSTRATING OUR NO. 10 ENGRAVING

Receiver elaborately embossed with figures and design in relief. Pearl background. Barrel, forearm tip and butt plate similarly engraved. Receiver, barrel and forearm tip inlaid with platinum lines.

Extra list for No. 10 engraving : : : **$50.00**

It will be observed that the stock and forearm have special checking to harmonize with the grape leaf design on the receiver.

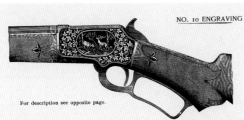

NO. 10 ENGRAVING

For description see opposite page.

This grade will, of course, be furnished in various designs. If desired the pictures will be omitted, and instead of the same may be substituted names and monograms in relief or inlaid with platinum. The general body design will be varied as far as possible to agree with any special instructions which may be furnished.

SPECIAL DESIGNS

We have engraved many rifles with special designs, from photographs or pictures and in some cases from heads of animals.

The cut on the opposite page gives only a meagre representation of one of these rifles.

The receiver is handsomely embossed, the figures, scrolls, and even the leaves and grass standing out in bold relief. The barrel is handsomely engraved. The forearm tip, butt plate and screw heads are all embossed with scrolls, while the above mentioned parts, as well as the hammer and lever, are inlaid with scroll lines of platinum and gold. The hammer and lever are also slightly engraved.

This makes a most handsome scene, and the beauty of the engraving is never dimmed by use owing to the fact of the figures being in such bold relief.

The reverse side is engraved in the same style; also the trigger plate, the top of the action and in short all the metal parts.

Extra list for engraving of this style : : : **$75.00**

CUT ILLUSTRATING RECEIVER PORTION OF OUR $75.00 LIST ENGRAVING

For description see opposite page.

The reverse side is engraved in the same manner with some scene represented on the receiver or lower part, while the breech bolt is handsomely engraved with scrolls in relief. If desired a monogram will be embossed in place of the scene or in the center of the breech bolt. If desired the monogram or initials will be executed in platinum instead of in relief as usual.

ENGRAVING AND INLAYING.

The effect of finely engraved work is often heightened by neat inlaying with platinum and gold. On this work we have made no regular prices, as it of course varies with the taste of the purchaser and character of the design. It will be observed that in all grades from our No. 10 upwards that inlaying is included as a part of the engraving.

In other grades, however, this may be added at moderate additional expense in case extra ornamentation and designs are desired, especially if required to show with greater prominence, as, for instance, initials, insignia, etc. Simple scrolls on butt plate, forearm tip, and lever add considerably to the appearance of a nicely engraved and highly finished rifle.

STYLES OF CHECKING.

No. A. This is the checking used on plain pistol grip stocks and forearms. This checking is amply illustrated in the first illustration of this book showing our pistol grip rifle. It may also be seen in the cut of the pistol grip take-down described on inside of back cover.

The extra list for plain pistol grip stock and forearm with our No. A checking is $5.00.

FANCY CHECKING ON SELECTED STOCKS.

 No. B. This cut illustrates our No. B checking which is the regular style of fine checking used on our rifles with selected walnut stock and forearm (either straight or pistol grip stock). The stocks will be found fully illustrated on preceding pages.

The extra list for selected pistol grip stock and forearm with No. B checking is $15.00.

SPECIAL CHECKING ON EXTRA SELECTED STOCKS.

The following are a few of the special checkings used on our extra selected stocks with special checking. These illustrations represent a few of the main styles which are varied from time to time, in view of the design of the engraving and special ornamentation which may be desired. The illustrations show only the forearm. It will be observed, however, from the preceding pages that the checking on the stock is exactly like that of the forearm.

The extra list for extra selected pistol grip stock and forearm with special checking is $20.00.

No. C.   No. D.

No. E. In this style, circles filled with extra fine checking are substituted for the diamond of No. D. In other respects the checking is exactly like No. D.

No. F. This is a combination of Nos. B and D. The diamond, however, is much larger than in D and there is but one covering the whole front of the forearm instead of one small diamond on each side of the forearm.

No. G. In this style the band is continued unbroken around the forearm. It is our No. B checking with addition of band.

EXTRA SPECIAL.

Our illustration of No. 10 engraving shows a stock and forearm, specially checked to accord with the grape leaf design of the engraving. In guns of this grade such extra special checking is considered a part of the engraving design, and there is no further charge over that quoted above for extra selected stocks with special checking.

SPECIAL RIFLES MADE TO ORDER.

There are many people who desire a rifle made with the same care, as regards length of stock, drop and other measurements, as they demand in the case of their shot-guns. We have always been prepared to make rifles with special length and drop of stock to order, but we have paid especial attention to this work of late in connection with our fancy engraved rifles with special stocks, etc. There is no reason why a person procuring a high grade rifle should not have the stock made to personal measurements as in the case of his shot-gun.

We are confident that any one ordering a rifle made expressly to his measurements will be thoroughly satisfied with the same, and will find that the slight extra expense is more than justified by the extra comfort he can obtain in using the rifle. It will of course be an excellent feature that a person can obtain a rifle and shot-gun with exactly the same length and drop of stock.

The extra list price for variations from the regular standards of length and drop of stock is $10.00.

GRIFFITH, HOLYOKE, MASS.

The Finest and Most Perfectly Balanced Repeater

for hunting purposes is the Marlin Take-down with half-octagon barrel, half-magazine and pistol grip stock with rubber butt plate.

Only $10.00 list, extra.

$5.00 for the Take-down; $5.00 for plain pistol grip stock checked.

Fancy pistol grip stock at extra prices quoted on preceding pages.

Marlin's engraving catalogue, published 1896 and thus predating Winchester's Highly Finished Arms by a year. Compare with complete catalogue, published in chapter III of the author's *Winchester: An American Legend.*

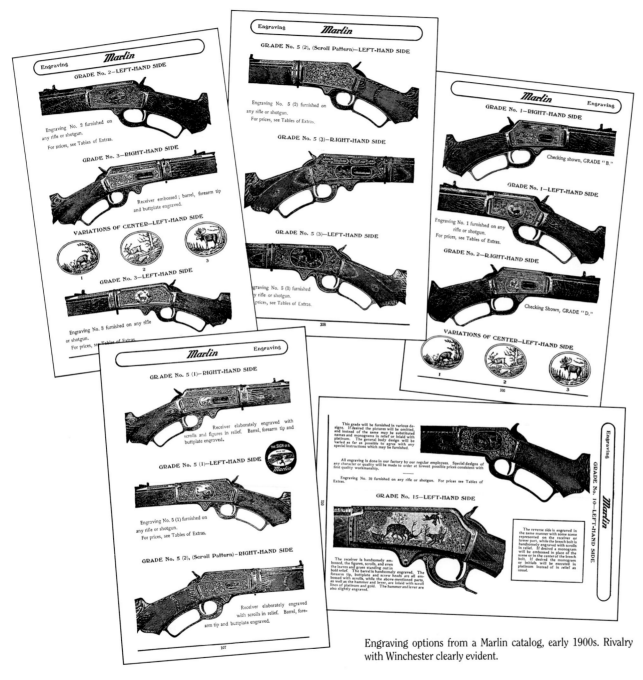

Engraving options from a Marlin catalog, early 1900s. Rivalry with Winchester clearly evident.

the 1876 Centennial Exposition admired the complete perfection of every detail. The perfectly executed perspective gave a true three-dimensional appearance to the scene. Costumes, anatomy, and every other feature were faultless.

Young carefully allowed breathing space around the scene, by engraving C-shaped border motifs that held the large scrolls in place as if they were ocean waves. Had the scrolls and borders been closer to the battle scene, much of the effect of atmosphere and depth would have been lost. His final triumph was to cut the scrolls and C-borders in a pattern that while forming the perfect oval to show off the Bunker Hill scene also reduced the ugly appearance of the humpbacked profile of the gun's frame at its top.

The other side of the rifle bore matching scroll and border layouts and a female figure representing prosperity and peace. In her left hand was a statue of Mercury, the messenger of the Roman gods as well as the god associated with cleverness, travel, commerce, eloquence, manual skill, and thievery. As in the Bunker Hill panel scene, the detail and quality were exquisite. The Providence Tool Company's patronage of Young resulted in not only one of the great American decorated firearms of all time, but a perfectly designed statement of the firm's patriotism, its hope for America's future, and its pride in its own fine craftsmanship and inventiveness.

Among other examples of richly engraved Peabody-Martinis is a superb Kill Deer model, probably engraved by Gustave Young, as are a Creedmoor Long Range, and two What Cheer Long Range rifles. These handsome pieces may well have been part of Providence Tool Company's Centennial Exposition display, along with the "Battle of Bunker Hill" rifle. Fine rifles built with inscribed frames revealing their model designation were the Creedmoor, the What Cheer, the Creedmoor Mid Range, the Kill Deer, and the Rough and Ready.

Other Makers

Engraved Allen & Wheelock single-shot rifles are quite rare. A .44-rimfire example exists, another fine Nimschke

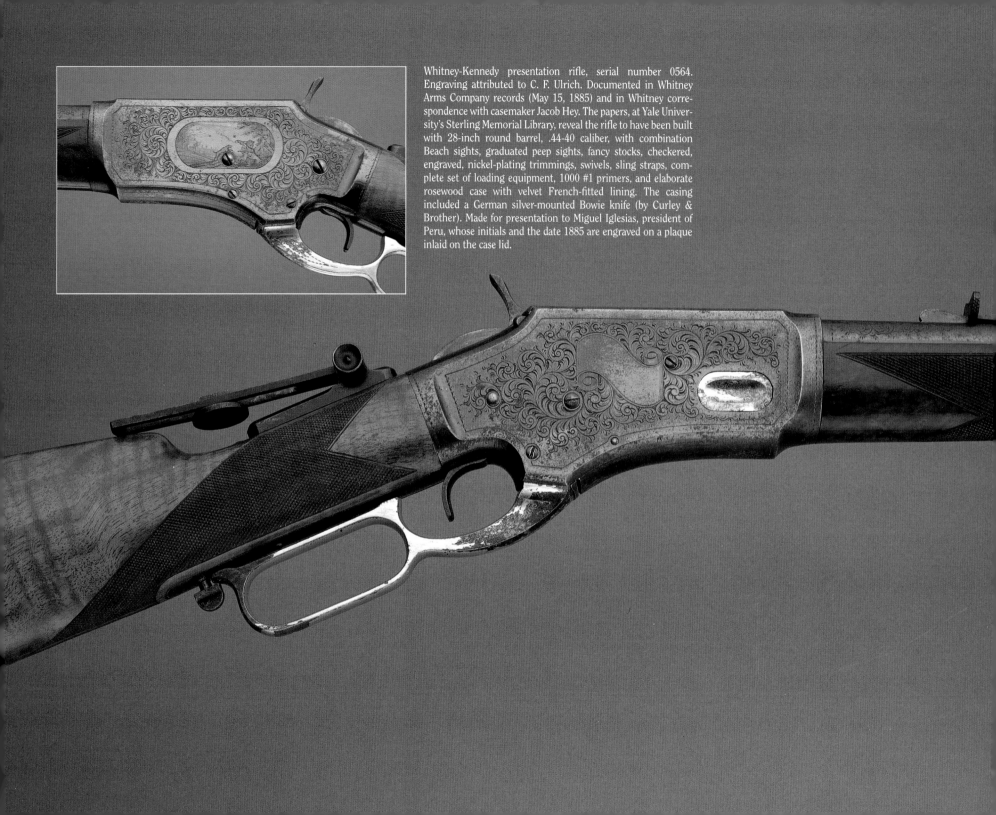

Whitney-Kennedy presentation rifle, serial number 0564. Engraving attributed to C. F. Ulrich. Documented in Whitney Arms Company records (May 15, 1885) and in Whitney correspondence with casemaker Jacob Hey. The papers, at Yale University's Sterling Memorial Library, reveal the rifle to have been built with 28-inch round barrel, .44-40 caliber, with combination Beach sights, graduated peep sights, fancy stocks, checkered, engraved, nickel-plating trimmings, swivels, sling straps, complete set of loading equipment, 1000 #1 primers, and elaborate rosewood case with velvet French-fitted lining. The casing included a German silver-mounted Bowie knife (by Curley & Brother). Made for presentation to Miguel Iglesias, president of Peru, whose initials and the date 1885 are engraved on a plaque inlaid on the case lid.

piece with game scenes and profuse scrollwork, bearing the serial number 2. Clear prints of what appears to be that rifle are on Nimschke's record book, on page 8; still another Nimschke-engraved Allen & Wheelock rifle is on page 10, and another can be found on pages 21 and 27.

Maynard rifles were finely constructed, though the tip-up action is not as attractive in form as many of its contemporaries. Production ran from the 1860s into the 1890s, in Chicopee Falls, at the Massachusetts Arms Company. Engraved Maynards are rare; among the few known is a Gustave Young–style percussion Sporting Rifle, with a game panel scene.

Marlin

During the period c. 1875–1913 most of the engraving on Marlin firearms was done by Conrad F. Ulrich. While brother John's artistry would dominate Winchester's engraving into the early twentieth century, C.F. occupied the same role at Marlin. A capstone of his creativity was the publication in 1896 of the advertising booklet, Special High Grade Marlin Repeaters. This minute, twenty-four-page pocket catalogue preceded by fifteen months the more elaborate thirty-page Winchester catalogue of 1897, Highly Finished Arms.

Measuring a mere 3⅝ by 5¹⁵⁄₁₆ inches, Marlin's booklet was free of charge, as noted in their August 1896 products catalogue: "If interested send for Book of Illustrations showing engraving and checking."

Marlin rated the grades of engraving from the minimum basic style No. 1, to grades No. 2, No. 3, No. 5, No. 10, and a top category they designated "Special Designs." Winchester, as would be expected, rated their engraving with Style No. 1 at the top, and then went down the scale with coverage decreasing as the numbers increased: 1 through 10.

In stockwork, Marlin offered styles A, B, C, D, E, F, G, and "Extra Special," the A-grade being their lowest-ranked pattern, and "Extra Special" their most deluxe. Winchester stock style designations were, again, the inverse: Winchester's A-grade was its fanciest and "H" its least fancy. In between were styles B, C, D, E, F, and G.

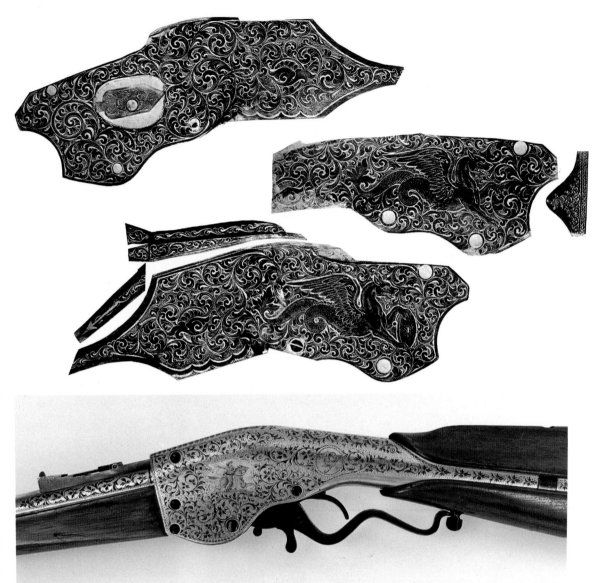

(*top*) Pulls by Nimschke from Evans Rifles embellished by him, and pictured on page 66 of his scrapbook.

(*bottom*) Evans lever-action repeating rifle, made for Porfirio Díaz, and with rare combination of engraving, enameling, and gold plating. Panels include PD monogram, mounted vaquero, Mexican eagle and snake, hunting dog, and hunter.

(*opposite*) Compare scrolls on Warner Civil War carbine *at top* (Ulrich flavor), and Remington Rolling Block *at center* (factory Nimschke-influenced decor), to Savage Model 99 of the 1980s (with even heavier Germanic influence than its nineteenth-century companions).

230

The dissimilarity stops as soon as the illustrations in the two publications are compared. The work of brothers John and C. F. Ulrich both show the profound influence of the master Gustave Young.

Highly Finished Arms and Special High Grade Marlin Repeaters are the only catalogues published up to that time by American gunmakers that were devoted solely to deluxe engraving and stockwork. These two rarities in firearms literature are also the first published works of Ulrich engraving. But at the time (c. 1896–97) no reference whatever was made in the catalogues to the identities of the craftsmen themselves.

Fortunately for both John and C. F. Ulrich, they were permitted by Winchester to sign their work. Not so at Marlin, and this writer has yet to observe a signed Marlin engraved piece from this period, nor had the late authority Lt. Colonel William S. Brophy.

Bullard Arms

Made in limited numbers from c. 1886 through 1890, the invention of James H. Bullard was unable to compete with the mighty Winchester and Marlin lever actions, and only a few thousand Bullard lever-action repeaters and single-shot rifles were made. A handful were engraved, the most stunning of these being a small-frame lever action decorated by Gustave Young and presented by the inventor to D. B. Wesson. A Bullard repeater with gold plaque inlay on the stock belonged to rancher Theodore Roosevelt; the motif was probably engraved with a game animal of a species T.R. intended to hunt with the rifle, which was of .50-115 caliber. An 1887 Bullard catalogue listed under "Extras" engraving work priced from five to one hundred dollars, "according to style." Special stockwork was also offered.

E. Remington & Sons, *et al.*

With the introduction of the rolling-block mechanism in the mid-1860s, Remington had a product that would sell in quantities totaling over 1,000,000 into the early twentieth century. But unlike Colt and Winchester, two of its chief rivals, Remington showed little interest in catering

Exquisite gold-inlaid Remington Rolling Block shotgun, made as showpiece in Liege, for Samuel Remington's use in Europe; features American eagle and shield device on top of breech; profuse inlays in gold and platinum. Rifle finest known deluxe model in Rolling Block series; formerly in Remington Gun Museum. Profuse factory engraving; nickel and blue finish; believed similar to presentation made by factory to Lt. Colonel George Armstrong Custer.

(*top and bottom left*) This page from the Nimschke record book shows his use of signature on frame side of Rolling Block (concealed beneath frame plate), and his mastery of layout and scrolls.

Advertising illustration used by Remington factory in promotion of new hammer shotgun, Model of 1882.

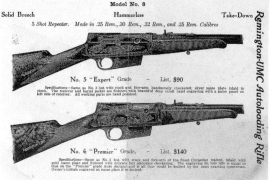

Factory catalogue of pre–World War I vintage, showing two of the fancy grades of the Model 8 autoloader rifle.

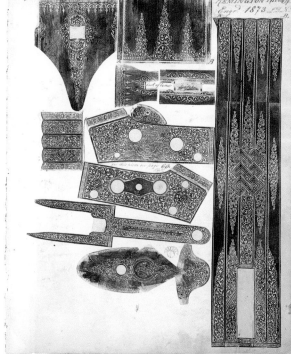

(*right*) Remington shotgun *at top* attributed to Wilbur Glahn, though style is in marked contrast to floral, leaf, and vine scroll on Colt automatic pistol slide *at bottom;* latter characteristic of his post-1919 work at Colt factory.

MODEL 16
MONARCH GRA

Calibers 25-35, 30-30, 303, 32-40 and 38-55.
The Monarch Rifle has a beauty of design distinctly
own, due to the graceful ivy leaf pattern, which is repr
highest degree of the engraver's and carver's
refully selected Circassian Walnut, ever t
brought out to clean finish.

SAVAGE

to the decorative wants of its clientele. Nevertheless, some handsome and distinctive arms were engraved by the factory, and L. D. Nimschke played a role in them.

Factory-engraved rolling-block rifles are among the most rarely encountered of all Remington firearms. Buffalo Bill Cody is pictured with a deluxe rifled musket, plated and engraved, in a publicity photograph for the stage from the late 1860s. A gun similar to that piece is illustrated, as is one of Nimschke's most elaborate longarms.

Remington factory catalogues make few references to engraving and plating. Therefore much of the informa-

S&W Double Barrel Shotgun, serial no. 1, made c. 1868 (prior to regular production) for presentation; thus, combination of DBW (D. B. Wesson) script monogram within shield motif on upper tang. Monogram CE (unidentified) intertwined on gold escutcheon inlaid on bottom of buttstock. Engraving by Gustave Young, with coverage on barrel breech, hammers, frame, barrel-release lever, triggerguard, forend mounts, and skeleton-style buttplate. Walnut stocks with rosewood insets.

Theodore Roosevelt was the proud owner of mid-1880s Edwin Thomas, Jr., Chicago, 10-gauge side-by-side shotgun; popular English scroll. Often fine shotguns of period were made in England or Belgium, but marked with American gun dealers' names for sale in United States. T.R. was such an enthusiast of fine guns that he wrote his sister Anna from the Dakota Badlands, August 1884, about setting off on an extended hunt: "I now look like a regular cowboy dandy, with all my equipments finished in the most expensive style." Among guns on trip was the Thomas shotgun, a Model 1873 Winchester deluxe, three deluxe Model 1876 Winchesters, a fancy Bullard repeating rifle, an L. C. Smith ranch gun, a Kennedy shotgun, and a Webley (English) double-barrel Express rifle.

Savage Model 99s engraved by Enoch Tue, an Englishman who had apprenticed with the London gunmakers, Churchill, and is known to have been Savage's master engraver from about 1900 to 1916. The Savage Arms Company catalogue for 1900 advertised engraving patterns in grades A, B, C, D, E, F, and G, and variations in stocks, with the most elaborate identified as "Extra Fancy Circassian Walnut . . ." The two rifles superposed are of grade D; those *below, from left,* are the Monarch (the company's superior grade) with gold-inlaid barrel bands, a G grade, and an F grade. Tue is estimated to have engraved not more than 600 guns in his tenure at the Savage factory.

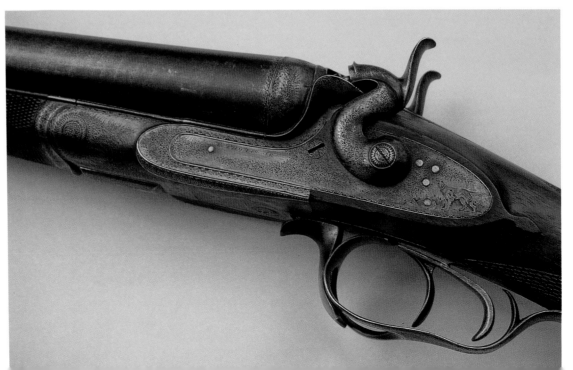

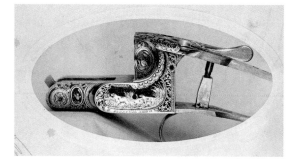

(*top*) Gunmaker's pulls attributed to Jacob Glahn, from various examples of his shotgun work; mainly receivers and trigger-guards; late nineteenth century.

(*bottom left*) Receiver from a Syracuse Arms Company shotgun; by one of the Glahns. Rare early photo, taken before parts finished and assembled. Blackening agent rubbed into lines for contrast.

From *Fur, Fin and Feather* magazine (1875). Most firearms engravers operated under their own names; the company name on the bold ad was quite out of the ordinary.

tion on the subject has been gleaned from surviving firearms, a few engraved pieces in the factory museum in Ilion, New York, and Nimschke's record book.

Remington's Model 1882 shotgun was advertised in six grades initially, with engraving of English style on the higher grades. The models that followed all offered hand embellishments, including the hammer types of 1883, 1885, 1887, and 1889, and the hammerless Models of 1894 and 1900. Owen De Lange, whose career at Remington began in 1880, is known to have engraved lockplates for Remington shotguns, and engraver Joe Loy joined the firm around 1895. Identities of other company engravers of the period remain unknown.

Only with their autoloaders and slide actions does the firm begin to show sustained interest in embellishment, and the Remington catalogues pictured some quite elegant and handsome examples. Some of the finest decorated Remington firearms were made after the introduction of the early model repeating shotguns, in the period up into the 1930s.

L. C. Smith Shotguns

The recognition given L. C. Smith shotguns needs to be tempered somewhat by the fact that four different firms manufactured these arms. In sequence, they are: (from 1877) W. H. Baker & Co., Syracuse, New York; (from c. 1890) the Hunter Arms Company, Fulton, New York; (from c. 1945) the L. C. Smith Gun Company, acquired by Marlin Firearms Company in 1945; and (from c. 1949) the Marlin Firearms Company.

For the period starting c. 1890, the special grades of L. C. Smith shotguns were—in descending order, starting with the most elaborate—the DeLuxe, the Premier, the Monogram (of 1913 and later), the A3 Monogram (pre-1913), the A2 Crown, the 5 Eagle, the A1 Gladiator, the 4 Whippet, the Pigeon Premier Skeet, and the three Trap models: the 1 Olympic, the 0 Ideal, and the 00 Field. Some of the more deluxe grades were so rare that only a handful were made. For example, only seventeen of the A3s with automatic ejectors were made between 1896 and 1915. The A2 automatic ejector, on the other hand, totaled some 200 guns in the years c. 1892–1913.

The late Lt. Colonel William S. Brophy's *L.C. Smith Shotguns* presents extensive details on all grades of L. C. Smiths, with illustrations showing the variety of patterns, coverages, and quality offered by the factory. Of the ultimate grade of L. C. Smiths, the DeLuxe (offered from 1913), the catalogue of that period noted:

> . . . a beautiful specimen of mechanical and artistic skill, the finest type it is possible to manufacture. The gold game birds in bas-relief on each lock plate, interlaced with the finest engraving, produced an effect that is most striking. We do not confine ourselves to the illustrated design; customer's own design will be carried out and inscriptions of any character carefully inlaid or engraved. . . . Selected workmen are employed on them and neither time nor money are spared in their manufacture. Specially suited for presentation purposes.

The engravers used several colors of gold, and a standard feature appears to have been the gold lightning bolt flush-inlaid on the barrels at the breech. Figures detailing the numbers of DeLuxe and other high grade L. C. Smith shotguns made appear in Appendix B of Brophy's book.

The engravers who embellished most of the L. C. Smith guns made in Syracuse, New York, were Jacob Glahn, Sr., and sons George, Gus, and Theo. Of these artisans, Jacob Sr. would sometimes sign lockplates within the background of a game scene. His signature has also been observed on the upper tang adjacent to the thumb lever. When the Smith gun was acquired by the Hunters, and the factory was set up in Fulton, New York, the Glahns moved as well.

Engraving brothers A. E. and Wilton Spangler were also employed at Syracuse, and they too moved to Fulton. The extent of their work on L. C. Smith guns was limited to a few years; both were succeeded by the Glahns and by Albert E. Kraus. A. E. Spangler, who worked on some Smiths, is better known for his work on Lefever guns.

Kraus is credited by Brophy with decorating most of the deluxe-grade L. C. Smiths, with gold-inlaid dogs a

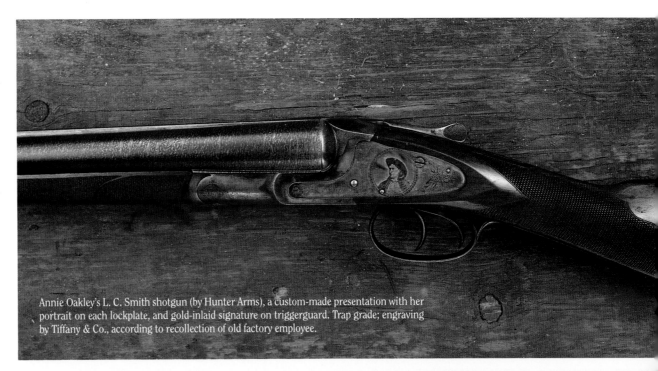

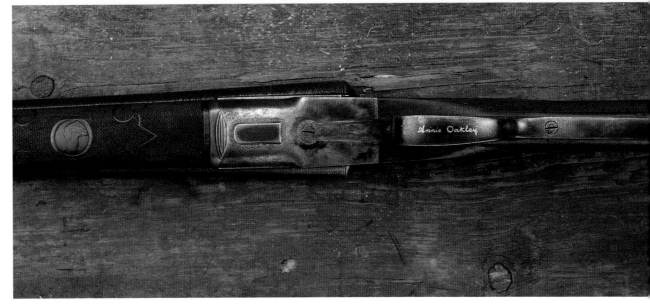

Annie Oakley's L. C. Smith shotgun (by Hunter Arms), a custom-made presentation with her portrait on each lockplate, and gold-inlaid signature on triggerguard. Trap grade; engraving by Tiffany & Co., according to recollection of old factory employee.

speciality. His career with the firm spanned the years c. 1890 through 1945. According to an article in the *Oswego Valley News* of January 28, 1964, Kraus had done custom engraving for "Gene Autry, Clark Gable, and J.P. Sousa," and he died at the age of ninety-one, in Geneva, New York. Apprenticed to Kraus was Charles H. Jerred.

This writer judges the finest of all L. C. Smith engravers to have been A. E. Spangler, though he has seen only one gun done by this master craftsman, a Lefever, made for presentation to U.S. president Benjamin Harrison.

The most historic and handsome L. C. Smith gun known to this writer is the 12-gauge Trap Grade hammerless double-barrel shotgun presented to Annie Oakley (c. 1899), with the world-famous markswoman's signature gold-inlaid on the triggerguard and engraved with her portrait on each lockplate. Credit for the engraving and inlaying has traditionally been ascribed to Tiffany & Co. Quoting Hunter Arms Company employee Charles L. Rogers: "When it came to the engraving work on the sidelock plates and the inlay work on the triggerguard . . . it was decided not to take any chances. . . . These parts were sent to Tiffany in New York, under guarantee of a perfect engraving job. . . . It had a real feminine look . . . the marvelous little *special* 16 [*sic*] gauge scatter-gun that probably had more care and pains in building and cost more than any other L. C. Smith gun that the Hunter Arms Co. of Fulton, New York, ever turned out."

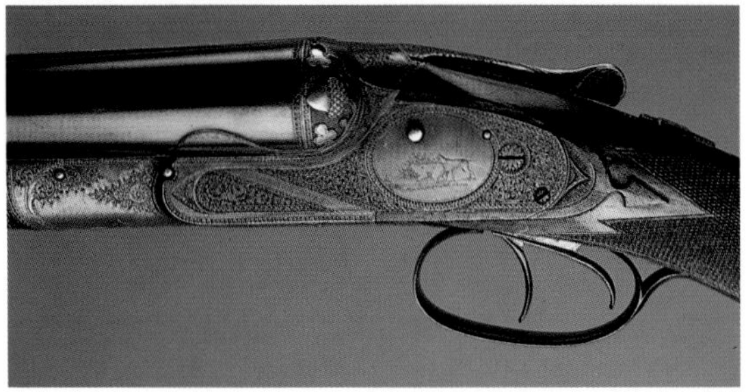

Lefever Optimus Grade double-barrel shotgun, presentation to President Benjamin Harrison, with gold-inlaid American eagle on triggerguard, and industrial protectionist inscription on banner in beak. Gold-inlaid BH monogram on forend release button. Signed by engraver, SPANGLER SC. on sideplate. One of the finest and most historic of nineteenth-century American shotguns. Acorn on recoil shield may symbolize growth of American industry.

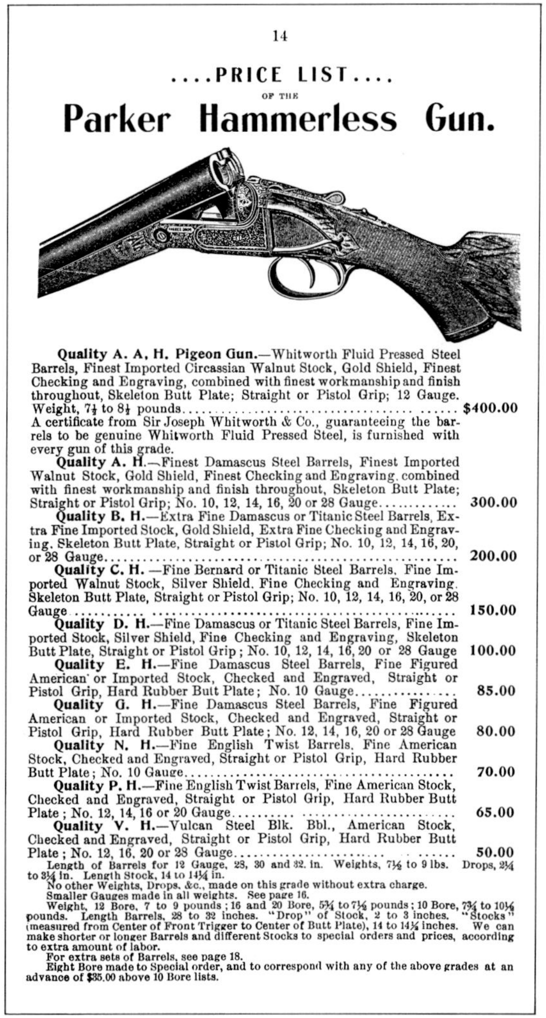

14

....PRICE LIST....

OF THE

Parker Hammerless Gun.

Quality A. A, H. Pigeon Gun.—Whitworth Fluid Pressed Steel Barrels, Finest Imported Circassian Walnut Stock, Gold Shield, Finest Checking and Engraving, combined with finest workmanship and finish throughout, Skeleton Butt Plate; Straight or Pistol Grip; 12 Gauge. Weight, 7½ to 8½ pounds.......... **$400.00**
A certificate from Sir Joseph Whitworth & Co., guaranteeing the barrels to be genuine Whitworth Fluid Pressed Steel, is furnished with every gun of this grade.

Quality A. H.—Finest Damascus Steel Barrels, Finest Imported Walnut Stock, Gold Shield, Finest Checking and Engraving, combined with finest workmanship and finish throughout, Skeleton Butt Plate; Straight or Pistol Grip; No. 10, 12, 14, 16, 20 or 28 Gauge.......... **300.00**

Quality B. H.—Extra Fine Damascus or Titanic Steel Barrels, Extra Fine Imported Stock, Gold Shield, Extra Fine Checking and Engraving, Skeleton Butt Plate, Straight or Pistol Grip; No. 10, 12, 14, 16, 20, or 28 Gauge.......... **200.00**

Quality C. H.—Fine Bernard or Titanic Steel Barrels, Fine Imported Walnut Stock, Silver Shield, Fine Checking and Engraving, Skeleton Butt Plate, Straight or Pistol Grip; No. 10, 12, 14, 16, 20, or 28 Gauge.......... **150.00**

Quality D. H.—Fine Damascus or Titanic Steel Barrels, Fine Imported Stock, Silver Shield, Fine Checking and Engraving, Skeleton Butt Plate, Straight or Pistol Grip; No. 10, 12, 14, 16, 20 or 28 Gauge **100.00**

Quality E. H.—Fine Damascus Steel Barrels, Fine Figured American or Imported Stock, Checked and Engraved, Straight or Pistol Grip, Hard Rubber Butt Plate; No. 10 Gauge.......... **85.00**

Quality G. H.—Fine Damascus Steel Barrels, Fine Figured American or Imported Stock, Checked and Engraved, Straight or Pistol Grip, Hard Rubber Butt Plate; No. 12, 14, 16, 20 or 28 Gauge **80.00**

Quality N. H.—Fine English Twist Barrels, Fine American Stock, Checked and Engraved, Straight or Pistol Grip, Hard Rubber Butt Plate; No. 10 Gauge.......... **70.00**

Quality P. H.—Fine English Twist Barrels, Fine American Stock, Checked and Engraved, Straight or Pistol Grip, Hard Rubber Butt Plate; No. 12, 14, 16 or 20 Gauge.......... **65.00**

Quality V. H.—Vulcan Steel Blk. Bbl., American Stock, Checked and Engraved, Straight or Pistol Grip, Hard Rubber Butt Plate; No. 12, 16, 20 or 28 Gauge.......... **50.00**

Length of Barrels for 12 Gauge, 28, 30 and 32 in. Weights, 7½ to 9 lbs. Drops, 2¼ to 3¼ in. Length Stock, 14 to 14¼ in.

No other Weights, Drops, &c., made on this grade without extra charge.

Smaller Gauges made in all weights. See page 16.

Weight, 12 Bore, 7 to 9 pounds; 16 and 20 Bore, 5¾ to 7½ pounds; 10 Bore, 7¾ to 10½ pounds. Length Barrels, 28 to 32 inches. "Drop" of Stock, 2 to 3 inches. "Stocks" (measured from Center of Front Trigger to Center of Butt Plate), 14 to 14¼ inches. We can make shorter or longer Barrels and different Stocks to special orders and prices, according to extra amount of labor.

For extra sets of Barrels, see page 18.

Eight Bore made to Special order, and to correspond with any of the above grades at an advance of $35.00 above 10 Bore lists.

Parker price listing c. 1904; engraving style accurately depicted in artist's rendering.

The Ithaca Gun Company

Ithaca Gun Company engravers were Joseph F. Loy, Edward Laytham, and William McGraw. Loy's years with Ithaca spanned 1890–95, after which he left to assume a position at the Remington Arms Company. Occasionally he would sign his work, not a common practice with most factory engravers in America until the 1970s.

Edward Laytham is known to have been an Ithaca engraver from the mid-1890s until about 1914. No signed examples of his work have been discovered to date. Laytham was succeeded by the best known of all Ithaca engravers, William McGraw, who began working there on a part-time basis in 1907, at age fourteen, becoming full time by age seventeen and continuing until his retirement in 1968. His talent was such that he was executing game scenes and the most critical of gold and silver inlays while still a teenager, eclipsing other engravers on the staff.

McGraw was a natural and developed a style peculiarly his own. He could boast a list of clients that included King Faisal of Iraq, Annie Oakley, Theodore Roosevelt, John Philip Sousa, Jack Dempsey, and Dwight David Eisenhower.

Daniel M. Lefever and the Lefever Arms Co.

Studying Lefever arms is complicated by Daniel M. Lefever's own restlessness over the years: in New York State, he spent the years 1848–53 in Canandaigua, 1854–73 in Auburn, and 1874–1906 in Syracuse, and in Ohio, the years 1903–04 in Defiance and 1905 in Bowling Green. Serial number 2X, a side-by-side double-barrel shotgun, by Dangerfield and Lefever (Auburn), is finely scroll-engraved in a style similar to Nimschke's popular style of the period. A review of the various grades of guns as detailed by R. W. Elliott and Jim Cobb in their book *Lefever: Guns of Lasting Fame* shows a generally admirable grade of engraving, inspired by the fine English scrolls of the period.

The finest grades of Lefevers were the A, the AA, and the Optimus: "For the money, no better gun can be built than our Optimus. The materials used and workmanship employed are of the very highest grade. . . . Stock. Finest Circassian or French walnut, selected with greatest care to produce the finest effect in coloring and figure superbly checkered and beautifully finished." Only about ninety Optimus-grade Lefevers were built, most with at least nine gold inlays.

A rare and historic Optimus was number 10784, presented to President Benjamin Harrison, with a gold-inlaid eagle motif on the triggerguard, the banner in its beak inscribed PROTECTION OF AMERICAN INDUSTRY. On the left lockplate, within a game-scene panel, is the engraver's minute signature: SPANGLER SC. The president wrote to Lefever in 1884, noting his delight with this gun: "I have shot it a great deal and with the most satisfactory results. . . ." Harrison had received the presentation as a token of thanks for his defense of American industry and his vigorous promotion of protectionist trade policies. In every respect, the Benjamin Harrison Lefever is one of the finest expressions of the gunmakers' art in America.

Even more deluxe than the Optimus was the Thousand Dollar Grade, of which only two examples appear to have been made, both c. 1910. Experts regard this class of Lefever in the same league as the Parker Invincible, the highest grade of that marque ever produced.

Certainly one of the most elaborate of all Lefevers was that pictured on an R. J. Kornbrath promotional illustration, a dated example of which indicates manufacture c. 1914.

Parker Brothers

Founded in 1866 or 1867, Parker Brothers very quickly joined the ranks of America's premier shotgun makers. With the development of their boxlock hammerless line, the firm rapidly earned a following among American sportsmen on a scale unequaled by any other U.S. shotgun maker of the last century. Parkers were advertised in

Parkers *at left and right* flank Ithaca Gun Company double; upper grade of guns indicates emphasis on quality in stocks, metalwork, engraving, and inlaying. Also demonstrates distinctiveness in style between one company and another.

specific grades, and had the advantage of handsome catalogues, an aggressive sales force, and high standards of design and workmanship. Among the engravers known to have been in their employ are Joe Loy (1884–88), Slim Rogers, and Robert R. Runge (the latter two from 1910).

The evolution of the various grades of these guns is too involved a story to be told here. An example of the degree of complexity may be found in the 1899 catalogue, which listed the line beginning with the U, and gradually moving up through the T, S, R, I, H, G, F, E, D, C, B, A, and AA Pigeon Gun. (Some of these grades were not leaps in quality, but simply variations in gauge or stock type, or other details.) At its finest, the 1899 Parker, the AA Pigeon Gun, boasted barrels of Whitworth fluid-pressed steel, the best Circassian walnut stock, gold-shield stock inlay, the finest in checkering, engraving, workmanship, and finish, a skeleton buttplate, and the stock straight or with pistol grip; the AA came in 12 gauge only.

The great mystery gun in Parkers is the high-grade double made for Czar Nicholas II of Russia. A nearly successful hoax was played with the fake, pictured on page 349. The author is aware of the existence of the genuine article and is intent on publishing that international gunmaking treasure in the future.

Ithaca Gun Company shotguns. *From top,* the Model 37 (with number 3 engraving pattern, introduced 1937, engraved and signed by Ralph Alpen); grade 6 Emil Flues model side-by-side (introduced 1908, engraving attributed to Ed Latham); and the grade 6 Flues Model Single Barrel Trap Gun (introduced 1914, engraved and gold-inlaid by one of several engravers, including possibly R. J. Kornbrath or Bill McGraw.)

Symbolic of the end of an age: Czar Nicholas II on a stand, awaiting driven birds with the Czarina Alexandra. His Excellency armed with matched set of boxlock Lebeau-Courally game guns, serials 31831 and 31832. Illustrated sidelock gun represents profile adopted by the English gunmakers as early as the 1880s.

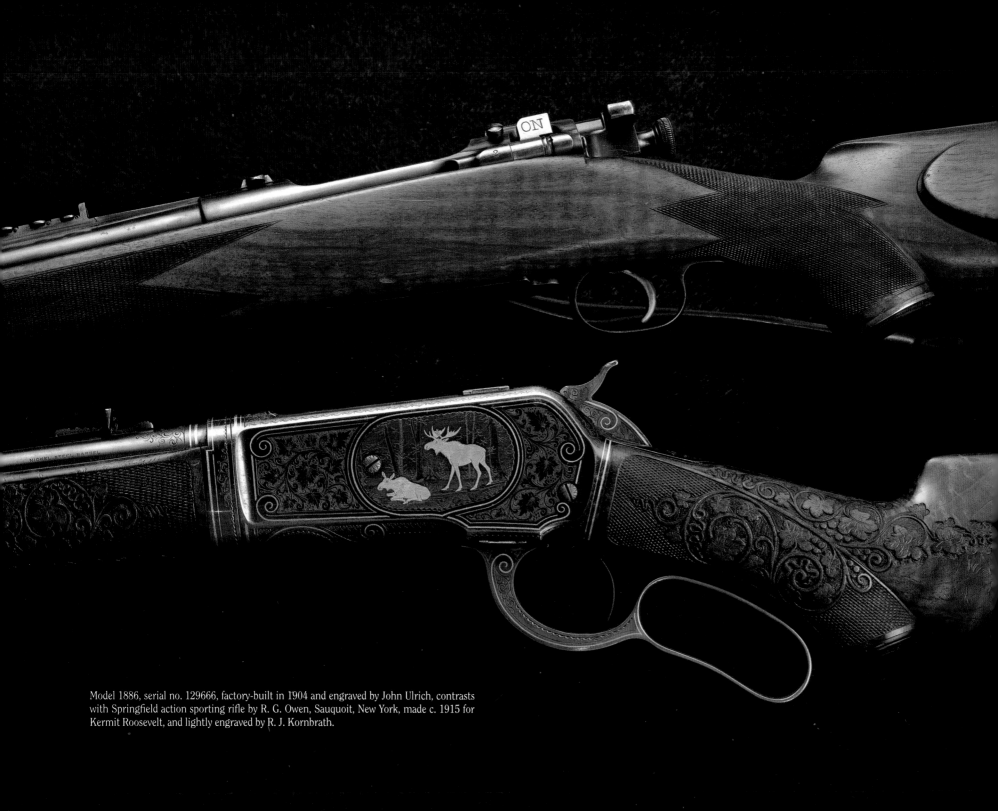

Model 1886, serial no. 129666, factory-built in 1904 and engraved by John Ulrich, contrasts with Springfield action sporting rifle by R. G. Owen, Sauquoit, New York, made c. 1915 for Kermit Roosevelt, and lightly engraved by R. J. Kornbrath.

Chapter 8
A Tradition in Flux:
1914–1960

World War I interrupted the commercial production of firearms by several manufacturers in the United States. Companies like Colt and Winchester ballooned in size almost overnight, reaching employee rosters of more than 18,000 and 25,000, respectively! Other gunmaking firms expanded dramatically as well, and for some (Winchester, for example) the rapid growth would ultimately lead to bankruptcy.

The push to meet wartime production quotas brought about many changes in manufacturing techniques and, most important, generally lowered standards of quality. Standards of shooting performance and mechanical reliability were high, but a distinct decline in finish and fit was noticeable. Needless to say, this period saw a marked slump in firearms engraving, the worst so far in America's history. The two major factors behind the slump were the shortage of craftsmen and a decrease in interest and demand by the shooting public.

Further, the Stock Market Crash of 1929, and the resulting Depression, severely interrupted the already slackened manufacture and sale of decorated weapons. To aggravate the situation further, steels were undergoing critical changes. Some attained such a degree of hardness that engraving tools often broke and lines were difficult to cut neatly or with depth. As a consequence, the time required to complete many engraving projects increased.

R. J. Kornbrath

Prominent artisans of this period were R. J. Kornbrath, Joseph Fugger, George Ulrich of Winchester, Wilbur Glahn of Colt, Bill McGraw of Ithaca Gun Company, and Harry Jarvis of Smith & Wesson. Of these, Kornbrath reigned supreme: word-of-mouth advertising by satisfied customers, published references by admiring writers, and the artist's own promotional acumen, contributed to the establishment nationally of his reputation as an extraordinary designer and engraver.

An immigrant from Ferlach, Austria, most of Kornbrath-engraved custom decorations were on a variety of types and makes of firearms. His peak years were in the 1920s and 1930s. About 1967 the author had the good fortune to purchase much of Kornbrath's archive of drawings, photographs, correspondence, and other records, from his widow. When knocking on her door in Hartford, one could not help but notice the name plate by the bell—KORNBRATH—engraved by the artist himself. These papers proved him a versatile and talented artisan, but, interestingly, the quality of his work seemed inconsistent. Subsequent research revealed that after suffering a stroke in 1937, he farmed out work to other engravers, representing it as his own. He died February 23, 1946.

Kornbrath continued the Germanic type of decoration that had dominated American arms engraving from the mid-nineteenth century. Many of his contemporaries were also immigrants from Germanic countries, and they too preferred to cut in their native fashion. Most of these men did not adopt any refinements nor did they attempt to Americanize the German style as had such predecessors as Gustave Young and L. D. Nimschke. For this reason, much of the output for the period 1914–45 appears to be European embellishment on products of American manufacture.

Alden George Ulrich and Winchester

George Ulrich was the last of the Ulrich family to embrace the engraver's craft. He began his career under

Kornbrath's own India-ink design drawing, for business letterhead, 1913. Among other drawings by this artist-craftsman was a design for a Single Action Colt for Tom Mix.

the tutelage of his father, Conrad F., at about the age of seventeen. In 1919, after nearly fifteen years at Marlin, George joined Winchester. This was about the time when Conrad and John were going into full retirement. George remained with the company until his death, in 1949.

George's masterpiece at Marlin had been a richly gold-inlaid and engraved shotgun, made for Czar Nicholas II of Russia. With the help of his father (who made the design drawing and carved the deluxe stocks), George completed the gun in 1913. In Russia, it was hand-delivered to the czar by William F. Gartland of New Haven.

Conrad is believed to have left full-time employment at Marlin sometime between 1907 and 1910, and thus it is possible George may have been the factory's chief engraver at the tender age of nineteen. According to

family tradition, George established himself as a master engraver in 1913 with the excellence of his engraving and inlaying work on the czar's shotgun.

Family history has it that George "engraved a gun for every United States president from 1913 on, with the exception of Hoover, for whom he engraved a fishing rod."

So the family could see his handiwork, George sometimes brought home pieces of which he was especially proud. At home he did wood carving, made his own golf clubs, and was fond of other handcrafts. However, he engraved only at the factory, never at home.

George was the first of the Ulrich engravers to receive published recognition of his work. Sadly, the article, in the form of an illustrated piece in *Outdoor Life* magazine, appeared in December 1950, a year after his death.

A humorous anecdote told by his son, George Jr.,

reveals the engraver's frustration at a slip of the graver—referred to in the trade as a "flyout." When he made such a slip, George would sometimes lose his temper and throw his graver out the window! Then a maintenance man would be summoned and sent crawling through the window, onto the roof below, to retrieve the lost tool!

What was the attitude of these highly skilled craftsmen toward their work? To quote George Jr.: "These Ulrichs, including my father, considered themselves shop hands. My father once said that to become a gun engraver it took a strong arm and a weak mind. This was hardly a true picture of these men, who were self-educated and thoroughly enjoyed all the arts."

Alden George Ulrich died October 18, 1949, at the age of sixty-one.

Leslie Borden Ulrich was one of the two sons of John Ulrich. (His mother, Esther Munsill, was a granddaughter of Gail Borden, developer of condensed milk.) According to New Haven directories, Leslie worked as an engraver during the period 1908–25. According to the family, Leslie also did stock carving and checkering at the Winchester factory.

The Kusmit Brothers, John and Nick

The Kusmits form a historical link with the Ulrichs: John was taught engraving and gold inlay as an understudy of George Ulrich, beginning at Winchester c. 1935, and Nick learned the art from brother John. Collectively, the Kusmits represent over one hundred years of experience in the field of arms embellishment. Through Winchester catalogues, advertising, gun and other sports magazines, newspapers, television, and word of mouth, the brothers have received about as much publicity as any of the present crop of practitioners of arms engraving in America, with the exception of Alvin A. White.

Jack Denton Scott's "Adventure Unlimited" column in the December 8, 1957, issue of the *New York Herald Tribune* proved a welcome bit of recognition for John:

We have just had an adventure in patience, craftsmanship and dedication up here in the Winchester Arms factory. In a civilization that is rapidly mechanizing

244

and automating everything from radar cooking the Sunday roast . . . to spanking the baby by auto-suggestion, it is reassuring to know that there is at least one process left that is being kept in the capable hands of the craftsman. A process of painstaking perfection called gun engraving.

John Kusmit, a lean, black-eyed, shy sort, whose parents came to America from the Ukraine, is our man. He has also been President Eisenhower's, Senator Harry Flood Byrd's, former Secretary of the Treasury Humphrey's, Walter Alston's, Robert Taylor's, President of Mexico Don Adolfo Ruiz Cortines', [Haile Selassie's, Chuck Connors', General Omar Bradley's, President Harry S. Truman's, Prince Ranier's, General Curtis LeMay's, John M. Olin's, Ted Williams'] and Leonard Hall's, the Republican National Chairman's man. At least he has engraved guns for them. He is, of course, completely his own man and one of a select few of talented gun engravers in the world. . . . We watched him lift a gun into a work of art. Pride of craftsmanship in action. We recommend it as a worthwhile adventure for anyone.

Younger brother Nick, who began at Winchester in about 1950, has decorated a broad array of types of firearms, in a variety of patterns and styles. Among the dignitaries for whom he has embellished guns are Britain's Prince Philip, Prince Rainier of Monaco, the king and queen of Thailand, former secretary of the treasury John Connally, Henry Ford II, Ernest Hemingway, John Wayne, Robert Montgomery, Roy Rogers, and General Omar Bradley.

Interestingly, Winchester company practice discouraged engravers from signing firearms. Nick, however, would occasionally sign his initials in tiny letters, NK, usually on a rock or other obscure area. Toward the end of his career he generally signed only Grand American grade Model 21 Winchesters, or other arms when the

R. G. Owen custom rifle, *left,* on Springfield action; Kornbrath engraved and sculpted, even on bolt handle. Mauser Kurz square-bridge-actioned rifle by New York City's Griffin & Howe, another example of Kornbrath artistry. High-relief carving reflects traditional Austro-German approach to some of the most deluxe scrollwork and game scenes.

customer requested he sign. Full-name signatures for John or Nick are therefore rare.

John Kusmit retired from Winchester in 1977, and Nick in 1981. Nick remains active, on a freelance basis.

Wilbur A. Glahn and Family

Of the several families that made their mark in arms engraving in America, one of the largest was the Glahns. Their genealogy is rather complex, but family records show the first engraving Glahn came to America from the Black Forest region of Germany, in 1828. This immigrant craftsman was George Glahn, and he became an employee of the American Bank Note Company. Family sources suggest that he was also a gun engraver.

Some of George's sons, grandsons, and great-grandsons became engravers. Among them was another George, who is believed to have been chief engraver at the Syracuse Arms factory; little is known of his career, however.

Jacob Glahn, who died in 1902, first worked for the American Bank Note Company, and at later dates engraved for several other firms, including Colt. Background data on his career was located in a letter in the Colt Collection of Firearms, which is housed in the Museum of Connecticut History. Jacob wrote to Colt on September 27, 1878, inquiring about work:

> [Among my previous employers are] the New Britain Lock Co., American Sterling Co. of Naubuc. Sharps Rifle Co. and Winchester Repeating Arms Co. . . . [and] the Defunct National Arms Co. of Brooklyn, N.Y. I had the Engraving contract under this firm for Six years. . . . Should you find me trustworthy I would be happy to receive your Guns, and I think I can satisfy you, or the most critical Judge of this kind of work.

A letter from the same period, from Joseph W. Livingston of the Nichols & Lefever gun company, Syracuse, to Colt, endorsed Jacob and noted that he had also been employed by the Parker gun company for the previous year: "I consider him one of the most Compleet artizens that is to be found to day, on his Speciality, Gun Engraving."

One of Kornbrath's most inspired creations; profuse scroll coverage and generous distribution of sculpted gold inlays. Eagle motif on top of slide with monogram; other side of slide depicts Native Americans in pursuit of buffaloes. Diamonds inset in bears' eyes, both sides of briarwood grips.

From Kornbrath's promotional brochure, entitled "Expert Gun Engraving." Text notes: "Kornbrath artistic engravure on your gun will enhance its value in the same degree that proper landscaping adds to the living worth of a home, or beautiful settings increase the loveliness of fine gems." Evidence of Kornbrath's artistic sensitivity and training is the well-developed sense of spatial depth on several guns.

Hugo Reuss design, post–World War I. Reuss worked three years for Helfricht, forming own business in 1887. After leaving Helfricht's employ, Reuss appears to have concentrated on die cutting, and on fine jewelry work. Kornbrath worked with Reuss for several years, sharing the same shop.

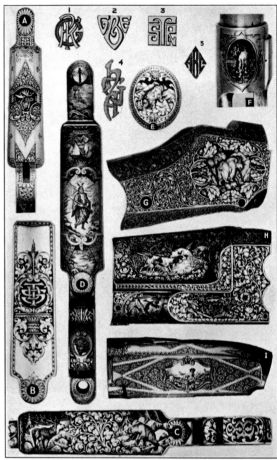

Research in the Colt factory ledgers reveals that the company did indeed send Jacob work, specifically Model 1878 hammer shotguns, serial numbers 250, 255, 256, 279, 280, 282, 284, 302, 309, 349, 385, and 394. Jacob also appears in the author's *L. D. Nimschke, Firearms Engraver* (page 95), with prints from a Moore revolver.

Theodore Glahn (c. 1857–1937) was an engraver for the Parker, Fulton, and Syracuse arms companies. While at Syracuse he was assigned the embellishment of a deluxe gun for Theodore Roosevelt. Still another Glahn, Gus, died prior to World War II; he is known to have

These massive, yet beautiful, Austrian-made Charles Daly guns (the larger a 4-bore measuring 37 inches, the other an 8-bore) were a set built for an American client and intended for serious wildfowl shooting. Such lavishly rich embellishments were an inspiration to American engravers. Double-W cartridge board and boxes examples of arms-related promotional arts at turn of century; board c. 1897 used for years thereafter in gun emporiums.

engraved for the Buffalo Arms Company and for Syracuse Arms.

The family member about which the most information is known is Wilbur A. Glahn. Born March 4, 1888, Wilbur learned the trade from his father, George, and was a general engraver, specializing in firearms. He is known to have worked for Fulton, for Remington (c. 1905–19), and for Colt. Wilbur also had a number of private clients, and occasionally took on projects for other arms companies, among them High Standard. Besides metal engraving, he was skilled in carving, enameling, and inlaying on pearl and ivory grips.

Wilbur came to Hartford in 1919 and was hired by the Colt factory. He worked at the plant through 1923, leaving in that year to set up an engraving workshop in his home, but continuing to do the bulk of Colt's work. In November of 1923 he set up a shop with E. R. Houghton, a jewelry engraver, at 11 Central Row, Hartford; their company was known as Houghton & Glahn.

After ending his association with Houghton, in about 1926, Wilbur moved his shop to 71 Asylum Avenue, Hartford, and adopted the name of the Aetna Stamp and Engraving Company (a firm that had been established c. 1890). Besides general engraving, he worked in mother-of-pearl and ivory, and sometimes handled custom grip assignments for R. J. Kornbrath. Wilbur was not a practiced die cutter, but could work in that field if need be.

From his arrival in Hartford in 1919, Wilbur continued to do most of the Colt company's engraving through the spring of 1950. He became ill at that time, and entered the hospital; he passed away February 6, 1951. Until about 1933, 90 percent of Wilbur's work was on firearms. He then entered into industrial engraving. Before long, guns settled into the background and the firm's largest customer was the Pratt & Whitney company. During this period he turned down work from the Remington and Ithaca companies but occasionally took on gun commissions from individual clients or from High Standard. Remington and Ithaca had been asking him to help with their engraving needs ever since Wilbur first came to Hartford.

The Fred Adolph Over and Under gun made as a present by the master gunsmith for Theodore Roosevelt, and published in the Genoa, New York, artisan's catalogue, c. 1914. At T.R.'s behest, gun was displayed at the Abercrombie & Fitch store, New York, with mirrors and magnifying glasses to accentuate detail. Adolph was touted in the press as "maker of the finest guns in America." Gun lost in tragic fire in Tanzania, August 1986, during filming of *In the Blood,* a documentary on hunting and wildlife conservation. Single Action Colt was T.R.'s favorite Western revolver, engraved with carved ivory grips by L. D. Nimschke, 1883.

12-2 *Engraving*

12-3 *Engraving*

John Kusmit–engraved special presentation, carrying on tradition of deluxe pieces with special numbers: 1,000,000th Model 94 rifle to President Calvin Coolidge (1927), 1,000,000th Model 92 rifle to Secretary of War Patrick Hurley (1932), 1,000,000th Model 12 shotgun to General Henry H. Arnold (1943), 1,500,000th Model 94 rifle to President Harry S Truman (1948), 1,000,000th Model 97 shotgun to John M. Olin (1951). Taylor and Olin guns engraved by John Kusmit; others attributed to Alden George Ulrich.

12-4 *Engraving*

12-5 *Engraving*

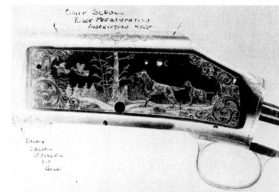

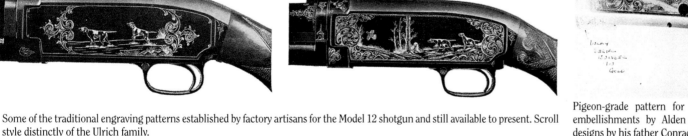

Some of the traditional engraving patterns established by factory artisans for the Model 12 shotgun and still available to present. Scroll style distinctly of the Ulrich family.

Pigeon-grade pattern for Model 1897 Winchester shotgun, embellishments by Alden George Ulrich, based on original designs by his father Conrad F., and uncle John.

Among special assignments by Wilbur for Colt were a Thompson submachine gun for Alvaro Obregón of Mexico, a pair of deluxe handguns for the king and queen of Siam, a handgun for the Prince of Wales, several guns for show business personalities (among them Tom Mix and stripper Sally Rand), guns for several Texas Rangers and other law enforcement officials, a pair of .45 automatic pistols for General Douglas MacArthur (Wilbur said that the general held up the invasion of the Philippines until he had received these guns!), a gold-inlaid automatic pistol for General George C. Marshall, another automatic for Connecticut governor John Trumbull, and an Auto Ordnance Thompson submachine gun for presentation to Joseph Stalin (the author has seen this gun, with silver presentation plaque, in a Moscow museum). For High Standard, Wilbur engraved and gold-inlaid two automatic pistols for Ted Williams, and for the Syracuse Arms Company Wilbur engraved a fancy shotgun for the king of Greece and another shotgun for Theodore Roosevelt. However, most of Wilbur's assignments for Colt were on grade A, B, and C handguns.

The Transition from Helfricht to Glahn

In preparation for the retirement of Cuno A. Helfricht,

21-3 *Engraving*

21-4 *Engraving*

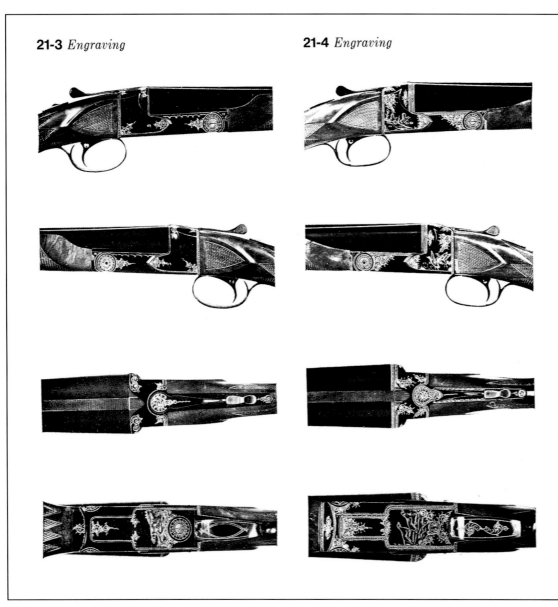

Selection of factory design patterns for Model 21 shotgun. Credit for most of these designs goes to Alden George Ulrich; designs first published in the 1930s. However, roots of some scenes and scrolls harken back to John and C. F. Ulrich.

Marlin slide-action shotgun made for Czar Nicholas II by Alden George Ulrich, and his father, C.F. Drawing by Conrad; whereabouts of gun presently unknown. Among premier of all arms made by Marlin.

the Colt factory had sets of blueprint-style drawings detailing the engraving styles and coverages for a variety of Colt handguns rendered. This was to provide continuity for the engraving department, with Helfricht's retirement impending. However, Glahn had his own style, and soon after Helfricht departed, Glahn dispensed with the drawings and engraved in his own style. For his own reference, Glahn made photostats (c. 1928–29) of several guns embellished by him and used them in place of the Helfricht blueprints. Serial numbers of a handful of guns by Glahn are known from these photostats, including Single Action Armys numbers 347208 and 347651, Government Model automatics C156705 and C156706, Model 1903 Hammerless automatics 494771 and 494813, and Model 1908 Hammerless .25 ACP automatics 377733 and 377719.

William H. Gough

Though he is not known to have worked in the Colt factory, William H. Gough appears in the firm's records frequently enough to indicate that he was something of a backup craftsman to Glahn and Kornbrath. Working as early as the first part of the twentieth century on Winchesters, Gough's name on photographs of several of that firm's firearms has helped record his work.

Gough had apprenticed in Birmingham, England, and worked at engraving jobs in Meriden, Connecticut (Parker Brothers), and Philadelphia (Fox Gun Company). Other clients included Aubrey (who made guns for Sears, Roebuck & Co.), Norwich Arms Corporation, Remington, and Hollenbeck. The Savage Arms Company was his employer before and during the early years of World War II.

Gough's style on Colts contrasted with the Germanic scrolls and beaded backgrounds standard to most of his contemporaries. However, at times his work is so close to the style of Wilbur Glahn that it is difficult to tell the two apart. One must also bear in mind that at his peak, there were employees in Gough's shop, engraving arms according to the style desired by the customer.

The death of Wilbur A. Glahn in 1951 marked the end

Official Police Colt sold to town of Chappaqua, New York, 1933. Grade-B scroll, with inscription, by Wilbur A. Glahn; representative of the customary style of embellishments done by him for Colt factory.

Photostat of Colt Single Action serial no. 347208, which served as a reference for grade 2½. From a series of copies made up from engraved guns of varying degrees of coverage. Preceded by blueprints, attributed to Cuno Helfricht.

Characteristic scrollwork by W. H. Gough, on Model 1908 .25 Automatic Colt, shipped 1914. Frame inscribed, beneath pearl grip: DES & ENG BY W.H. GOUGH. Shipped to Utica, New York, for engraving; then returned to Colt, then sent to dealer Murta Appleton, in Philadelphia. The design betrays a stiffness that is not seen in the flow and execution of Kornbrath's work.

Alvin F. Herbert at his bench, Colt factory, c. 1953. In his vise, the presentation Single Action Army for President Dwight D. Eisenhower.

of America's family dynasties of gun engravers. The Youngs and Helfrichts had faded from the picture as early as the 1920s, and the Ulrichs as late as the 1940s. Of these four families, only the Ulrichs can claim any of the current crop of engravers as their protégés; and of the Kusmit brothers, Nick alone remains active.

Nevertheless, the Germanic influence of the family dynasties, and of such contemporaries as Nimschke, Kornbrath, and Fugger, left a permanent imprint on the stylistic preferences of America's clientele for engraved firearms. The high standards of quality, design, and style set by these exceptional craftsmen will forever serve as the benchmark by which gun engravers of the present and future will be measured. It is a valuable legacy, and an indisputable reason for the appreciation of quality antique arms by collectors whose specialties would otherwise be limited only to the modern gun.

Alvin F. Herbert

Al Herbert's career at Colt spanned only about fifteen

years (c. 1954–69), but in that time he turned out more than most engravers could in a twenty-five-year period. While working a full week for Colt, he also maintained an outside shop, where he took in jewelry engraving, presentation inscriptions, and, occasionally, guns from private parties and from other gunmakers. For many years he was one of the sources of lettering for A. A. White Engravers, and the author spent many an hour on Saturdays in Al Herbert's upstairs shop on State Street, in downtown Hartford.

Initially trained in jewelry engraving, he was especially talented at lettering and monograms. He admired the work of Kornbrath, and his favorite scroll style was based on one of that master's best Germanic patterns.

Ebony and *Guns* magazines published feature articles on Herbert and his work. Thousands of gun enthusiasts and the general public saw him demonstrate gun engraving at the New England States' Expositions, at various sportsmen's shows, and on television. He enjoyed giving interviews, and was always happy to be photographed.

Herbert's life was capsulized in an obituary published in a Springfield, Massachusetts, newspaper, September 5, 1969:

> Alvin F. Herbert, 68, of 190 Northampton Ave., who achieved international fame as a gun engraver, decorating weapons for the late President Dwight D. Eisenhower and Gen. Charles De Gaulle, among others, died Thursday in Wesson Memorial Hospital.
>
> He was born in Saint Vincent, West Indies, January 3, 1901, and had been a resident of this city for 41 years, moving to Springfield from Cambridge. . . . He was employed as a gun engraver at Smith & Wesson, later worked at Colt's Patent Firearms as a master engraver, not only for guns, but delicate work on jewelry and trophies. His masterpiece was an embossed Colt revolver which commemorated the Colt firm's 125th anniversary. He also engraved guns for Sammy Davis, Jr., former chief of police of Springfield Raymond P. Gallagher, Mayor La Guardia of New York, ex-Cuban president Fulgencio Batista and many movie stars. . . .

Al Herbert was also the first black engraver to achieve

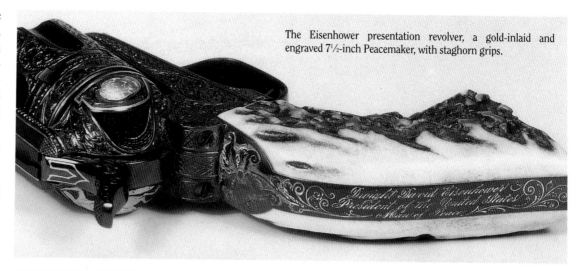

The Eisenhower presentation revolver, a gold-inlaid and engraved 7½-inch Peacemaker, with staghorn grips.

Smith & Wesson .44 Magnum, by Alvin A. White, for the factory, c. 1955. Note sculptural quality of elk motif. Commencing in the 1960s, the demand for S&W engraved arms equaled that of period before 1900. A revival also evident to the Colt and Winchester factories, and to numerous freelance engravers.

Robert P. Runge at his Remington Arms workbench in Ilion, New York.

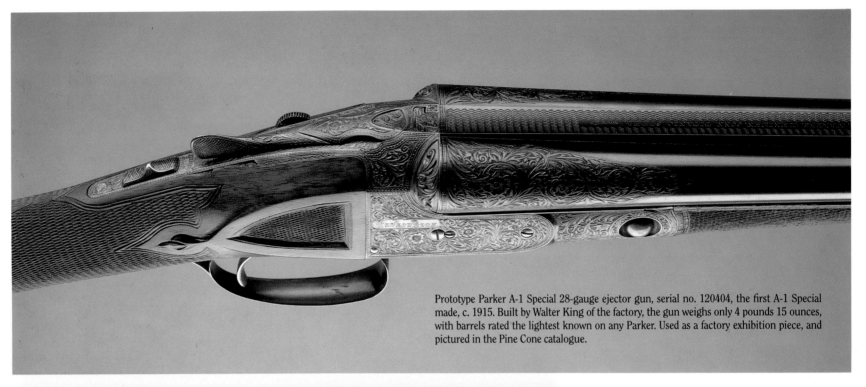

Prototype Parker A-1 Special 28-gauge ejector gun, serial no. 120404, the first A-1 Special made, c. 1915. Built by Walter King of the factory, the gun weighs only 4 pounds 15 ounces, with barrels rated the lightest known on any Parker. Used as a factory exhibition piece, and pictured in the Pine Cone catalogue.

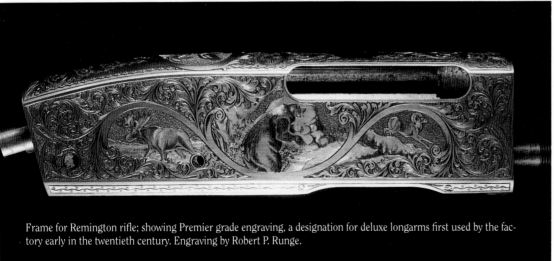

Frame for Remington rifle: showing Premier grade engraving, a designation for deluxe longarms first used by the factory early in the twentieth century. Engraving by Robert P. Runge.

recognition in the arms field. His output at Colt overlapped with that of Alvin A. White and A. A. White Engravers, beginning on an active basis c. 1961.

Hand Engraving from Smith & Wesson

Research by Smith & Wesson historian Roy G. Jinks has unraveled much of the complex story of S&W engraving. A landmark tribute to the firm's craftsmanship was the 1991 publication of Jinks's book *Artistry in Arms: The Guns of Smith & Wesson,* in association with the traveling loan exhibition of the same title. After opening at the Connecticut Valley Historical Museum, Springfield, Massachusetts, it went to the Gene Autry Western Heritage Museum, to the National Cowboy Hall of Fame, and to such other institutions as the Buffalo Bill Historical Center, the Tennessee State Museum, the Dallas Historical Society, the North Carolina Museum of History, the

Quincy Museum of Natural History and Art, and then to foreign institutions, including, most importantly, the Royal Armouries–H.M. Tower of London.

The Young family's reign at S&W ended in 1912, and the successor engravers included Harry Jarvis, Leon Goodyear, R. J. Kornbrath, and A. A. White. Russell J. Smith was another factory engraver, as was Alvin Herbert. As universally true with U.S. gunmakers, World War I and the Depression saw a diminishing demand for S&W engraving. In the 1960s the demand returned, at a level rivaling that of the years before 1900.

Remington Arms Company and Parker Brothers

Very little is known of Remington Arms Company engraving in the period covered by the present chapter; the same is true of Remington guns made in previous years. Record-keeping at Remington was lax, and the best one can state is that hand engraving continued to be offered, as evidenced by such special presentation arms as a .30-caliber Model 8F semiautomatic rifle, engraved and inscribed to Tom Mix from friends, and still another similarly embellished as a gift from the factory to Frank Hamer, the Texas Ranger credited with the ambush of the notorious Bonnie Parker and Clyde Barrow. These superb Remingtons were presented in 1911 and 1922, respectively.

Among the craftsmen whose careers have been recorded with Remington are Anda Hardy (1933–46), Slim Rogers (1920s–30s), Bill Gough (1946–50), Robert R. Runge (1934–46), his son Robert P. Runge (1938–1980s), Carl Ennis (1937–1980s), Jack H. Caswell (1946–50 and 1969–70s), and Leo Bala (1967–80s). Of these, Anda Hardy, Slim Rogers, Robert R. Runge, Robert P. Runge, and Carl Ennis are also known to have worked on Parkers.

While researching a gun-engraving article for Petersen's *Guns & Ammo Annual 1977,* the author met the factory engraving staff at Remington Arms, including Robert P. Runge. Runge's father, a factory engraver at Parker Brothers, Meriden, Connecticut, moved to Ilion,

Austrian master engraver Albin Obiltschnig probably responsible for this Low Wall Winchester; frame and lever finished in gray to accentuate carving in high relief. Foxes and grouse on opposite side of frame. Pre–World War II German commercial proof markings. Obiltschnig and son Hans were highly popular with American clientele.

New York, when the company was acquired by Remington, in 1934.

Several handsome catalogues and brochures were published by the Parker Brothers in promotion of their various grades of shotguns. These prove useful in identifying all manner of Parkers with hand engraving, but are of little assistance in trying to identify the engravers themselves. Nevertheless, a 1929 Parker brochure includes a picture of the senior Runge at his engraving bench beside the heading "Three Generations of Master Gunmakers Have Made the Parker Gun World Famous"; a 1934 Remington brochure continued the same theme.

At their peak, the established grades of Parkers began with a standard model known as the Trojan (first made in 1915); from that base gun, they graded up to the ultimate of all Parkers: the Invincible. In between were VH, PH, GH, DH, CH, BH, AH, AAH, and A-1 Special; if the model featured an automatic ejector, the letter E was added to the grade designation.

Numerous illustrations of engraved and specially stocked Parkers appear in Larry L. Baer's book *The Parker Gun*, but even his extensive research was unable to identify by name, date, and style all the firm's engraving staff. However, Baer does offer the reader a valuable guide to prevent the purchase of Parkers that have been upgraded (or faked) from the original grade in which each gun was sold. Some Parkers were decorated with richly detailed scrolls, and with equally fine game scenes. A-1 Specials and other high-grade Parkers are among the most sought-after of all American collector's firearms.

Griffin & Howe custom rifles, engraving and gold inlaying by Joseph Fugger. *From left:* .35 Whelen on Mauser action, made 1947; .30-06 pre-1964 Winchester Model 70, from 1949; .375 H&H Magnum Brevex Magnum Mauser action, made 1961. Note minutely detailed scenes and scrollwork, and Art Deco monograms.

Historic Model 99 Savage reached the milestone of one million rifles in 1960.

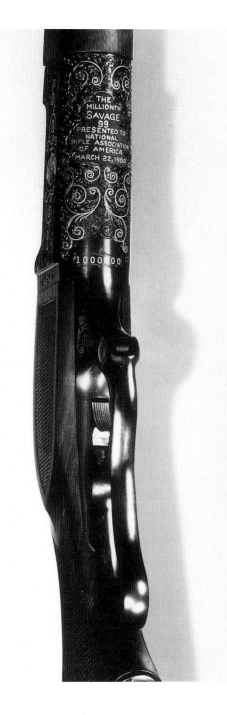

The Ithaca Gun Company

Thanks to the talents of William McGraw, the Ithaca Gun Company maintained a high standard of engraving. In 1915, McGraw was joined by apprentice Jay Leech, then sixteen years old. Leech described the department at that time:

> Jim Hallam was the boss. Bill McGraw was there and I sat next to him.
>
> There was a fellow by the name of Jack Clance. Jack was from Meriden, Connecticut. There was Sam Rogers. Sam was from Ilion, New York. Percy Clapp was an engraver who did work from time to time. I engraved the line and scroll work up to the grade 4. Bill McGraw did all the fancy work, the game scenes, all the gold and silver inlays.

Leech remained in the engraving department until about 1923, when he moved over to a manufacturing capacity.

Still another of the Ithaca engravers in the late 1920s and early 1930s was J. C. Shoemaker. Author and researcher Walter Claude Snyder discovered an advertisement by this craftsman in the March 21, 1931, *Sportsmen's Review:* "Engraving: Shotguns, Rifles, etc., all work guaranteed; Reasonable rates, J.C. Shoemaker, 432 N. Titus Av., Ithaca, N.Y." McGraw followed this advertisement two weeks later with one of his own in the same publication: "Have your initials inlaid in pure gold on trigger guard of your gun. My price for a limited time, $7.50. Embossed $9.00. Wm. McGraw, 102 West Falls St., Ithaca, N.Y."

Following World War II, McGraw's nephew Paul took an apprenticeship at Ithaca's engraving department, staying until about 1950. Two other apprentices in the shop at the time were David Hurd (brother-in-law of Bill McGraw) and Bill Johanson. These craftsmen could do journeyman's work but not the critical projects assigned to their talented master.

Still another Ithaca engraver was Justin Michelina, a Florida resident contracted in the 1950s and continuing into the mid-1960s. Later on, Ralph Alpen was hired at the factory, where he worked during the years 1967–71, having the advantage of working with McGraw before his 1968 retirement.

The L. C. Smith and Lefever Arms Companies

An indication of the production figures for hand-engraved L. C. Smith guns is the fact that from about 1913 through 1945, 80 percent of the company's production (a total of 141,844) was in field-grade guns. These guns had no engraving and were comparable to the Parker Brothers Trojan grade. Adding to the existing DeLuxe, Premier, Monogram, Crown, Eagle, and Gladiator grades of L. C. Smith, their better quality and more profuse engraved and/or inlaid doubles, the firm proudly brought out the Single-Barrel Trap Gun in 1917, and it remained in production through about 1950. Only three of these were made in DeLuxe grade, two in Premier, and fifteen in Monogram.

Engraving After World War II

The years following World War II are characterized by a renaissance in engraving interest among the gun public, accompanied by a noticeable increase in the number of craftsmen. Many of these artisans were returning from wartime service. A half-dozen of the postwar engravers had been active prior to the war, including William McGraw, Joseph Fugger, and the youthful virtuoso Alvin White. A few of the new crop were European born, and some American clients would continue to send their arms to Europe and Britain for embellishment.

By 1960, approximately fifty engravers were active in the firearms field in the United States, most of them working independently. Their output was augmented by the many thousands of imported engraved guns by Browning and other continental and British manufacturers. A few export firms were sending pieces abroad for decoration, despite the costs and involvements of shipment and customs.

A vital factor in the crescendoing demand in postwar America for engraved arms was the recognition that quality decorated arms represented a good investment.

At bottom, Holland & Holland double-barrel rifle, .375 H&H Magnum, serial no. 35288, gold-inlaid, engraved, and with sculpted steel motifs of the wildlife of India, by Joseph Fugger, with gold-inlaid RML monogram on lid of pistol-grip cap; 24-inch barrels. *At top,* James Purdey & Sons double-barrel rifle of .465 caliber, no. 26550; 25-inch barrels. Gold-inlaid, engraved, and with sculpted steel African motifs by Fugger; gold-inlaid RML monogram on lid of pistol-grip cap. Each rifle with detailed barrel inscription attesting to custom-made nature. Circumstances surrounding building of these superb rifles are told in the words of the patron, Robert M. Lee:

In 1955, on return from my first safari in East Africa, I stopped in to see Harry Lawrence, who, at the time, was Managing Director at Purdey's. I had met Harry prior to my departure for Africa and had corresponded with him previous to our first meeting.

Harry was the Dean of English gunmakers, and was certainly the only Managing Director in the London gun trade who could, in fact, make a "best London gun" lock, stock, and barrel!

Above all, Harry was a gentleman, and undoubtedly knew more about the London gun trade and "best London guns" than any man alive at the time.

In any case, having shown Harry a sample of Joe Fugger's work, in the form of a Mauser floorplate, he agreed to undertake the making of a special .500/.465 double-barrel rifle, to be engraved in New York by Joe Fugger. This was to be the first time in Purdey's history that a gun or rifle was sent overseas for engraving.

It took nearly two years for the gun to be ready for shipment to the States, "in the white." Joe Fugger spent about eighteen months on the engraving, which commenced after many discussions and trips to the picture section of the New York Public Library.

African game scenes were selected for the theme of this rifle, and I decided that since the rifle was intended for hard use, gold inlays should be minimized. In fact, the only gold inlay is a cobra on the opening lever.

I elected, instead of gold, to have the work done in high relief.

Additionally, I wanted to have the action finished in what is now referred to as the "old coin" finish rather than color case-hardened. This was a problem in that Purdey had never attempted to do this bright, case-hardened finish in the past. Nevertheless, Harry agreed to investigate the process and during the engraving period, he sent me several test pieces, the last of which was acceptable.

The rifle was finally returned to Purdey and was ready to be picked up prior to my 1959 safari.

When I arrived at Purdey's, Harry Lawrence had the new rifle on the big table in the famous "Long Room." He was beaming as he handed it to me. What a magnificent rifle!

On asking Harry what he thought of it . . . he smiled and said, "Bob, this is the most magnificent rifle of our time!"

I took the rifle to Africa and on a number of safaris and shikars.

I neglected to mention that the stock was designed by the late Monty Kennedy, who had completed a number of Mauser stocks for me in the past. Monty was, in my opinion, one of the half-dozen best stock makers in America, if not in the world. His book *Checkering and Carving of Gun Stocks,* is a classic, and no one could checker better than Monty.

It was agreed that the wood would be left unfinished, and while Joe Fugger was doing the engraving, Monty would finish and checker the stock.

After securing Harry Lawrence's agreement to build the rifle, I visited Leonard Pierce, who at the time was Managing Director of Holland & Holland. This was at Holland's old location on Bond Street.

I had previously been trying to convince Leonard to build a .375 H&H Magnum double rifle for me, again to be engraved in New York by Joe Fugger.

He said that he would discuss it with his Board of Directors. In due time, Leonard advised me that H&H would agree to build the rifle.

The .375 was finished in 1961 and incorporates a scope mount which I had designed earlier and which was based on Griffin & Howe's double lever locking system. All Griffin & Howe mounts, up until the mid-50s, were simply side bracket mounts.

After many discussions with Seymour Griffin, he agreed to allow Robert Heym, Griffin & Howe's best metalsmith, to work with me and develop my idea of a top-mount incorporating dovetail blocks and the Griffin & Howe double lever system. The first top mount, with the front base built flush into a short rib, was completed for me on a .375 H&H Magnum magazine rifle in the mid-1950s. I later came up with a modification that would allow building the front base integral with the rib rather than as a set-in piece. Since that time, Griffin & Howe has made a number of top-mounts and short ribs incorporating front-mount bases for me and for other clients. It produces the cleanest look and is low, fool-proof, and rugged.

I decided that Asian game scenes would be appropriate for the .375. Again, several trips to the picture section of the New York Public Library produced some good references and the result was a work of art at least the equal of the Purdey. Of course, Monty Kennedy did the final stock finish and checkering.

This rifle too was given the "coin finish" case-hardening treatment. Leonard Pierce was quick to state that, in his opinion, this H&H double rifle was certainly the finest example ever produced by Holland & Holland and at least on a par with my Purdey!

This, then, is "A Tale of Two Rifles" that are absolutely unique and can never be duplicated.

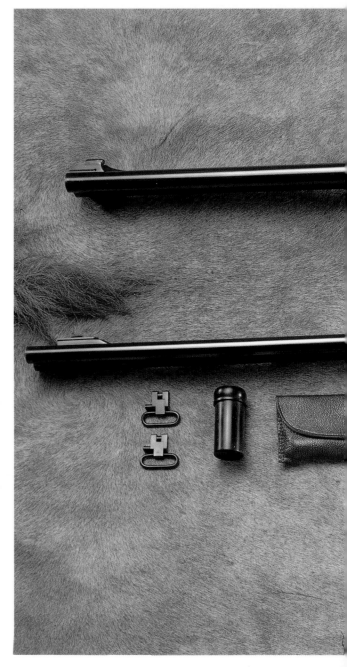

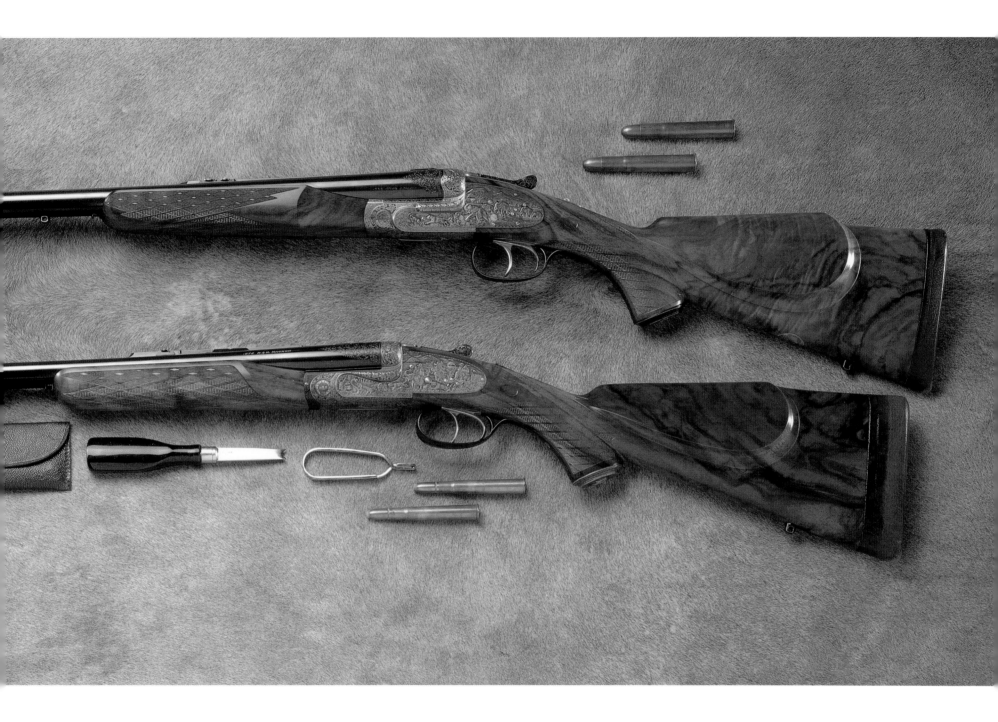

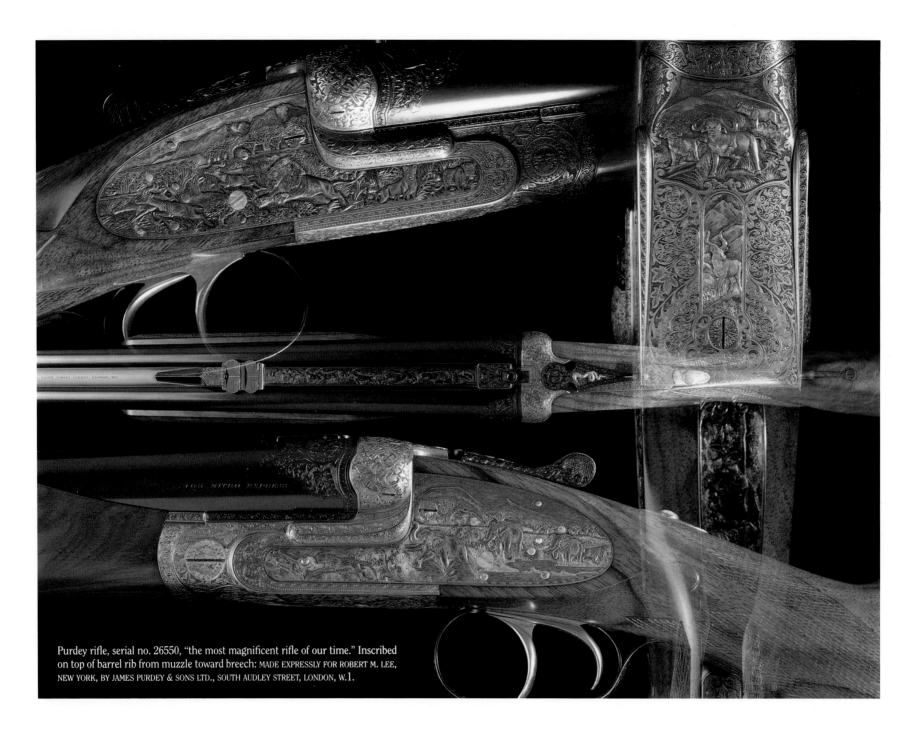

Purdey rifle, serial no. 26550, "the most magnificent rifle of our time." Inscribed on top of barrel rib from muzzle toward breech: MADE EXPRESSLY FOR ROBERT M. LEE, NEW YORK, BY JAMES PURDEY & SONS LTD., SOUTH AUDLEY STREET, LONDON, W.1.

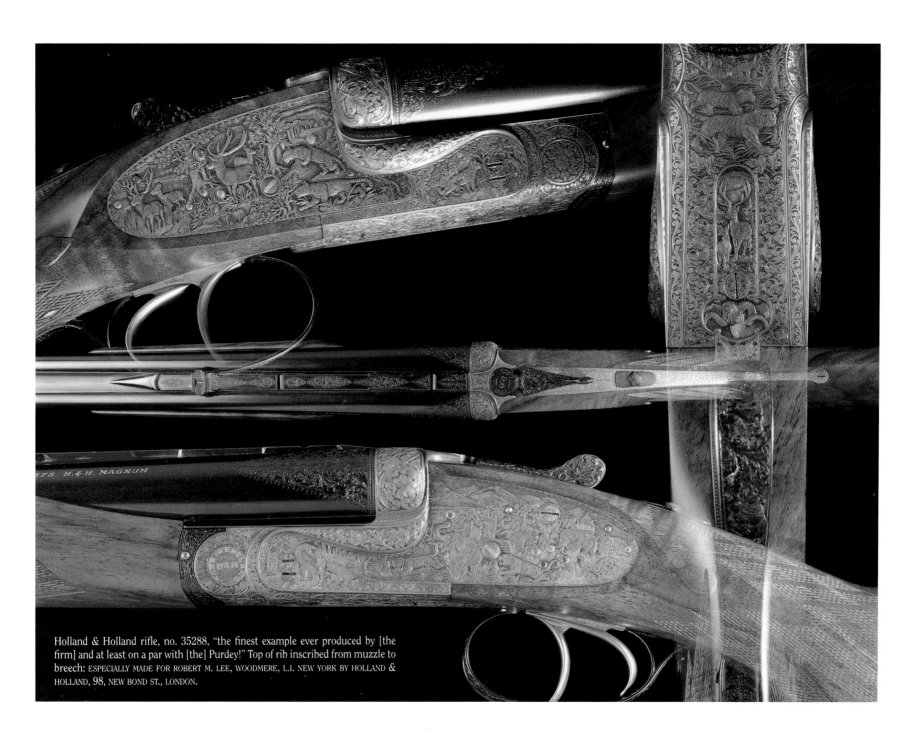

Holland & Holland rifle, no. 35288, "the finest example ever produced by [the] firm] and at least on a par with [the] Purdey!" Top of rib inscribed from muzzle to breech: ESPECIALLY MADE FOR ROBERT M. LEE, WOODMERE, L.I. NEW YORK BY HOLLAND & HOLLAND, 98, NEW BOND ST., LONDON.

America entered into the modern age of the collector, where investment value was as important a consideration for purchase as any other factor.

This new collecting age—and rage—meant a number of changes from previous periods of arms engraving. Artistically, the diversification of styles was considerable. Engravers, always alert to design influences, were confronted increasingly with new pictorial sources. The output of their colleagues was now readily available through magazines, arms shows, and the like, and such exposure inspired considerable variation in decoration.

The most evident difference between post–World War II arms engraving and that of earlier periods is the great variation in quality. Only a handful of the postwar engravers were true masters. Of the balance, several were quite able, though they still fell short of the highest standard in major areas—usually in the execution of finely detailed animal, bird, or human-figure motifs, and often in scrollwork, in addition to overall design. Not a few of this postwar group were of only average ability. Unfortunately, that state of affairs was representative of a postwar period in which quality had taken a backseat to quantity. All too often the customer was partly at fault, failing to recognize or insist on the highest standards.

Also all too common were craftsmen of limited versatility. In the second half of the nineteenth century it had not been unusual for the master engraver to also be an accomplished die cutter, a carver of wood, mother-of-pearl, ivory, and ebony, as well as a silver- and goldsmith. In marked contrast, many of the postwar engravers were hardly qualified to cut in more than one or two styles of scrollwork.

Neither was "progress" in the science of metallurgy of much help to the postwar engraver (including those active at this writing). Problems arose with investment castings (wherein the metal proved extremely tough), or with zinc-aluminum alloys, whose "painted" (anodized) finish filled in the engraved lines and ate away part of the detail, thus robbing it of the appearance of being hand cut. Some steels could only be cut with the greatest of effort; and the problem of porosity in the castings of some companies meant that the engraver often had to vary his design in order to conceal that irritating defect.

In a way, these problems and shortcomings were representative of the trials and tribulations that have become so commonplace in the "modern world." The engraver, a proud and independent soul, loves his work and does the best he can. One cannot help but feel that most of these men were born too late. Their era was, at the most recent, the late nineteenth century, and most of them would fit into the past effortlessly, and probably without objection.

Demands on the post–World War II engraver grew as the clientele became more and more educated. To avoid having to turn down commissions, most craftsmen tried to keep as many projects under way at a time as possible. The major source of work came from the individual client, since factories like Colt, Winchester, S&W, and Remington maintained only small engraving shops up until about 1960. On occasion some of the major manufacturers found it necessary to farm out work when in-house production lagged behind. Private patrons might wish a custom design on a pet handgun, rifle, or shotgun. And the growing number of custom gunmakers (mainly bolt-action rifles) turned work over to engravers for decorating special pieces. In assessing totals of arms engraved in the United States in the period 1945–60, the number would just about equal the figure for the period 1914–40. By contrast, the post–1960 years have been tremendously productive, a subject dealt with in detail in chapter 10.

Who were those craftsmen who set the standards of style and quality in those fifteen years following World War II? The best of them became much more renowned in their time than earlier craftsmen could ever have hoped to become in their own lifetimes. Gun magazines and books, and the swiftness of modern travel and communication all spread reputations at high speed. The foremost American artisans of those fifteen critical years were Joseph Fugger and Alvin White.

Fugger, in the employ of what was then the most distinguished sporting goods store in America, Abercrombie & Fitch—its gun division was known as Griffin & Howe—was creating some of the most exquisite firearms embellishments seen in any era in American history. And Alvin White's wide range of talents attracted clients from all over the United States, and his original eye led him to decorations—particularly on handguns—that tell a story. For example, White executed an engraving depicting Lt. Colonel George Armstrong Custer and the 7th Cavalry (for client and friend John S. duMont), and another of J. Edgar Hoover and the FBI (for another client and friend, William O. Sweet). These two gifted artist-engravers, along with craftsmen such as John E. Warren and E. C. Prudhomme (both frequently featured in the engraving section of John T. Amber's annual publication *Gun Digest,* and in magazines like the *American Rifleman, Guns,* and Robert E. Petersen's *Guns & Ammo*) kindled an ever-increasing interest in finely decorated firearms.

The stage was set for the veritable explosion of interest in the post-1960 period that continues today.

At bottom, c. 1960–period Griffin & Howe Mauser bolt-action sporting rifle; gold-inlaid and engraved by Joseph Fugger; RML monogram on pistol-grip cap; Weatherby scope, express sights, Griffin & Howe marking and no. 2219 on top of barrel; 7mm caliber; 23-inch barrel; double set trigger; checkered steel buttplate; horn forend. *At top,* W. Glanznig, Ferlach, Austria, three-barrel rifle and shotgun combination (Drilling); with scope by Zeiss; serial 101. Signed by maker in script on top barrel rib. Engraved by J. Deflorian (and so signed in script behind the right trigger), including matching steel buttplate. Note gold borders on forend stock screws on left side. Right trigger set for the rifle barrels; left trigger for the shotgun; 20-gauge barrel on top, with right-center barrel in 5.6 × 50R Magnum caliber and bottom barrel in 9.3 caliber; 24-inch barrels; automatic ejectors. Glanznig only contemporary maker capable of doing such a complex three-barrel mechanism of such superb quality.

Chapter 9
Tiffany Treasures

The opulence of Victorian art and of revivals of earlier eras, the elegance of Art Nouveau, the ebullience of an expanding nation epitomized in the doctrine of Manifest Destiny, and the universal fascination with a host of technological developments merged in mid- and late-nineteenth-century America to produce a form of decorative arts that has enthralled and delighted collectors and students ever since.

That medium was weaponry, from swords and Bowie knives to the revolvers of Colt and later Smith & Wesson and the lever-action repeaters of Winchester. The roster of artists included distinguished European (principally German) immigrant arms engravers, native sculptors, and, to an as yet undetermined degree, the prestigious firm of Tiffany & Co., of New York City.

Colt Industries' chairman, George A. Strichman, commissioned Tiffany & Co. to create this fantasy Colt Peacemaker; serial GAS-O/TIFFANY, subsequently donated by chairman for benefit auction at Christie's, on behalf of The Metropolitan Museum of Art's Arms and Armor Department. Oil painting by Alvin A. White; most of the decorative objects by Tiffany & Co.; revolver designed by Paul Epifanio of Tiffany's Corporate Division.

By the early nineteenth century, when a veneer of civilization had settled over both the Old World and the New, the highly refined small sword and pocket pistol were fulfilling the dual role of personal sidearm and gentleman's wardrobe accessory. Not surprisingly, therefore, in America at this time, jewelers' shops had joined more typical sources like hardware and sporting goods dealers as places where pocket pistols and edged weapons could be purchased—a direct reflection of their relationship to the wardrobe.

The house of Tiffany (founded in New York City in 1837), having soon established its reputation for providing the exquisite to people of means, was destined to become associated with the finest in personal arms. Charles Lewis Tiffany and his partner, friend, and neighbor from Danielson, Connecticut, John B. Young, first called the firm Tiffany & Young. When Jabez L. Ellis joined the company, the name was changed to Tiffany, Young & Ellis. The firm's original inventory of stationery and fancy goods was soon augmented with imported luxury items. In 1841 direct ties to European sources were strengthened and eventually branch stores were opened in Paris and London.

Examples of silver accessory items being offered by the firm appeared in its first catalogue, which was published in 1845 and was the forerunner of the famous Tiffany Blue Book, which began annual publication in 1877. Included in that first listing of 1845 were silver thimbles, card cases, pens and pencils, snuff boxes, and even silver-handled parasols.

Presentation Swords

The Mexican War produced a new crop of heroes, and the tradition of awarding suitably inscribed presentation swords was expanded and given greater design attention. Even minor figures, who were, nonetheless, authentic hometown paladins, were recognized with martial arms, while many of the leading lights received a substantially new form of presentation sword, one with an all-metal hilt that provided yet another surface (in addition to the blade and scabbard) for the artisan to embellish.

It was the Civil War, however, that elevated the presentation sword to the realm of high art, and Tiffany quickly became the leading name in its manufacture. The firm had begun its own direct involvement in silver manufacturing in 1851, when New York silversmith

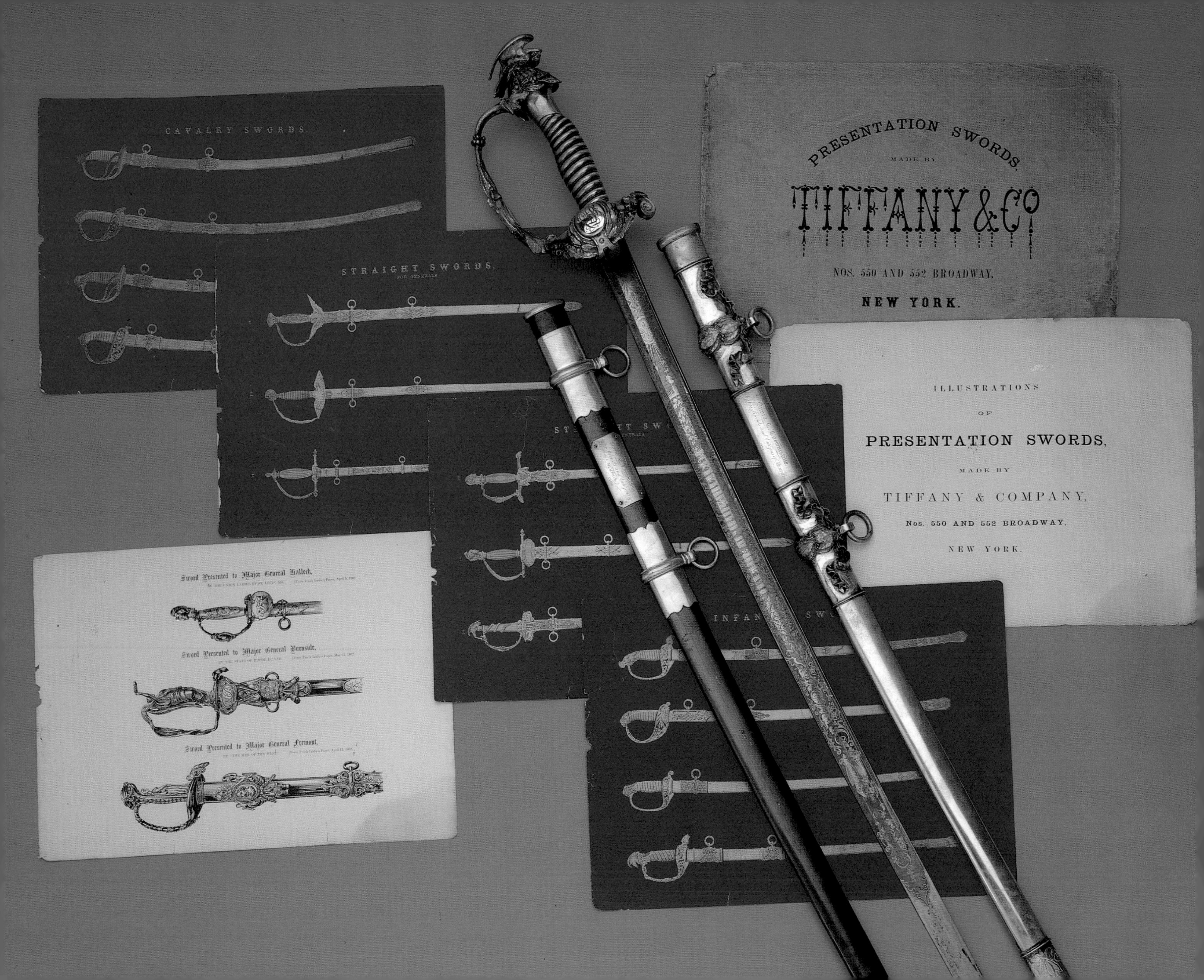

CAVALRY SWORDS.

STRAIGHT SWORDS,
FOR GENERALS

PRESENTATION SWORDS,
MADE BY
TIFFANY & CO.
NOS. 550 AND 552 BROADWAY,
NEW YORK.

ILLUSTRATIONS
OF
PRESENTATION SWORDS,
MADE BY
TIFFANY & COMPANY,
Nos. 550 AND 552 BROADWAY,
NEW YORK.

Sword Presented to Major General Halleck,

Sword Presented to Major General Burnside,

Sword Presented to Major General Fremont,

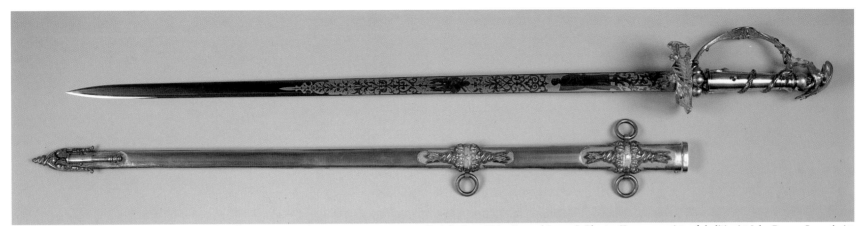

A modest inscription on the cannon barrel hilt identifies presentation from L & MC TO MAJ. GEN. J.G.B. Recipient was Major General James G. Blunt, a Kansas associate of abolitionist John Brown. Same design given to Major General John C. Robinson by his friends in New York, July 4, 1865. Among the presenters was Charles L. Tiffany.

(*right*) Two swords in rosewood cases, gold embossed in the lids: MANUFACTURED BY / TIFFANY & CO. / AND BY THEM PRESENTED TO THE / METROPOLITAN SANITARY FAIR. The Army sword, *at top,* presented to General Grant, raised $100,000 for Civil War charity through the sale of votes at one dollar each; blade by Collins & Co., Hartford. The Navy sword, *at bottom,* presented to Admiral Farragut. Still another Tiffany sword was presented to Admiral Farragut, by members of the Union League Club of New York, April 23, 1864. Considered most notable of the Civil War naval swords in the National Museum of American History (Smithsonian Institution), this latter boasts a pommel inspired by a Phrygian helmet, on its front a large anchor with gold wreath.

(*opposite*) Tiffany catalogue of 1862, showing three of their most deluxe commissions, and four pages of production designs for officers. The silver and silver-gilt sword, with its two scabbards, inscribed to David C. Loewenstine. Cased in rosewood, the set was given by "his many appreciative friends" (quoting from the *Memphis Daily Bulletin* of July 6, 1864). "The sword is from the manufactory of Tiffany, New York, and is of exquisite workmanship, eclipsing in splendor anything of the kind ever brought to Memphis" (from an article, "The Jews of Memphis: 1860–1865," in *The West Tennessee Historical Society Papers,* No. III, 1949). Tiffany catalogue sheets measure 14 by 10 inches.

Major General John McAllister Schofield received the "Washington Pattern" sword, which he clutched in rare photograph, "From the Citizens of St. Louis, Mo. Jany. 30th 1864." Inscribed on scabbard. Tiffany catalogue described this popular pattern as "Octagon Grip of silver, surmounted by head of Washington in gilt. Knuckleguard heavy gilt, with medallion relief of Hercules in silver. Wrist-guard, a crosspiece, with ram's head finials, and draped with flags. Scabbard chased and etched. Blade etched and gilt."

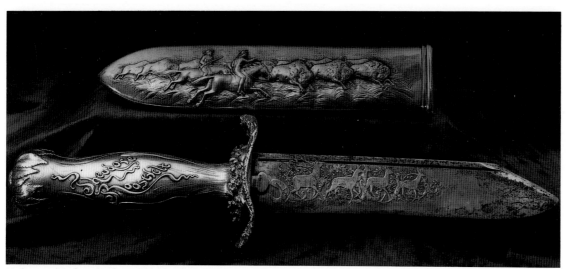

Made on order of rancher-huntsman Theodore Roosevelt, c. 1884, Bowie knife boasts hilt and scabbard of sterling silver, the blade relief engraved with game scenes and floral scrolls. Other side of hilt carries depiction of frontiersman in buckskins; 7½-inch blade; scabbard marked TIFFANY & CO. M STERLING.

John C. Moore agreed to produce exclusively for Tiffany. John Moore retired shortly afterward, but his son, Edward C. Moore, took his place and became the prime mover in Tiffany's climb to prestige. In 1853, Charles Tiffany took total control of the business, giving it the name of Tiffany & Co.

In 1861, under Moore's supervision, Tiffany began a series of swords that were among the most effectively embellished of the time and are today the most highly prized by museums and collectors. Among the most exquisite were elaborate Civil War presentations commissioned for Generals U. S. Grant and William Tecumseh Sherman and Admiral David G. Farragut, and a gold-mounted sword and scabbard presented (c. 1886) by Arizona admirers to General Nelson A. Miles. Tiffany itself stated that "in real artistic excellence" this latter was "one of the best, if not the very best" sword the firm had ever made.

An 1893 publication by Tiffany & Co. could boast: "The products of Tiffany & Co.'s workshops that could be classed under this heading ["War Testimonials"] are so numerous that only those associated with historic incidents or of general interest are mentioned below. . . ." The brochure listed the most noteworthy but also added that "hundreds of richly mounted testimonial swords were made, many of them set with precious stones and costing from $500 to $10,000." Among the recipients listed, in addition to several of those already noted, were Generals G. B. McClellan and J. C. Fremont and Major Generals H. W. Halleck and Ambrose E. Burnside.

Three splendid swords from the late period are the presentations for Admiral George Dewey, Captain John W. Philip, and Commander Richard Wainright. All were designed by Paulding Farnham, a sculptor and designer, a protégé of Edward C. Moore, and one of the directors of Tiffany & Co. All were sumptuous examples of Tiffany's traditional excellence in edged weaponry while adhering to the configuration of the regulation Naval dress sword of the period.

Shooting Trophies

One of the several shooting trophies by Tiffany is recorded in the files of the original client, the National Rifle Association. As last reported (c. 1947) the Grand Centennial Trophy was in a federal warehouse! A miniature version of the award, known as the Palma Trophy, is in the collections of the National Firearms Museum, at NRA Headquarters. Target shooters comprised a likely clientele for Tiffany, judging from a full-page advertisement in the program for the nineteenth annual fall prize meeting of the association, at Creedmoor, Long Island (September 1–5, 1891). The Tiffany advertisement offered chronographs of various types, in sterling silver and 18 karat gold.

Firearms

The Civil War also saw firearms added to Tiffany's wares, and the company sold Colt revolvers, and other products of various gunmakers, in addition to other military goods. Sometime in 1863, Tiffany & Co. entered into a contract with the Philadelphia gunmaker Henry Deringer to act as sole New York and New England agent for his by then famous pocket pistol. A Tiffany advertisement in the December *Army and Navy Journal* of that year announced the fact, and alluded to a curious phenomenon in the history of personal arms. The ad notes that the arrangement "has become necessary on the part of Mr. Deringer, in order to protect the public from spurious articles assuming to be his wares, and that purchaser only, wholesale or retail, will be safe who appreciates this fact."

Deringer's diminutive large-caliber pistols were exactly what were needed as frontier boom towns settled into respectability. The wearing of an exposed holster arm was often considered a provocation, but at the same time, no one was safe unarmed. The Deringer pistols, usually carried in pairs, rested unobtrusively in a gentleman's coat or waistcoat pockets, or in a lady's handbag or muff. Their extreme power made them deadly in close-range encounters. The fact that Deringer was the only gunmaker whose name has become a generic term is but one indication of the popularity of his pistols.

Inevitably, hundreds of other makers copied the

This design attributed to Paulding Farnham. Recipient of this elegant sword was Admiral Robley D. Evans, the gift a subscription (at a cost of $1,500) raised by the state of Iowa. Evans was the hero of the Battle of Santiago, where he was in command of the USS *Iowa;* his triumph prompted enormous pride from the citizens of that state.

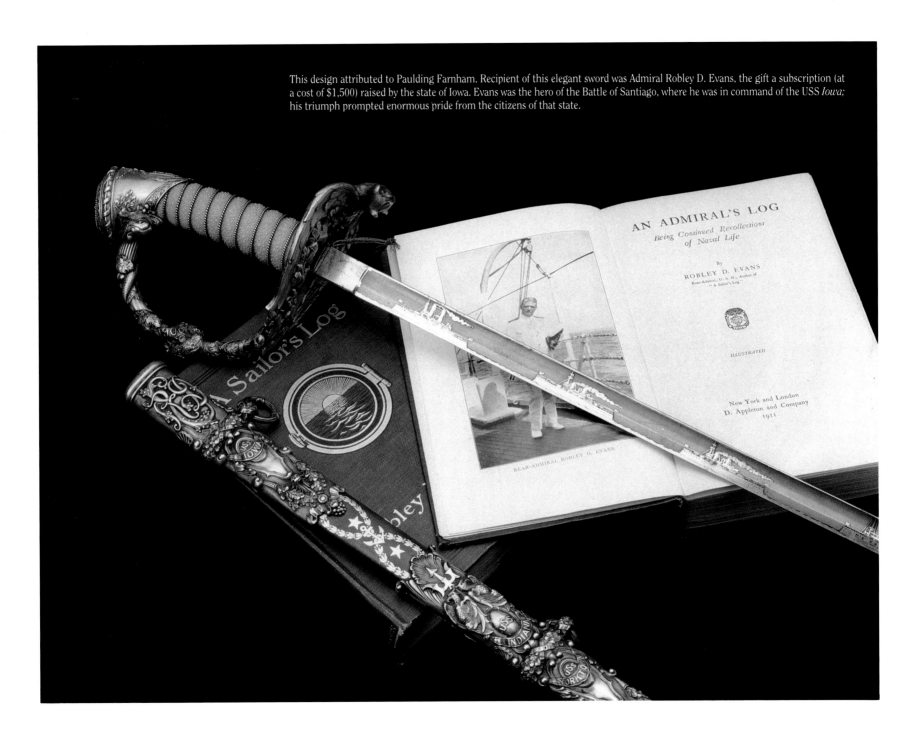

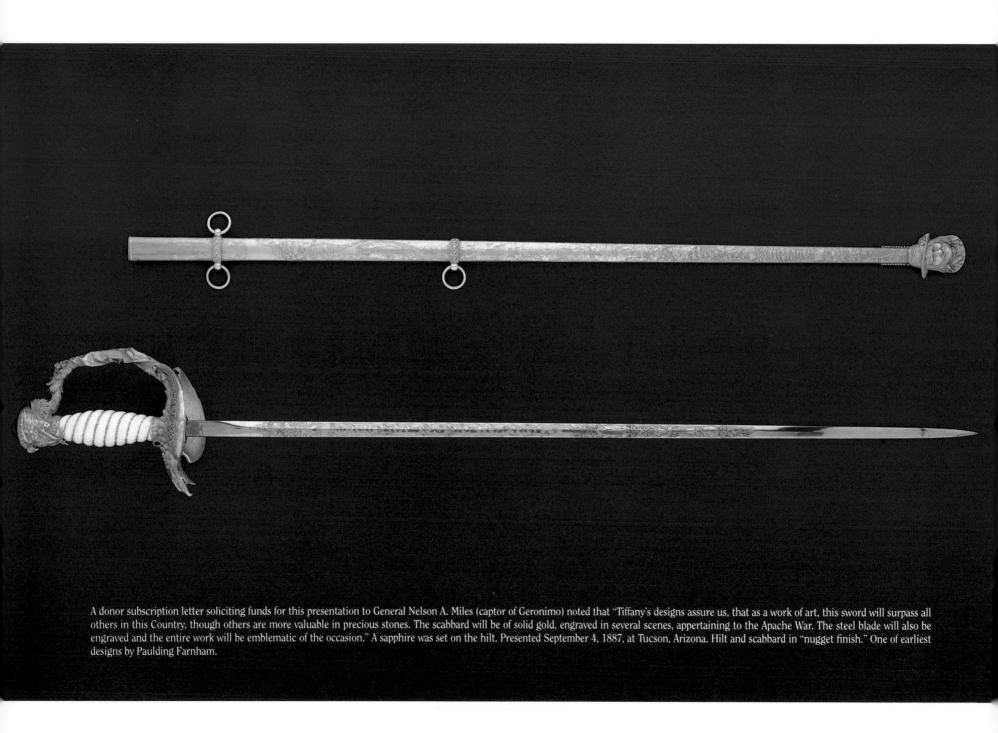

A donor subscription letter soliciting funds for this presentation to General Nelson A. Miles (captor of Geronimo) noted that "Tiffany's designs assure us, that as a work of art, this sword will surpass all others in this Country, though others are more valuable in precious stones. The scabbard will be of solid gold, engraved in several scenes, appertaining to the Apache War. The steel blade will also be engraved and the entire work will be emblematic of the occasion." A sapphire was set on the hilt. Presented September 4, 1887, at Tucson, Arizona. Hilt and scabbard in "nugget finish." One of earliest designs by Paulding Farnham.

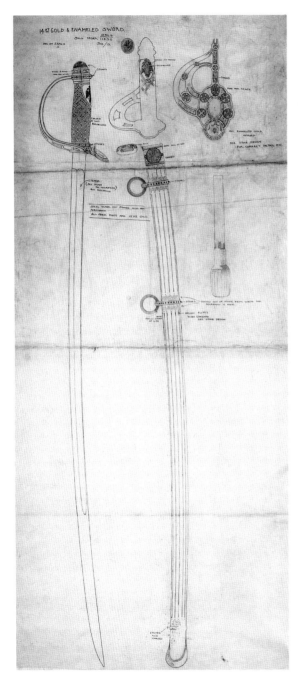

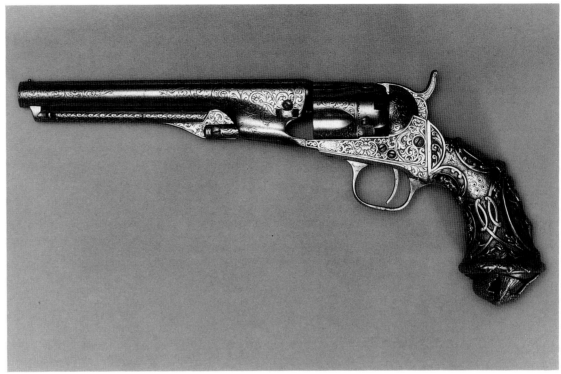

Arabesque and scroll decor by L. D. Nimschke, on Colt Model 1862 Police revolver, serial no. 27931. Prints from this revolver appear on page 33 of the Nimschke record book. The gold-plated "Tiffany grip" was cast in the John Quincy Adams Ward style of an eagle with figure of Justice. Remainder of pistol plated in gold and silver.

Design for a 14 karat and enameled sword, with stone mounts, and etched and gilded steel blade, period of World War I. Believed ordered as a presentation for French military figure Marshal Foch.

Advertisement for the Deringer pistol in the *Army and Navy Journal,* 1864. A genuine Deringer with Tiffany & Co. markings has yet to be viewed by the author.

Probably gold-inlaid and engraved by Gustave Young, serial no. 38549 Model 1862 Colt Police revolver has gold or gold-plated grips designed by J.Q.A. Ward, and is quite similar to the cased pair of revolvers of the same model, presented by President Lincoln to Kibrisili Pasha, 1864.

Deringer style, only to find that without the cachet of DERINGER/PHILADELA stamped on breech and lock, even a superior gun (and many, in fact, were technically better and more finely wrought) was doomed to obscurity. Outright counterfeiting became common, as well as such subterfuges as one perpetrated by some former Deringer employees. They took a fortuitously named Philadelphia tailor in partnership and began stamping their pistols J.DERINGER/PHILADELA. There is no evidence that John Deringer, the tailor, ever set foot in a gun shop.

Deringer pistols, as produced by Henry Deringer, were iron-barrelled, with case-hardened locks, walnut stocks, and German-silver mountings. A few, however, were made with coin-silver mountings, and fewer still with gold. While there is no proof in existing records, it is possible that Tiffany remounted some Deringers to particular customers' specifications.

"Tiffany Grips"

The firm *was*, however, directly involved in the manufacture of silver grips for revolvers made by the Colt factory, and both Samuel Colt and D. B. Wesson were Tiffany & Co. clients.

In 1847, an order to the Colt factory from the arms-dealing firm of Moore & Baker resulted in the Colonel George Washington Morgan pair of Whitneyville-Hartford Dragoon revolvers, with inscribed and engraved silver grips. These early grips were faithful to the design of standard-model revolver handles, rendered in wood. But starting with the 1860s, a style of cast-metal grip appeared on presentation revolvers that is more reminiscent of the hiltings on presentation swords of the period. Among collectors, this style of grip has acquired the name "Tiffany," primarily because it exhibits the lush Victorian taste in embellishment that can be found not only on swords but on many of Tiffany's other silver pieces. To assume that all such arms were Tiffany products, however, would be a mistake. In fact, most were not.

Three designs predominated during the period 1861–75: the American and Mexican eagle, the Civil War

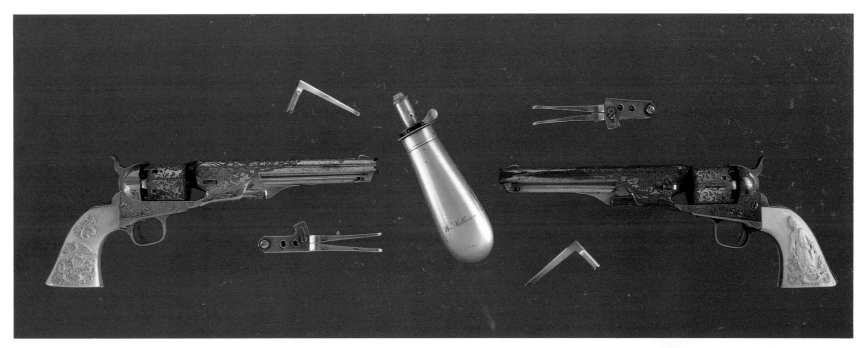

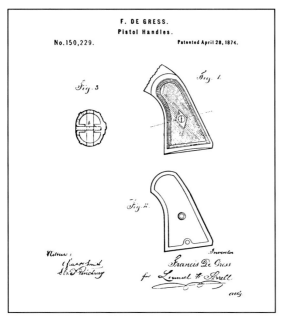

Presentation set of Colt Model 1861 Navy revolvers, given in 1867 to Kansas hero William Mathewson (considered by many to be the original "Buffalo Bill") for saving a train of 147 wagons from the Indians. Mahogany casing, etching, silver plating, inscribing (on case lid and buttstraps) and relief-carved ivory grips attributed to Tiffany & Co. Comparison should be made with the ivory-stocked Henry Deringer pistols on page 90, and Lt. Colonel George Armstrong Custer's pair of Smith & Wesson etched pistols (see the author's *The Peacemakers,* page 98).

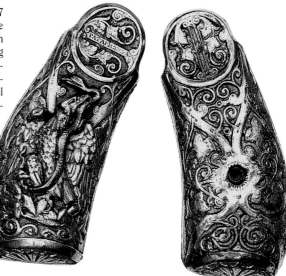

A patent for "Improvement in Pistol-Handles," cast metal grips, granted to Francis DeGress, of Bloomfield, New Jersey. Grips made for Colt, Marlin, and other makes of handguns.

Best grade known to author of DeGress grips. Note patent date, April 28, 1874, marked at top of grip *at left*.

battle scene, and a design that has been called the "missionary and child" by collectors, but which is actually a figure of Justice and an American eagle. All three types have a presentation escutcheon just behind the hammer. They are nearly always cast in bronze and subsequently plated in gold or silver.

The Justice-and-eagle design, rarest and most striking of the three, has been traced to sculptor John Quincy Adams Ward, who designed it on commission from the U.S. government. The occasion was a presentation from President Abraham Lincoln to Kibrisili Pasha, governor of Adrianople, in 1864. Ward directly supervised the work, which was carried out on a pair of Colt Model 1862 Police revolvers (serial numbers 25513/E and 25514/E). A State Department record, Instruction No. 68 of January 11, 1864, noted: "The designs for the handles, which are of solid silver (oxidized) and those on the barrels were made by Mr. Ward, a young and promising sculptor of New York, who also superintended the workmanship, which as you will perceive is of the finest description." The revolvers were subsequently returned to the United States in 1945, as a gift to Franklin Delano Roosevelt, and are currently in the Franklin Delano Roosevelt Library Museum, Hyde Park, New York.

The identical design appears on the grips of certain other deluxe Model 1862 Police revolvers, which were, without doubt, cast from the same mold. In the early 1860s, Ward was also employed by the Ames Sword

The Jewelers' Review published an engraving of this Smith & Wesson No. 3 New Model Double Action Navy revolver in an article on the Chicago World's Fair of 1893. Revolver illustration identified with a caption that noted: "Silver Handle, studded with turquoise." In addition to the sixty-eight turquoise cabochons on petal-form bases, two lapis slabs were set by the frame hinge on either side, with a large lapis slab within a sunflower motif on the buttcap. Serial no. 23060; etched sight, barrel, and cylinder; finished "in the white." Marked TIFFANY & CO. STERLING and with special exposition cartouche on bottom of frame.

Etched, silver-plated, and with carved ivory and sterling silver grips, this Tiffany Smith & Wesson was decorated with Moorish motifs. Typical of designs Edward C. Moore was creating in the mid-1880s.

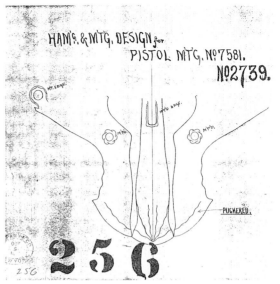

Rare 18 karat gold grips on Smith & Wesson Safety Hammerless revolver. Factory shipping records indicate revolver went to New York City jobber; eventually reached Tiffany & Co. Wine label features selected modern designs by Tiffany & Co., Corporate Division, for special-order revolvers. Vineyard owned by Tiffany chairman William R. Chaney.

Tiffany design for S&W, indicating technique of wrapping grip around form to obtain final shape, which is soldered together. References show system of mounting to revolver. Other designs for handgun grips have been observed in Tiffany archives, among them a salamander style and a dragonfly, both influenced by Japanese art.

Silver-mounted Winchester Model 1886 takedown rifle, serial no. 120528, with Tiffany markings on buttplate, indicating display at Exposition Universelle, 1900. (A design drawing from Tiffany archive marked "GUN MTG. No 11657" either shows a variant preceding this rifle or is of a completely different Winchester Model 1886—note straight stock configuration.) Rosewood stock; scalloped detail to top of forend. For bottom view, see frontispiece.

(*opposite*) Factory samples from the S&W Collection, decorated by Tiffany, c. 1892, for the World's Columbian Exposition. Commissioned by D. B. Wesson, and a departure from the norm of using only in-house engraving for displays. Frames and grips overlaid with silver; etched cylinders and barrels. All Tiffany-made S&W revolvers bear the jeweler's marking and registration number.

Hand Ejector S&W revolvers, .32 caliber, c. 1896–1903. Swept-profile sterling silver grips etched with police and thug motif *at left* and American West theme *at right*. S&W exhibited these arms at such events as the Exposition Universelle, Paris (1900) and the Pan-American Exposition, Buffalo, New York (1901).

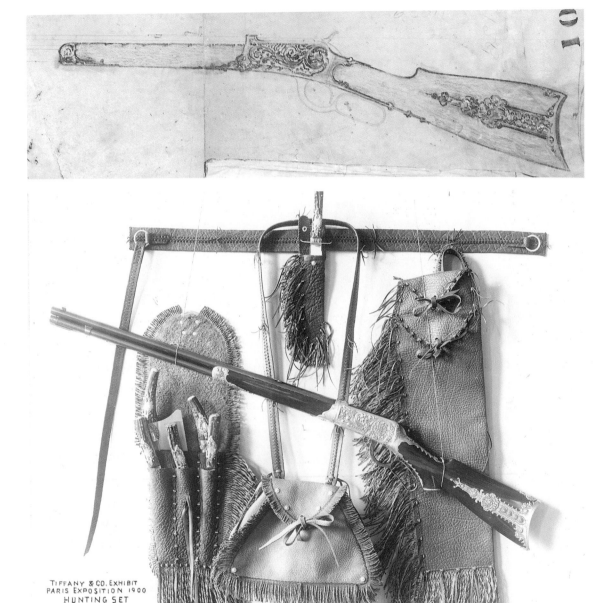

TIFFANY & CO. EXHIBIT
PARIS EXPOSITION 1900
HUNTING SET

NEG. NO. 1949

⅕ FULL SIZE

Company in the design of sword hilts. The Colt records of October 1866 note a gold-mounted and engraved Model 1862 Police pistol made for James T. Ames of the Ames firm. While the serial number is not given, the 5½-inch barrel length noted is the same as that of the gold-inlaid and engraved revolver number 38549. The Colt records, however, make no specific mention of deluxe grips.

If Ames was associated with the New York retail and jobber firm of Schuyler, Hartley and Graham, prestigious vendors of military goods during and after the Civil War, that might account for the source of most of the cast grips on percussion and early cartridge Colt revolvers (their 1864 catalogue illustrates three such arms). The barrel and frame engraving on these revolvers is strongly suggestive of L. D. Nimschke, active in the New York area at that time—and associated primarily with Schuyler, Hartley and Graham.

Lewis I. Sharp's *John Quincy Adams Ward, Dean of American Sculpture* notes: "After Ward had set up a studio in the Dodsworth Building in New York in 1861 the Ames Manufacturing Company employed him to model presentation swords and small art objects that included cane tops, pistol mounts, and table bells." One of his most important and elaborate sword commissions was the presentation for General U. S. Grant, for which the citizens of Jo Daviess County, Illinois, paid the Ames Manufacturing Company $2,000.

The association of Ward with Ames, of Nimschke with Schuyler, Hartley and Graham, and the association of all

Handsomely rendered design drawing shows Kentucky rifle–style decoration on left side of rosewood buttstock of Model 1894 Paris Exposition takedown Winchester. The most profuse and elaborate Art Nouveau embellishment for an American longarm of that time.

In Tiffany's display at the Paris Exposition of 1900, a Model 1894 Winchester was enriched in elaborate fashion, the decor with embossed sheet sterling silver. Design drawing reveals pains for the most profuse and precise treatment. Hunting sets bore Tiffany & Co. blade stamps, likely from dies cut by the Young family.

of them with cast-grip Colt revolvers; the Ames Company's involvement in casting presentation-sword hilts and revolver handles; and the fact that miscellaneous bronze castings from the Ames estate show a high degree of diversity and sophistication—all of these factors combine to suggest that most of the so-called Tiffany Colt grips may have been made by the Ames Company.

What then of Tiffany? It began to appear as though no cast grips were ever made by the firm for Colt revolvers, but Charles H. and Mary Grace Carpenter, while researching their comprehensive book *Tiffany Silver,* uncovered an entry in the Tiffany plant journal no. 1, dated January 6, 1863, referencing a "Pistol Mounted Colts Navy size A.W. Spies" (Spies was a New York firearms dealer and a jobber in Colts). The Carpenters noted further that no Tiffany plant records existed of Civil War presentation swords, and there may have been a separate account book that has since been lost. There may also have been a separate account book for firearms. Former Tiffany & Co. archivist Janet Zapata located several design drawings for deluxe swords, most of them by Edward C. Moore, but was unable to find any ledger documentation on Civil War period deluxe firearms in addition to the Carpenters' find.

However, a note in the February 6, 1864, *Hartford Evening Press,* following the Colt factory fire two days earlier, stated that "The splendid pistols made for presentation to Gen. Grant, were not destroyed, having been sent a few days ago, to Tiffany & Co., New York, to receive their gold mountings." The newspaper's reference to "gold mountings" could only mean metal grips, not plating or inlay, or even overlay. Being a distinguished retail and manufacturing firm, it is logical that Tiffany would have signed such work, especially a pair of pistols for one of the most important officers in the Union Army. The

Details of the left side of frame and buttstock, showing embossed silver. Rifle lent to The Metropolitan Museum of Art, along with selection of Tiffany-mounted S&W revolvers, on occasion of reopening of the Arms and Armor galleries, November 1991.

Matched pair of Colt Peacemaker revolvers, decorated on order of George Strichman by Alvin A. White, with gold inlays, engraved and sculpted steel, and silver and gold grips, their original pattern made by White, the castings by Joel Meisner & Co. Now exhibited in the Gene Autry Western Heritage Museum, Los Angeles.

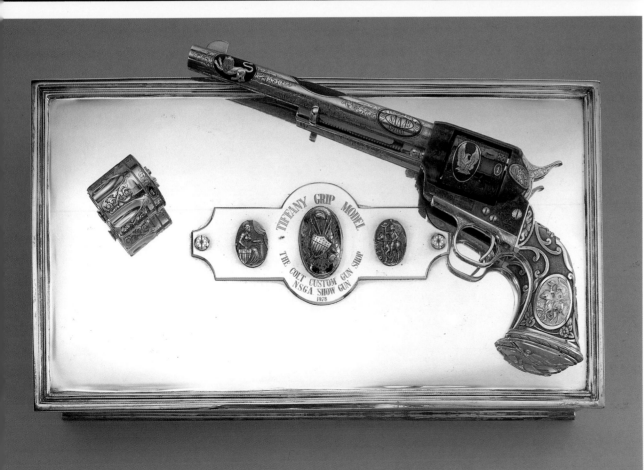

By the Colt factory for the National Sporting Goods Association 1978 Gun Show; the design theme was "Tiffany grips." Author aided Colt's Al DeJohn in creating design, and on behalf of firm approached Tiffany to request their manufacture of the silver and gold casing. The Design Department's director at the time, John Brown, agreed to take the job, and began sketching while the author was still at Tiffany. Case lid plaque and gold and silver grips by A. A. White; gun inlaid with details from Tiffany revolver grips made prior to 1900.

whereabouts of General Grant's Tiffany Colts remains a mystery, unless it is the elaborate set pictured on page 142.

Art Nouveau Arms

The period from the mid-1880s to the early 1900s saw silver-gripped Colts and Smith & Wessons, at least two silver-mounted Winchester rifles, and one silver-mounted Bowie knife (for the young rancher Theodore Roosevelt). Some of these exotic arms are documented in Tiffany records. The Tiffany catalogues (Blue Books) for 1900 through 1909 advertised "Revolvers of the most improved types, mounted in silver, carved ivory, gold, etc. with rich and elaborate decorations, $50.00 to $300.00. Cases, boxes, belts and holsters made in appropriate styles for presentations." Several examples have already been noted and were exhibited by Smith & Wesson at the 1893 World's Columbian Exposition in Chicago. Only one Colt from the period, a New Army and Navy Model double action revolver, from the mid-1890s, with Tiffany-marked, etched silver, bag-shaped grip, is extant. The engraving on the steel parts appears to be contemporary with the grip, but was unlikely to have been executed by Tiffany.

Examples of these arms from the late nineteenth century onward have always been found marked with the firm's name, usually reading TIFFANY & CO. MAKERS STERLING stamped in small letters on the silver in a relatively obscure place. On at least one example, the marking was positioned on a separate plate which was soldered to the front of the gripstrap, directly behind the triggerguard. The distinctive marking on a rare gold-gripped Smith & Wesson is indicated in its picture caption.

The procedure used in creating the cast grips was considerably different from the more traditional method of arms engraving. Decoration by an engraver involved laying out the design on the metal, and then cutting the intricate motifs into the steel surfaces with hammer and graver. By comparison, the cast Art Nouveau grips were carefully fitted silver sheaths, and if necessary the frame of the gun was even cut or reshaped so that the handle could be formed in the desired design. The decoration itself was generally chased for more precise detail, after casting. Some grips were etched with the decoration after casting. And others were made from sheet silver, cut and formed to the final grip contour, and then etched (and sometimes engraved) with decorations.

Not all the revolvers, most of which were Smith & Wessons, had cast or formed sheet-silver grips. Some with wooden or ivory grips were further embellished with silver latticework, skillfully pierced and decorated, then fitted over the grip so the wood or ivory showed through. Others were in niello, and a Tiffany design drawing records another in enamel.

The two Winchester rifles known, a Model 1886 and a Model 1894, were decorated in two contrasting degrees of coverage, and in two contrasting techniques. Design drawings for both rifles have survived, as well as the rifles themselves. The Model 1886 was more simply decorated with cast and chased fittings, whereas the Model 1894 was sheathed in repoussé silver on the frame, with the balance richly appointed with cast and chased mountings. Both Winchesters were displayed by Tiffany at the Paris Exposition Universelle of 1900, as evidenced by minute touchmarks on each rifle: a TCO monogram superimposed on a feather.

Also displayed at the Paris Exposition, a world's fair of considerable moment, were sets of hunting and skin-

The Colt Diamondback birthday gift commission from George Strichman for his wife, Sandy, had same vermeil grip as pictured, but floral gold inlays on steel, in contrast to Art Nouveau style shown here on gun made for author. Both designs by April Flory. The Purdey shotgun encrusted in gold by K. C. Hunt, on order of American client.

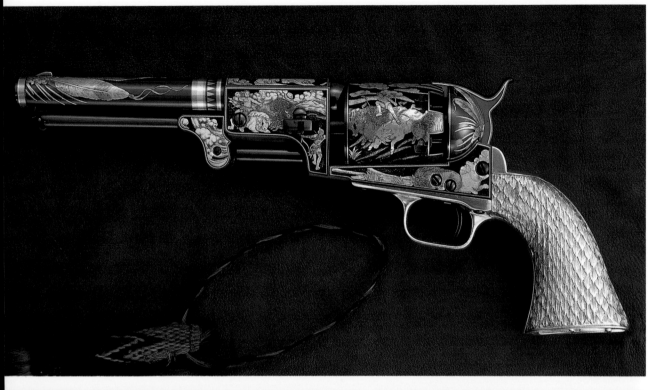

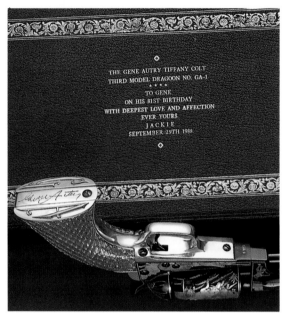

Gene Autry's eighty-first birthday gift, which rendered the normally loquacious singing cowboy momentarily speechless. Gold and silver overlay and inlay, with vermeil grips; GA monogram on butt. Snakeskin-motif grips by V. Ubaldo, craftsman who executed grips for George and Sandy Strichman. Design by Larry Wojick.

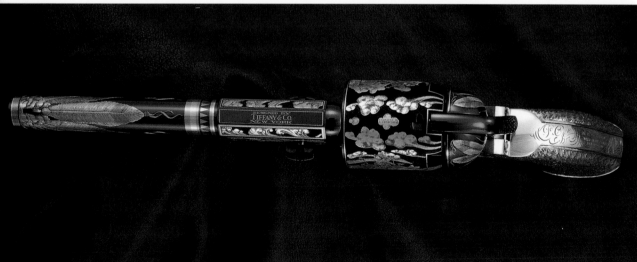

ning knives, in leather scabbards, and with matching hunting bags, made by Tiffany & Co. for its hunting clients.

After the start of World War I, the firm was commissioned to design and produce an elegant sword, "gold and enamelled." The design exists in the Tiffany Archives, but whether or not the sword was completed remains unknown. A simple silver plaque was made for a Colt Model 1911 Automatic pistol, with the embossed inscription: F.R. APPLETON, JR. 2ND LIEUT FROM 'G' FIRST TRAINING REGIMENT PLATTSBURG, NY. AUGUST 1915. Design drawings for this commission are also in the Tiffany & Co. archives. The bottom edge of the plaque bears the stamped marking: TIFFANY & CO., probably struck by a die cut by Gustave Young or one of his sons, Oscar or Eugene.

Probably due to the Sullivan Act, passed in 1911 to eliminate guns from the criminal element in New York City but actually serving primarily to keep them out of the hands of the city's law-abiding citizens, Tiffany & Co. dropped out of the arms business soon after completing the Colt Automatic and the gold and enamel sword commissions. It was not until 1983 that the firm returned to the field of fine firearms with a series of projects that equal or surpass the most demanding and beautiful of arms in American history.

Revival of a Tradition

The modern phase of the arms of Tiffany & Co. began when the author suggested to Colt Industries' board chairman, George A. Strichman, that he should enquire of Tiffany's chairman, William R. Chaney, about the feasibility of making a special commission Colt revolver. Within a week after Strichman's letter, not only had Chaney responded favorably, but he had arranged for Paul Epifanio, of Tiffany's Corporate Division Design Department, to visit the Colt Industries offices on Park Avenue, New York. George Strichman and the author discussed the commission with Paul Epifanio, and the initial design drawings were completed six months later.

The availability of Colt Industries' arms collection and gun library and the private arms collection of George Strichman proved advantageous to Tiffany's understanding of the extraordinary history and traditions of American arms engraving, and the special role of Tiffany & Co. in that field.

This first design, using George Strichman's yacht *The Peacemaker* as its theme, was so extraordinary that a pair of revolvers was ordered, followed by another. This last was to replace the gift by Strichman of one of his matched pair to The Metropolitan Museum of Art, for a Christie's benefit auction sponsored by the Armor and Arms Club of New York. The revolver sold at a figure twice Strichman's cost. He was so thrilled with every facet of the Tiffany commissions that he ordered still another revolver: a birthday present for his wife, Sandy. Tiffany corporate designers Paul Epifanio, April Flory,

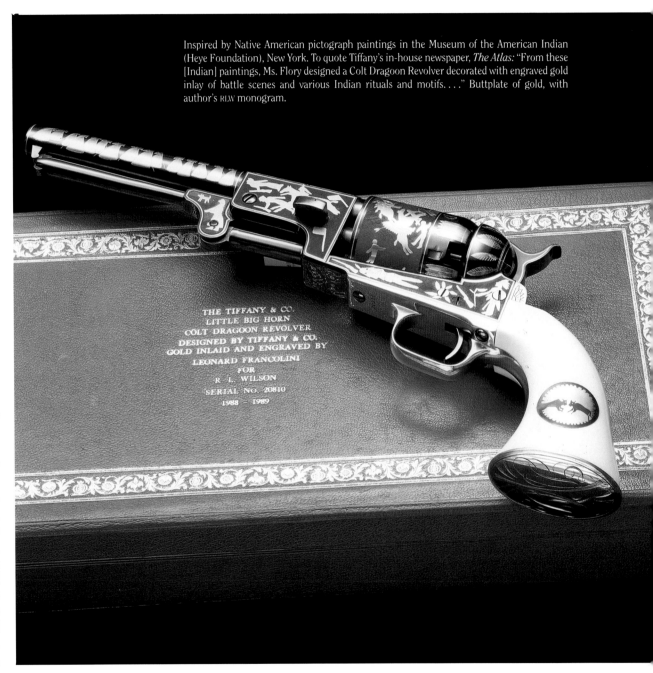

Inspired by Native American pictograph paintings in the Museum of the American Indian (Heye Foundation), New York. To quote Tiffany's in-house newspaper, *The Atlas:* "From these [Indian] paintings, Ms. Flory designed a Colt Dragoon Revolver decorated with engraved gold inlay of battle scenes and various Indian rituals and motifs. . . ." Buttplate of gold, with author's RLW monogram.

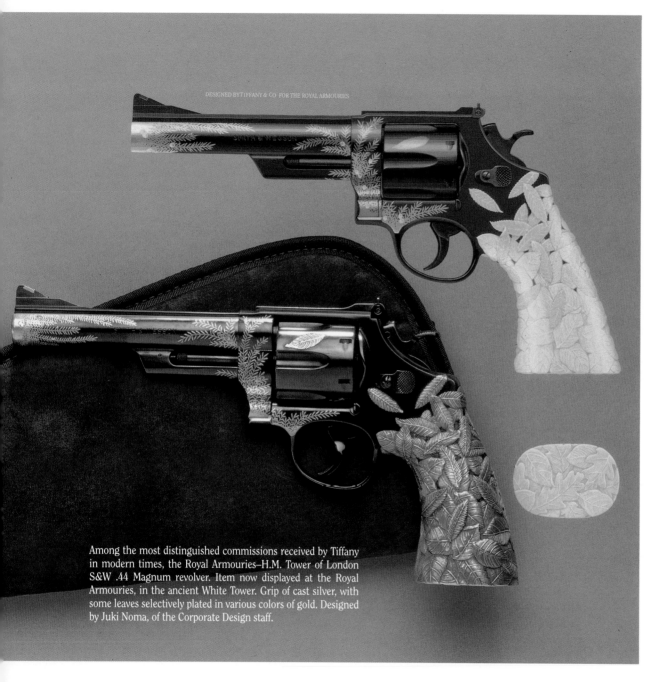

Among the most distinguished commissions received by Tiffany in modern times, the Royal Armouries–H.M. Tower of London S&W .44 Magnum revolver. Item now displayed at the Royal Armouries, in the ancient White Tower. Grip of cast silver, with some leaves selectively plated in various colors of gold. Designed by Juki Noma, of the Corporate Design staff.

and Larry Wojick paid a call at the Strichman home in New Rochelle, New York, ostensibly to see their collections of guns and art—though Tiffany's real purpose was to gather personal research information in order to create the design for the Sandy Strichman revolver.

Completed in 1985, the new revolver, a Colt Diamondback .38, featured an orchid theme, the grip in vermeil (gold-plated sterling silver), in a Tiffany blue-leather-and-velvet case in the form of a book. The piece was quite stunning, and—with the client's permission—the author commissioned a similar revolver, but with a differing design for the gold-inlaid barrel, cylinder, and frame.

Next came an order from the author for a Colt Dragoon, the designers having been given only the themes of the Battle of the Little Bighorn and cowboys and Indians. Of the two designs—each beautiful and captivating—the author commissioned the former, while Jackie Autry commissioned the latter as an eighty-first birthday present for her husband, Gene. Accompanying the present was a letter of congratulations from Chairman Chaney, which also made reference to Tiffany's historic tradition of artistic arms.

The Little Bighorn revolver was the subject of an article in Tiffany's employee publication, *The Atlas,* documenting the design inspiration as follows:

> The Colt's designs are based on Indian paintings of the famous battle of the Little Bighorn. . . . While researching the project at the American Indian Museum in Manhattan, Tiffany designer April Flory found pictorial versions of the fight by the Sioux, Kicking Bear, and Red Horse, and the Cheyenne, Two Moon. These battle scenes are abundantly detailed, depicting such intricate elements as the departing spirits of the dead soldiers and the slain Custer with his hat, pistol and brass bullet shells scattered next to him.

John Loring, Tiffany's senior vice president and design director, approves all designs and has been instrumental in inspiring the high level of achievement of the Corporate Design Department and the craftsmen who execute the commissions. Most of the initial projects were under

The American Eagle by Tiffany, commissioned by the U.S. Historical Society; designed by April Flory.

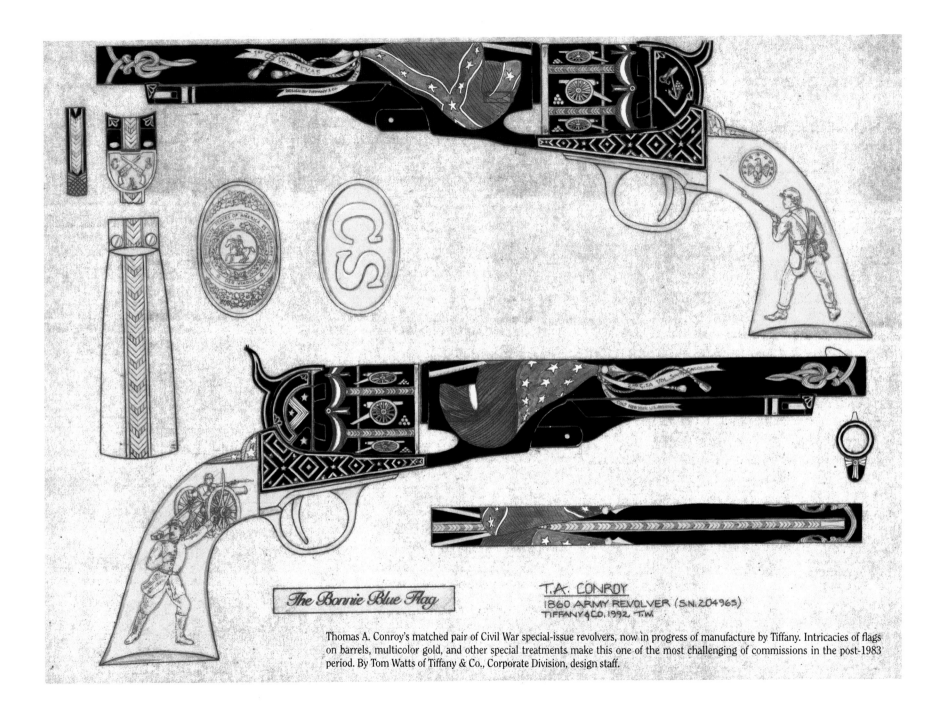

The Bonnie Blue Flag

T.A. CONROY
1860 ARMY REVOLVER (S.N. 204965)
TIFFANY & CO. 1992 T.W.

Thomas A. Conroy's matched pair of Civil War special-issue revolvers, now in progress of manufacture by Tiffany. Intricacies of flags on barrels, multicolor gold, and other special treatments make this one of the most challenging of commissions in the post-1983 period. By Tom Watts of Tiffany & Co., Corporate Division, design staff.

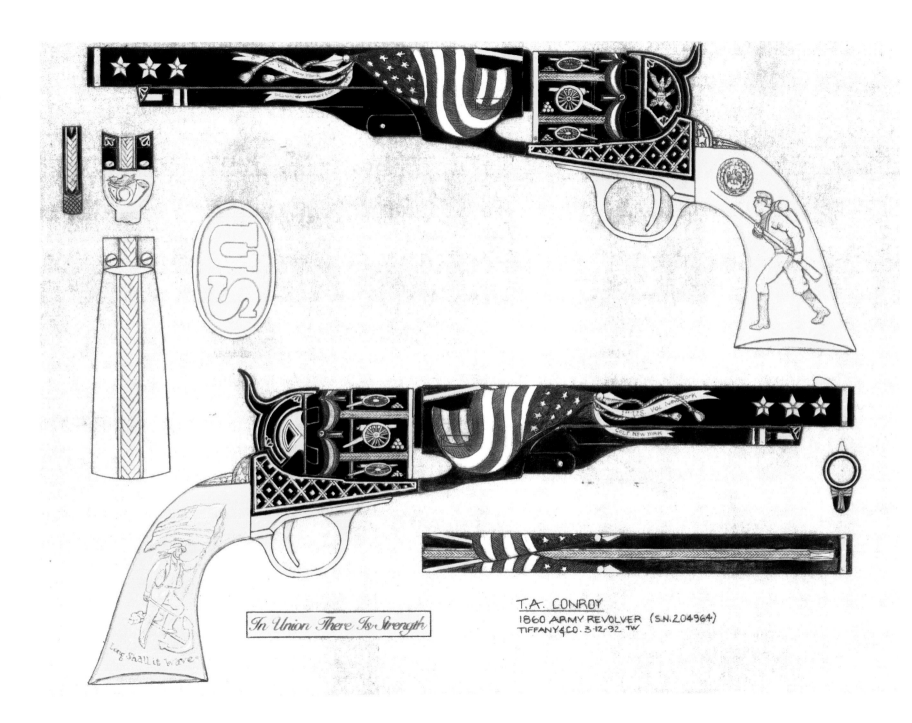

In Union There Is Strength

T.A. CONROY
1860 ARMY REVOLVER (S.N. 204964)
TIFFANY & CO. 3-12-92. TW

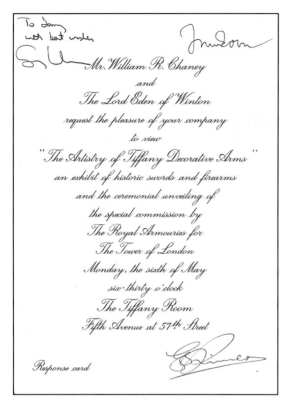

the aegis of Sandra M. Alton, director of special design sales, and later the firm's director of international sales. Nancy Goldberg assumed the management of special design projects in 1990, and she in turn was succeeded by Victoria Reynolds, in 1993.

Next in the evolving modern masterworks of Tiffany was a Smith & Wesson Model 29 .44 Magnum revolver, commissioned by the Royal Armouries–H.M. Tower of London. While visiting in London, 1988, the author showed Guy Wilson, Master of the Armouries, and Graeme Rimer, Keeper of Firearms, a Tiffany & Co. brochure that pictured and described Sandy Strichman's deluxe Colt. The next day the Royal Armouries indicated its interest in a special Tiffany commission, and over the course of the next year the Corporate Division designed the uniquely exquisite revolver pictured on page 284.

On completion, the revolver was so striking, and the event of such significance in the history of arms decoration, that Tiffany arranged a special retrospective loan exhibition at its New York store, 1991: "The Artistry of Tiffany Decorative Arms." Organized by Janet Zapata, the display drew from the wealth of presentation swords, the Winchester Model 1886 rifle, various Art Nouveau Smith & Wesson revolvers, the Colt .45 Automatic pistol, and all the creations of Tiffany's Corporate Division, beginning with the George Strichman Peacemaker Colts, and ending with the Royal Armouries' Smith & Wesson.

The very evening the show opened, the author met with Robert H. Kline, the chairman of the U.S. Historical Society, and Tiffany corporate officials, to approve the next deluxe design: The American Eagle Colt Model 1860 Army revolver. At this writing, designs have been completed for a David Miller & Co. Winchester Model 70 rifle, a pair of Civil War–theme Colt 1860 Army revolvers, and a Colt Peacemaker revolver. The author has ordered an elaborate Bowie knife, and other clients have assumed positions in line, expressing their desire for specially designed arms by Tiffany.

The most renowned of American arms, made into true works of art for a galaxy of enthusiastic and sometimes famous clients, are as much a hallmark of Tiffany & Co. as their signature on more familiar examples of fine silver flat- and hollowware and fabulous gems and jewelry. In the process, the New York firm has claimed an enviable niche in the centuries-old tradition of arms embellishment.

Designed and at this writing being built for arms specialist Norm Flayderman, Colt Single Action Army shows influence of the Empire style, with Boutet-inspired buttplate. Grip option of mother-of-pearl, gold and ebony inlays, or blued-steel inlays and bright silver, on vermeil. Design by Tom Watts.

DETAIL SHOWING FRONT OF BARREL & CHAMBER

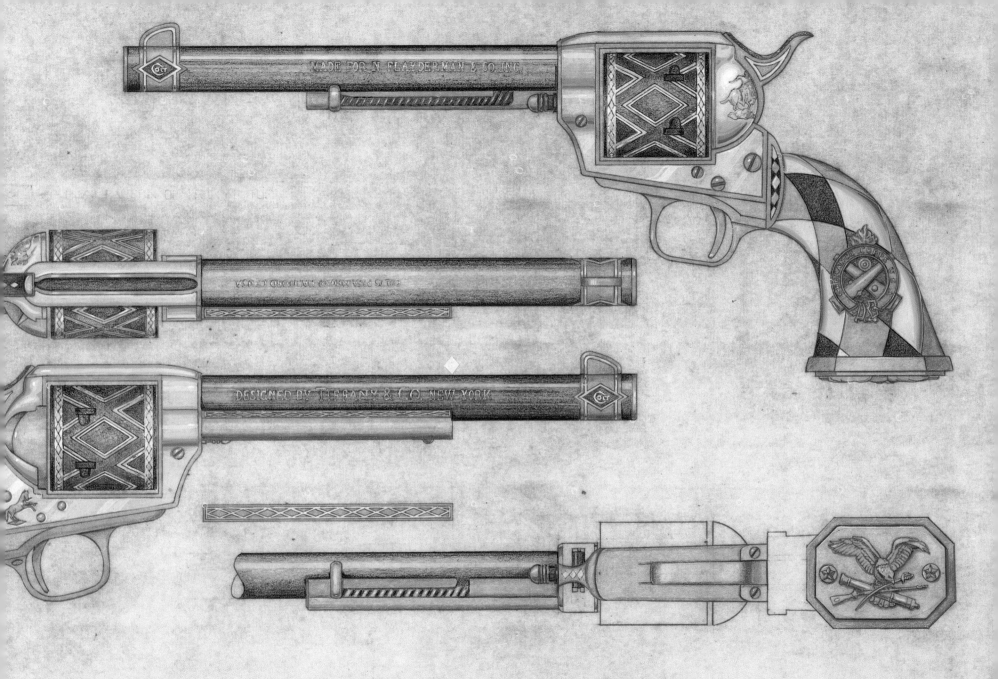

MADE FOR N. FLAYDERMAN & CO. INC

COLTS PAT'A MFG CO HARTFORD CT USA

DESIGNED BY TIFFANY & CO. NEW YORK

— MR. NORMAN FLAYDERMAN —
©TIFFANY & CO. 1992 TW
`COLT 45`, 7½` BARREL

The Leopard Winchester Model 70, the David Miller Company deluxe cased rifle set, which realized $201,000 at fund-raising auction of Safari Club International in 1986. In quality, craftsmanship, and design, a masterpiece of the art of the gunmaker. Case of South American ironwood; accessories engraved by Steve Lindsay; gold inlay and antiqued brass hardware by Ray Wieglus; Steve Hoel made the knife. See also page 296.

Chapter 10
The Golden Age Rekindled:
1960 to the Present

The early 1960s mark the threshold of embarkation into the modern fine arms renaissance. The field had been building up to this explosion of talent and patronage since the end of World War II. But a number of factors led to a revival that has exceeded in dedication and creativity even the golden age of American gunmaking.

Despite the prevalence of junk art, junk food, throwaway products, and planned obsolescence, a return to handcraftsmanship and to precision has taken place in a number of fields: hand bookbinding, ceramics, silver- and gold-smithing, quilting, miniatures, dolls, luggage, and replicas of Wild West–period costumes and leather (especially holsters), to name a few.

Though seemingly quite apart from most of these fields, the decoration of fine arms and the making of custom guns and knives is no exception to this revival of excellence. In the author's opinion, the art of the gun- and knifemaker is presently at the highest level of achievement in history.

Contemporary craftsmen in guns and knives, and engravers thereof, have previously unknown opportunities to study objects made by their predecessors and con-temporaries, through books, periodicals, museums, private collections, arms shows, and videos, as well as by exchanging pictures and ideas through personal visits and correspondence. The advice of a colleague is as close as a phone call; modern transportation makes going anywhere in the world a matter of only one or two days' travel; and word of mouth about talented craftsmen spreads with amazing rapidity.

The wealth of books and periodicals that promote fine arms continues to grow, and organizations such as the National Rifle Association, the Firearms Engravers Guild of America, the American Custom Gunmakers Guild, and the American Knifemakers Guild provide avenues for exchanging ideas, drawing specialists together in annual shows devoted to excellence.

A crucial contribution to the engraving field was the establishment of the NRA Gunsmithing Schools in the mid-1970s, wherein hobbyists and professionals alike could take professional, comprehensive courses in the gunmaking arts. These schools were located in selected major colleges, among them the Rochester Institute of Technology, site of the prestigious School for American Craftsmen. In the ensuing years, hundreds of craftsmen have attended these courses, and among the distinguished alumni are John K. Barraclough and Lynn Wright.

Neil Hartliep played a vital role in the NRA Gunsmithing School programs devoted to engraving. His book, *The Basics of Firearms Engraving,* published in 1985 by the NRA's Education and Training Division, is a masterfully thought out, detailed primer. That profusely illustrated, 106-page volume has launched the careers of several arms engravers, while satisfying the needs of many gunsmiths and hobbyists.

Connoisseurship amongst patrons of fine arms has spiraled upwards to a level unequaled in history. Even antique arms collectors aspire to an ever-greater degree of perfection as they pursue the best of firearms and edged weapons.

Furthermore, the unending pressures by antigun and antihunting groups have inspired gun, knife, and hunting enthusiasts to purge their ranks and to upgrade quality and behavior in every respect. And why should not the finest weapons made rival such exquisite objects as a watch by Patek Philippe, luggage by Hunting World or Hermès, or jewelry by Tiffany, Cartier, or David Webb?

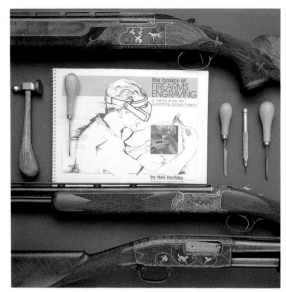

Neil Hartliep's NRA-published engraving text, accompanied by guns from his workbench. *From top*, Model 3200 Remington, with stocks by Fred Wenig; Ruger Red Label with relief chiseled stainless-steel frame and factory stocks; and Remington Model 31 pump, also stocked by Wenig. In 12, 20, and 20 gauges respectively.

The Major Manufacturers

The custom shops at Winchester and Colt are presently operated at levels unequaled in any previous period since the nineteenth century. Smith & Wesson's present engraving quality is at its best since the days of Gustave Young and sons, and the same is true with the Remington Arms Company. Although Marlin does not maintain a custom shop, three of the finest rifles in the firm's history were built in 1984, 1989, and 1990, all gold inlaid and deluxe engraved by Alvin A. White: the 2,000,000th Model 39 .22-caliber lever-action; the Model 1889 Centennial lever-action, serial number 1889-1989; and the 25,000,000th Marlin, a Model 1894 lever-action.

Though these rifles had elements reminiscent of nineteenth-century Marlins, each was an original concept, superbly realized in gold, steel, and wood.

Sturm, Ruger & Co., youngest in years of all the

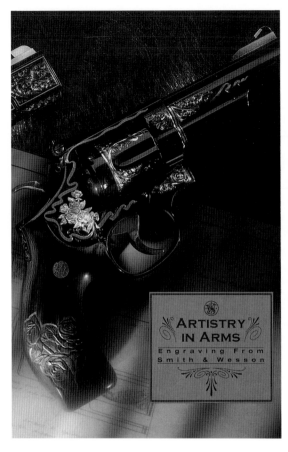

The Artistry in Arms engraving brochure from Smith & Wesson, 1993. With their active support of the traveling exhibition and book of the same title, S&W has assumed key role in fine guns revival. Roses mark a departure from traditional hunting and wildlife-oriented motifs.

Winchester's Custom Guns brochure even incorporated patterns by the Ulrichs, from the glorious period of nineteenth-century custom arms. The catalogues of Browning Arms Co. (owners of U.S. Repeating Arms Co.–Winchester as of 1990) include richly presented section on engraving and superior stockwork.

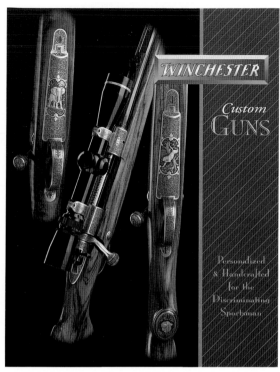

major U.S. gunmakers, though seasoned in wisdom, innovation, and marketing brilliance, have built their own sensational special-grade arms. The 1,000,000th Standard Automatic .22 pistol, engraved and inlaid by Ray Viramontez (with ivory grips by Bob Purdy), served as a fund-raising vehicle for the International Shooter Development Fund, to benefit the 1980 U.S. Olympic Shooting Team. The handsome pistol realized in excess of $27,000 at sealed-bid auction. The 1,000,000th Security Six was scroll-engraved and gold-inlaid with the serial number and inscriptions, its ivory grips with sterling silver buttcap decorated in red enamel. This piece, by Paul Lantuch, was donated by Sturm, Ruger & Co. to the National Shooting Sports Foundation, for the 1984 Shooting and Hunting Outdoor Trade Show fund-raising auction, where it went for over $25,000. Additionally, the 1,000,000th and 1,000,001st Model 77 rifles and the

A. A. White and American Master Engravers, Inc.

Alvin A. White's career began in the Depression Era, and he is the only prewar engraver of major rank still active in modern times. White was saluted in the January 1967 issue of *American Rifleman* magazine, in an article from the series "America's Leading Gunsmiths":

A worker in precious metals, fine woods, ivory, and pearl is a rather rare breed of firearms craftsman today. Yet Alvin A. White . . . has been a professional engraver for 20 years, his active interest in this precise skill extending back to his boyhood.

Today White is a master engraver for Colt [which retains his services through an exclusive contract with the firm of A. A. White Engravers, Inc.]. White's ornamentation has included gold and silver inlaid handguns, the Samuel Colt Sesquicentennial guns in both deluxe and custom models, and Colt's 3 standard grades of engraving. . . . White got his first professional training in his home city of Attleboro [Massachusetts] during the depression when a jewelry trade school was opened. . . . [He also] took courses at the Rhode Island School of Design at Providence in design and in shaping or modeling. . . . Besides collecting firearms and armor of colonial times, White occasionally restores antique firearms and edged weapons. He also has an interest in antique furniture, wood decoys, glass, and Japanese art.

Alvin White's style of scrollwork is influenced by British taste of the late flintlock period, and in many instances does not include beaded or punched dot backgrounds. His standard scroll is of a medium size, and is finely shaded, often with lined background cuts. Gold-inlaid subjects are invariably done in 18 karat, allowing for extra detail and greater wear and durability in comparison to softer gold (22 karat, for example). The author has observed White beating a relief-inlaid 18 karat gold elk with a mallet of solid walnut—the gold remained undamaged. A collector of Oriental art, White is an ardent admirer of Japanese metalwork, the influence of which can be seen in the style of his finely chiseled and engraved birds and animals.

Signatures appear on nearly all work done personally by White. His most distinctive markings are gold-inlaid rectangles, relief-stamped from dies of his own manufacture. The two major variations are AA WHITE/ENG. and COLT'S A.A. WHITE ENG. The same stamps are also used for marking silver and gold buckles, and appear on other non-firearm items made by White. On some occasions his signature is engraved. In a few instances two or more signatures have appeared on extra-fancy commissions. The usual location of his signature is on the left side of the triggerguard strap or receiver, beneath the grips. White's quality and style are distinctive, and, like the work of any expert craftsman, cannot be duplicated exactly.

Inspector stamps were sometimes used by the A. A. White Engravers company, and these were AW or WE, in tiny letters. These markings do not often appear on work done by White himself but usually represented engraving by other members of the firm. Over the years 1961–73, these craftsmen included Denise Thirion, Siegfried Rentschke, Daniel Cullity, Tom Freyburger, and even such artisans as Hans Obiltschnig, K. C. Hunt, Rene Delcour and Philip Grifnee.

Oakleaf · *Nimschke* · *English* · *American* · *German* · *Vine*

From Colt's spiral-bound custom shop catalogue, The Personal Touch, issued in 1977 and revised 1979, most elaborate of presentations by U.S. gunmakers on engraving, inlaying, special stocks, casings, finishes, and so on. Sample done by Alvin White on order of Colt's Al DeJohn, for many years manager of their custom gun department. Updated brochure issued 1993.

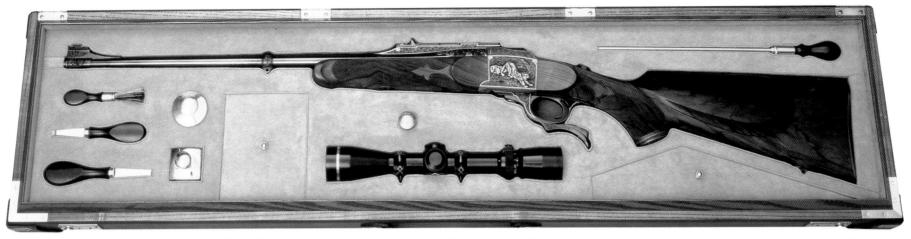

Second from Sturm, Ruger & Co. limited edition of North American big game No. 1 Single Shot rifles, serial no. 132-65199, honors the mountain lion. Engraving and gold inlaying by Franz Marktl.

Master artisan Alvin A. White is the maker of every object in this photograph.

Premier-grade Model 742F Automatic Rifle, from promotional photograph by Remington Arms Co. Continuing tradition, Remington, not as active in custom guns itself, continues the tradition by way of Parker Gun, which it revived in the early 1990s.

2,000,000th Mk I automatic pistol were gold-inlaid and engraved by Paul Lantuch, and are in a private collection.

In 1995 Ruger launched its own engraving program, featuring the Woodside over-and-under shotgun with hand-engraved patterns, made possible by the development of an engraving department at the Newport, New Hampshire, factory.

The North American Big Game wildlife series, announced in 1985, offered twenty-one elaborate No. 1 Rifles, matching oil paintings, and signed and limited-edition numbered prints, and was the most ambitious of all Ruger issues. The first of these, with scenes of bighorn sheep, was donated by Sturm, Ruger & Co. to an auction at Christie's to benefit The Metropolitan Museum of Art's Arms and Armor Department, and realized $52,000. An Alvin White gold-inlaid and engraved Security Six revolver (originally commissioned by William B. Ruger, Sr.) was donated to the Buffalo Bill Historical Center and raised approximately $12,000 at a 1984 Christie's fund-raising auction. In the years 1979 through 1991, the Ruger firm put together a private collection of exquisitely deluxe pieces of all their models then in production. These magnificent guns rival any commissions done by any gunmaker in American history.

White's creativity and versatility have earned him a unique place in the pantheon of arms engravers and craftsmen. Flintlock guns made from scratch; the patchbox reminiscent of the golden-age Kentuckys; locks formed in his own forge, as featured in BBC-TV documentary *The Gun Industry in America*.

Private Collectors and Conservation Groups

An extraordinary private collection has been assembled by Robert E. Petersen, one of America's foremost publishers of books and periodicals, ranging from off-the-rack shooting guns to the most exquisite custom handguns, rifles, and shotguns. Wishing to remain anonymous is a leading maker of sporting clothes, fishing and hunting accessories, and fine luggage, well on his way to assembling the finest private collection of antique and modern firearms in the world. And the patronage of a number of other dedicated enthusiasts help to support the new cadre of artist-engravers and craftsmen who are dedicating their lives to making the finest of fine arms.

Annual trade shows like the Shooting and Hunting Outdoor Trade Show, the NRA Annual Meetings and Exhibits, the Gun Engravers Guild, the Custom Gunmakers Guild, the Custom Knifemakers Guild, and Europe's International Trade Fair for Hunting and Sporting Arms and Accessories (in Nuremberg) provide showcases for gun- and knifemaking skills. Safari Club International's annual meeting, traditionally in Reno or Las Vegas, in addition to attracting gunmakers, dealers, and engravers, also features custom guns at fund-raising auctions. Prices realized by a *single firearm* have reached $201,000, and the profits are directed into wildlife conservation projects.

These conservation fund-raising projects have been of such merit that they were the subject of a feature article in the National Audubon Society's *Audubon* magazine (November 1987 issue). On the subject of man's veneration of masterpiece firearms, the article quoted at

On the Tiffany & Co. presentation case, selection of artifacts, most by White. White's associate, Andrew Bourbon, made the gold-bedecked Swiss Army knife *at right,* as well as rings and Roman coin *at left.*

Decorative art from the White workbench; netsuke tribute to Japanese mastery of ivory carving. Praying mantis entirely of gold. Rolex wristband one of only five made, each with unique design. Aborigine bust from sperm-whale tooth. Miniature wheel-lock, built from scratch, has over thirty-five parts.

Details from one of the most exclusive grade of Model 21 Winchester, the Grand Royal, the first from the series having been built for John M. Olin and completed shortly after his death. Serial no. W33104 made for John Olin's friend, William E. Simon; nos. W33121 and W33105 made for the author. Alvin White designed and executed the John Olin gun (W9190), and serial no. W33103, while the balance of the guns were jointly by White and Andrew Bourbon, the latter playing an increasingly significant role. Stocks by master stockmakers and checkerers Fred Wenig, Elbert Smith, and Darrell Smith. Longtime Winchester employee Carl Hummel came up with the Grand Royal designation (original spelling had the extra *e*). See also page 362.

American Master Engravers, Inc., sample case. The firm employs half a dozen master craftsmen, with wide variety of commissions and special orders, including annual Gala Colt Single Action Army revolver for Gene Autry Western Heritage Museum fall fund-raiser.

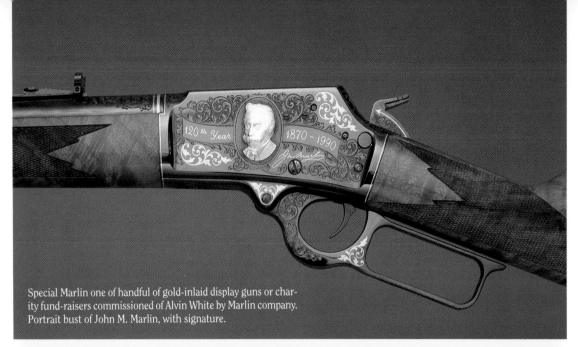

Special Marlin one of handful of gold-inlaid display guns or charity fund-raisers commissioned of Alvin White by Marlin company. Portrait bust of John M. Marlin, with signature.

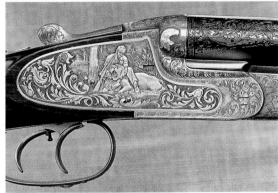

(*above*) Dumoulin & Deleye .375 H&H Magnum double rifle, made for author c. 1970 and used on safari in Kenya, Tanzania, Central African Republic, Botswana, and Ethiopia. Locks by K. C. Hunt, breech by Alvin White, pistol grip cap and forend by Denise Thirion, barrels by Rene Delcour and Philip Grifnee, and gold stock oval by Hans Obiltschnig. Each craftsman worked in a favorite style.

(*left*) Every item pictured is by an engraver of firearms, except William Randolph Hearst's armorer's touchmark on brass disc. Frank Hendricks made prototypes for Hunting World buckle series; shield device and rings by Andrew Bourbon; gold pocket watch by K. C. Hunt; bighorn sheep buckle by Alvin White; stork by Leonard Francolini; and Paterson Colt money clip by Horacio Acevedo for Thomas Haas's Guns Unlimited.

298

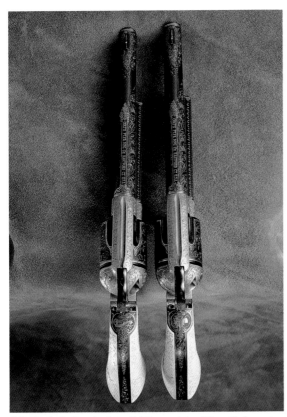

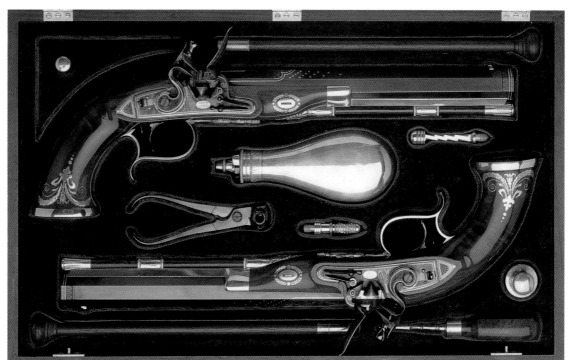

Colt Single Actions by John E. Warren, late of Cape Cod, master stockmaker, gunsmith, and engraver. Germanic scroll styling; influence of Kornbrath *et al.* prevalent in Warren's fine guns.

Elaborate set of dueling pistols, built entirely by Daniel Cullity, in a style influenced by American gunmakers the likes of Simeon North and James Haslett; completed on commission for client William "Pete" Harvey, in 1975. Mounts of 18 karat gold, with 24 karat gold and platinum inlays on steel, and 24 karat gold inlays on the select walnut stocks; in .54 caliber, with 10¼-inch barrels rifled up to within 2 inches of the muzzles. Blued steel bullet mold; silver flask and silver-mounted cleaning accessories and case.

S&W commissioned of White by prominent Eastern ruler; floral motifs in multicolored gold, low relief; *Playboy* nude with 18 karat gold finials. Casing in leather and velvet by Arno Werner, for many years chief binder for the rare-book collection at Harvard University's Houghton Library.

Lynton McKenzie's distinctive scrollwork, with game motif, on S&W Model 29 revolver. An Australian who traveled extensively in Europe and England to study engraving before coming to America in the late 1960s, McKenzie received early support and encouragement from patron Stanley Diefenthal, late owner of New Orleans Arms Co.

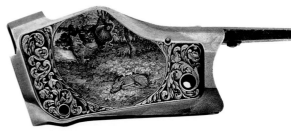

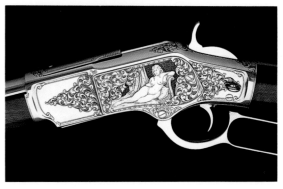

(*top*) High Wall Winchester action, by Robert Swartley, a protégé of Joseph Fugger. Swartley also issues limited-edition prints, and is known for subtly executed panel scenes and an individual scroll style.

(*bottom*) Winchester Model 1873 by Martin Rabeno, with classic barroom nude.

(*opposite bottom left*) Selection of creations by Paul Lantuch, multitalented artist and craftsman. Note bloodstone set in sterling silver buttcap on brown-finished revolver's ebony grip. Versatility of styles and precision are hallmarks of this gifted original.

(*opposite bottom right*) Engraving and inlaying by Sam Welch; knife by Curt Erickson. Germanic roots evident in scrolls; game scene on lock rendered in effective and distinctive style. Damascus blade technique revived by contemporary craftsmen.

Classic styling by D'Arcy Echols on large-ring Model 98 Mauser custom rifle; metalwork done in collaboration with Jasper Rabourn. Built for client to take on buffalo hunt in Zimbabwe.

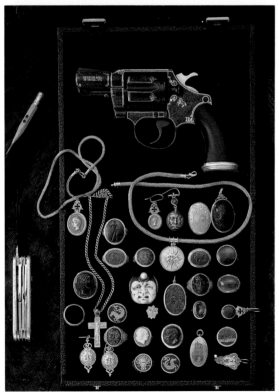

Miniature arms have come into their own, with displays at the Royal Armouries–H.M. Tower of London and the National Museum of American History (Smithsonian Institution). The Miniature Arms Society exhibits at the annual NRA Gun Collector competitions, where members compete for ten silver medals awarded for finest guns. U.S. Historical Society Colt issues done with factory involvement. Sheriff's Model by Uberti & Co. Tiny wheel-lock and flintlock pistol by Alvin White. Cannon by William O'Neal. Helmet by the English couple of Magnus and Byrne McLeod. Rampant colts by Leonard Francolini. Cape Buffalo by Robert Glen, of Kenya.

Custom Dakota Model 76 rifle by Paul G. Dressel, Jr., with unique broken ribbon-point checkering pattern. Dressel often works with other artisans, including his wife, Sharon Farmer-Dressel, a designer and builder of custom guns.

Browning Citori 12-gauge; design and stock- and metalwork by Sharon Farmer-Dressel. California English walnut, checkered by husband Paul. Jon Robyn's engraving, Roger Kehr's metal finishing.

(*opposite*) Oberndorf Mauser–action dangerous-game rifle in .425 Westley Richards; made by Mark Silver, engraved by Robert Swartley, cased by Marvin Huey, and case-hardened by Saint Regis, in Britain. Gunmaker Silver states that via his study and training in the decorative art forms in gun work of the seventeenth through nineteenth centuries, he has developed a stylistic vocabulary that he is often able to apply to twentieth-century projects. He "finds expression in the overall architectural shaping of both wood and metal, and the detailing that defines and refines transitions from one area to another. This work is usually carried out by hand filing, but occasionally by relief chiseling." Best-quality rifle done in pre–WWI Edwardian, an extension of Victorian style from the 1860s. Note profile of cheekpiece molding (inspired by a c. 1785 flintlock rifle by Mortimer, London), fluted borders to checkering, and warthog ivory bars in rear of express sights and on face of flip-up front sight (secured by gold rivet). Engraving of relief chiseled scenes on steel floorplate and triggerguard and bulino scenes on receiver ring.

MARK SILVER
GUNMAKER
CEDAR, MICHIGAN, USA
ENGRAVED BY ROBERT SWARTLEY

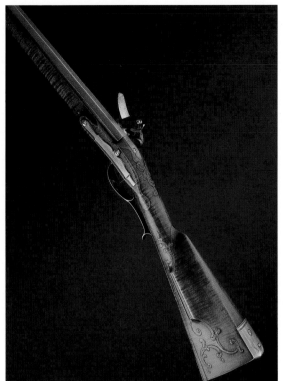

Superb American longrifle by Mark Silver, in style of Isaac Haines (Lancaster County, c. 1770). Done not only in re-creation of currently well-understood decorative art form of the longrifle, but also as an exploration of less well-understood finishing methods used by eighteenth-century gunmakers. Curly maple stock finished by scraping with a steel-bladed scraper, producing a slight "washboard" effect on surface, very different from sanding. Bright iron barrel and brass mounts finished by burnishing, quite different from polishing with abrasives. As noted by Silver: "Isaac Haines' rifles reflect the highest levels of American work of the period but are still very 'provincial' renditions of the art produced in the baroque and rococo periods of Paris gunmaking."

Selection of custom big-game rifles, with gold-medal red deer taken in Hungary in 1985. The rack a world record 17.2 kilograms. *From top center,* two bolt-actions by Griffin & Howe, then a takedown single-shot by Hunting World; *center left* and *lower right,* single-shots by Darwin Hensley; *far right,* double rifle by Ludwig Borovnik; *lower left,* Mauser bolt-actions by Hartmann & Weiss and, *far left,* by Thomas Burgess. Calibers range from .22-250 to .340 Weatherby.

Magnificent guns by Monte Mandarino, contemporary tributes to European and American gunmakers of the seventeenth and eighteenth centuries (also featured in back endpaper). *From top:* one of a pair of Louis XIV Parisian holster pistols, as from c. 1690, with mate and a gold-mounted fowling piece; gold-inlaid and chiseled en suite; 14-inch smoothbore barrels of 20-bore. Maple-stocked and relief-carved American longrifle, of transitional style from shorter Jaeger to Kentucky. German longrifle, as from c. 1720, relief-carved stock with silver-wire inlay and showing influence of French baroque style of twenty-five years earlier; engraving by Daniel Goodwin.

Frank Klay Navy with patriotic American-eagle theme, engraved by Alvin White. Klay Colts have proven popular with antique arms collectors, as well as devotees of modern gunmaking, their quality standards being strictly equal to those of products from Sam Colt's own lifetime.

From Colt's 1970 series Blackpowder revolvers, these Third Model Dragoons pay homage to Colonel Colt (*top*) and his son Caldwell. Embellishments by Colt master engraver Steven Kamyk, for a private collector. Scrollwork inspired by Nimschke and Gustave Young.

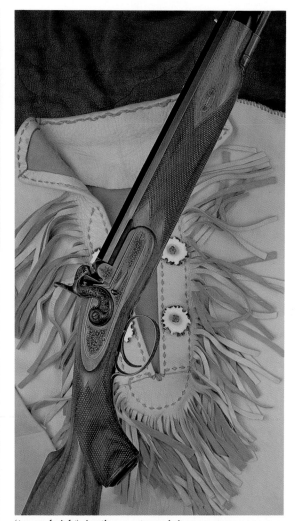

(*top and right*) Another masterwork by a contemporary gun-maker, in tribute to earlier craftsmen: .450 percussion mid-nineteenth-century English-style sporting rifle by Stephen Alexander, engraving by Lynton McKenzie; made for the author; completed 1988. Rifles of this perfection are used by Alexander's clients on African safari; they prove deadly accurate.

length from the 1970 book *Death as a Way of Life* by animal authority Roger Caras:

> If the mechanical perfection of a firearm doesn't convince you that man loves his guns, perhaps art will. A modern rifle can cost anywhere from twenty-five dollars to several thousand, depending on style, place of manufacture, and embellishment. Older guns can sell for many, many thousands, and leading art museums display firearms as appropriate and significant works of art. . . . Gold-and-jewel-encrusted presentation models are sought after at auction today the way masterpieces of painting and the choicest first editions are. . . . Gold, silver, ivory, jade, stones both precious and semi-precious, have adorned endless examples of the gun craftsman's skill down through the centuries. Neither the can opener, the plow, or even the automobile has been so honored. In plain fact man has ridden off to war and on his hunts with exquisite works of art for tools. It has not been an accident that this is so. It is a crystal-clear expression of man's attitude toward his gun—love and respect.

Who are the clients for the contemporary masterpieces and for those arms that qualify as superior in craftsmanship and artistry? Most of these patrons are hunters or trap, skeet, or sporting-clay shooters. Some are collectors of commemoratives, some are collectors of antique arms and/or modern arms, and a few are nonshooters acquiring a deluxe gift for a friend who is an arms fancier. Some who collect "first generation" guns of a

Gold charms and floorplate show precision and beauty of Winston G. Churchill's engraving.

TO
MR. BOB
FROM
PAUL A. BENKE

W. B. Wetmore

THE HERITAGE GUILD
L. D. NIMSCHKE
FIREARMS ENGRAVER
1832—1904
THE ONE OF FIFTY DRAGOON

R. L. WILSON
From his friend
TOM OVERBEY

COLT
The Legend Lives

HANSEN
Cartridge
Company

particular make, like Colt or Parker, are also dedicated to the later, contemporary generations. Most buyers are city dwellers, many of them from areas where they must undergo irritating amounts of official paperwork to allow for the legal possession of any firearm—engraved or otherwise. On the whole, the contemporary buyer of fine arms is knowledgeable and discerning.

Even today, with the arms renaissance in full swing, American engraving on these objects has been so heavily influenced by European craftsmen that there is not a single widely used style from the past two hundred years which could be termed purely native. All show the imprint of Europe, and of Germany in particular. There are engraving styles identified as "American," but these invariably show specific foreign roots, and generally they were designed by immigrant European craftsmen, mostly in the period 1850–1900. Our post–World War II arms decoration shows some departure from the past, but popular tastes dictate the styles and patterns of workmanship. Most clients are traditionalists, and the same is true of the engravers themselves. Thus it is highly unlikely that future years will reveal any major changes in the appearance of hand-engraved arms designs—with the notable exceptions of the influence of Tiffany & Co. designers, and such stalwart originals as

Over-and-under game gun, 20-bore, by Ivo Fabbri; engraving and gold inlaying by Churchill. Scenes and scrolls require careful study to appreciate the intense dedication to detail and style. Some details sculpted in relief, such as scrolls on breech behind barrel.

Colt Automatic with masterful scrolls and colt scenes, by Winston Churchill.

(*opposite*) Selection of inscriptions, etchings, pantograph and roll engraving, gold embossing on leather, stampings, castings, and engraving into anodyzed aluminum. Franklin Mint issue of General George S. Patton Single Action has *cast* "engraving," made in Japan; among series of replica arms issued by Pennsylvania collectibles giant. Shaw and Leibowitz etching on Randall knife. Prominent firm currently supplying photo-etching and plating services to arms industry is Baron Technology, Trumbull, Connecticut, operated by the father-son team of Frank and David Baron.

The Safari Club International Winchester Model 70 Leopard Rifle, built by David Miller Company (Miller, Curt Crum and Dale Drew), with engraving and inlaying by Lynton S. M. McKenzie. Leopard motif on floorplate (not illustrated) taken from wildlife art by Guy Coheleach.

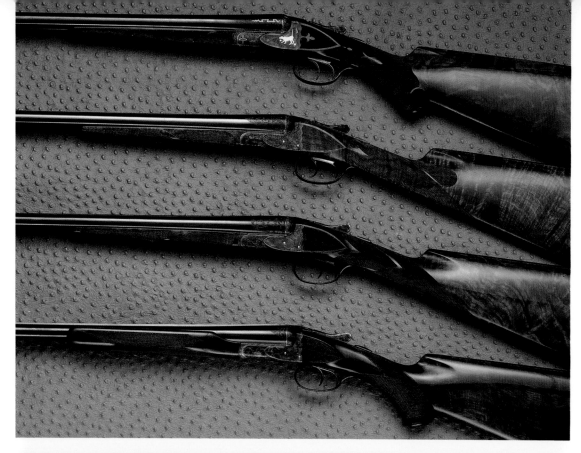

Raymond Wielgus, Tucson, Arizona, whose Art Deco– and Art Nouveau–influenced designs are represented in The Art Institute of Chicago's arms and armor department.

Certainly the promise of a continuing renaissance in the field of American arms embellishment is strong, barring only economic disaster or unreasonable antigun and antihunting legislation of a comprehensive, national nature. The future of arms engraving—that surviving aspect of weaponry bonded so closely to tradition—is one of vigor and promise, such that all who appreciate embellished firearms and knives can take heart.

The revival of the A. H. Fox double-barrel shotgun, by Tony Galazan and Dick Perrett and their Connecticut Shotgun Manufacturing Company, of New Britain. Introduced in 1993, four of the firm's top-of-the-line guns are the FE Grade (*starting at top*), the DE, the XE, and the CE. Brochure notes: "Annual shipments are estimated to be less than one hundred guns . . . all [with] the prerequisites necessary to attain their place as American classics and to provide their owners immense satisfaction as excellent investments."

Recognized for his creativity, artistry, and craftsmanship by an exhibition at The Art Institute of Chicago, Raymond Wielgus has charted new territory for enthusiasts of fine guns. To quote the late Dr. Leonid Tarassuk, in the publication accompanying the show:

> Pistols decorated by Raymond Wielgus (born 1920) show an entirely new approach both to the art of the gun decorator and to the selection of ornamental motifs . . . mostly inspired by Art Nouveau and Art Deco [and] elements found in the primitive art that he has studied and admired. Not content with simply applying decoration to a plain standard-issue weapon, Wielgus normally refines a pistol's shape by remodeling its component parts with files . . . [creating] a lighter and more elegant form that is subsequently emphasized by linear gold-damascened decoration along the pistol's edges.

Baby Dragoon Colt replica completed in 1993.

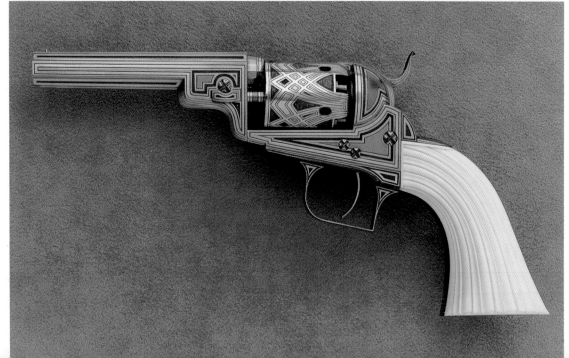

L. C. Smith 20-gauge upgrade, from "field" grade to "deluxe" grade. European walnut stocks by Toby Leeds; engraving and metal work by Jim DeRunck; case hardening by Doug Turnbull. Inlays done in three colors of gold; charcoal-blued triggerguard; rust-blued barrels. Serial no. 87595. Built as an auction fund-raising special gun for the Lake Plains chapter of the National Wild Turkey Federation, 1994.

Colt Industries' donation to the 1985 benefit auction for The Metropolitan Museum's Arms and Armor Department. Designed, engraved, and gold-inlaid by Alvin White. Among minute 18 karat gold details: portrait bust of Dr. Bashford Dean (near-legendary founder and first curator of the department), Japanese tsuba, Negroli Renaissance helmet, and American eagle on steel buttcap. One of the most inspired of handguns by Alvin White.

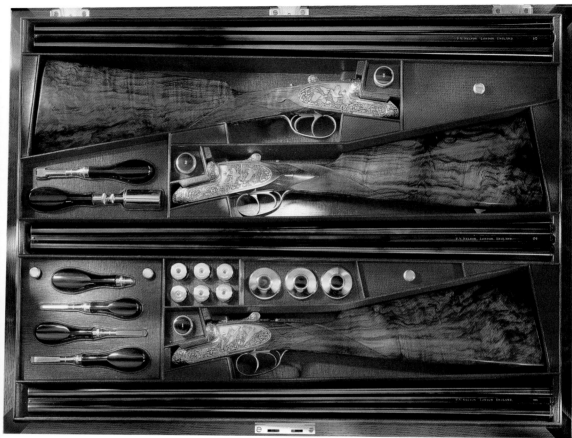

Brilliant U.K. gunmaker Peter Nelson, formerly of J. Purdey & Sons, with vignettes from his career (including 1953 apprentice photograph with Tom Purdey, Hon. Richard Beaumont, and Harry Lawrence), selected stock blanks, engineering drawings, in-white over-and-under and side-by-side guns, and other memorabilia, with interior of case lid, for three-gun self-opener set *at left and right*, among several built or on order for American client. Engraving by K. C. Hunt (1991) with sculpted game scenes and relief scrollwork. Elaborate brassbound oak Hunting World case, lined in the firm's exclusive London-grain leather; overcase of Hunting World's black Battue, trimmed in the same leather. Specially designed hinge by Bob Lee to allow easy removal of lid. Sidelocks on blue velvet *at right* are assisted-opening, over-and-under, and standard-opener.

314

(*opposite*) Set of 20-bore Purdey game guns, serial nos. 28244 and 28245, with deep-chiseled engraving by K. C. Hunt. *At top* 28-bore Purdey, no. 28576, similarly engraved and deep-chiseled. All three guns with 26-inch barrels. Hunt's genius has served to inspire an entire generation of engravers in America, Britain, and on the Continent. When he began his apprenticeship at Purdey's (along with such craftsmen as Peter Nelson and the now U.S.-based stockmaker David Trevallian) his teacher was John Kell. Hunt mastered his craft quickly, absorbing much, in addition, from studies at the great arms museums of London. The majority of clients for fine guns of British manufacture are Americans.

Holland & Holland double rifles of .375 H&H, .577, and .470 calibers, luxuriously embellished by K. C. Hunt, each from equally luxurious cases. Extra locks in crystal case for *center* rifle. Leopard from Mozambique safari, c. 1960.

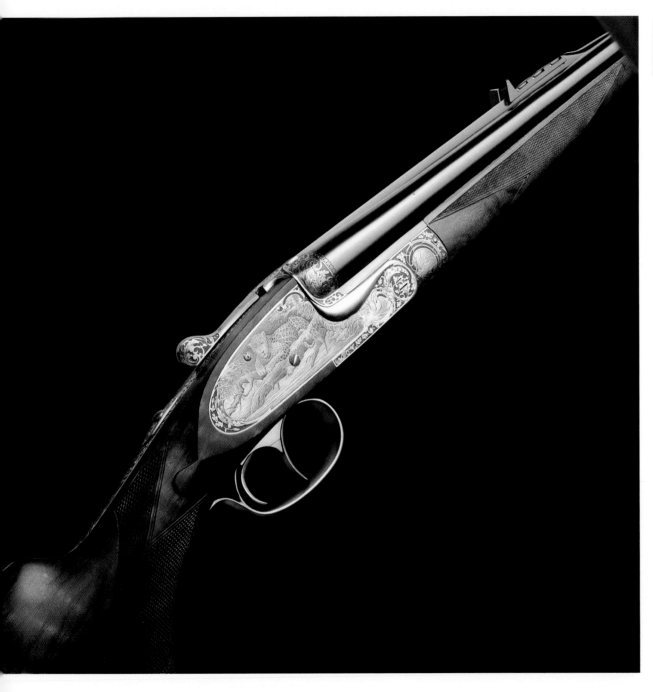

Purdey side-by-side 20-bore game gun, with sculpted steel embellishments by K. C. Hunt. Made for the author, c. 1980. In 1988, Tiffany & Co. completed design drawings for engraving and inlaying a set of Holland & Holland game guns, also for author. Game scenes were created in which the accompanying borders and scrolls evolve from favored habitat of each species. Cartoon drawn by Hunt while he and his family, on a visit to U.S., were guests at author's home. Hunt's daughter Alison and son Marcus are now accomplished engravers in their own right, working freelance for the English gun trade.

Elegant double rifle, engraved for Asprey by G. Pedersoli. Marking of maker and place (London) in logo style on bottom of frame, rather than traditional location on sideplates. Both company chairman John Asprey and cousin Edward, managing director of gunmakers, are keen shots and thoroughly devoted to the making of fine rifles, shotguns, and handguns. By exclusive arrangement with tailors Gieves & Hawkes, they have added sporting clothing to their line.

From the Broadlands set of four, by Holland & Holland, 1984 (known as the "Mountbatten guns"). Bulino engraving by the Brown brothers, prodigies who suddenly appeared on the London gunmaking scene in the 1970s, and have since embellished some of the finest guns made. Among other shotgun specials by Hollands have been the 1968 Set of Five, the 1970 Set of Five, the 1977 Queen's Jubilee Set of Four, the 1983 Set of Six Wildfowl and Wader Guns, the 1985 Set of Three Sesquicentennial Guns, the 1987 Set of Four British Field Sports Guns, and the 1990 American Civil War Set of Four. The African Hunter Series of double rifles includes creation of the 1987 Sir Samuel Baker and the 1988 Selous. In most instances, clients for these have been American.

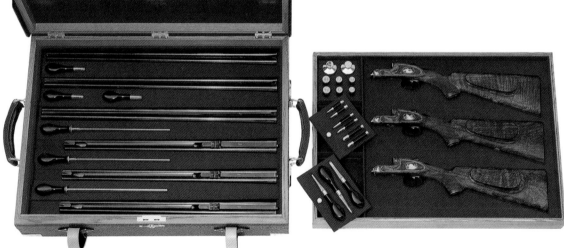

By appointment, goldsmiths, silversmiths, and jewelers to H. M. Queen Elizabeth II and to H.R.H. the Prince of Wales, Asprey launched their own gunmaking enterprise in 1991, opening an elegant showroom, at 23 Albemarle Street. Their best-quality arms joined those of the other British firms, none of them older than Asprey (founded 1781, and, to quote Director Edward Asprey, "the oldest family business in the United Kingdom making guns"). The firm can also draw on experience and tradition in luxurious goods in precious metals, leather, and other elegant materials; they even supply their own range of shotshells, from .410 to 12-bore.

Unique set of Asprey combination guns: a .470 double rifle with exchange 12-bore game-gun barrels; a .30-06 with 20-bore barrels; and a .243 with 28-bore barrels. Gold inlays of game motifs, by one of the firm's engraving staff. Note Turkish walnut, preferred by company over French select woods. Casing from Asprey's own workrooms.

Pair of Aztec-motif 20-bore Hollands, made for dove-shooting devotee Alain Wertheimer, owner of Holland & Holland. Print pulled from an earlier gun by K. C. Hunt, who has kept scrapbooks with photographs and impressions of numerous special guns over the years.

(*opposite*) Extraordinary gunmakers Hartmann & Weiss built sporting rifle, serial no. 8641, in .30-06 caliber, with 23½-inch barrel; gun reclines on lid of its leather and felt case. Exquisite stock, of superbly grained select walnut. Top of barrel with gold-inlaid inscription: HARTMANN & WEISS: HAMBURG. American craftsman Ralph Bone engraved and gold-inlaid this rifle in a Celtic style, c. 1993.

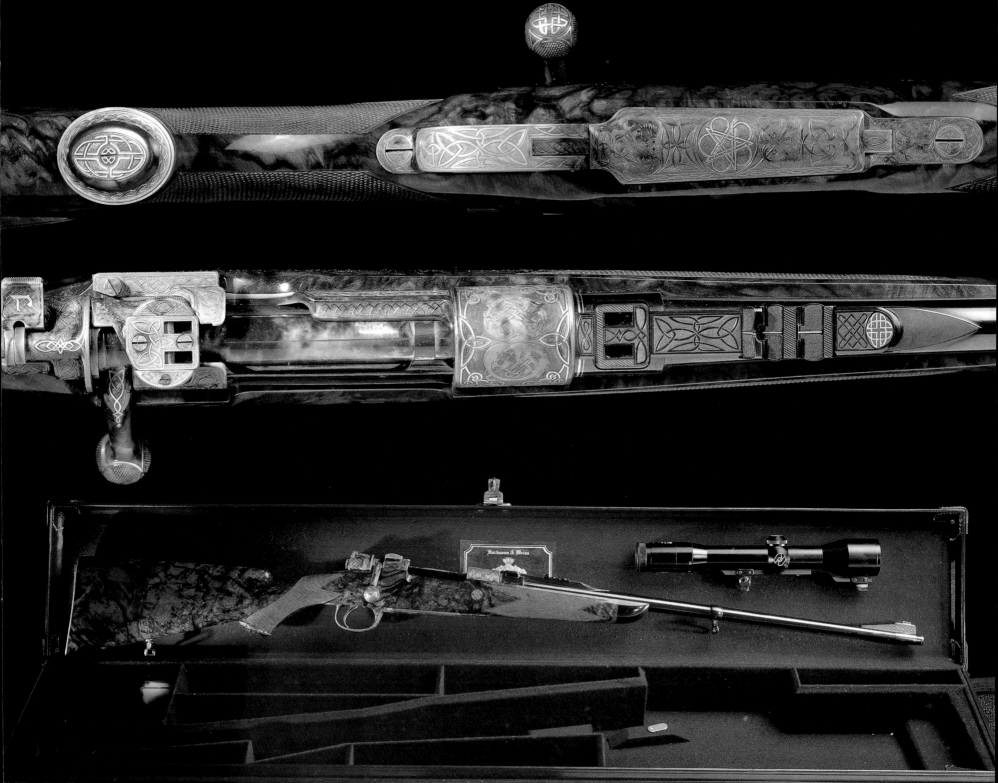

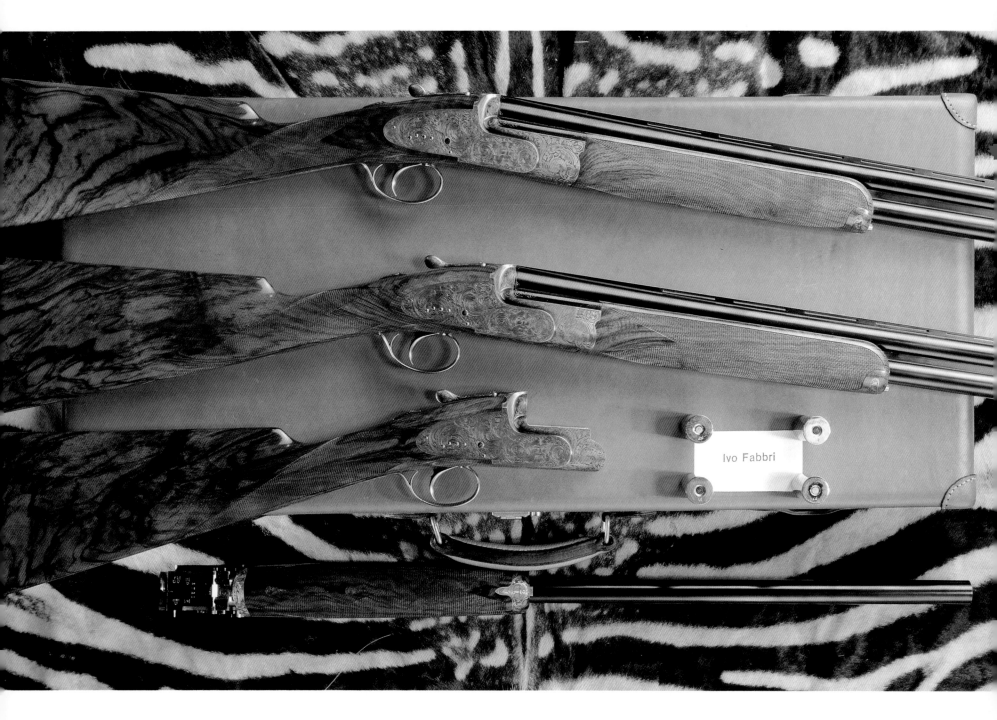

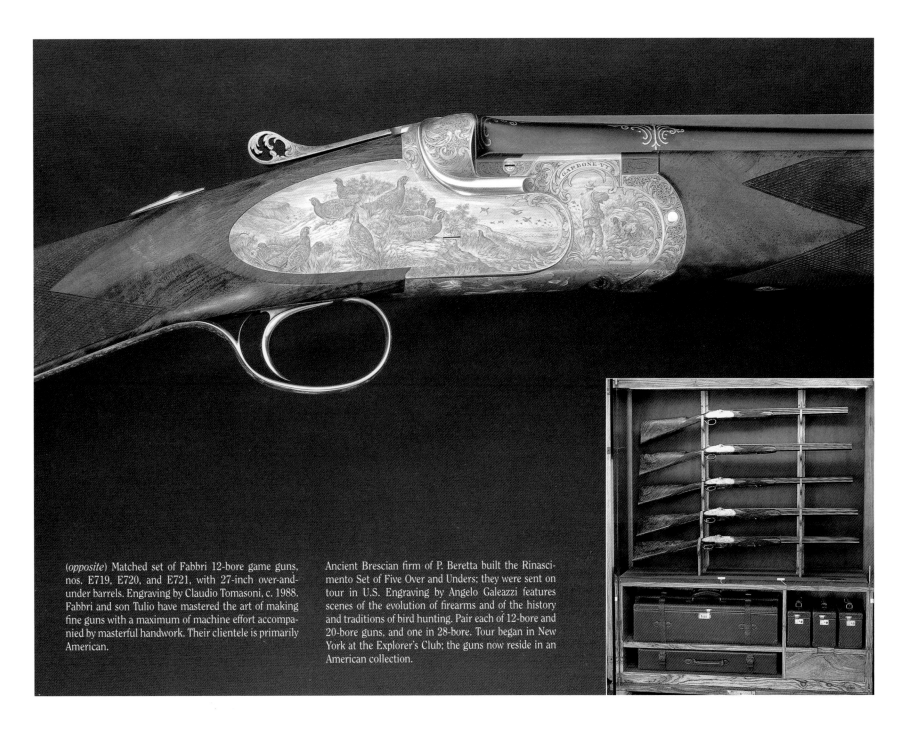

(*opposite*) Matched set of Fabbri 12-bore game guns, nos. E719, E720, and E721, with 27-inch over-and-under barrels. Engraving by Claudio Tomasoni, c. 1988. Fabbri and son Tulio have mastered the art of making fine guns with a maximum of machine effort accompanied by masterful handwork. Their clientele is primarily American.

Ancient Brescian firm of P. Beretta built the Rinascimento Set of Five Over and Unders; they were sent on tour in U.S. Engraving by Angelo Galeazzi features scenes of the evolution of firearms and of the history and traditions of bird hunting. Pair each of 12-bore and 20-bore guns, and one in 28-bore. Tour began in New York at the Explorer's Club; the guns now reside in an American collection.

By Thierry Duguet, Belgian engraver from l'Ecole d'Armurerie de Liege (and a partner in the firm Albemarle Fine Arms), with marketing under the direction of University of Virginia Professor of Environmental Sciences Mahlon G. Kelly. Gun by Lebeau-Courally.

Bulino technique at its finest, by the master Firmo Fracassi. An inspiration to engravers worldwide, Fracassi makes his humble studio in his apartment near Brescia. Frame from Famars shotgun.

Bottom of Famars (of Italy) shotgun frame, showing vignette based on art by Guy Coheleach, an unusual collaboration of artist and engraver, G. Pedersoli.

Created for President Richard M. Nixon in 1970 but never presented, Browning's 2,000,000th Automatic Shotgun was subsequently donated to the National Shooting Sports Foundation, for which it raised $50,001 for educational projects at public auction (in 1986). By master engravers José Baerten and G. Vandersmissen, from designs, c. 1930, by Felix Funken.

Fighting knife by Steve Johnson; grip of ram's horn.

(*left*) The damascus blade on this ivory-handled Buster Warenski dagger measures 7½ inches. Wife Julie carved the ivory and inlaid the gold, both flush and relief. The Warenskis are the reigning maestros of fine knives and their embellishment in America.

Welcome to the world of knife art.

Masterworks by contemporary creators of exquisitely crafted and decorated edged weapons, in a collection by the guru of custom knives, Jim Weyer. The author and publisher of the *Knives: Points of Interest* series, Weyer photographs extraordinary knives in a fashion equal to the perfection of his subjects. He selected this gallery from his matchless collection of color transparencies of knives by America's finest makers.

In the preface to *Knives: Points of Interest* (volume II), Weyer stated:

> Edged weapons are making a spectacular comeback, for purposes never dreamed of by the ancient armorers who forged the steel that won the day on a thousand battlefields.
>
> Though never intended for combat there's nothing "symbolic" about these new blades. They are weapons of superb craftsmanship and stunning beauty, but certainly not meant for parade-ground pomp and ceremony.
>
> They have become a new art form. And they are taking their places in the pantheon of artistic endeavors that include such pursuits as painting, sculpture, music and literature. . . . No more than 50 years ago American knifemakers began producing edged weapons that were a lot more than well-made, useful and efficient. They were beautiful—some of them stunningly so—and they certainly fitted Webster's definition of art as the "conscious use of skill and imagination in the production of aesthetic objects."

324

Folding knife made and engraved by Tim Herman; handle of gold, with opal inlay.

One of the finest knives ever made, Buster Warenski's re-creation of the King Tut dagger. Granulation and cloisonné on knife, and repoussé on the sheath; 32 ounces of gold used in this tour de force.

Folders of horn and ivory, by Jess Horn; engraving and scrimshaw by Gary Blanchard.

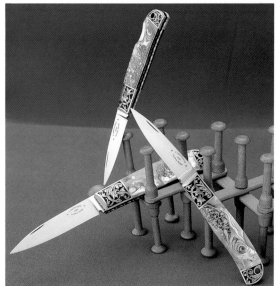

Folders by Frank Centofante, each with abalone handles. Engraving by Old Dominion.

An elegant dagger by Fred Carter, suspended in one of Weyer's imaginative environments.

Double exposure by Weyer of a Ron Lake folder; handles of stag. Pet bulldog engraved by Pedretti for client.

Damascus dagger by Jim Ence, including buttcap and cross-guard. Fluted ivory handle mounted with nickel-silver rings and spacers. Blade measures 8½ inches. The revival of damascus is but one of the stellar achievements of contemporary American knifemakers.

Wolfe Loerchner made the "Diana Special," its blade 7 inches long, the twisted ivory handle with wire wrap 3¾ inches.

One of the best-known of contemporary knifemakers, Bob Loveless made this sub-hilt fighting knife.

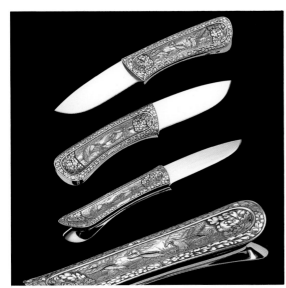

In this multiple exposure, Weyer shows all of T. M. Dowell's integral hunter, with dished-out handles. Gold-inlaid and engraved by Ron Skaggs.

Herman Schneider knife with fluted ivory handle, mounted with twisted gold wire; 6-inch blade. Deep-relief engraving by Gary Blanchard.

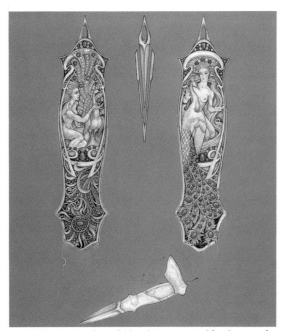

Four of the world's finest folding knives, created for the one-of-a-kind establishment of Barrett-Smythe, Ltd., New York, by artisans exclusive to the firm's atelier. Details supplied by Donald C. Mendelson. (*top right*) The salmon and trout appear swimming in a stream, the technique known as spectrum-coloring. Boat-tail knife by Durvyn Howard, the decoration sculpted by Gary Blanchard, similar to the way Japanese lacquer was made over the centuries.

(*center right*) Napoleon Bonaparte knife by Durvyn Howard, engraved and gold-inlaid by Jon Robyn. Scenes based on paintings by David, in 24 karat gold. Tweezer and toothpick in gold.

(*bottom right*) The art of Henri Rousseau was an inspiration for this Jon Robyn–engraved knife with the Arabic theme of the Falconer of the Maghreb. Emeralds and diamonds are part of the decor, along with gold and platinum inlaying and engraving.

(*above*) Jon Robyn's design drawing of another masterwork in progress, to be engraved and inlaid by Robyn; the knife itself being built by Durvyn Howard. Platinum or high-karat gold exterior set with canary diamonds, sapphires, and emeralds. Gold swinging panel for hidden (erotic) engraving beneath. Patented locks to secure each side of front handle and blades, in a unique system never before accomplished. Tweezer and toothpick in gold.

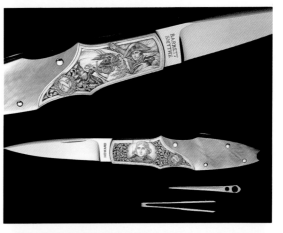

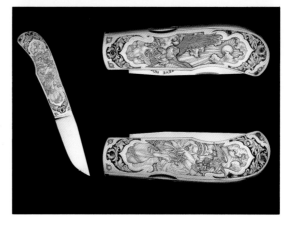

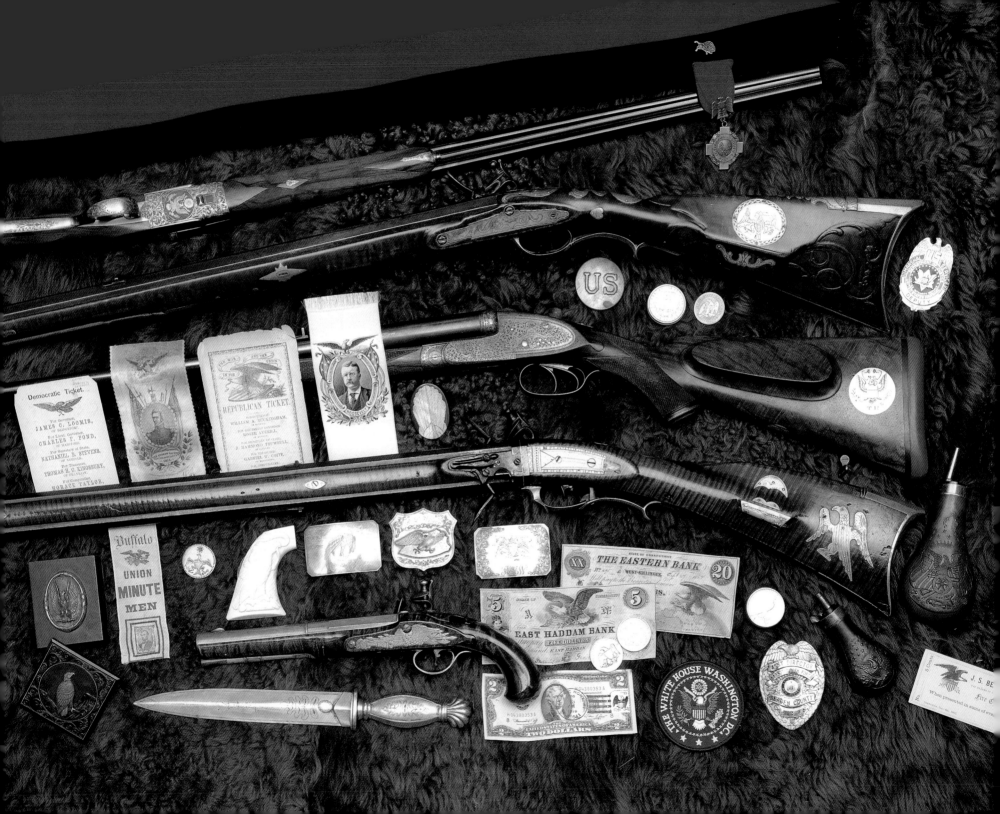

Chapter 11
Pursuing the Ultimate

I n collecting fine arms, the aficionado shares a passion that dates back to the original collectors, the British and continental European aristocrats who were not only shooters, but frequently devoted students and impassioned collectors. The collecting of valued objects of art, craftsmanship, and curiosity is an

Patriotism is a recurring theme throughout the history of American arms. Note the eagle, evident on firearms as well as other American decorative arts, from the visual arts and advertising to coins and currency, and more. *From top,* Rizzini .410 game gun made for author; John Armstrong Kentucky rifle; Theodore Roosevelt's Holland & Holland double rifle; over-and-under Kentucky by Christian Derr, Jr.; and brass-barreled Kentucky pistol replica by A. A. White. Eagles are located on various parts from frame sides and bottoms, to cheekpieces, and other areas on stocks, sideplates, ad infinitum.

"The Weapons Fool," seventeenth-century German poem. English translation:

> I'm an upright citizen
> Can't stand the smell of powder even,
> Yet I own all kinds of weapons
> Bringing me but few laudations,
> Since I know not how to use them
> Just see that rust does not suffuse them.

Apropos for many arms collectors; some things never change.

Der Gewähr-Narr.

Ich bin ein braver bürgers Mann,
Der fast kein pülver riechen kan;
Doch schäff ich mir viel rüstgewehr,
Die mir doch bringen wenig Ehr;
Weil ich, nicht anderst weiß, zu Nützen
Als daß ich mag den Rost weg büßen,

occupation as ancient as civilization itself. But only with the cultural blossoming of the Renaissance did such collecting become quite widespread, systematic, and, to some extent, specialized. At that time every royal and princely family in Europe possessed hereditary treasures that included precious metals and stones, valuable works of art, and other prized memorabilia—and among these valuables, a notable place belonged to arms and armor. Besides valuing specimens in actual use, many princes undertook to preserve the arms and armor of their ancestors and those taken as trophies of war.

Prominent in the phalanx of these dedicated aristocratic collectors (in addition to those previously mentioned) were: Maximilian I, Henry VIII, Charles V, Philip II, Ferdinand (Archduke of Austria), August of Saxony, Christian I and Christian II (also of Saxony), Peter the Great (and his father Czar Aleksey Mikhailovich), Empress Elizabeth (Peter the Great's daughter), Catherine the Great, the Princes Radziwill, Czars Nicholas I and Alexander II, Frederick III (Denmark), Napoleon I and his nephew Napoleon III, Count de Nieuwerkerke (a director of the Louvre), King George IV, Prince Albert, King George V, Sir Walter Scott, Edward, Prince of Wales (later King Edward VII), Baron Ferdinand de Roths-

The Peter Pech double-barrel combination wheel-lock and matchlock gun, made for Holy Roman Emperor Charles V. Traditions begun as early as the sixteenth century by gunmakers of this quality still affect the dedication, goals, and sometimes details of decorative style of contemporary craftsmen. Etched and gilt barrel, lock, and mounts; complex mechanism; engraved staghorn richly inlaid on stock.

child, the Duke of Edinburgh, and the Sultan of Brunei.

A smattering of arms collectors from the ranks of merchants, high-ranking military officers, and others of means (concentrating mainly on Americans) is equally fascinating: George Washington, Thomas Jefferson, Colonel Samuel Colt, Oliver F. Winchester, William F. Cody, Captain Jack Crawford, Theodore Roosevelt, J. Pierpont Morgan, Clarence H. Mackay, William Randolph Hearst, Henry H. Harrod, Henry Ford, Tom Mix, William S. Hart, William K. Vanderbilt II, Charles Addams, William E. Simon, Ronald Lauder, Russell Barnett Aitken, William B. Ruger, Sr., Samuel Cummings (Interarms), John Mecom, Ken Behring, Robert E. Petersen, Robert M. Lee, and members of the Ford, Mellon, Lilly, du Pont, Phillips, Olin, Donnolley, Tufts, and Woolworth families.

Add to the above a selection of devotees from the world of show business: John Wayne and his sons Patrick and Michael, Gene Autry, Monte Hale, Johnny Cash, Hank Williams, Jr., Mel Torme, John Entwistle (of The Who), Sammy Davis, Jr., Clark Gable, Ernie Kovacs, Buddy Hackett, Elvis Presley, Robert Conrad, Erik Estrada, Charlie Callas, Steve McQueen, Peter Fonda, John Milius, Blake Edwards, Steven Spielberg, George Lucas, Sylvester Stallone, Ted Nugent, and Jerry Lewis. And from the ranks of the literati: author and publisher Michael Korda, New York radio commentator Barry Gray, Dan Greenburg, Dr. Hunter S. Thompson, David Mamet, and Tom Clancy.

It was Thomas Jefferson, writing to George Washington, who observed, "One loves to possess arms," reflecting an American passion with roots that stretch back to the seventeenth century.

British and Continental Fine Guns

Attempting to collect the finest of antique arms under this broad umbrella oftimes means competing with

Louis XIII, the "Gun King," being crowned by Victory; from the school of Rubens. Arms from his collection were accurately painted, indicative of his absolute devotion to collecting. Collection of the Royal Armouries–H.M. Tower of London.

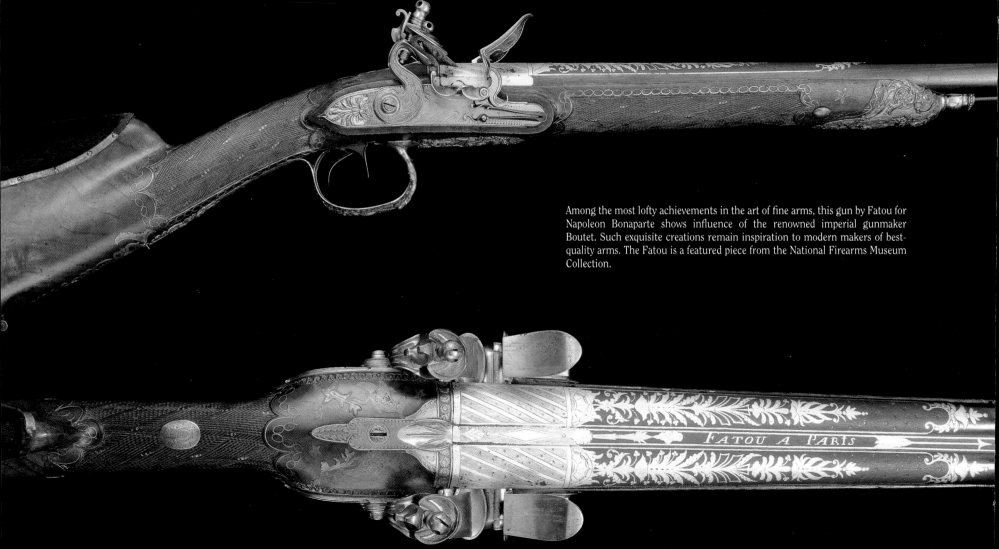

Among the most lofty achievements in the art of fine arms, this gun by Fatou for Napoleon Bonaparte shows influence of the renowned imperial gunmaker Boutet. Such exquisite creations remain inspiration to modern makers of best-quality arms. The Fatou is a featured piece from the National Firearms Museum Collection.

FATOU A PARIS

JOHN BOND HIS HORN / BRIMFIELD MAY 1779 engraved with rich geometric and scroll designs, boldly executed. Desirable as well to collector due to Revolutionary War date.

Long fowler by Phineas Sawyer, Harvard, Massachusetts, c. 1770. Engraved lock, barrel breech, buttplate heel, triggerguard, and sideplate; stock lightly carved. Overall length 70½ inches.

existing ancestral and national or municipal collections in Europe, or such mega-collections as The Metropolitan Museum of Art, in New York. Although wars and such factors as economic need have liberated objects from princely and public European collections over the centuries, a great many of those institutions have survived and the best a collector can do is make pilgrimages to admire their holdings.

Objects still surface, but they are inclined to disappear quickly into another collection. As is true of virtually all areas of arms collecting, dealers, agents, and auction houses keep a flow of objects circulating. The fall and winter antique shows in New York's Seventh Regiment Armory provide opportunities to meet top dealers (at this writing, Peter Finer, William Guthman, and Peter Tillou are likely to be at one or both events), as do such shows as the spring event in Baltimore, sundry fairs in England and on the Continent, and the best collectors' arms meet in the world: the Las Vegas Antique Arms Show, produced by Wallace Beinfeld at the Hotel Sahara.

For auctions of European fine guns, Christie's, Lon-

don, consistently offers outstanding pieces with reasonable estimates, with the result that the buyer is competing with other bidders and not with an owner's reserve price. Experts Peter Hawkins (a protégé of the famed collector, the late W. Keith Neal) and his associate David Williams seem to know where every fine object of arms and armor in the world is located and eventually bring most of those available into their historic sales rooms.

Alas, this is a task increasingly difficult, since most of the grand pieces are already secure in permanent collections. The American-based collector *must* see the arms and armor display at The Metropolitan Museum of Art, repeatedly if possible. Other American museums worthy of visits for their collections of European arms are: the National Museum of American History (part of the Smithsonian Institution), the Buffalo Bill Historical Center (Cody, Wyoming), The Art Institute of Chicago (the George F. Harding Collection), the Higgins Armory Museum (Worcester, Massachusetts), the Cleveland Museum of Art, the City Art Museum of St. Louis, the West Point Museum, and the Milwaukee Public

Museum. In Canada, the Royal Military College, in Kingston, Ontario, has the Porfirio Díaz Collection, but this may not always be available for public viewing.

Internationally the most significant collections are the Royal Armouries–H.M. Tower of London and the Wallace Collection (both in London), Paris's Musee de l'Armée, Madrid's Real Armería, Copenhagen's Tojhusmuseet, Vienna's Kunsthistorisches Museum, St. Petersburg's Hermitage Museum, Moscow's Kremlin Armoury, and Turin's Armería Reale.

A handy reference book, *International Guide to Museums of Arms and Armor* (by the author and Brooke Anne Chilvers), which will include a comprehensive listing of every institution in the world with worthwhile arms and/or armor collections, is now in preparation.

The Colonies to the Kentucky Rifle

Colonial arms and the Kentucky rifle, and their accoutrements, present a particular challenge to the collector. These arms are viewed in a different light than later specialties, such as Colts and Winchesters. Restoration is more acceptable in the early arms, whereas in the latter

types it has much stricter limitations. Learning these ins and outs is part of the collecting challenge. It is not unusual, for example, for a Kentucky to have been converted in its period of use from flintlock to percussion. Often a latter-era collector will have reconverted the piece back to flintlock; some such alterations are better done than others. Reconversions are generally accepted by enthusiasts, but they should be done by specialists. Other acceptable repairs and alterations might be a restoration of the muzzle end of barrels and stocks to what was probably the original length, replacement of locks or missing inlays, and filling in of missing wood. Some tomahawks may have replacement hafts; and powder horns may have replacement plugs.

As in all other areas of fine arms, however, pieces remain to be dug out of attics and storage, and some treasures remain forgotten in dusty historical societies and libraries. The collector usually feels that a piece is better appreciated (and by more people) in private hands than if hidden away in storage and virtually inaccessible, as is the case with many public institutions.

I. Perkins flintlock pistol, of elegant form and high-quality workmanship, and having important historical association with the first Quartermaster General of the United States, whose name is inscribed on butt.

On an eighteenth-century English chair, an extraordinary grouping of pipe tomahawks, Great Lakes curly maple war club, and antler-handled knife, c. 1790–1840. Most of this array of tomahawks were built by riflemakers; some mounted in silver.

Utilitarian objects need not be unattractive; these Kentucky rifles meant life and death, food for the pot, and civilization to their owners. *From top left down,* by Philip Heckert, Jacob Gumpf, John Schneider (dated 1776), John Armstrong, and Jacob Sell; and *from top right,* Stofel Long, Nicholas Beyer, John Sheetz, Adam Angstadt, and John Noll.

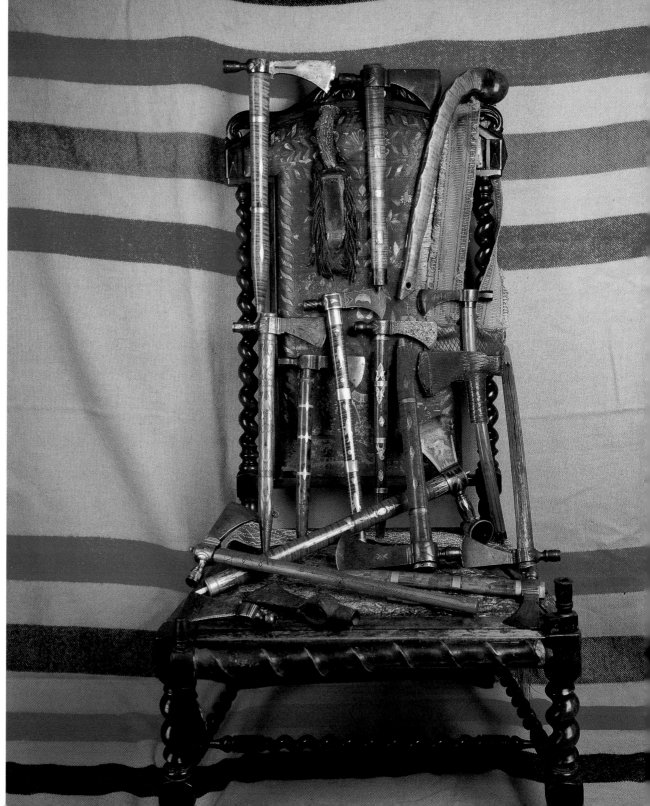

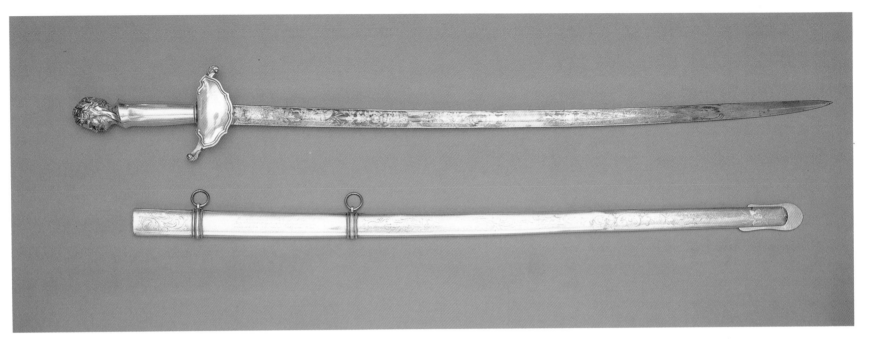

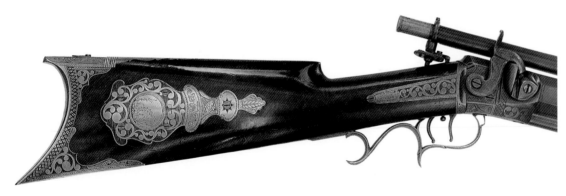

Sword by Ball, Tompkins & Black, New York (predecessors to the jewelry concern Black, Starr & Frost), presented by state of Illinois to Major Thomas S. Levingston, for gallant service in the Mexican War; drew on a Roman prototype for design inspiration. Bust sits on top of grip, which serves as plinth.

Wesson-marked heavy-barrel New England target rifle, c. 1840. German-silver mounts; lock and breech with stylized scrolls, borders, and lined background. Engraver probably also worked on silver and other decorative objects of the period.

The organization most actively promoting the study and appreciation of Colonial and Kentucky arms is the Kentucky Rifle Association (KRA). Although made up of only a few hundred members, this group, which is dedicated to research and collecting, was a sponsor of a major exhibition at the museum of the Historical Society of York County (Pennsylvania) in 1972. Much of the show was documented in Merrill Lindsay's *The Kentucky Rifle,* published the same year. The KRA has sponsored books, monographs, and seminars, and presents a coveted Distinguished Service Medal to the "member who has contributed the most to the perpetuation of the Kentucky Rifle and the Association." An annual meeting, held in June in Carlisle, Pennsylvania, is their major event of the year.

The major exhibition of powder horns, based on William H. Guthman's *Drums A'beating, Trumpets Sounding,* reflects the degree of dedication shared by Association members. Several traveled to New England to view the display, virtually a pilgrimage. Like the annual meetings, the exhibition is a learning experience in aesthetics, craftsmanship, connoisseurship, and American history and culture.

Dawn of the Industrial Revolution

Living history helps bring subjects alive for devotees of the Colonial and the Kentucky periods and of arms-collecting themes throughout the nineteenth century. The proliferation of battlefield sites, reenactment groups, museums and historical societies, television programs, movies (for example, *The Last of the Mohicans* in 1992), and a wave of books and other publications offer unprecedented opportunities for study and enjoyment. The Kentucky rifles made in the gunshop at Colonial Williamsburg are in such demand that the wait is about as long as for a Purdey or Holland & Holland shotgun: approximately three years. And not only are the Springfield Armory and Harpers Ferry prominent museums, but they are part of the comprehensive National Park Service network. The former houses thousands of firearms (though most are in storage) in what is the oldest arms collection in America. Despite its military orientation, a great many decorated arms are to be seen there. Both institutions also offer insights on how guns were made before, during, and after the Industrial Revolution.

Buckskinners and the National Muzzle Loading Rifle Association encourage interest in the craft of gunmaking. Surely more replica Hawken rifles have been made in the twentieth century than were originally made by the Hawkens. Encampments are sure to inspire a better understanding of antique arms because they foster research in their broader cultural aspects. Visiting a reenactment site is a sure treat for ladies and gentlemen and children of all ages.

A thirty-minute video produced by the BBC Open University, *The Gun Industry in America,* which is aired on British television yearly, explains the evolution, from handcraftsmanship to mass production, of the American firearms industry. Alvin White is featured in this production, as is the American Precision Museum (in Windsor,

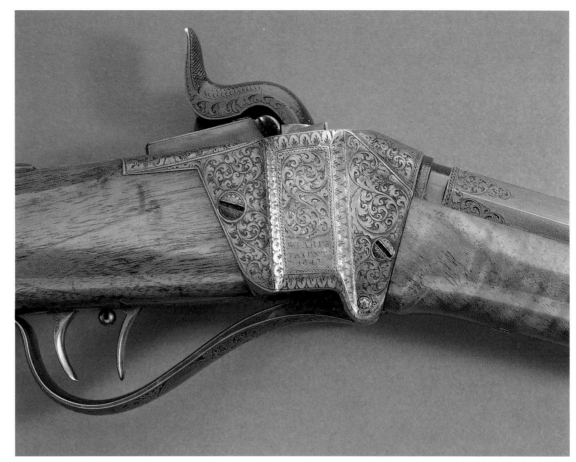

The Left-Handed Sharps Model 1853 sporting rifle; remarkably, this Gustave Young–engraved tour de force survived almost like new; its right-handed mate, which is known, is not in same superb condition.

Samuel Colt's use of Buhl-style casing evident on Model 1855 Sidehammer revolver, decorated with extra-fancy grade of Young-style scroll and border engraving.

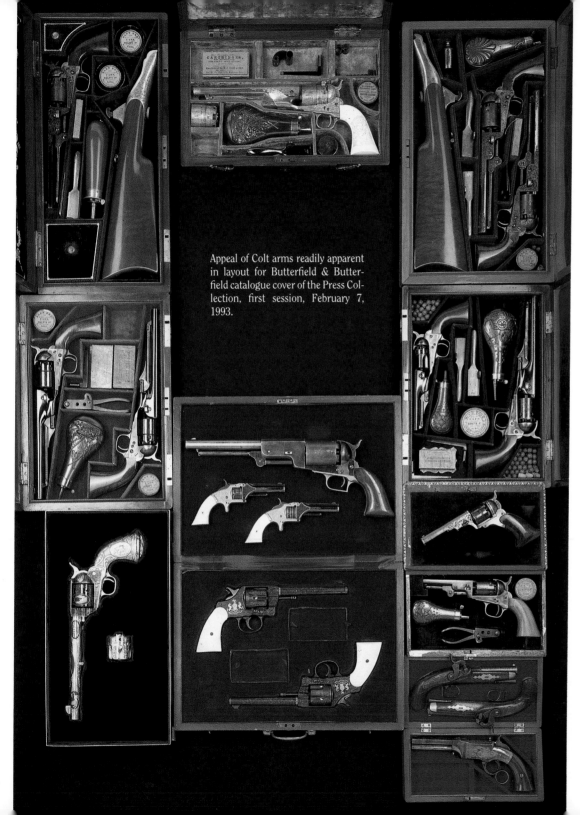

Appeal of Colt arms readily apparent in layout for Butterfield & Butterfield catalogue cover of the Press Collection, first session, February 7, 1993.

Vermont) and the old Winchester Custom Shop. Made in the mid-1980s, the production has yet to be equaled in this period. Efforts are presently under way by John O'Donnell, of Central Park Media (in New York), to assemble a collection of arms-related videos for a presentation of this multifaceted story of American ingenuity and craftsmanship.

Other programs have already been made by various producers, covering the subjects of Colt, Winchester, Bowie knives, and gunmaking at Williamsburg. They include the Hoyt Axton–narrated *Guns of the Old West,* and A&E's Kenny Rogers–narrated *The Guns That Won the West.* Though none of these concentrates exclusively on the "steel canvas," the author is hopeful that such production will result from the planned museum exhibition, "The Art of American Arms," sponsored by the Royal Armouries–H.M. Tower of London.

Arms collectors' clubs and private entrepreneurs produce a myriad of weekend shows across the country, each offering an opportunity to see and handle fine arms and to discuss them with experts, fellow collectors, and gunmakers. Although these meetings run the gamut from the rough-and-tumble to the refined, they offer a maximum of exposure in a short amount of time to the field of fine arms. Anyone who attends such an event must keep the warning *caveat emptor* very much in mind. This subject is covered well in *Flayderman's Guide to Antique American Firearms . . . and Their Values,* a "must" book for the arms collector. Although it does not cover embellished arms in any detail and contains little information for the period after 1900, this guide is an essential text.

The best periodical for the collector is Mowbray Publishing's bimonthly *Man at Arms,* which concentrates primarily on American firearms and edged weapons, and is the official collecting journal of the National Rifle Association.

The Arms of Colonel Colt

Following the trail blazed by Samuel Colt, the first Colt collector, was the subject of several chapters in the

Intricately carved screen from the Charter Oak, with ivory panels, commissioned by collector and arts patron, Colonel Samuel Colt. Tiny revolvers serve as adjustments for rod mount; light source from behind gave added dimension to patriotic, martial, armory, Charter Oak, and rampant-colt themes. Height, approximately 24 inches.

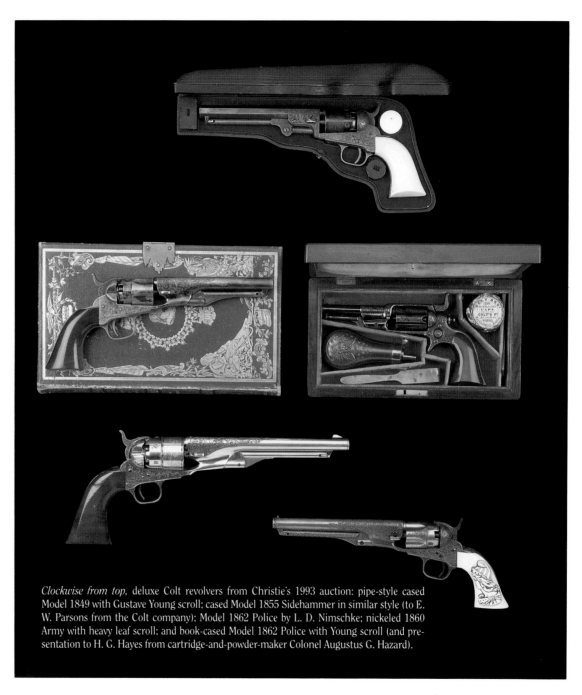

Clockwise from top, deluxe Colt revolvers from Christie's 1993 auction: pipe-style cased Model 1849 with Gustave Young scroll; cased Model 1855 Sidehammer in similar style (to E. W. Parsons from the Colt company); Model 1862 Police by L. D. Nimschke; nickeled 1860 Army with heavy leaf scroll; and book-cased Model 1862 Police with Young scroll (and presentation to H. G. Hayes from cartridge-and-powder-maker Colonel Augustus G. Hazard).

Single Action Army (*at top*), one of fifty "The Peacemakers" Colt revolvers planned for issue by the United States Society of Arms and Armour, with a matching numbered edition of *The Peacemakers* book. Prototype revolver engraved by Alvin White, based on original Single Action, no. 91936, part of the same shipment of fifty "soft" pistols to Hartley & Graham, New York, which included Theodore Roosevelt's favorite revolver from his ranching days. Engraving on T.R. and *Peacemakers* cover Colts attributed to L. D. Nimschke.

12 Cartridges,
FOR
Colt's Revolver, Cal; .45.
Powder, 30 grains.   Bullet, 250 grains.
FRANKFORD ARSENAL
May, 1874.

History and craftsmanship combine with technical merit in presentation Henry rifles for Secretary of the Navy Gideon Welles (*at top*), and Secretary of War Edwin M. Stanton; low nos. 9 and 1 respectively.

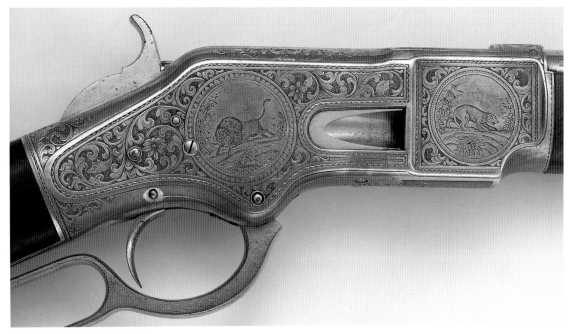

Previously misidentified on occasion, this early 1870s photo-graph shows Captain Jack Crawford, the Poet Scout, believed taken while he was in Hartford on show tour. A keen arms collec-tor, he sports presentation gold- and silver-inlaid Model 1871 Remington Rolling Block pistol (pictured on page 186).

Model 1866 Winchester carbine no. 100360, attributed to John or C. F. Ulrich, was factory-built for promotional purposes; has his-tory of display at the Centennial Exhibition of 1876. Later pre-sented to Mariano Ignacio Prado, president of Peru. Example of richly laid out and executed scrolls, with game scenes stylized (still evolving in sophistication). Gold- and nickel-plated, with select walnut stocks.

Signed J. ULRICH, Model 1873, 1 of 1000, shipped engraved, gold-plated, with 26-inch octagonal barrel, set trigger, and fancy stock (and so documented in factory records). Awarded silver medal at NRA annual meetings, 1961.

author's *The Colt Heritage* and *Colt: An American Legend.* An exciting possibility, which would enshrine Colt firearms' history and artistry in an unequaled way, is now in the planning stages: the rampant-colt sculpture and the old Colt Armory building may well figure as catalysts in the renaissance of the South Meadows area of Hartford, within the extraordinary estate and factory complex created by Colonel Samuel Colt.

Hartford real estate developer Thomas K. Standish and West Point graduate and former director of government affairs for Colt, James L. Griffin, together with this author, have been promoting an imaginative and exciting project that would completely renovate the Colt factory complex to its former grandeur, as well as create a unique museum of world importance. Standish has already restored a number of Hartford buildings, and did so with such style and impact that he was referred to by the late Marion Hepburn Grant as "Colonel Colt reincarnated." Griffin, a former White House and U.S. Senate staffer, is currently president of Economic Development Associates and has close ties with the Connecticut Development Authority and the State Department of Economic Development.

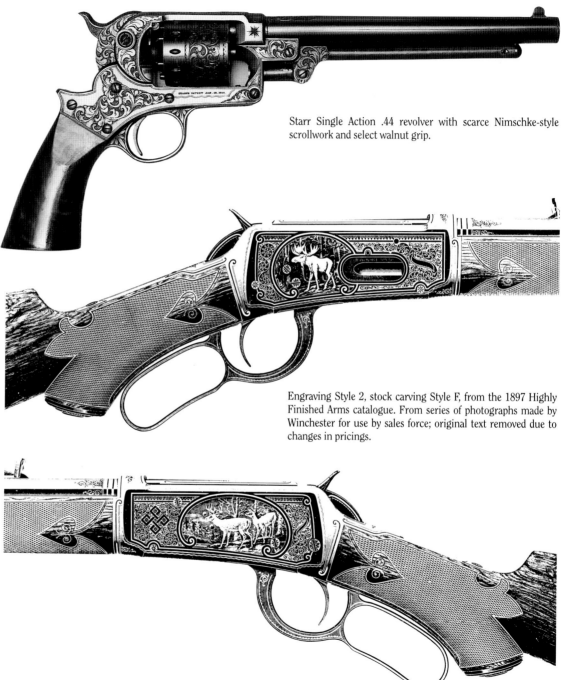

Starr Single Action .44 revolver with scarce Nimschke-style scrollwork and select walnut grip.

Engraving Style 2, stock carving Style F, from the 1897 Highly Finished Arms catalogue. From series of photographs made by Winchester for use by sales force; original text removed due to changes in pricings.

Statuary-hilted Civil War presentations, colorful examples of heavily decorated, gaudy swords typifying the apex of flamboyance during that period. *From left,* historic gift to General John F. Reynolds, Union officer killed by sniper on eve of Battle of Gettysburg; made by W. H. Horstmann; gilt-bronze hilt and mounts to iron scabbard. To Lt. Colonel George Sangster, from former prisoners of war; gilt-bronze hilt with thirty rubies mounted on guard; silver-plated bronze scabbard with gilt-bronze mounts. To Colonel George H. Biddle; gilt-bronze mounts with silver Native American motif grip; Fredericksburg, Virginia, scene on counterguard; silver scabbard with gilt-brass mounts; by Horstmann. To Colonel Thomas Stephens; silver and gilt figure of war grip, with multiheaded hydra on shield held in left hand; rubies on guard and on German-silver scabbard with gilt-bronze mounts. To Captain G. W. Harrison; gladiator hilt motif in silver and silver gilt; silver-plated bronze scabbard, with gilt-bronze mounts; recipient killed in action at Petersburg, Virginia, a few days before end of war. Blades of each sword profusely decorated with etched patriotic, martial, and scroll designs, sometimes augmented with floral motifs.

Julius Meyer set up shop in frontier Nebraska, catering to collectors and travelers, with full line of artifacts and souvenirs. Example of early fascination with collecting objects of the frontier, including fancy arms; here: Native American tomahawks.

Accompanying the restoration of the Colt factory site would be the development of the area into a combination firearms museum and civic complex, complete with a walkway over U.S. Route 91 (which is adjacent to the factory) and a luxury high-rise apartment building. Including its dome, the Colt factory is some five stories high and five hundred feet long. A national landmark structure, it is accompanied by substantial parking space. Furthermore, there is the huge Colt Park across the street, and Colonel Colt's private estate, Armsmear (now a home for widows of Episcopal ministers). Further, the Connecticut River Recapture program is restoring much

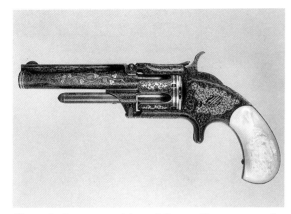

Ulysses S. Grant was recipient of Gustave Young presentation S&W Model 1½ Second Issue revolver, given August 1870; no. 41993. Mother-of-pearl grips carved in relief; barrel decorated with ivy wreath motif.

of the once unspoiled and beautiful environment of the area. The Colt Armory is easily the most distinguished historic landmark building along Highway 91, and an estimated one million people drive by the building daily.

The museum concept incorporates not only Colt displays, but also arms and memorabilia from other American gunmakers, primarily of the Connecticut River Valley. Further, it is proposed that the Colt factory would maintain a presence in the complex, in the form of its Historical Department (which answers about 15,000 letters on firearms collecting annually) and the Custom Shop (behind one-way glass, to allow the workers to engrave, polish, and gunsmith in view of the public).

The proposal has been made to the Royal Armouries–H.M. Tower of London that their satellite museum, planned for America, be part of the Colt factory restoration. Master of the Armouries Guy Wilson, and his Keeper of Firearms, Graeme Rimer, have already visited Hartford to discuss the possibilities. The concept has added interest insofar as Samuel Colt was the first American industrialist to establish a factory outside the United States—and that site was London. (Colt became, in effect, his own export manager, spending a significant amount of time traveling in Europe promoting his arms

Bowie knives of three distinct types. *From left,* California dress knife by Michael Price, San Francisco, with ivory hilt mounted in silver and gold; silver scabbard; 12 inches overall, c. 1860. Silver-mounted Sheffield-made exhibition knife, the mother-of-pearl grip carved with portrait bust of George Washington; blade etched in exacting detail with Mount Vernon and Native American devices within scroll borders, c. 1870; achieved record price at 1992 auction. American gold-mounted Bowie with silver scabbard, ivory grip, c. 1835.

Influence of Gustave Young on Herman, John, and C. F. Ulrich evident in Sharps
rifle from shop of former and Model 1866 Winchester from shop of latter.

to potential markets. Important tools on his travels were the elaborate exhibition-grade and presentation arms that served to open many doors abroad to the renowned Connecticut entrepreneur.)

The development of the Colt factory site and the potential of a Royal Armouries U.S.A. may well be tied in with the long-standing quest for an international traveling loan exhibition, to be titled "The Art of American Arms." A joint concept of Paul Rovetti (director, William Benton Museum of Art, University of Connecticut), art expert and collector Peter Tillou, collector-antiquarian-author Norm Flayderman, and this author, the project has already garnered pledges of support from the Royal Armouries, as well as from the Hermitage Museum, the latter agreeing to the loan of their Colt treasures and requesting that the exhibition schedule include their historic institution in St. Petersburg, Russia. A site in Japan is also under discussion, as are sites within the United States. An accompanying video is also a consideration, in addition to a detailed illustrated catalogue.

Winchester's Finest

The author's *Winchester: An American Legend* devoted one chapter (XII) to the subject of collecting these fine guns. Since the book appeared, in 1991, some spectacularly successful auctions have been held that offered major pieces of both Colt and Winchester super-guns, the blue chips of American arms collecting. The John R. Woods Collection, offered by San Francisco's Butterfield & Butterfield auction house in October 1991, set new records for Winchesters. The top price realized was $517,000 for the Colonel Gzowski cased Model 1876 presentation rifle. Made up of less than 170 lots, with forewords by Greg Martin and actor-collector James Stewart, the sale totaled over $2.9 million and set a raft of price records.

Next, Butterfield's offered the Warren Anderson Col-

Marlins from the Ulrich workshop, each attributed to C.F.; *at top,* three takedown models, in varying patterns of gold inlay, scroll placement, and stockwork; *at bottom,* .22, rare specimen of half-gold finish, with select wood.

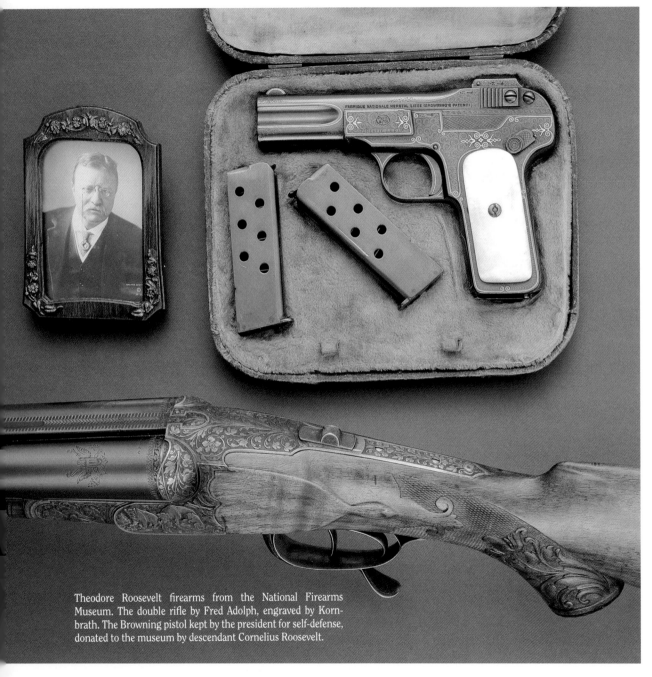

Theodore Roosevelt firearms from the National Firearms Museum. The double rifle by Fred Adolph, engraved by Kornbrath. The Browning pistol kept by the president for self-defense, donated to the museum by descendant Cornelius Roosevelt.

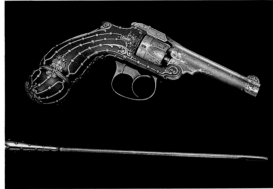

S&W topbreak revolver from the personal collection of Rudolph J. Nunnemacher, Milwaukee Public Museum. Custom embellished for the pioneer collector at the turn of the century by Tiffany & Co. Silver and copper grip; barrel and cylinder finely etched; casing of felt-lined oak, with silver- and copper-mounted cleaning rod (not illustrated).

lection, consigned by the Australian magnate, and so rich and varied that the material was sold in sessions in March and July 1992. Records were set for Colts and Winchesters, the highlight being the price of $1,045,000 fetched by the unique 1877 Schuyler, Hartley & Graham display board of forty-seven Colts, followed by the $770,000 realized by a cased and engraved Paterson Colt, and the $484,000 paid for the presentation B. Tyler Henry rifle. A cased pair of deluxe Colt Third Model Dragoons realized $572,000. The July session totaled $6.2 million, a world record for a single-day auction session of historic firearms.

As part of the March 1992 Warren Anderson sale, Butterfield's offered the Antique Bowie Knife Collections of Robert Berryman and Charles Schreiner III. Another bonanza, this event set several new records, the highest figure being $132,000 for the Wostenholm & Sons IXL Washington Hunting Knife (see page 345).

What many regard as the last great private collection of American arms, that of the Press family, was Butterfield's first arms sale for 1993. Again new records were achieved, among them $165,000 for a presentation Paterson Colt carbine, $275,000 for a cased deluxe Model

1866 Winchester, and $374,000 for the Ivory Stocked Model 1866 carbine of Porfirio Díaz.

Several commentators on art and antiques have observed that collecting fine guns is the hottest speciality for the 1990s, bearing out predictions made by Greg Martin early in 1990. This growth in activity reflects the myriad attractive qualities of fine arms as well as the fact that collectors are quickly realizing that these collectible guns are a finite resource.

Handguns and Longarms, 1860–1914

Certainly among the reasons why Colts and Winchesters are so popular is that both companies continue to produce arms (and thus to promote them), and that serial-number records offer documentation for substantial numbers of their products. This is also true of Smith & Wesson and Marlin, though only partially true of Remington, the oldest of all the American armsmakers but the one with the least complete production records. In addition to the Colt Collectors Association, the Winchester Club of America, the Winchester Collectors Association, the Marlin Firearms Collectors Association, the Remington Society of America, and the Smith & Wesson Collectors Association, with their sizable memberships, are quite a few smaller organizations: the American Single Shot Rifle Association, the Browning Collectors

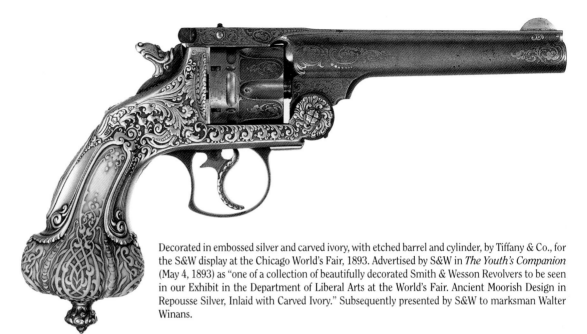

Decorated in embossed silver and carved ivory, with etched barrel and cylinder, by Tiffany & Co., for the S&W display at the Chicago World's Fair, 1893. Advertised by S&W in *The Youth's Companion* (May 4, 1893) as "one of a collection of beautifully decorated Smith & Wesson Revolvers to be seen in our Exhibit in the Department of Liberal Arts at the World's Fair. Ancient Moorish Design in Repousse Silver, Inlaid with Carved Ivory." Subsequently presented by S&W to marksman Walter Winans.

Two superb *fake* Parkers! Larger-frame gun upgraded from an A-1 Special to assume role of the Invincible made for Czar Nicholas II, including inscription on barrel rib: MADE TO ORDER FOR / TSAR NICHOLAS II EMPEROR OF ALL THE RUSSIAS / PARKER BROS. MAKERS, MERIDEN CONN. U.S.A. WHITWORTH STEEL. Gold-inlaid on barrel rib at breech: TSAR NICHOLAS II. Sculpted serial no. 165750 on lower tang. Relief gold-inlaid Romanoff eagle forward of triggerguard; gold crown on triggerguard and front sight. Elaborately sculpted and engraved skeleton buttplate. When author researched this gun at request of dealer, the Parker records indicated original shipment as an A-1 Special to a party in Colorado! Since the czar was not accustomed to vacationing in that state, suspicions were immediately aroused. The case ended up in court, the dealer claiming he had been duped by the maker and the maker stating the dealer knew all along the gun was bogus! Accompanying gun was a bogus .410 A-1 Special, with gold-inlaid serial no. (240638) on lower tang and gold-inlaid Parker Bros. marking on frame bottom.

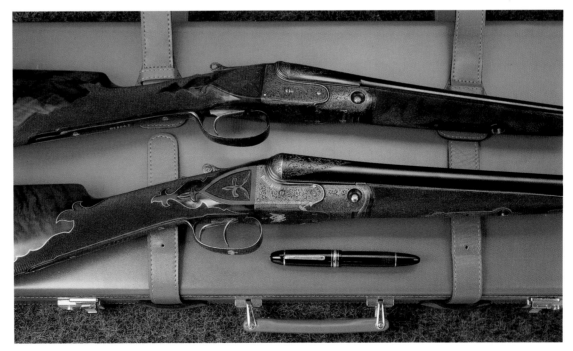

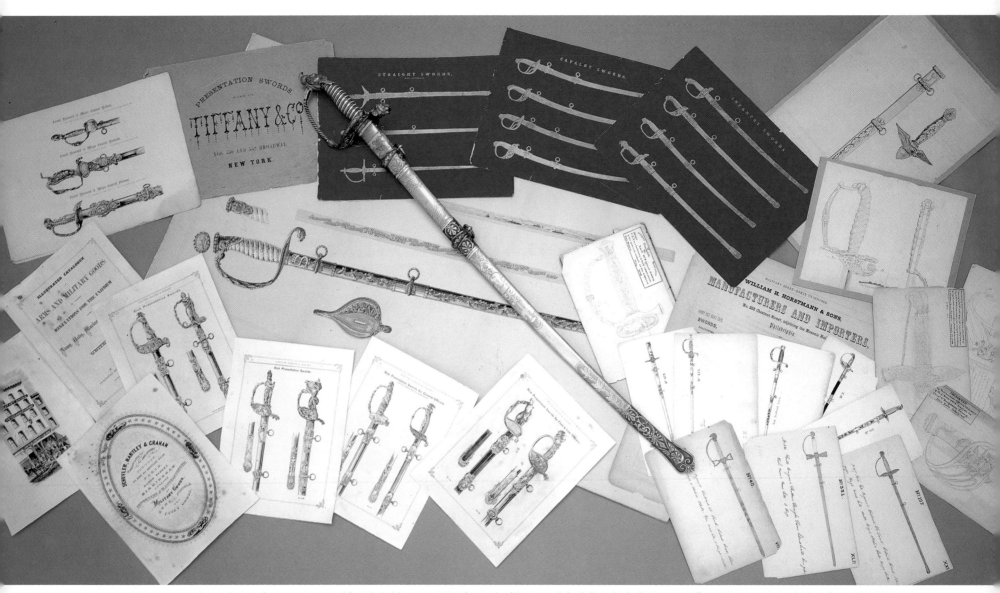

At center, full-size watercolor rendering of presentation sword for Admiral Sampson, USN, for Battle of Santiago, Cuba; believed to be by Ames or Tiffany & Co.; inscription laid out for etching blade. *Lower left,* seven pages from Schuyler, Hartley & Graham 1864 catalogue offering presentation-grade swords. *Lower right,* watercolor paintings, pen-and-ink and pencil drawings from showroom pattern book of W. H. Horstmann & Sons; most dated 1851, some 1852, and a few in late 1840s. Pencil sketches for Mexican War presentations. Broadside from 1855. *Upper right,* original designs for American swords, from Ames factory archives; the one in watercolor for North Carolina Captain Magrath, c. 1850. *Upper left and center,* cover and four pages of 1862 Tiffany catalogue, illustrating swords made by the firm for famous Union generals; blades could be ordered of German, English, or American manufacture, while the mountings of the blades will be "in all cases executed within the establishment." Tiffany sword with silver grips and knuckle bow and gilt-bronze mounts, inscribed to Lt. Colonel Mark Flanigan on gilt scabbard with engraved silver mounts.

Author's Colt Diamondback revolver with Tiffany & Co. grips and Art Nouveau gold inlay. *Lower left,* buttcap motif from Royal Armouries commission; *lower center,* George Strichman buttcap motif from Single Action Army; and emanating from muzzle, buttcap from U.S. Historical Society American Eagle, all Tiffany & Co., Corporate Division, creations. Silver Tiffany pocket calculator engraved by K. C. Hunt. Photo composition by Peter Beard on spread from *Windows at Tiffany's: The Art of Gene Moore.*

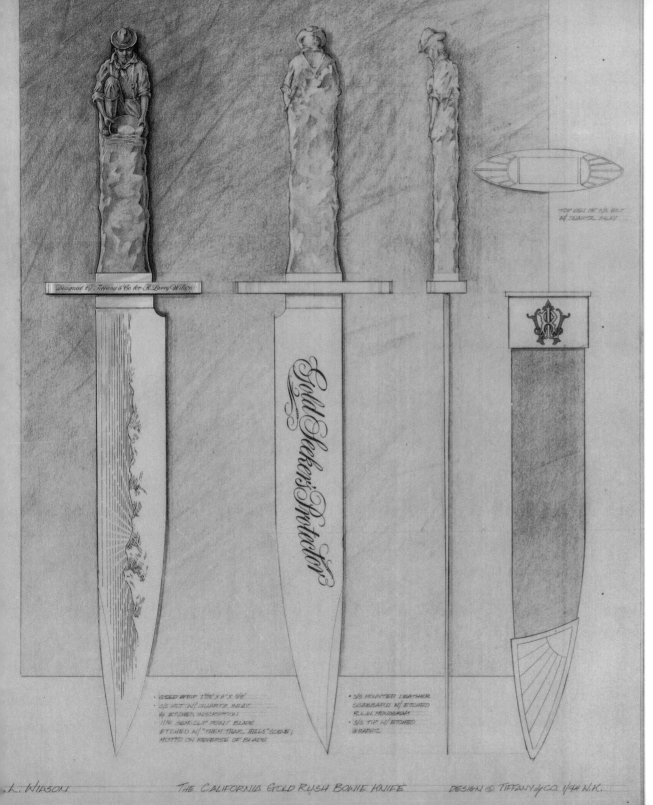

Designed by Tiffany & Co for R. Larry Wilson

Gold Seekers Protector

TOP DES. OF S/S HILT
W/ QUARTZ INLAY

• GOLD STRIP 1⅛" X 6" X ⅝"
• S/S HILT W/ QUARTZ INLAY
• W. ETCHED INSCRIPTION
• 11¼" SEMI-CLIP POINT BLADE
  ETCHED W/ "THEM THAR HILLS" SCENE;
  MOTTO ON REVERSE OF BLADE

• S/S MOUNTED LEATHER
  SCABBARD W/ ETCHED
  R.L.W. MONOGRAM
• S/S TIP W/ ETCHED
  GRAPHIC

L. WILSON   THE CALIFORNIA GOLD RUSH BOWIE KNIFE   DESIGN © TIFFANY & CO. H/H W.K.

Association, the Harrington & Richardson Gun Collectors Association, the Miniature Arms Collectors/Makers Society, the National Automatic Pistol Collectors Association, the National Muzzle Loading Rifle Association, the Ruger Collectors Association, the Southern California Schuetzen Society, and the Weatherby Collectors Association. All of these organizations are affiliates of the National Rifle Association, which maintains an office of gun-collector relations and a gun collectors' division. The NRA also promotes fine guns by their national silver medal award program at the annual meetings. The National Firearms Museum organizes special exhibitions—such as rare Colts and Winchesters from the Robert E. Petersen Collection—for the institution's display area at 11250 Waples Hill Road, Fairfax, Virginia.

NRA Headquarters includes the National Firearms Museum, with approximately 15,000 square feet of exhibits, and another 5,000 square feet devoted to library, office, and storage space. A major donation made in 1993 was the 200-piece American Liberty Firearms Collection of Dr. William L. and Collette N. Roberts. The museum displays some 2,400 firearms, a presentation rivaling that of any arms exhibit in America. In some fifteen galleries, the story of firearms in American history, technology, and culture is presented in a fresh and original manner. Further, the research records of the museum and the NRA's reference library offer a vital source on American arms.

Some rich correspondence on Sharps has survived, as well as the detailed factory ledgers in the collection of Dr. R. L. Moore, Jr., which corroborate several specially decorated Sharps rifles of the post–Civil War period. Some records also exist of arms from the years 1856 through 1869 in the archives of the Connecticut State Library, but these are primarily production arms, not engraved.

The author has been developing his own archive on

Bowie knife by Tiffany & Co., celebrating the California Gold Rush, commissioned by the author; executed in silver, gold, and gold quartz; the blade (by the legendary Buster Warenski) of etched and engraved steel. The first arms design by the Corporate Division's Ward Kelvin, and believed the first Tiffany & Co. Bowie since Theodore Roosevelt's commission of c. 1884.

fine American guns (as well as miscellaneous European arms), incorporating a library of several thousand volumes, thousands of catalogues, price lists, and advertising fliers, and over 50,000 color transparencies and black-and-white photographs. These files include individual documentation of thousands of fine guns he has examined over more than forty years in the field. Part of the collection consists of records and correspondences assembled by the late James E. Serven, William O. Sweet, William Goodwin Renwick, and Merrill K. Lindsay.

Collectors in pursuit of single-shot rifles need to be aware that some actions were decorated at later dates when custom gunmakers rebuilt rifles that were often originally without engraved decoration. The collector value of these arms depends heavily on the quality of the engraving, the stock work, and their shooting performance—as well as the identities of the maker and engraver.

As with the super-guns of Colt and Winchester, collecting in this period can yield some pieces of artistic interest that boast the added attraction of special histories. The Stevens-Lord No. 36 Target Pistol, given by Buffalo Bill Cody to Ben Thompson, is thus of far greater interest and value than the standard handgun of that model. Of course, the value is boosted greatly by documentation of the history, and identification of the engraver, donor, and recipient. As one collector has put it: "A 7 is always a 7, but a 10 is the best." In other words, if you buy the best, you can never go wrong.

Tiffany's Fine Guns

Collecting Tiffany & Co. firearms and edged weaponry is probably as exotic a category of American arms collecting as exists. So exclusive are their creations that only one collector has been able to specialize, and he owns by far most of their known examples in firearms: over thirty pieces at this writing. The collection is of such splendor that portions were included in Tiffany & Co.'s May 1991 loan exhibition, and five pieces, at this writing, are on display at The Metropolitan Museum of Art's Arms and Armor galleries.

Unique matched pair of Model 1911A1 pistols, masterpieces from R. J. Kornbrath's career. For over sixty years these pistols lay unknown but to the family of the original owner, rancher and oil man Guy Waggoner. Waggoner's father, W. T., known as the richest man in Texas, was initially upset when oil was discovered on his ranch, because "cattle couldn't drink it"—he needed water, not oil. Kornbrath's pride in the set is evident from his use of one of the pair in his advertising brochure. Colt factory ledgers document delivery to Kornbrath, and shipment on completion to Texas dealers Wolf & Klar; the work performed was gold inlaying, engraving, 4½- to 4¾-pound trigger pulls, and special diamond-mounted ivory grips. Inset shows Hereford steer from Three D ranch; their brand is gold inlaid on opposite side of receivers. Serial numbers C160986 and C160988.

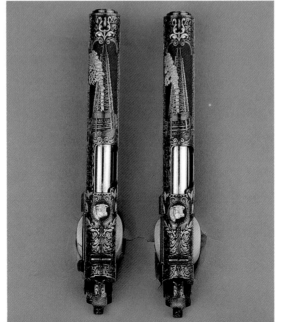

Winchester Model 61 pump-action .22 rifle, engraved and gold-inlaid for Arthur D. Leidesdorf, by Joseph Fugger, c. 1935; signed on bottom of frame above gold-inlaid serial number. Gold-inlaid on top of barrel: NO 2213 GRIFFIN & HOWE, INC. NEW YORK. Leidesdorf was a good friend and client of Drew Holl, whose gallery, Crossroads of Sport (founded 1939), pioneered the sale of sporting art, limited-edition prints, decoys, and related memorabilia, for clients throughout the United States. Located for most of its period of operation at 5 East Forty-seventh Street, Crossroads was literally that for sporting artists (such as David Maas, Chet Reneson, Ogden Pleissner, Maynard Reese, Guy Coheleach, and Bob Kuhn—several of whom got their first major recognition through the gallery), and for collectors (the likes of Mellons, Wideners, Firestones, and the ultimate enthusiast, Russell Barnett Aitken). The gallery preceded such giants of today as Wild Wings and Collector's Covey in issuing limited-edition wildlife prints and promoting the best of wildlife artists. Drew Holl received a call one day from Mr. Leidesdorf concerning the sale of the latter's amazing collection, kept in an elegant Park Avenue duplex apartment. Apparently the keen collector had a new girlfriend who had other interests—and the collection had to go. With some regret, Drew liquidated the collection, one of the grandest holdings sold in his entire career in sporting art.

Monte Mandarino's contemporary artistry. *From top,* Georgian rifle in c. 1740 mode, with pattern-welded barrel; inlaid English walnut stock; English rococo chiseled steel mounts. Louis XIV Parisian fowling piece c. 1790; inlaid English walnut stock; French baroque–style heavily chiseled steel mounts. Longrifle of American style of Lancaster County school, c. Revolutionary War; relief-carved maple stock. (See also back endpapers.)

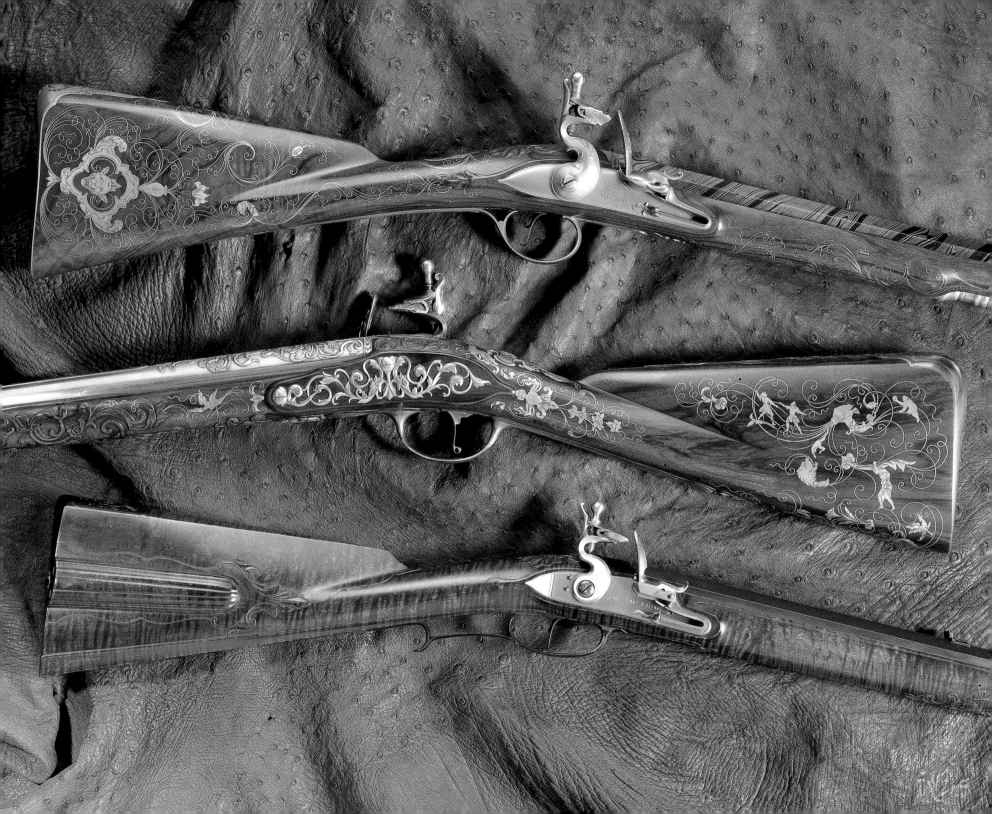

A miscellany of issues by the U.S. Historical Society and its successor for arms issues, the United States Society of Arms and Armour. *Clockwise from top:* General Chuck Jaeger Bertuzzi shotgun; Mel Torme special issue; Henry Deringer matched pair; Gene Autry premier edition; Texas Ranger Museum Dragoon; Jim Bowie knife; Royal Armouries–H.M. Tower of London Dragoon; Texas Paterson revolver; Thomas Jefferson–Monticello flintlock pistol (one of pair); and U.S. Navy Cutlass. Charles Addams cartoon (in larger, limited-edition print form) accompanied Merrill Lindsay–Eli Whitney Museum special-issue Dragoon. Photograph *at right* shows Society Chairman Robert H. Kline and author presenting Lindsay-Whitney Museum revolver to Addams, portions of his arms collection in background. A 1992 Single Action honored champion stock-car racer Richard Petty, a keen collector of Society special issues.

On a leatherbound copy of *Armsmear,* topbreak S&W with rare Tiffany & Co. Art Nouveau gold grip contrasts with Paul Lantuch tribute to Gustave Young. Miniature double gun case, also by Tiffany.

VINCIT QUI PATITUR

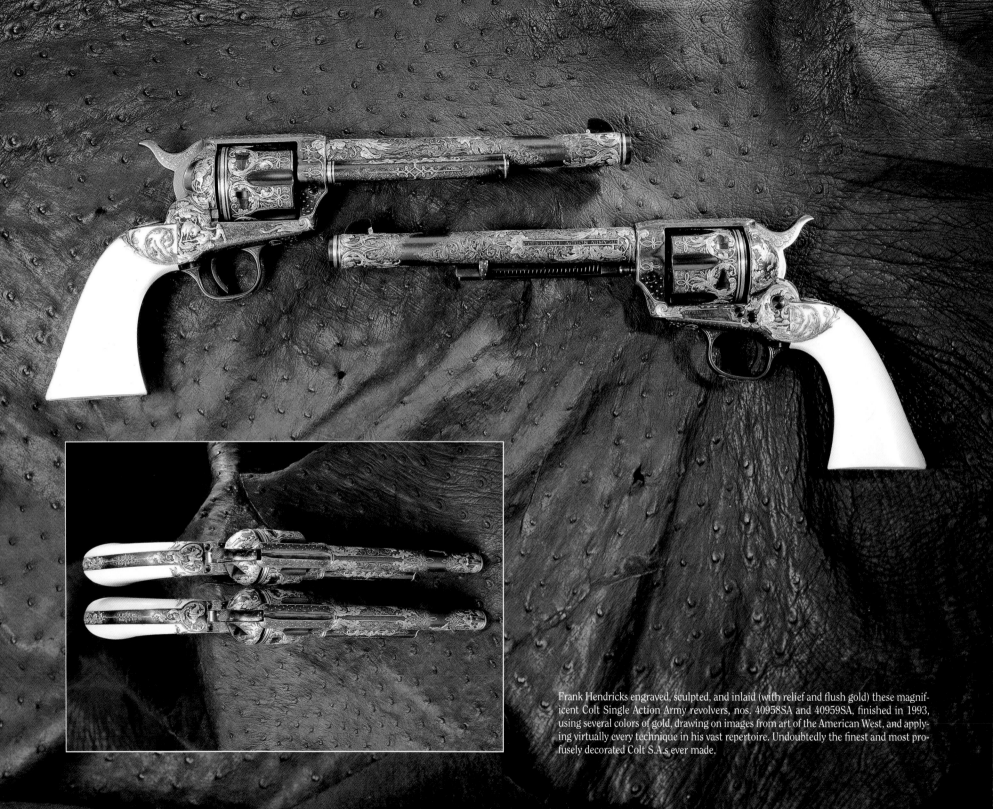

Frank Hendricks engraved, sculpted, and inlaid (with relief and flush gold) these magnificent Colt Single Action Army revolvers, nos. 40958SA and 40959SA, finished in 1993, using several colors of gold, drawing on images from art of the American West, and applying virtually every technique in his vast repertoire. Undoubtedly the finest and most profusely decorated Colt S.A.s ever made.

The National Museum of American History, part of the Smithsonian Institution, has no less than seven superb Tiffany presentation swords, the best grouping known. Not more than half a dozen important Tiffany presentation swords have come onto the market in the last twenty years. And there appears to have been only one nineteenth-century Tiffany silver-mounted Bowie knife, made for Theodore Roosevelt.

As a keen client of Tiffany's fine guns, the author can speak with conviction: these are among the most beautiful, original, and finely wrought arms made anywhere in the world today, or in any past era. Furthermore, it is exciting to be the patron and ultimate owner of a modern work of decorative art that is descended from an American legend.

Every Tiffany piece designed before publication of *The Arms of Tiffany,* a joint project of Janet Zapata, former archivist of Tiffany & Co., and this author, will be featured in that upcoming volume.

A Tradition in Flux and the Golden Age Rekindled

Collecting semimodern and modern fine guns offers a different challenge from most antiques. First, record-keeping must be meticulous, since transfer and shipping require either a collector's or a dealer's federal firearms license. Dealers who sell antique arms often do not handle anything post-1898, due to the record-keeping requirements, considered a nuisance by most. The degree of devotion to these fine guns is proven by the fact that some of the leading dealers are in major metropolitan areas: most particularly Griffin & Howe, in New York City since 1923.

Both Christie's and Sotheby's market twentieth-century fine guns, as do Butterfield's, Julia, and others. Christopher Austyn of Christie's, London, has put on some of the best sales of modern times, while rival Windi Phillips of Sotheby's has been actively promoting the genre in America. David Condon & Co. not only sell antique and modern guns of quality, but also hold their own auctions. Over 275,000 federal firearms licenses are

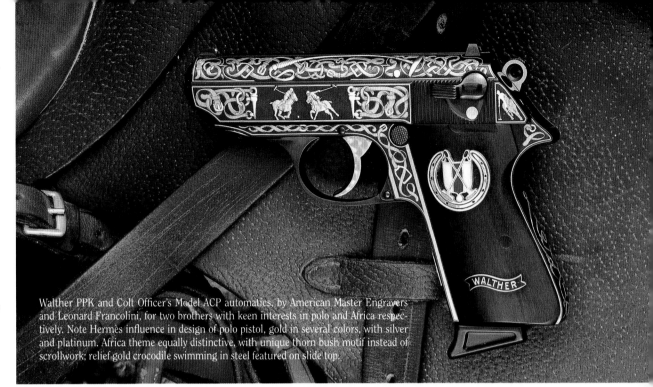

Walther PPK and Colt Officer's Model ACP automatics, by American Master Engravers and Leonard Francolini, for two brothers with keen interests in polo and Africa respectively. Note Hermès influence in design of polo pistol, gold in several colors, with silver and platinum. Africa theme equally distinctive, with unique thorn bush motif instead of scrollwork; relief gold crocodile swimming in steel featured on slide top.

(*left and center top*) The Dallas Gun, specially made on order of Larry Hagman. Holland & Holland's brochure on this fabulous creation quotes the client: "On May 3, 1991, *Dallas* aired its final episode in the U.S.A.—one of 357 over a period of 13 years. *Dallas* played in 87 countries and in many different languages . . . and for years was the highest-rated show ever on television in the U.S. . . . I decided to have a present made for myself to commemorate *Dallas* which would be both beautiful and functional. [The result was] one of the most striking and exquisite guns ever made by the best gunmaker in the world, Holland & Holland. . . . The gun took three years in the making, and, needless to say, combines both function and beauty." Completed 1991.

(*center bottom*) A master of bulino, Giancarlo Pedretti is especially known for knives and guns executed with that highly sophisticated technique. He is also one of the few engravers outside of England to have embellished a Purdey gun at the time of its original manufacture, in this case at the request of the buyer.

(*right*) Imaginative female-peacock motif by Manrico Torcoli on Fabbri shotgun, c. 1992, popular with Continental and American clients.

held in America. Not a few of these dealers and dealer-collectors locate, market, or make best-quality arms.

Fueling the frenzy of the legions of keen collectors are not only events like the Las Vegas Antique Arms Shows (a misnomer, since quite a bit of the displays are twentieth-century pieces of quality) and the Custom Knifemakers' Guild Show, but also publications like *Gun List, CADA Journal,* and *Shotgun News,* and ads in such periodicals as *American Rifleman, American Hunter, Petersen's Hunting, Guns, Guns & Ammo, Rifle, Safari,*

360

Curt Erickson made this exquisite dagger; engraving by Buster Warenski.

Master craftsman and teacher Neil Hartliep not only inlaid and engraved these Remington Model 870 and Winchester Model 21 shotguns but also wrote the engraving guide for the NRA's Education and Training Division. Under auspices of the NRA, Hartliep worked with Division Director H. Wayne Sheets in developing educational summer sessions on the college level. The educational program began in 1978 and remains active, counting among its graduates John Barraclaugh, Cecil Mills, Lynne Wright Winchester, Larry Parker, James Delaney, Terry Loesch, Tandy Morgan, Robert Rollifson, Rose Wessinger, Donald Cassavant, and Glen and Thomas Hartliep. Neil Hartliep and the NRA's educational programs, along with *American Rifleman* magazine, have been instrumental in accelerating the growth of interest in engraved firearms in America.

Pocketknives in steel and titanium, by Paul Lantuch for collector John R. Woods, in Celtic, Art Nouveau, Italian Renaissance, and Gustave Young styles.

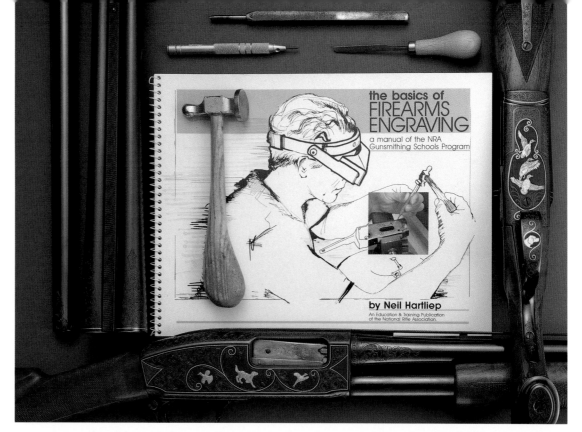

The Blade, The Engraver (journal of the Firearms Engraving Guild of America), *Gun Week, Gun World, Knife World, Muzzle Blasts, Muzzleloader, Shooting Times, Shotgun Sports,* and *Shooting Classics,* all of which contribute to the international passion for fine American arms.

Exhibits at U.S. shows such as Safari Club International (SCI) generally attract the British makers Holland & Holland, Westley Richards, P. V. Nelson, and J. Rigby, as well as Germany's Hartmann & Weiss, from Hamburg; Britain's James Purdey & Sons sends emissaries to major client cities.

Finally, the revival of arms by Tiffany & Co., and the entry of the London firm of Asprey & Co. (another SCI exhibitor) into the world of manufacturing fine arms—their New York showroom is on the same block of Fifth Avenue as Tiffany—are exciting endorsements of the field for its exclusive clientele. The modern arms renaissance continues to evolve, and the artistry and craftsmanship keep spiraling upwards.

From Henry VIII to the Fords and Mellons, fine arms collectors share an especially rich heritage. All have found captivating the unique attraction of arms, their artistry and beauty, craftsmanship and engineering, history and romance. What collectibles can equal this rich and fascinating heritage, and what objects can boast of such a role in the past five hundred years of decorative arts?

(*opposite*) Winchester Grand Royals, nos. W33104, W33105; (*right*), no. W33121. Gun at *right* the most deluxe in series, with .410-, 28-, and 20-gauge barrels. Made for the author's collection, with gold inlay and engraving by Andrew Bourbon, stocks by Fred Wenig, Elbert Smith, and Darrell Smith. See also page 297.

Selected contents of the Royal Armouries–H.M. Tower of London, symbolic of treasures of arms and armor, interpreted by artist Litizia Petigliani, in picture commissioned by author. The proposed Royal Armouries satellite museum in America will help to bring the art of European and American arms to a much broader public. While maintaining displays at the Tower of London, and at Fort Nelson in Portsmouth, the Royal Armouries is moving its headquarters to a new museum and research center at Leeds.

Eclectic display of arms, accessories, and memorabilia inspired by Peter Beard's picture layouts for *The Peacemakers* and the present book.

Six-month-old Greta Martin clutches her first gun, a U.S. Historical Society Colt Model 1861 Navy miniature, surrounded by treasures mainly from the collection of her famous father, antique arms specialist Greg Martin. *Clockwise from top right:* Annie Oakley Stevens rifle; Colt president C.L.F. Robinson's 00 Helfricht-engraved automatic; Captain Jack Crawford's Remington Rolling Block; Greg Martin's Freedom Arms .454 Casull (with which he dispatched a charging California wild boar from a distance of eight feet); gold-mounted Swiss Army knife by Andrew Bourbon; Rolex with custom gold band by Alvin White; author's Tiffany & Co. Dragoon; and Gustave Young gold-inlaid Sharps shotgun. Mother, wife, and kindred Wild West devotee Petra Martin assisted photographer Douglas Sandberg in unprecedented baby picture.

Glossary

acanthus A semistylized leaf motif appearing throughout the history of art; named for a plant widespread in the Mediterranean area. At times used in a variant form with leaves resembling thistle, parsley, celery, or dandelion.

arabesque A style of linear ornament, composed of interlaced lines or scrolls, at times with fruit-flower, leaf, and animal motifs interspersed. Most are curvilinear and flowing, though some are angular. Not to be confused with Arab styles, known as Moorish.

Art Deco Decorative art style from 1920s featuring geometric motifs, curvilinear forms, and crisply delineated outlines.

Art Nouveau Fine and applied art style from late 19th and early 20th centuries, featuring curvilinear motifs often based on natural forms.

banderol A decoration in form of a ribbon or long scroll, sometimes inscribed.

baroque The style that dominated European art and architecture throughout the seventeenth century, continuing in some regions up through c. 1750. A theatrical and dynamic style using illusionism, ornate forms, realism, and a blending of arts for effect.

bead A punched dot or tiny circle used for backgrounding or bordering.

billet A checkerboard pattern.

cartouche An engraved, sculpted, or cast ornament enclosing a plain central space, usually oval or lozenge-shaped; used for inscriptions.

chasing Ornamenting a metal surface with indentations with a striking or punching tool; name given to the resulting decoration. *Cf.* repoussé.

checkerboard Billet; pattern of dark and light squares.

chevron A repeated decorative device similar to the V-shaped stripes on a military uniform (sergeant). Sometimes known as herringbone.

cinquefoil Five small arcs, which, joined together, compose points (or cusps), creating a decorative effect; especially popular in Victorian decoration.

damascene Inlaying one metal with a more precious metal, usually silver or gold (sometimes both together).

damascus Method of making gun barrels, in which iron is wrapped around a central rod (under intense heat), then hammered and heat-welded, often leaving striking designs. Method of making blades, in which the iron is hammered and folded frequently, creating striking patterns in the metal.

egg Decorative motif in the shape of an egg. Usually found in borders, such as the so-called egg and dart (banded design of alternating egg and arrowhead shapes).

emboss Technique in which raised decorations or figures are done in relief.

engrave Process of incising a design, figures, or inscriptions on a hard surface with a sharp tool termed a graver.

escutcheon A shield or shieldlike surface, usually used for inscriptions; or an ornamental plate, usually inlaid on wood, ivory, or other stock material.

fascile A cross-ribbed bundling motif favored by L. D. Nimschke.

festoon Decorative design composed of gracefully curved lines done in loops; usually a garland of leaves, fruit, and flowers arranged in a loop between two points. Wavy vinelike extensions or ribbons may extend from the foliage and floral devices. Sometimes called a swag.

finial An ornament serving as the crowning detail, as at the front of a triggerguard, likely to be a pineapple or acorn.

foil One of several minute arcs that join together to make points (sometimes called cusps), for decorative effect. See also trefoil, quatrefoil, and cinquefoil.

foliate Decorative motifs of foliage designs or leaves.

fretwork Geometric border ornament of straight lines turning at right angles, arranged in regular, repeated pattern. Same as Greek key pattern.

garland A wreath or festoon of flowers or leaves.

guilloche Repeated double-serpentine design.

herringbone Two short straight lines that meet at an angle and repeat equally, much like the backbone of a fish. Sometimes referred to as fishbone. Similar to chevron.

imbrication Overlapping design resembling shingles or roof tiles, neatly arranged.

inlay Insertion of thin pieces of metal, usually gold or silver, into cuts or insertions made in steel or iron. Sometimes iron is inlaid in steel, and vice versa (rare on arms).

key Border ornament of straight lines turning at right angles, in regular repeating pattern; also termed fret or fretwork.

motif A recurring subject, theme, or idea in design detail or engraved device.

Moorish Arabic design details.

overlay Damascene decoration, in which the metal (usually gold or silver) is hammered onto scribed lines on the surface of (usually) iron or steel. In contrast to inlay.

quatrefoil Four small arcs joined together, making cusps. Generally done as borders.

repoussé Decoration of the metal by hammering or punching from the back or reverse surface. Sometimes further refined by chasing.

rinceau Repeated serpentine foliage design, usually grapevine scrollwork.

rococo Style of art and decoration from the eighteenth century, primarily during reign of Henry XV of France. An elegant and delicate refinement of the elaborate and curvilinear forms of Italy's High Baroque reduced to smaller scale. A reaction against heavy, ornate classicism of arts under Louis XIV.

Romanesque Bold pattern of scrolled leaves surrounding flowers.

scriber Engraving tool used for marking a design in metal.

scroll Decorative motif made up of any of a variety of spiral, coiled, or convoluted forms, similar to cross-section of a loosely rolled strip of paper. Scrollwork is the most widely used decorative element in arms engraving.

sculpt Carving or chiseling in metal, usually inlays, but sometimes base materials like steel or silver.

tongue Tongue-shaped design element, usually arranged in multiples, side-by-side.

trefoil Three small arcs joined together, making cusps. Generally done as borders.

trellis Decorative device like latticework.

volute A scroll-shaped ornament; found in pairs on Ionic capitals.

wave Decorative border like a wavy line.

vignette A decorative device with substance or subject of its own.

366

Though now heralded as "artist-engravers," the pliers of the centuries-old craft of arms engraving have had their ups and downs in terms of recognition and respect for their skills.

The lack of signatures on most of the American engraved arms predating c. 1945 has been the major reason why identifying the engravers of particular decorated arms can be extremely challenging. Of the craftsmen and women on the following list, the work of all the contemporaries can be identified, many by style (if they have developed a particularly individual approach to the craft), or at the least by locating initials or signatures, or even by referral to the careful firearms records that each must keep under federal, state, and local laws.

A great many of the earlier craftsmen have yet to be identified by the style and quality of their work. Time will tell how many of those remaining craftsmen can be identified beyond merely a name and other limited information.

Note: CE refers to the books *Colt Engraving* and *The Book of Colt Engraving* (both by the author), wherein the engraver is discussed. WE refers to *Winchester Engraving* and *The Book of Winchester Engraving* (also by the author). These works have special indexes devoted to engravers. Several of the contemporary craftsmen are members of the Firearms Engravers Guild of America, whose listing service and secretary Robert Evans have been helpful in providing information on present-day artisans. Ken Warner's annual *Gun Digest* lists engravers and engraving tools. The publication has been a consistent promoter of fine guns since its founding days under custom gun and engraving aficionado John Amber.

Appendix:
American Arms Engravers from Colonial Times to the Present

A

Acevedo, Horacio   contemporary, Kankakee, Illinois

Adair, Bill, Custom Shop   contemporary, Carrollton, Texas

Adams, John   contemporary, East Dennis, Massachusetts

Adams, John, Jr.   contemporary, East Dennis, Massachusetts

Aetna Stamp and Engraving Company   CE, 20th century

Agee, Cole   CE, 20th century

Albemarle Fine Arms   contemporary, Charlottesville, Virginia

Alfano, Sam   contemporary, New Orleans, Louisiana

Alpen, Ralph   contemporary, West Grove, Pennsylvania

American Gun Engraving Company   CE, 19th century (Jacob Glahn)

American Master Engravers, Inc.   contemporary, Hadlyme, Connecticut

Anderson, Conrad S.   contemporary, Orofino, Idaho

Anthony and George, Ltd.   contemporary, Evington, Virginia

Armurier Hiptmayer   contemporary, Eastman, Quebec, Canada

Aubray, William   CE, 19th century

Aurum Etchings   contemporary, Garland, Texas (photoengraving)

Averill, Ed   contemporary, Cooperstown, New York

Avery, William   CE, 19th century

B

Bakewell, Thomas W.   contemporary, Hancock, New Hampshire

Barbetti, Paolo   contemporary, Seattle, Washington

Barlow, Thomas   CE, 19th century

Baron Technology   contemporary, Trumbull, Connecticut (photoengraving)

Barraclough, John   contemporary, Gardena, California

Bates Engraving   contemporary, Decatur, Alabama

Bayer, Joseph C.   contemporary, Princeton, New Jersey

Bee, Angelo   contemporary, Chatsworth, California

Beebe, Bruce   contemporary, Akron, New York

Bell, Sid   contemporary, Tully, New York

Betrosoff, Bruce A.   contemporary, Bonaire, Georgia

Bieu, Earl   contemporary, address unknown

Blair, Jim   contemporary, Wright, Wyoming

Bledsoe, Weldon   contemporary, Fort Worth, Texas

Bleile, C. Roger   contemporary, Cincinnati, Ohio

Bleile, Carl B.   contemporary, Cincinnati, Ohio

Bodenstein, Hermann   CE, 19th century

Boice, Elden   contemporary, Chicago, Illinois

Bone, Ralph   contemporary, Owasso, Oklahoma

Bonham, Henry   contemporary, Brewster, Massachusetts

Boucher, Richard   contemporary, Edwards, Missouri

Bourbon, Andrew   contemporary, Brewster, Massachusetts

Bratcher, Dan   contemporary, Carthage, Missouri

Bridges, B. Bryan   contemporary, Tucson, Arizona

Brgoch, Frank   contemporary, Bountiful, Utah

Brooker, Dennis   contemporary, Derby, Iowa

Brownell's, Inc.   contemporary, Montezuma, Iowa (source of engraving tools)

Bruehl, Max   WE, 20th century

Budge, LaVere   contemporary, Venice, Florida

Burgess, Byron   contemporary, San Luis Obispo, California

Burt, Robert B.   contemporary, Burlington, Connecticut

C

CAM Enterprises   contemporary, Prescott, Arizona

Cargnel, Gino   contemporary, Simi Valley, California

Carmody, Michael A.   contemporary, Mary Ester, Florida

Cassavant, Donald H.   contemporary, Hyde Park, New York

Christopher Firearms Company, Inc.   contemporary, Miamitown, Ohio

Churchill, Winston G.   contemporary, Proctorsville, Vermont

Clark Firearms Engraving   contemporary, San Marino, California

Cole, E. A.   WE, 19th century

Conrad, David   contemporary, Lynnwood, Washington

Conroy, Frank L.   contemporary, West Hartford, Vermont

Creek Side Metal & Woodcrafters   contemporary, Fishers Hill, Virginia

Crocker Engraving   contemporary, Los Alamos, New Mexico

Cullity, Daniel contemporary, East Sandwich, Massachusetts

Curtis, Henry C. CE, 19th century

Custom Gun Engraving contemporary, Phoenix, Arizona

D

Delaney, James L. contemporary, Delevan, New York

Delcour, Rene contemporary, Fleron, Belgium (has worked in U.S. in California, Texas, and Connecticut)

Dooley, Herbert E. contemporary, Dayton, Nebraska

Dove, Howard M. 20th century, Christiansburg, Virginia

Doyle, John J. contemporary, Chula Vista, California

Dubber, Michael contemporary, Evansville, Indiana

Duguet, Thierry contemporary, Albemarle Fine Arms, Charlottesville, Virginia

E

Engraving Artistry contemporary, Burlington, Connecticut

Ennis, Carleton 20th century, Ilion, New York

Evans, Robert contemporary, Oregon City, Oregon

Eyster, Ken contemporary, Centerburg, Ohio (Heritage Gunsmiths, Inc.)

F

Fassio, Melvin contemporary, Bonnerla, Montana

Flannery, Jeffrey W. contemporary, Union, Kentucky

Floatstone Manufacturing Company, Inc. contemporary, La Crescenta, Calif. (L. Francolini)

Fountain Products contemporary, West Springfield, Massachusetts

Flood, Ken contemporary, Stamford, Connecticut

Forte, Giuseppi contemporary, Rawlins, Wyoming

Francolini, Leonard contemporary, La Crescenta, Calif. (Floatstone Manufacturing)

Frank, Heinrich H. contemporary, Whitefish, Montana

Freund, Frank W. 19th and early 20th centuries, Nebraska, Colorado, Wyoming, New Jersey

Fugger, Joseph 20th century, formerly Griffin & Howe and Abercrombie & Fitch

G

Gamraelt, William contemporary, Missoula, Montana

Gene's Custom Guns contemporary, White Bear Lake, Minnesota

George, Christy contemporary, Evington, Virginia

George, Tim contemporary, Evington, Virginia

Gerin, Max CE, 19th century

Glahn, George CE, 19th century

Glahn, Gus, CE, 20th century, possibly late 19th century as well

Glahn, Jacob CE, WE, 19th century

Glahn, Theodore CE, 19th and 20th centuries

Glahn, Wilbur A. CE, WE, 20th century

Glaser, Donald contemporary, Emporia, Kansas (Gravermeister, Gravermax)

Glimm, Jerome C. contemporary, Conrad, Montana

Gold, Eric contemporary, Flagstaff, Arizona

Golden Age Arms Company contemporary, Ashley, Ohio

Goodwin, Daniel contemporary, Kalispell, Montana

Goodyear, Lester 20th century

Gough, John WE, 20th century

Gough, William H. CE, WE, 20th century

Gournet, Geoffroy contemporary, Easton, Pennsylvania

Grant, Howard V. contemporary, Lac du Flambeau, Wisconsin

Grant, Malcolm F., Jr. contemporary, Grand Prairie, Texas

Green, Elliott L. CE, 19th century

Grencavich, William contemporary, Conyngham, Pennsylvania

Griebel, Arnold CE, WE, 20th century

Griffin & Howe, Inc. contemporary, Bernardsville, New Jersey, and New York, New York

Groff, Noel E. contemporary, Carson City, Nevada

GRS Corp. (Gravermeister Tool) contemporary, Emporia, Kansas

Grunewald, Augustus CE, 19th century

Grunewald, possibly Augustus WE, 19th century

Gun Room, The contemporary, Muncie, Indiana

Guns contemporary, Hudson, Ohio

Guns Unlimited contemporary, Spencer, Indiana

Gurney, F. R. contemporary, Edmonton, Alberta, Canada

Gwinnell, Bryson J. contemporary, Rochester, Vermont

Gwinnell, Jan L. contemporary, West Hartford, Connecticut (Colt factory)

H

Haga, Eric contemporary, Bellvue, Washington

Hahn, William CE, 19th century

Hand Engravers Supply Company contemporary, Albany, Georgia

Harrington, Fred A. contemporary, Mount Morris, Michigan

Harris Hand Engraving contemporary, San Antonio, Texas (Paul A. Harris)

Hartliep, Glen contemporary, Tucson, Arizona

Hartliep, Neil contemporary, Tucson, Arizona, and Fairmont, Minnesota

Harwood, Jack O. contemporary, Blackfoot, Idaho

Hayhurst, Sol contemporary, Truth or Consequences, New Mexico

Helfricht, Charles J. CE, 19th century

Helfricht, Cuno A. CE, 19th and 20th centuries

Henderson, Fred D. contemporary, Forest Park, Georgia

Hendricks, Frank E., Jr. contemporary, Dripping Springs, Texas

Henshaw, Richard B. CE, 19th century

Herbert, Alvin F. CE, 20th century

Hiptmayer, Heidemarie contemporary, Eastman, Quebec, Canada

Hiptmayer, Klaus contemporary, Eastman, Quebec, Canada

Hoggson & Pettis WE, 19th and 20th centuries

Hoggson, Samuel J. WE, 19th century

Horvath, Kurt contemporary, Fayetteville, Tennessee

Houghton & Glahn CE, 20th century

Houser, Jesse contemporary, Troyoe, North Carolina

Huff, Stephen E. contemporary, Missoula, Montana

Hurst, Ken contemporary, Lynchburg, Virginia

I

Ingle, Ralph W. contemporary, Rossville, Georgia

Inshaw, Richard Bates 19th century, Springfield, Massachusetts

J

Jaeger, Paul, Inc. contemporary, Grand Junction, Tennessee (subsidiary of Dunn's)

Jarvis, Harry 20th century (Smith & Wesson)

Jlantonio, Robert contemporary, Venice, Florida

Joaquim, Domingos contemporary, Woronoco, Massachusetts

Johns, Bill contemporary, McAllen, Texas

Johnson, Adolph WE, believed 19th and into 20th century

Johnson, C. WE, believed 19th and into 20th century

Johnson, W. B. CE, 19th century

K

Kain, Robert C. contemporary, address unknown

Kamyk, Steven   contemporary (Colt factory)
Kane, Edward   contemporary, Ukiah, California
Kasper, Peggy Sue   contemporary, Sussex, Wisconsin
Kaye, Tommy J.   contemporary, Beaumont, Texas
Kellogg, A. J. G.   CE, 19th century
Kelly, Lance   contemporary, Decatur, Georgia
Kelso, Jim   contemporary, Baring, Washington
Kies, Dennis   contemporary, East Hartford, Connecticut
Kissler, Larry   contemporary, Reno, Nevada
Kleinguenther's   contemporary, Segin, Texas
Koevenig, E. J.   contemporary, Keystone, South Dakota
Kolouch, Walter   contemporary, McMinnville, Oregon
Kontout, Al   contemporary, Waterbury, Connecticut
Kornbrath, R. J.   CE, WE, 20th century
Kummer, Charles   CE, 19th century
Kusmit, John   contemporary (retired from Winchester factory), New Haven, Connecticut
Kusmit, Nick   contemporary (retired from Winchester factory), New Haven, Connecticut

L

Lageose's Engraving   contemporary, Kalispell, Montana
Lane, Ben G., Jr.   contemporary, Estes Park, Colorado
Lantuch, Paulius L.   contemporary, New Haven, Connecticut
Leibowitz, Leonard   contemporary, Pittsburgh, Pennsylvania (etcher)
Letschnig, Franz   contemporary, Martintown, Ontario, Canada
Lindsay, Steve   contemporary, Kearney, Nebraska
Lombardy, Carmen   contemporary, Attleboro, Massachusetts
London Guns, Ltd.   contemporary, Santa Barbara, California
Long, Gene M.   contemporary, Salt Lake City, Utah
Love, Daniel E.   contemporary, Arthur, Iowa

M

McGraw, Bill   CE, 20th century (mainly Ithaca Gun Co.)
Machu, Edward Joe, Jr.   contemporary, San Antonio, Texas
McKenzie, Lynton   contemporary, Tucson, Arizona
McManis, Charles   contemporary, Las Vegas, Nevada
Mains, William   contemporary, Las Vegas, Nevada
Maki, Robert, School of Engraving   contemporary, Glenview, Illinois
Marek, George   contemporary, Westfield, Massachusetts

Marek, Rudy   contemporary, Banks, Oregon
Marktl, Franz   contemporary, Phoenix, Arizona
Martin, F. W.   19th century (Smith & Wesson)
Martin, Fred M.   CE, 19th century
Master Engravers, Inc.   contemporary, Dripping Springs, Texas
Mason, Ed   contemporary, Memphis, Tennessee
Medairy, John   CE, 19th century
Mele, Frank   contemporary, Granville, Tennessee
Merritt, S. T.   19th century (Smith & Wesson)
Meyer, Christian   contemporary, Ridgefield, New Jersey
Mittermeier, Frank   contemporary, New York, New York (tools)
Morba, Hans   CE, 19th century
Moschetti, Mitchell R.   contemporary, Denver, Colorado
Mountain States Engraving   contemporary, Wenatchee, Washington
Muller, Louis   CE, 19th century
Murphy, Thomas D.   contemporary, Phoenix, Arizona

N

New Orleans Arms Company   c. 1969–79 (Lynton McKenzie)
NgraveR Company (MagnaGraver tool)   contemporary, Bozrah, Connecticut
Nimschke, Louis Daniel   CE, WE, c. 1850–1904, New York (see also L. D. Nimschke, Firearms Engraver)
Nott, Ron   contemporary, Summerdale, Pennsylvania
Novak, Jonathan   contemporary, Reading, Pennsylvania

O

O'Brien, C. C.   CE, 19th century
Old Dominion Engravers   contemporary, Lynchburg, Virginia
Olin, Stephen   contemporary, Mexico, New York
Olmdahl, Jamie   contemporary, Valley City, North Dakota
Ormsby, W. L.   CE, 19th century
Overbey, Tom   CE, WE, contemporary, Richmond, Virginia

P

Pachmayr, Ltd.   contemporary, Pasadena, California (formerly Los Angeles)
Palmgren Steel Products   contemporary, Chicago, Illinois
Parker, Larry A.   contemporary, Belmont, Ohio

Parker, William   CE, 19th century
Patchbox, The   contemporary, Kalispell, Montana
Patterson, C. H.   contemporary, College Station, Texas
Pedersen, C. R. and Son   contemporary, Ludington, Michigan
Pedini, Marcello   contemporary, Dix Hills, New York
Pengh, Edward   contemporary, Ukiah, California
Perlowin, James   contemporary, Laguna Hills, California
Peters, Larry   contemporary, Milwaukie, Oregon
Pfeiffer, Hans   contemporary, Elmhurst, Illinois
Phillips, Ray   contemporary, Bozrah, Connecticut
Pierce, Barbara R.   contemporary, Hermiston, Oregon
Pilkington, Scott   contemporary, Monteagle, Tennessee
Piquette, Paul R.   contemporary, Springfield, Massachusetts (Smith & Wesson)
Pitetti, Arthur   contemporary, Denver, New York
Plante, Eugene T.   contemporary, White Bear Lake, Minnesota
Popovits, Joseph   contemporary, Laguna Hills, California
Potts, Wayne E.   contemporary, Denver, Colorado
Pranger, Ed   contemporary, Anacortes, Washington
Prudhomme, Edward C.   20th century, Shreveport, Louisiana

R

Rabeno, Martin   contemporary, Ellenville, New York
Rankin, William H.   contemporary, Bloomfield Hills, Michigan
Regan, Daniel   CE, 19th century
Reno, Karen   contemporary, Aurora, Colorado (scrimshander)
Reno, Wayne   contemporary, Aurora, Colorado (scrimshander)
Rentzschke, Siegfried   contemporary, Springfield, Massachusetts
Reuss, Hugo   CE, 19th and 20th centuries
Richardson, William   CE, 19th century
Roberts, J. J.   contemporary, Manassas Park, Virginia
Rohner, Hans   contemporary, Boulder, Colorado
Rohner, John   contemporary, Boulder, Colorado
Rose, Adam (pseudonym)   WE, contemporary, St. Louis, Missouri
Ruden, Henry   WE, 19th and 20th centuries
Rundell, Joe   contemporary, Clio, Michigan
Rundell's Gun Shop   contemporary, Clio, Michigan
Runge, Robert P.   contemporary, Ilion, New York (formerly Remington factory)

Russell, Charles M. 19th century (artist of the American West who tried his hand at arms engraving; somewhat primitive work)

S

Salazar, Rudolph contemporary, Denver, Colorado
Salerno, Jasper contemporary, New Haven, Connecticut (formerly Winchester factory)
Sampson, Roger contemporary, Mora, Minnesota
Sanford, Lockwood WE, 19th century, New Haven, Connecticut
Scarberry, Don A. contemporary, Fairbanks, Arkansas
Schrzan, Thomas A. contemporary, Shawnee, Oklahoma
Schonhaar, Harry CE, 19th century
Shaw, Bruce contemporary, Pacific Grove, California
Shaw's Finest in Guns contemporary, Escondido, California
Sherwood, George contemporary, Roseburg, Oregon
Shostle, Ben contemporary, Muncie, Indiana
Showalter, Paul CE, 20th century, Tucson, Arizona
Simmons, Don contemporary, Jenkintown, Pennsylvania (with Paul Jaeger, Inc.)
Sinclair, Burt contemporary, Shallowater, Texas
Smith, Mark A. contemporary, Sinclair, Wyoming
Smith, Ron contemporary, Fort Worth, Texas
Smith, Russ J. contemporary, Springfield, Massachusetts (retired from Smith & Wesson factory)
Smokey Valley Rifles contemporary, Scandinavia, Wisconsin
Spring, George B., Jr. 20th century, Essex, Connecticut
Spring, George B., III contemporary, Chester, Connecticut
Soares, Hennry A. contemporary, Petaluma, California
Stanford, Norm contemporary, Shell Beach, California
Stokes, Angelo J. WE, 20th century
Stokes, William E. WE, 19th and 20th centuries
Strosin, Robert contemporary, Wisconsin Rapids, Wisconsin
Swartley, Robert contemporary, Napa, California

T

Telio, Epaminonda contemporary, Sylmar, California
Tennessan, Joan L. contemporary, Washburn, Wisconsin
Theis, Terry E. contemporary, Fredericksburg, Texas
Thirion, Denise contemporary, Graton, California
Ticehurst, Leonard contemporary, San Jose, California

Tiffany & Co. CE, WE, New York, New York (acid etching, casting, engraving)
Timm, Robert H. contemporary, Castle Rock, Colorado
Timme, Augustus CE, 19th century
Timme, E. A. 19th century (Smith & Wesson)
Tomlin, Lisa contemporary, Huddleston, Virginia
Trindle, Barry contemporary, Earlham, Iowa
Tue, Enoch contemporary, Utica, New York (Savage Arms Company)
Turner, C. Hunt contemporary, St. Louis, Missouri

U

Ulrich, A. F. WE, 19th and 20th centuries
Ulrich, Alden George WE, 20th century
Ulrich, Conrad F. CE, WE, 19th and 20th centuries
Ulrich, Herman L. CE, WE, 19th and 20th centuries
Ulrich, John CE, WE, 19th and 20th centuries
Ulrich, Leslie B. WE, 20th century
Ulrich, Rudolph E. WE, 20th century

V

Valade, Robert B. contemporary, Cove, Oregon
Vest, John contemporary, Susanville, California
Viramontez, Ray contemporary, Albany, Georgia
Vorhes, David contemporary, Napa, California

W

Wallace, Terrill Lee contemporary, Vallejo, California
Warenski, Buster contemporary, Richfield, Utah
Warenski, Julie contemporary, Richfield, Utah
Warren, Floyd E. contemporary, Cortland, Ohio
Warren, John E. 20th century, Eastham, Massachusetts
Warren, Kenneth W. contemporary, Wenatchee, Washington
Warren, W. T. "Dub" contemporary, Fairbanks, Alaska
Welch, Sam contemporary, Moab, Utah
Wells, Rachel contemporary, Prescott, Arizona
Wessinger Custom Guns & Engraving contemporary, Chapin, South Carolina
White, A. A. contemporary, Sandwich, Massachusetts
White, A. A. Engravers, Inc. c. 1961–72, Manchester, Connecticut
Whitmore, Jerry contemporary, Oakland, Oregon
Wielgus, Raymond contemporary, Tucson, Arizona
Williams, A. E. contemporary, Aberdeen, Mississippi
Williams, Robert L. contemporary, Salem, Oregon
Wolfe, Bernie contemporary, El Paso, Texas

Wood, Mel contemporary, Santa Maria, California
Wright, Dwain R. contemporary, Bend, Oregon

Y

Yendell, P. S. 19th century (Smith & Wesson)
Young, Eugene CE, 19th and 20th centuries
Young, Gustave CE, WE, 19th century
Young, Oscar CE, 19th and 20th centuries
Young, Robert CE, 20th century
Young Brothers, Engravers CE, 19th and 20th centuries

Z

Ziety, Dennis contemporary, Kenosha, Wisconsin

Published materials on the decoration of American firearms are limited in number. The field is a highly specialized one, and many aspects of it remain unexplored. The present book is based nearly entirely on original research in unpublished sources. But the items listed in the following selected bibliography will be of further interest to the reader, even though many do not deal specifically with arms embellishment except through illustrations. An exhaustive bibliography on arms decoration, with the emphasis on European sources, appears in Stephen V. Grancsay's *Master French Gunsmiths' Designs* (1970). The reader should consult that volume for information beyond the scope of *Steel Canvas*.

Miscellaneous Unpublished Sources

Archives and memorabilia of the following engravers: R. J. Kornbrath, Wilbur A. Glahn, Cuno A. Helfricht, A. F. Herbert, L. D. Nimschke, John and C. F. Ulrich, Alden George Ulrich, other members of the Ulrich engraving dynasty, and Gustave, Eugene, and Oscar Young. Some of this material is from the engraving collection of Richard C. Marohn, M.D., and some from the archival material in the author's collection. Several descendants of the above engravers were interviewed for data; numerous contemporary engravers have been interviewed by the author, beginning c. 1961.

Shipping and inventory ledgers of the Colt's Manufacturing Company, Inc., 1861 through the twentieth century, at Colt's Hartford office, as well as assorted Winchester shipping ledgers, and miscellaneous records of other American gunmakers.

Colt company ledgers, correspondence, catalogues, photographs, firearms, and various memorabilia in the Colt collections at the Connecticut Historical Society, Wadsworth Atheneum, and Museum of Connecticut History, and in various private collections, and in the author's archives.

The John Hintlian Library (largely broken up over the years), which contained a nearly complete collection of catalogues and price lists of American gunmakers, from the early nineteenth century into the twentieth.

The *Hartford Courant* and *Hartford Times* newspapers, various issues from 1847 through 1865. The Hartford and New Haven city directories, 1847 through 1950. Numerous city directories from eastern and southern cities.

The four original nineteenth-century pattern books from the L. D. Nimschke archive, in the collection of Richard C. Marohn, M.D. An additional pattern book in the William H. Myers Collection.

Bibliography

The author's privately funded American Archive of Arms and Armor, which concentrates on American and European arms and armor, with information, photographs, books, memorabilia, and documents. The collection includes a substantial section of arms engraving photographs, documents, catalogues, correspondence with numerous engravers, and miscellaneous related material. The ever-expanding research facility is maintained at the author's residence and office, in Hadlyme, Connecticut.

Miscellaneous documents, records, and arms from numerous private collections, and museums, and tens of thousands of firearms examined at collectors' firearms shows, from 1951 to the present.

General Titles

Abbiatico, Mario. *Modern Firearms Engraving.* Gardone, Valtrompia, Italy: Edizioni Artistiche Italiane, 1980.

Abbiatico, Mario, Gianoberto Lupi, and Franco Vaccari. *Grandi Incisioni su Armi d'Oggi.* Florence, Italy: Editoriale Olimpia, 1977.

Achtermeier, William O. *Rhode Island Arms Makers & Gunsmiths.* Lincoln, Rhode Island: Andrew Mowbray, 1990.

Adams, Bill, Terry Moss, and J. Bruce Voyles. *The Antique Bowie Knife Book.* Conyers, Georgia: Museum Publishing Co., Inc., 1990.

Albaugh, William A., III. *Confederate Edged Weapons.* New York: Bonanza Books, 1960.

Amber, John T., ed. *Gun Digest.* Chicago: The Gun Digest Company, various editions feature gun engraving (annual first appeared in 1947). Several of the volumes carry articles by E. C. Prudhomme on engraving. Amber was succeeded by Ken Warner, c. 1979.

Austyn, Christopher. *Modern Sporting Guns.* London: The Sportsman's Press, 1994.

Baer, Larry L. *The Parker Gun.* North Hollywood, California: Beinfeld Publishing, Inc., 1980.

Barber, Edwin Atlee. *The Ceramic Collectors' Glossary.* New York: Da Capo Press, 1967.

Beaumont, The Hon. Richard. *Purdey's, the Guns and the Family.* Pomfert, Vermont: David and Charles, 1984.

Bergling, J. M. *Art Monograms and Lettering.* Coral Gables, Florida: V. C. Bergling, 1964 (20th edition).

Bergling, J. M., and A. Tuston Hay. *Heraldic Designs and Engravings.* Coral Gables, Florida: V. C. Bergling, 1966.

Bivens, John. *Longrifles of North Carolina.* York, Pennsylvania: George Shumway, 1988.

Blackmore, Howard L. *Royal Sporting Guns at Windsor.* London: Her Majesty's Stationery Office, 1968.

Bleile, C. Roger. *American Engravers.* North Hollywood, California: Beinfeld Publishing Co., 1980.

Bowers, William S. *Gunsmiths of Pen-Mar-Va.* Mercersburg, Pennsylvania: Irwinton Publishers, 1979.

Brophy, Lt. Col. William S. *L. C. Smith Shotguns.* Highland Park, New Jersey: The Gun Room Press, 1979.

_____. *Marlin Firearms: A History of the Guns and the Company That Made Them.* Harrisburg, Pennsylvania: Stackpole Books, 1989.

Brown, M. L. *Firearms in Colonial America.* Washington, D.C.: Smithsonian Institution Press, 1980.

Buchele, William. *Recreating the American Longrifle.* York, Pennsylvania: George Shumway, 1983.

Burton, Kenneth J. *A Sure Defence: The Bowie Knife Book.* Balmain, Australia: K. J. Burton & Co., 1988.

Carpenter, Charles H., Jr., with Mary Grace Carpenter. *Tiffany Silver.* New York: Dodd, Mead & Co., 1978.

Carpenter, Charles H., Jr., and Janet Zapata. *The Silver of Tiffany & Co., 1850–1987.* Boston: Museum of Fine Arts,

1987. Catalogue of an exhibition held at the Museum of Fine Arts, September 9–November 8, 1987.

Chandler, Roy F. *Kentucky Rifle Patchboxes & Barrel Marks.* Duncannon, Pennsylvania: David E. Little, 1971.

Condry, Ken, and Larry Jones. *The Colt Commemoratives 1961–1986.* Dallas: Taylor Publishing Co., 1989.

Cooper, Edith G. *The Kentucky Rifle and Me.* Port Royal, Pennsylvania: Edith G. Cooper, 1977.

Cromwell, Giles. *The Virginia Manufactory of Arms.* Charlottesville, Virginia: University of Virginia Press, 1975.

Demeritt, Dwight B., Jr. *Maine Made Guns and Their Makers.* Hallowell, Maine: Paul S. Plumer, Jr., 1973.

Dillon, Captain John G. W. *The Kentucky Rifle.* York, Pennsylvania: Trimmer Printing, 1959.

Dresser, Christopher. *The Art of Decorative Design.* Watkins Glen, New York: American Life Foundation, 1977. Reprint of the London edition of 1862.

duMont, John S. *American Engraved Powder Horns.* Canaan, New Hampshire: Phoenix Publishing, 1978.

Durant, Stuart. *Ornament from the Industrial Revolution to Today.* Woodstock, New York: Overlook Press, 1986.

Elliot, Robert W., and Jim Cobb. *Lefever: Guns of Lasting Fame.* Lindale, Texas: Robert W. Elliot, 1986.

Elman, Robert. *The Great American Sporting Prints.* New York: Alfred A. Knopf, 1972. Introduction by Hermann Warner Williams, Jr., director emeritus, The Corcoran Gallery of Art.

Flayderman, Norm. *Flayderman's Guide to Antique American Firearms . . . and Their Values.* Northbrook, Illinois: DBI Books, Inc., 1990.

———, ed. *Illustrated Catalogue of Arms and Military Goods.* New Milford, Connecticut: N. Flayderman & Co., 1961. Reprint of the 1864 Schuyler, Hartley & Graham company catalogue.

Garavaglia, Louis A., and Charles G. Worman. *Firearms of the American West, 1803–1865.* Albuquerque: University of New Mexico Press, 1984.

———. *Firearms of the American West, 1866–1894.* Albuquerque: University of New Mexico Press, 1985.

Garton, George. *Colt's S.A.A. Post War Models.* North Hollywood, California: Beinfeld Publishing Co., 1979.

Goldschmidt, Friedrich. *Kunstlerische Waffengravuren Ferlacher Meister.* Schwabisch Hall: Journal-Verlag, 1978.

Graham, Ron, John A. Kopec, and C. Kenneth Moore. *A Study of the Colt Single Action Army Revolver.* La Puente, California: published by the authors, 1976; revised edition, 1979.

Grancsay, Stephen V. *American Engraved Powder Horns: A Study Based on the J. H. Grenville Gilbert Collection.* New York: Metropolitan Museum of Art, 1945.

———. *Master French Gunsmiths' Designs of the Mid-Seventeenth Century.* New York: Greenberg, 1950.

———. *Master French Gunsmiths' Designs.* New York: Winchester Press, 1970.

Grant, James J. *More Single-Shot Rifles.* Highland Park, New Jersey: The Gun Room Press, 1976.

———. *Still More Single-Shot Rifles.* Union City, Tennessee: Pioneer Press, 1979.

———. *Boys' Single-Shot Rifles.* Prescott, Arizona: Wolfe Publishing Co., 1991.

———. *Single-Shot Rifle Finale.* Prescott, Arizona: Wolfe Publishing Co., 1992.

Grant, Madison. *The Kentucky Rifle Hunting Pouch: Its Contents and Accoutrements as Used by the Frontiersman, Hunter and Indian.* York, Pennsylvania: Madison Grant, 1977.

———. *The Knife in Homespun America and Related Items.* York, Pennsylvania: Madison Grant, 1984.

———. *Powder Horns and Their Architecture and Decoration as Used by the Woodsman, Soldier, Indian, Sailor and Traders of the Era.* York, Pennsylvania: Madison Grant, 1987.

Gusler, Wallace B., and James D. Lavin. *Decorated Firearms, 1540–1870.* Williamsburg, Virginia: Colonial Williamsburg Foundation, 1977.

Guthman, William H. *March to Massacre.* New York: McGraw Hill, 1975.

———. *Drums A'beating, Trumpets Sounding: Artistically Carved Powder Horns in the Provincial Manner 1746–1781.* Hartford, Connecticut: Connecticut Historical Society, 1993.

Haedeke, Hanns-Ulrich. *Metalwork.* New York: Universe Books, 1969.

Hamilton, John D. *The Ames Sword Company, 1829–1935.* Providence: Mowbray, 1983.

Hanson, Charles E., Jr. *The Plains Rifle.* Highland Park, New Jersey: The Gun Room Press, 1989.

Harriger, Russel H. *Longrifles of Pennsylvania, Volume 1: Jefferson, Clarion & Elk Counties.* York, Pennsylvania: George Shumway, 1984.

Harris, Dr. Fredric A. *Firearms Engraving as Decorative Art.* Seattle: Barbara R. Harris, 1989.

Hartliep, Neil. *The Basics of Firearms Engraving.* Washington, D.C.: NRA, Education and Training Division, 1985.

Hartzler, Daniel D. *Arms Makers of Maryland.* York, Pennsylvania: George Shumway, 1975.

Hartzler, Daniel D., and James B. Whisker. *Maryland Longrifles.* Bedford, Pennsylvania: Old Bedford Village Press, 1991.

Hawkins, Peter, Christopher Brunker, and R. L. Wilson. *Colt/Christie's Rare and Historic Firearms.* New York: Christie, Manson & Woods International, Inc., 1981.

Hayward, John F. *The Art of the Gunmaker.* London: Barrie & Rockliff, 1962–63. Two volumes.

Heckscher, Morrison H., and Leslie Greene Bowman. *American Rococo, 1750–1775: Elegance in Ornament.* New York: Metropolitan Museum of Art; and Los Angeles: Los Angeles County Museum of Art, 1992. Distributed by Harry N. Abrams, Inc., New York.

Heskett, John. *Industrial Design.* London: Thames & Hudson, 1980.

Holland, Margaret. *Phaidon Guide to Silver.* Englewood Cliffs, New Jersey: Prentice-Hall, 1983.

Hood, Graham. *American Silver: A History of Style, 1650–1900.* New York: Praeger, 1971.

Hornung, Clarence P. *Treasury of American Design.* New York: Harry N. Abrams, Inc., 1976. Two volumes.

Houze, Herbert G. *Winchester Repeating Arms: Its History and Development from 1865 to 1981.* Iola, WI: Krause Publications, 1995.

Howe, James Virgil. *The Modern Gunsmith.* New York: Funk & Wagnalls Company, 1941.

Huddleston, Joe D. *Colonial Riflemen in the American Revolution.* York, Pennsylvania: George Shumway, 1978.

Hutslar, Donald A. *Gunsmiths of Ohio, 18th & 19th Centuries, Volume I: Biographical Data.* York, Pennsylvania: George Shumway, 1973.

Isaacson, Philip M. *The American Eagle.* Boston: New York Graphic Society, 1975.

Jamieson, G. Scott. *Bullard Arms.* Ontario, Canada: Boston Mills Press, 1989.

Jervis, Simon. *Art and Design in Europe and America, 1800–1900*. New York: E. P. Dutton, 1987.

Jinks, Roy G. *Artistry in Arms*. Springfield, Massachusetts: Smith & Wesson, Inc., 1991.

——. *History of Smith & Wesson: No Thing of Importance Will Come Without Effort*. North Hollywood, California: Beinfeld Publishing, Inc., 1977.

Jinks, Roy G., and Robert J. Neal. *Smith & Wesson, 1857–1945*. New York: A. S. Barnes & Co., 1975.

Jones, Owen. *Grammar of Ornament*. New York: Van Nostrand Reinhold Company, 1982. Reprint of London edition of 1856.

Kauffman, Henry J. *The Pennsylvania-Kentucky Rifle*. Harrisburg, Pennsylvania: The Stackpole Co., 1960.

Kennedy, Monty. *Checkering and Carving of Gun Stocks*. Harrisburg, Pennsylvania: Stackpole Books, 1962.

Kentucky Rifle Association. *The Kentucky Rifle: A True American Heritage in Pictures*. Alexandria, Virginia: The Forte Group of Creative Companies, Inc., 1985.

——. *Kentucky Rifles and Pistols, 1750–1850*. Delaware, Ohio: Golden Age Arms Co. and James R. Johnston, 1976.

Kindig, Joe, Jr. *Thoughts on the Kentucky Rifle in Its Golden Age*. York, Pennsylvania: George Shumway, 1984.

King, Peter. *The Shooting Field with Holland & Holland*. London: Quiller Press, 1990.

Latham, Sid. *Knifecraft*. Harrisburg: Stackpole Books, 1978.

——. *Great Sporting Posters of the Golden Age*. Harrisburg, Pennsylvania: Stackpole Books, 1978.

Lenk, Torsten. *The Flintlock: Its Origin and Development*. London: Holland Press, 1965.

Levine, Bernard R. *Knifemakers of Old San Francisco*. San Francisco: Badger Books, 1977.

——. *Levine's Guide to Knives and Their Values*. Northbrook, Illinois: DBI Books, 1989.

Lindsay, Merrill. *One Hundred Great Guns*. New York: Walker & Company, 1967.

——. *Miniature Arms*. New York: Winchester Press, 1970.

——. *The Kentucky Rifle*. New York: Arma Press; and York, Pennsylvania: Historical Society of York County, 1972.

——. *The New England Gun*. New York: David McKay Company; and New Haven: New Haven Colony Historical Society, 1975.

Logan, Herschel C. *Underhammer Guns*. Harrisburg, Pennsylvania: Stackpole Books, 1965.

Loring, John. *Tiffany's 150 Years*. Garden City, New York: Doubleday & Co., 1987.

McIntosh, Michael. *Best Guns*. Traverse City, Michigan: Countrysport, Inc., 1989.

Madis, George. *The Winchester Book*. Lancaster, Texas: Art and Reference House, 1961.

Maryon, Herbert. *Metalwork & Enamelling*. New York: Dover, 1971.

Mayer, Ralph. *A Dictionary of Art Terms and Techniques*. New York: Thomas Y. Crowell, 1969.

Meek, James B. *The Art of Engraving*. Montezuma, Iowa: Brownell's Inc., 1974.

Minnis, Gordon B. *American Primitive Knives, 1770–1870*. Bloomfield, Ontario, Canada: Museum Restoration Service, 1983.

Moore, Warren. *Weapons of the American Revolution . . . and Accoutrements*. New York: Promontory Press, 1967.

Mowbray, E. Andrew. *The American Eagle Pommel Sword: The Early Years, 1793–1830*. Lincoln, Rhode Island: Man at Arms Magazine, 1988.

Neumann, George C., and Frank J. Kravic. *Collector's Illustrated Encyclopedia of the American Revolution*. Secaucus, New Jersey: Castle Books, 1975.

Nobili, Marco E. *Il Grande Libro Delle Incisioni*. Milan: Il Volvo Srl, 1989. Preface by Firmo Fracassi.

Peterson, Harold L. *The American Sword, 1775–1945*. New Hope, Pennsylvania: Robert Halter, The River House, 1954.

——. *Arms and Armor in Colonial America, 1526–1783*. Harrisburg, Pennsylvania: The Stackpole Co., 1956.

——. *American Knives*. New York: Charles Scribner's Sons, 1958.

Phelps, Art. *The Story of Merwin, Hulbert & Co. Firearms*. Rough and Ready, California: Art Phelps, 1991.

Prudhomme, E. C. *Gun Engraving Review*. Shreveport, Louisiana: E. C. Prudhomme, 1961.

Rattenbury, Richard. *Packing Iron: A Survey of Military and Civilian Gunleather on the Western Frontier*. Millwood, New York: ZON International Publishing, 1993.

Riling, Ray. *The Powder Flask Book*. New Hope, Pennsylvania: Robert Halter, The River House, 1953.

Rosa, Joseph G. *Colonel Colt London*. London: Arms and Armour Press, 1976.

Russell, Carl P. *Guns of the Early Frontiers*. Berkeley: University of California Press, 1957.

——. *Firearms, Traps & Tools of the Mountain Men*. New York: Alfred A. Knopf, 1967.

Schwing, Ned. *Winchester's Finest, The Model 21*. Iola, Wisconsin: Krause Publications, Inc., 1990.

Sellers, Frank. *The William M. Locke Collection*. East Point, Georgia: The Antique Armoury, 1973.

——. *Sharps Firearms*. North Hollywood, California: Beinfeld Publishing Co., 1978.

——. *American Gunsmiths*. Highland Park, New Jersey: The Gun Room Press, 1983.

Sharp, Lewis I. *John Quincy Adams Ward: Dean of American Sculpture*. Newark: University of Delaware Press, 1985.

Sheldon, Lawrence P. *California Gunsmiths, 1846–1900*. Fair Oaks, California: Far West Publishing Co., 1977.

Shumway, George. *Rifles of Colonial America*. York, Pennsylvania: George Shumway, 1980. Two volumes.

——. *George Schreyer, Sr & Jr, Gunmakers of Hanover, York County, Pennsylvania*. York, Pennsylvania: George Shumway, 1990.

Snyder, Walter Claude. *The Ithaca Gun Company: From the Beginning*. Marceline, Missouri: Walsworth Publishing Co., 1991.

Speltz, Alexander. *The Styles of Ornament*. New York: Dover Publications, 1959.

Stroud, David V. *Inscribed Union Swords: 1861–1865*. Kilgore, Texas: Pinecrest Publishing Co., 1983.

——. *Civil War Sword and Revolver Presentations as Reported in the Boston Daily Evening Transcript, 1861–1865*. Kilgore, Texas: Pinecrest Publishing Co., 1984.

Swayze, Nathan L. *Engraved Powder Horns of the French and Indian War and Revolutionary War*. Yazoo City, Mississippi: Gun Hill Publishing Co., 1978.

Tarassuk, Leonid. *Antique European and American Firearms at the Hermitage Museum*. Leningrad, U.S.S.R.: Iskusstvo Publishing House, 1971.

Trolard, Tom. *Winchester Commemoratives*. Plano, Texas: Tom Trolard, 1985.

Untracht, Oppi. *Metal Techniques for Craftsmen.* Garden City, New York: Doubleday & Company, Inc., 1968.

Warner, Ken, ed. *Gun Digest.* Northbrook, Illinois: DBI Books, Inc., published annually.

———. *The Gun Digest Review of Custom Guns.* Northbrook, Illinois: DBI Books, Inc., 1980.

Weil, Robert. *Contemporary Makers of Muzzle Loading Firearms.* Dallas: Taylor Publishing Co., 1980.

Whisker, James B. *Gunsmiths of West Virginia.* Bedford, Pennsylvania: Old Bedford Village Press, 1987.

———. *Ohio Long Rifles, Volumes I and II.* Bedford, Pennsylvania: Old Bedford Village Press, 1988 and 1990.

———. *Gunsmiths of York County, Pennsylvania.* Bedford, Pennsylvania: Old Bedford Village Press, 1990.

Whisker, James B., and Roy F. Chandler. *Arms Makers of Eastern Pennsylvania: The Colonial Years to 1790.* Bedford, Pennsylvania: Acorn Press, 1984.

Whisker, James B., and Vaughn Whisker, Sr. *Gunsmiths of Bedford, Somerset and Fulton Counties.* Bedford, Pennsylvania: Old Bedford Village Press, 1991.

Whisker, James B., and Stacy B. C. Wood, Jr. *Arms Makers of Lancaster County, Pennsylvania.* Bedford, Pennsylvania: Old Bedford Village Press, 1991.

Wilkerson, Don. *The Post-War Colt Single Action Revolver.* Apple Valley, Minnesota: Don Wilkerson, 1978.

———. *Colt's Single Action Army Revolver Pre-War Post-War Model.* Minneapolis: Don Wilkerson, 1991.

Wilson, R. L. *Samuel Colt Presents.* Hartford, Connecticut: Wadsworth Atheneum, 1961.

———. *L. D. Nimschke, Firearms Engraver.* Teaneck, New Jersey: John J. Malloy, 1965.

———. *The Book of Colt Engraving.* Studio City, California: Beinfeld Publishing Co., 1972.

———. *The Book of Winchester Engraving.* Studio City, California: Wallace Beinfeld Publications, 1974.

———. *Colt Handguns.* Tokyo: World Photo Press, 1979.

———. *The Colt Heritage.* New York: Simon & Schuster, 1979.

———. *Colt Engraving.* North Hollywood, California: Beinfeld Publishing Co., 1982.

———. *Winchester: The Golden Age of American Gunmaking and the Winchester 1 of 1000.* Cody, Wyoming: Buffalo Bill Historical Center, 1983.

———. *Colt: An American Legend.* New York: Abbeville Press, 1985.

———. *Winchester: An American Legend.* New York: Random House, Inc., 1991.

———. *Winchester Engraving.* Palm Springs, California: Beinfeld Publishing Co., 1991.

———. *The Peacemakers: Arms and Adventure in the American West.* New York: Random House, Inc., 1992.

———. *The Book of Colt Firearms.* Minneapolis: Blue Book Publishing, Inc., 1993.

———. *Ruger and His Guns.* New York: Simon & Schuster, Inc., work in progress.

Wilson, R. L., ed. *Antique Arms Annual.* San Antonio, Texas: S. P. Stevens, Leo Bradshaw, and the Texas Gun Collectors Association, 1971.

Wilson, R. L., and L. D. Eberhart. *The Deringer in America, Volume I: The Percussion Period.* Lincoln, Rhode Island: The Mowbray Company, 1985.

———. *The Deringer in America, Volume II: The Cartridge Period.* Lincoln, Rhode Island: The Mowbray Company, 1993.

Wilson, R. L., and R. E. Hable. *Colt Pistols.* Dallas: Jackson Arms, 1976.

Wilson, R. L., and Philip R. Phillips. *Paterson Colt Pistol Variations.* Dallas: Jackson Arms, 1979.

Articles and Monographs

Bazelon, Bruce S., ed. *Swords from Public Collections in the Commonwealth of Pennsylvania.* Lincoln, Rhode Island: Andrew Mowbray Inc., 1984.

Cullity, Brian. *Arts of the Federal Period.* Sandwich, Massachusetts: Heritage Plantation of Sandwich, 1989. Catalogue of a loan exhibition, May 7–October 30, 1989.

Dow, Richard Alan, and R. L. Wilson. "The Czar's Colts." *Nineteenth Century,* Winter 1980.

Dyke, S. E. *Thoughts on the American Flintlock Pistol.* York, Pennsylvania: George Shumway, 1974.

Elisofon, Eliot. "Sam Colt's Pistols." *Life,* March 2, 1962.

Gill, Harold B., Jr. *The Gunsmith in Colonial Virginia.* Williamsburg, Virginia: Colonial Williamsburg Foundation, Williamsburg Research Studies, 1974.

Grancsay, Stephen V. "The Craft of the Early American Gunsmith." *Arms & Armor Essays by Stephen V. Grancsay from the Metropolitan Museum of Art Bulletin 1920–1964.* New York: Metropolitan Museum of Art, 1986.

———. "An Exhibition of Colt Percussion Revolvers." *Op. cit.*

———. "The J. H. Grenville Gilbert Collection of American Powder Horns." *Op. cit.*

Guthman, William H. "Decorated Military Americana." *Antiques,* July 1966.

———. "Powder Horns of the French and Indian War, 1755–1763." *Antiques,* August 1978.

———. "Frontiersmen's Tomahawks of the Colonial and Federal Periods." *Antiques,* March 1981.

———. "Decorated American Militia Equipment." *Antiques,* July 1984.

Guthman, William H., ed. *Guns & Other Arms.* New York: Mayflower Books, 1979.

Hamilton, John D. "A Roland for an Oliver, Swords Awarded by the State of New York During the War of 1812." *American Society of Arms Collectors Bulletin,* 1987.

Houze, Herbert G. *The Sumptuous Flaske: European and American Decorated Powder Flasks of the Sixteenth to Nineteenth Centuries.* Cody, Wyoming: Buffalo Bill Historical Society, 1989.

———. " 'The Appearance of Evidence': A Brief Examination of the Life and Work of Herman Leslie Ulrich." *Armax,* volume IV, number 2, 1993.

Keener, William G. *Bowie Knives.* Columbus, Ohio: Ohio Historical Society, 1962. Knives from the Robert Abels and Ohio Historical Society collections, on exhibition April 1962.

Kindig, Joe K., III. *Artistic Ingredients of the Longrifle.* York, Pennsylvania: George Shumway, 1989.

McKenzie, L.S.M. "Old New Orleans Presents." Catalogue of the New Orleans Arms Co., c. 1972, published by the late Stanley Diefenthal.

Martin, Greg. *Historic American Swords.* Los Angeles: Butterfield & Butterfield, 1989. Catalogue of an auction of swords, November 20, 1989.

———. Miscellaneous auction catalogues, including the John R. Woods Collection (October 22, 1991), the Warren Anderson Collection (March 23 and July 14, 1992), and the Press Collection (February 7, August 3, 1993, and December 6, 1994). San Francisco: Butterfield & Butterfield.

———. *The Antique Bowie Knife Collections of Robert*

Berryman & Chas. Schreiner III. San Francisco: Butterfield & Butterfield, 1992. Catalogue of an auction of Bowie and related knives, March 23, 1992. A videotape was produced based on the auction contents.

Ogan, Ronald A., and Ben Lane, Jr. "Colt Factory Single Action Engraving Techniques." *The Gun Report,* March 1978.

Parsons, John E. "New Light on Old Colts." Harrison, New York: John E. Parsons, 1955.

Rattenbury, Richard. *Winchester Promotional Arts*. Cody, Wyoming: Buffalo Bill Historical Center, 1978.

Ross, Andrew G. "Gun Engravers Turn Fine Sporting Arms into Works of Art." *Outdoor Life,* December 1950.

R. W. Norton Art Gallery. "Artistry in Arms." Catalogue of engraving and gunsmithing display at the Norton Art Gallery, Baton Rouge, Louisiana, May 16–June 27, 1971.

————. "E. C. Prudhomme, Master Gun Engraver." Catalogue of work of Prudhomme, on display at the Norton Art Gallery, April 1–May 13, 1973. Foreword by John T. Amber.

Ryan, Bill. "Our Most Excellent Rifles." *The American Sportsman,* Fall 1968.

Tarassuk, Leonid. "Arms and Art: American and European Firearms Decorated by Raymond J. Wielgus." Art Institute of Chicago, March 16–June 12, 1988.

Toffolon, Siro. "Gunsmiths and Silversmiths." *The Kentucky Rifle Association.* Spring 1987.

————. "The Kentucky Rifle and Its Ornamentations." *The Kentucky Rifle Association.* Winter 1980.

Wardwell, Allen. "Guns in Black Tie." *Connoisseur,* August 1986.

Wilson, R. L. "L. D. Nimschke, Firearms Engraver." *American Rifleman,* January 1966.

————. "Is There Proof That Joseph Wolf Engraved Firearms?" *The Gun Report,* October 1967.

————. "Colt's Army .45." *The Gun Report,* June 1968.

————. "The Youngs: Standouts in the Gun Engraver's Heyday." *American Rifleman,* May 1968.

————. "A. A. White Engravers, Inc." Catalogue of engravings and gold inlaying offered by the firm, 1969.

————. "Enterprising Sam Colt's Profitable Presentations." *American Rifleman,* July 1969.

————. "Fifty Years of Gun Engraving at Colt's." *American Rifleman,* October 1969.

————. "Gold Inlaid Colt Revolvers." *Arms Fair '69 Guide,* London: 1969.

————. "Pocket Guide to Good and Bad Firearms Engraving." Brochure published privately by A. A. White Engravers, Inc., 1969.

————. "Some Nimschke-Engraved Colt Pistols." *The Gun Report,* March 1969.

————. "Engrave Your Favorite Gun." *Guns & Ammo Annual 1970.* Los Angeles: Petersen Publishing Co., 1970.

————. "Gunmetal Mastery." *Sports Afield,* August 1971.

————. "Masterpieces of the Gun Engraver's Art." *Guns & Ammo Annual 1971.* Los Angeles: Petersen Publishing Co., 1971.

————. "Gun Engraving." *Guns & Ammo Annual 1969.* Los Angeles: Petersen Publishing Co., 1969. Reprinted in the Petersen Publishing Co. book, *Guns of the World* (1972).

————. "The History of Gun Engraving in America." *Guns & Ammo Annual 1972.* Los Angeles: Petersen Publishing Co., 1972.

————. "A Most Select Collection of Colts." *Guns & Ammo,* April 1973.

————. "Engraving Secrets." *Basic Gun Repair.* Los Angeles: Petersen Publishing Co., 1973.

————. "Firearms Engraving in Nineteenth Century America." *The Bulletin of the American Society of Arms Collectors,* Fall 1973.

————. "Gun Engraving [in Europe]." In *Guns of the World.* Los Angeles: Petersen Publishing Co., 1973.

————. "A. A. White Engravers, Inc." Brochure of engravings offered by the firm, 1974.

————. "Colt Engraving." *Arms Gazette,* April and July 1974. An article in two parts.

————. "Fine Engraving Is Still Taught." *Guns & Ammo Annual 1974.* Los Angeles: Petersen Publishing Co., 1974.

————. "When You Say 'Engraved Winchester'—Ulrich Is the Name." *Arms Gazette,* October 1974.

————. "A Masterpiece of Modern Gunmaking." *Shooting Times,* December 1975.

————. "Engraving from the Big Four." *Guns & Ammo Annual 1977.* Los Angeles: Petersen Publishing Co., 1977.

————. "The Colt Custom Gun Shop." *Colt American Handgunning Annual 1978.*

————. "The New Collecting Breeds." *Man at Arms,* July–August 1979.

————. "A. A. White, Prince of Craftsmen." *Man at Arms,* September–October and November–December 1980. An article in two parts.

————. "A Return to Tradition: The Paris Show Gun." *Man at Arms,* July–August 1980.

————. "The Van Syckel Dragoons." *Man at Arms,* March–April 1980.

————. "American Arms Engravers, c. 1830–1981." *Man at Arms,* November–December 1981.

————. "Les armes et les artistes." *L'oeil,* October 1989.

————. "The Solid Silver Winchester." *The Winchester Repeater,* Winter 1990.

Wilson, R. L., and Richard Alan Dow. "The Art of American Arms." *The American West,* July–August 1986.

Wilson, R. L., and Herb Glass. "The Art of the Gun Engraver." *Shooting Times,* September 1968.

Wilson, R. L., and Roy Jinks. "Tiffany Stocked Firearms." *Antique Arms Annual,* 1971.

Wilson, R. L., and Edward R. Ricciuti. "A Canvas of Steel." *Audubon,* November 1987.

Wilson, R. L., and Dr. Leonid Tarassuk. *The "Russian" Colts.* North Hollywood, California: Beinfeld Publishing Co., 1979.

————. "Gun Collecting's Stately Pedigree." *American Rifleman,* July 1981.

————. "Aristocratic Arms Collectors." *Man at Arms,* January–February and November–December 1983. An article in two parts.

Zapata, Janet. "The Rediscovery of Paulding Farnham, Tiffany's Designer Extraordinaire." *The Magazine Antiques,* March and April 1991. An article in two parts.

Acknowledgments, Photographic Note, and Owner Credits

ACKNOWLEDGMENTS

To John R. Woods, President, and H. Wayne Sheets, Executive Director of the NRA Foundation, for their encouragement and support of this book and other projects.

To Robert M. Lee, for his inspiration, cooperation, and assistance, and for his insights into the fine points of engraving, stockmaking, casemaking, gold and silver inlaying and damascening, ivory carving, and the myriad other challenging crafts required to make the finest of firearms. His connoisseurship has played a key role in setting a new standard of excellence in the arms field.

To Anne Brockinton, Scott Bergan, Karen Sheldon, Michael Amrine, Dena Durant, Justin Heath, and Peggy Sanders for their help with some of the most challenging photography and special effects.

To Janet Zapata, former Archivist, Tiffany & Co., for reviewing the photographs selected for *Steel Canvas* and commenting on its direction; also for reading the manuscript for further comments. Her expertise on American art, style, and craftsmanship, on terminology, and on the relationship of arms to other decorative arts has been invaluable.

To Guy Wilson, Master of the Armouries, Royal Armouries–H.M. Tower of London, and to Graeme Rimer, Keeper of Firearms, for their support of the concept of "The Art of American Arms" traveling loan exhibition. And to Paul Rovetti, Director, The William Benton Museum of Art, University of Connecticut, and to Larry Doherty, President, Fine Arts Express, and to Peter Tillou, of Peter Tillou Fine Arts, for their efforts on behalf of that project.

To Norm Flayderman and his photographer Rick Oltmans for the several exquisite photographs of fine and rare guns, taken with the most meticulous care and artistry.

To Peter Hawkins, David Williams, Christopher Austyn, and Natasha Hanscomb, of Christie's Arms and Armour and Gun departments, for supplying several color transparencies of fine guns sold through their firm, both in London and New York, over the years.

To Bernard J. Osher, John Gallo, and Greg Martin, at Butterfield & Butterfield, for their assistance with color photography, and for making treasures from the Press and other collections available in Connecticut and in San Francisco. And to Petra Martin for her patience and imagination in the setting up of Greta's charming baby picture, taken by Douglas Sandberg.

To Martin J. Lane, collector and dealer in antique arms, for bringing rare Colt and other arms to Hadlyme for special photography, for lining up other pieces for the front of the dust jacket, and for several other critical photographs.

To Siro Toffolon, for his expertise on the Kentucky longrifle in reviewing text and pictures from chapter 2.

To Robert E. Petersen, Chairman, Petersen Publishing Company, for his cooperation in permitting publication of pieces from his collection, and for permission to publish material previously appearing in various issues of the *Guns & Ammo Annual*.

To Morris Hallowell, of Hallowell & Co., Greenwich, Connecticut, for bringing to Hadlyme beautiful and rare firearms for photography by Peter Beard and Allan Brown.

To Anne A. Grimes, Curator, USS *Constitution* Museum, Robert T. Delfay, President, National Shooting Sports Foundation, Richard and Diane Ulbrich, John K. Watson, Jr., Matthew Isenburg, Christian deGuigne IV, Vern Eklund, David Berghoff, William H. Guthman, Mathias Oppersdorf, Alice Stillinger, Paul Carella, Peter J. Buxtun, and William F. Parkerson III, Editor, *American Rifleman*, for their cooperation and special efforts in photography, and for permission to use material previously published in articles on Gustave Young, Cuno Helfricht, and L. D. Nimschke.

To Nancy E. Goldberg, formerly Director, Special Design Sales, Corporate Division, Tiffany & Co., and to Paul Epifanio and his staff at Corporate Design, Tiffany & Co.

To William H. and Joan Myers and their daughter Sarah, David Hansen, David Currie, Thomas L. Parker, Fred and Beverly Beck, and Ken Hanna for making possible the Peter Beard and Jonathan Shorey shoot in Perrysburg, Ohio. And to William Jaqua, George H. and Camille Jaqua Ranzau, David Hartzell, and Neal Kathrens of Jaqua's Fine Guns, for their hospitality as we continued the shoot in Findlay.

To Martin S. Huber, Historian Emeritus, Kathleen Hoyt, Historian, and Beverly Rhodes, of the Historical Department, Colt Manufacturing Company, Inc., for cheerfully responding to research pleas.

To Roy G. Jinks, Historian, Smith & Wesson, Inc., for supplying critical color photographs of special pieces displayed in the loan exhibition "Artistry in Arms," and for the benefit of his expertise in the evolution and identification of S&W engravers.

To Roger Mitchell, Vice Chairman, Holland & Holland, Ltd., and David Winks, for supplying color transparencies of the Larry Hagman, the Saurian, the .700 Nitro Express Double Rifle, and other special guns. To Peter Nelson for making available the extraordinary set of three Ken Hunt–engraved and –inlaid P. V. Nelson guns, for special photography. To collectors Ronald Holden and William Feldstein, patrons of the world's finest gunmakers, for their interest and cooperation.

To Edward Asprey of Asprey, London, for color transparencies and prints,

and for his edification of the author on the firm's creation of a gunmaking department.

To Dr. Richard C. Marohn, for making available selections from L. D. Nimschke's engraving scrapbook and the Nimschke collection of pattern books for examination and special photography.

To William E. Simon, Sr., for his cooperation in permitting the special photography of the Theodore Roosevelt presentation Holland & Holland .500/.450 double-barrel rifle, by Peter Beard with Allan Brown.

To Jim Weyer, Weyer International, Toledo, Ohio, for his special selection of color transparencies from his unequaled series of knife studies, which cover the extraordinary work of contemporary knifemakers.

To Donald C. Mendelson, of Barrett-Smythe, Ltd., New York, for a review of the artistry of the firm's exclusive craftsmen and artists, and for assistance in supplying color transparencies and information on their creations.

To Tom James, T. J. James, and custom knifemaker Lynn Erickson, of Fort Knox Security Products, Orem, Utah, for their continued promotion of the writer's books, and for the world's finest personal safes.

To Gary Reynolds, whose Hamburg Cove emporium has served as a point of rejuvenation and inspiration for the author, for his assistance in collecting firearms and illustrations.

To Hans W. Schemke, for his wizardry at finding rare engraved guns for publication in this and other books.

To Richard Alan Dow, for assistance in authoring chapters 1 and 9, originally written for magazine publication.

To Robert Morrison, of Smith & Wesson, U.S. Repeating Arms Co., Colt, and Bianchi International, who coined the phrase "steel canvas." And to Les Line, who first published that title in *Audubon,* November 1987.

To Christopher and Stephen Wilson, in recognition of their fascination with the magical world of arms, for assistance during Peter Beard's shoots in Hadlyme, and for their patience while Dad wrote "one more book."

To Basil Charles, his industrious and delightful daughter Elizabeth, and the staff at Basil's Bar, and to Lilyian and Raymond Polynice, and the staff at the Cotton House, Mustique, St. Vincent, the West Indies, for the week in paradise that saw the final touches put on *Steel Canvas*.

And to Robert Loomis and colleagues at Random House, and to Martin Moskof with George Brady, designers, who again produced a complex volume in record time.

PHOTOGRAPHIC NOTE

Peter Beard's work has appeared in *Vogue, Life, Playboy,* and a number of other publications, and his books to date are *The End of the Game, Eyelids of Morning,* and *Longing for Darkness.* Books in progress are *Beyond Gauguin* and *Last Word from Paradise.* His photography was featured in *The Peacemakers: Arms* and *Adventure in the American West* and Gilles Turle's *The Art of the Maasai,* both published in 1992.

His photographic technique for this project was creative design and layout for over one hundred 4 × 5 transparencies, of over five hundred objects of firearms, edged weapons, and accessories, at interior and exterior locations. His customary photography is with Leica cameras, lenses, and accessories. Allan Brown and Jonathan Shorey assisted with their equipment as described below.

Allan Brown's work has appeared in the editorial pages of *Outdoor Life, Audubon, Colonial Homes, Saturday Evening Post, Yankee, American Rifleman, Man at Arms, Quest,* and numerous other periodicals and books. He played a major role in *Winchester: An American Legend* and *The Peacemakers.* For firearms photography, Brown uses a 4 × 5 Combo View Camera almost exclusively. He prefers Kodak Ektachrome film (either daylight for outdoors or tungsten for studio work) for consistent quality. His color development is by R. J. Phil of East Hampton, Connecticut.

For lighting, Brown uses Lowell tungsten lights, 3200° Kelvin, in the studio. The combination of these lights along with diffusion materials and reflectors produces the lighting he finds complimentary to weaponry. Tungsten lights have the added benefit over strobes of allowing one to see the exact lighting that the film will record.

Douglas Sandberg is a graduate of California College of Arts and Crafts, in Oakland. Much of his skill in photographing works of art was learned at the auction gallery Butterfield & Butterfield in San Francisco, where he was Director of Photography for seven years. In 1987 he created his own company, Comprehensive Photography, in South Park, San Francisco. His clients range from Christie's to WordStar, from Pebble Beach Co. to Electronic Arts, and more. An artist as well with a brush, his paintings of antique and modern cameras have been on show at galleries. Equipment used for this book was primarily a Toyo 4 × 5 View Camera and Balcar Electronic Flash system. Strong and direct lighting were used to bring out subtleties of engraving, with soft low-light filling in shadow detail. He has recently experimented as well with a fiber-optic paint-with-light system, an effective and dramatic means of showcasing detail. This system is called Hosemaster, and was created by Aaron Jones of New Mexico. A high-powered light wand allows the photographer to place light where it is nearly impossible to do so conventionally. The final effect gives the object a lighted-from-within glowing appearance and very fine detail. For this book Douglas Sandberg drew on every photographic technique in his repertoire. His choice of film: Ektachrome 100 Plus.

John Shorey studied art in Boston and is a self-taught photographer with studios in New York City. He uses a Linhof 4 × 5, with Balcar Electronic Flash system. His light system is modified with extensive filtration, in addition to using tungsten light to bring out colors. Kodak Ektachrome or Fuji films are preferred, depending on the subject. His clients range from Kenneth Cole to Lehman Brothers. He has been experimenting with Polaroid transfer printing and cross-processed films for computer manipulation.

Other photographers who assisted or shot photographs for *Steel Canvas* are Russell B. Aitken; Mustafa Bilal; Butterfield & Butterfield's Terry Allen, Matthew Fertel, Herman Mallard, Chris Paris, and Jose Ysaguirre; Robert Benson, E. Irving Blomstrann, Edward Lee Diefenthal, Herbert G. Houze, Sid Latham, Dick Marsh (Asprey), George Matthews, Ed Muno (National Cowboy Hall of Fame and Heritage Center), Carl B. Neustrand (Director, Photography Staff, *American Rifleman*), Bruce Pendleton, Steffany Rubin, Turk Takano, Hikaru Uesaka, Ricardo Vargas (National Museum of American History, Smithsonian Institution), Arthur Vitols (Helga Photo Studio), Sam Welch, Jim Weyer, David Wesbrook, David Wharton, and John Robert Williams.

Index

Note:
Page numbers in *italics*
refer to illustrations.